Consumer Behaviour in Tourism

Consumer Behaviour in Tourism

John Swarbrooke and Susan Horner

OXFORD   AUCKLAND   BOSTON   JOHANNESBURG   MELBOURNE   NEW DELHI

Butterworth-Heinemann
Linacre House, Jordan Hill, Oxford OX2 8DP
225 Wildwood Avenue, Woburn, MA 01801-2041
A division of Reed Educational and Professional Publishing Ltd

ℛ A member of the Reed Elsevier plc group

First published 1999
Reprinted 1999

British Library Cataloguing in Publication Data
Swarbrooke, John
Consumer behaviour in tourism
1. Consumer behaviour   2. Tourist trade
I. Title   II. Horner, Susan
658.8'342

ISBN 0 7506 3283 6

FOR EVERY TITLE THAT WE PUBLISH, BUTTERWORTH-HEINEMANN
WILL PAY FOR BTCV TO PLANT AND CARE FOR A TREE.

Composition by Genesis Typesetting, Laser Quay, Rochester, Kent
Printed and bound in Great Britain

Contents

Preface   vii

Part One   Context   1

1 Introduction   3
2 The history of tourist behaviour   12
3 Main concepts in consumer behaviour, including models of
   consumer behaviour which have been adapted for tourism   41

Part Two   The Purchase-decision Process   51

4 Motivators   53
5 Determinants   62
6 Models of the purchase decision-making process   69

Part Three   Typologies of Tourist Behaviour   83

7 Typologies of tourist behaviour and segmentation of the
   tourism market   85

Part Four   Tourism Demand and Markets   103

8   The global pattern of tourism demand   105
9   National differences – domestic, outbound, inbound   121
10 The nature of demand in different segments of the tourism
    market   146
11 Consumer behaviour and markets in the different sectors of
    tourism   157

Part Five   Consumer Behaviour and Marketing   167

12 Researching tourist behaviour – marketing research   169
13 The marketing mix and tourist behaviour   180

Part Six   Topical Issues in Consumer Behaviour   195

14 The green tourist – myth or reality?   197
15 The rise of the global/Euro tourist?   209
16 The emergence of new markets and changes in tourist demand   225
17 Quality and tourist satisfaction   236

Part Seven   Conclusions and Future   **249**

18   Conclusions   251
19   The future of tourist behaviour   255

Part Eight   Case Studies   **265**

Case study 1   PGL Adventure Holidays   267
Case study 2   Flying Colours Holidays Limited – Club 18–30   277
Case study 3   The segmentation of the outbound Japanese market   285
Case study 4   The Savoy Group of hotels   287
Case study 5   Cathay Pacific Airways   297
Case study 6   First Choice Holidays – all-inclusive package   315
Case study 7   Carnival Cruise Lines – the cruise market   323
Case study 8   Wensleydale Creamery, Hawes, North Yorkshire   335
Case study 9   Société Roquefort, Roquefort, France   342
Case study 10   Industrial tourism in France   346
Case study 11   British Airways – environmental policy   349
Case study 12   TUI, Germany – environmental policy   362
Case study 13   Ragdale Hall – health hydro   372
Case study 14   The international spa market   380
Case study 15   Granada Studios Tour   383
Case study 16   easyJet   390
Case study 17   Las Vegas, Nevada, USA   398
Case study 18   Rural tourism in France   416
Case study 19   Inbound and outbound tourism in the USA –
                breaking the myths   419
Case study 20   Taiwan – the emergence of a new major outbound
                tourism market   421
Case study 21   Susi Madron's Cycling for Softies   423
Case study 22   Currency exchange rates as a determinant of
                tourist behaviour   430

Part Nine   Glossary of Terms   **433**

Bibliography and further reading   439
Index   451

Preface

This book is designed to provide a concise overview of consumer behaviour in tourism. The authors feel, from their own teaching experience and the comments of colleagues in the tourism field, that there is a need for such a text. It will hopefully play a small part in focusing attention on this increasingly important area, as well as helping to give students the necessary underpinning for learning more about the phenomenon of tourism as a whole.

Consumer behaviour is clearly a crucial issue today, in an era when:

1 Marketing theory is dominated by the concept of consumer- or market-led marketing, where organizations must meet the demands of their customers if they are to thrive. How can they do this unless they understand the behaviour of their customers?
2 The conventional wisdom is that, increasingly, 'mass' markets are fragmenting into niche markets. Marketers have to be able to find ways of identifying and targeting these markets.
3 Most theorists and practitioners are talking about consumers becoming ever more sophisticated and demanding, and this idea is driving much new product development in tourism.
4 Consumer tastes are changing and developing, perhaps, faster than ever before.

This book attempts to:

- provide an introductory text on consumer behaviour in tourism
- look at the subject from an international perspective, as far as possible in a book of this length, and bearing in mind that both authors are British
- highlight topical issues in the subject area and bring together, for the reader, the latest research findings in the field
- link theory to practice and show the implications of consumer behaviour theory for marketing practice
- offer a range of up-to-date detailed case studies to illustrate points made in the text
- give lecturers and tutors a truly interactive text that they can use to develop student-centred teaching.

To achieve these objectives, the book is divided into a number of parts, as follows:

- Part One sets the context by offering some definitions of key terms, introducing the basic concepts of general consumer behaviour, and briefly outlining the historical development of tourist behaviour. There is also a chapter that identifies the characteristics of tourism, which make the study of consumer behaviour in tourism a particularly complex subject.
- Part Two concentrates on the factors that influence the individual purchase decision, including motivators, determinants, tourist perceptions and external influences such as the media, friends and the actions of the tourism industry.
- Part Three looks at the typologies of tourist behaviour that have been developed.
- Part Four focuses on actual tourism demand and different markets. It explores the pattern of tourism demand across the world, highlighting major differences between regions of the world and between individual countries. There is also a chapter on the market for different sectors of tourism such as tour operations, airlines, attractions and accommodation.
- Part Five examines some topical issues in the field of tourist behaviour, including the ideas of the 'green consumer' and the global tourist, together with the idea of quality. One chapter also explores emerging markets such as adventure holidays and industrial tourism.
- Part Six discusses the link between consumer behaviour and marketing practice, notably the marketing mix, and marketing research.
- Part Seven offers some conclusions, as well as taking a look into the future.
- Part Eight contains a number of major case studies drawn from around the world, to illustrate points made in the text.
- Part Nine consists of a glossary of terms for readers who may be unfamiliar with some of the terms used in consumer behaviour and/or in tourism.

Each chapter features conclusions, discussion points and essay questions, and exercises, at the end, to help tutors direct student-centred learning and to allow the reader to check their understanding of what they have read. Some also contain mini case studies on the specific topic covered in the chapter.

Due to its limited length, the book cannot offer an in-depth treatment of every aspect of consumer behaviour in tourism. However, a full list of further reading is provided for those who would like to delve deeper into a particular subject.

We hope that the text will be valuable for a number of audiences including students, lecturers and practitioners. However, our greatest wish in writing it is that it should stimulate the reader's interest in this fascinating, but so far largely under-valued, area of tourism studies and tourism management.

The writing of this book as been an enjoyable experience. However, it would have been less so had it not been for our son John, whose bright eyes and wide smile make life a joy, even on grey, wet days in Sheffield!

We would also like to recognize the debt we owe to our parents, but we know it is a debt we can never repay. They gave us what strengths we have but bear none of the blame for our weaknesses.

Our friend, Judith Mitchell, deciphered our awful handwriting, typed the manuscript magnificently, and helped us keep the whole project in proportion.

We would also like to take this opportunity to thank those students who have stimulated and inspired us; wherever they are, we wish them well.

As for ourselves, we are just pleased that we have completed the book without recourse to divorce lawyers!

For us, the writing is over, but for you, the reading is about to begin. We sincerely hope that you find something of value in these pages and that the book serves to encourage you to explore this fascinating subject further.

John Swarbrooke and Susan Horner

Part One
Context

Part One sets the scene for the rest of the book, through three chapters, as follows:

1 An introduction that includes key definitions and explores the importance of consumer behaviour in tourism as a subject.
2 This chapter provides a history of consumer behaviour in tourism, both in terms of different types of tourism and the various regions of the world.
3 Discusses the main general concepts in consumer behaviour that were developed from other industries and/or industry as a whole. At the end of the chapter, there is a brief consideration of the specific characteristics of tourism that make it difficult to apply general consumer behaviour concepts and markets to tourism.

1   Introduction

The subject of consumer behaviour is key to the underpinning of all marketing activity which is carried out to develop, promote and sell tourism products. Clearly, if we are to optimize the effectiveness and efficiency of marketing activities, we must try to understand how consumers make their decisions to purchase or use tourism products. If we understand their behaviour patterns, then we will know when we need to intervene in the process to obtain the results that we want. We will know who to target at a particular time with a particular tourism product. More importantly, we will know how to persuade them to choose certain products which we will have designed more effectively to meet their particular needs and wants. An understanding of consumer behaviour is therefore crucial to make marketing activity more successful.

The problem with the academic disciplines of consumer behaviour, however, is that while many general models of consumer behaviour have been advanced, there has been little empirical research conducted in order to test these models against actual behaviour patterns. This is especially true in the tourism sector where research on consumer behaviour is very much in the early stages of development. Despite a lack of empirical research, however, there have been several examples of models of consumer behaviour in tourism which have been suggested. It is important, in this book, that we consider these models and consider the stage at which the development of the subject has reached. This will allow us to identify further areas of research and will offer the reader some judgements as to how useful the research is to date, for the application to practical marketing activities.

Consumer behaviour is a fascinating but difficult subject to research. This statement is particularly relevant in the tourism field, where the decision to purchase by a consumer is of emotional significance. Purchase of a holiday, for example, involves the consumer in a large spend. The holiday that the consumer buys will probably provide the consumer with the major highlight of the year – a chance to escape from work and grey skies and revitalize the spirit. Consumers are influenced in their decision-making processes by many internal and external motivators and determinants when they choose products. It is very difficult to research how these many motivators and determinants affect the consumer when they are making their choices. They may be affected in different ways, according to the type of product or service that they are purchasing. The experience of purchasing a holiday, for example, will be very different from the experience of purchasing an everyday food item in a supermarket. It is likely to take much more time, and involve more careful consideration and selection, particularly as the purchase of a holiday usually involves a high proportion of income.

Before we get into the detail, however, it is necessary for us to define some of the key terms.

We can start with a definition of tourism. Definitions of tourism were explained by Horner and Swarbrooke (1996) as having several components as well as considerable overlap with hospitality and leisure.

Tourism is defined as a short-term movement of people to places some distance from their normal place of residence to indulge in pleasurable activities. It may also involve travel for business purposes. Horner and Swarbrooke (1996) continue to discuss the reasons for tourism not being a simple concept:

It does not encompass the lucrative field of business tourism where the main purpose of the trip is for work rather than play. We also have difficulty in deciding how far you have to travel to be a tourist or how many nights you have to stay away from home to be classified as a tourist.

Tourism can be described as an activity which is serviced by a number of other industries such as hospitality and transport. The rise of the mass package tourism business with the development of package holiday companies and retail travel agencies is probably the nearest that tourism comes to being an industrial sector.

Tourism also incorporates the hospitality sector. Collin (1994) defines hospitality as 'looking after guests well'. The term 'hospitality' is becoming increasingly used in Europe to replace more traditional terms such as 'hotel and catering'. This is because the word 'well' suggests a qualitative dimension which is a fashionable concept in a time when quality management is growing in importance as a discipline. Hospitality therefore includes all organizations which provide guests with food, drink and leisure facilities. Not all hospitality is concerned with tourism, however. It may just involve people going to a leisure centre or out for a drink.

Horner and Swarbrooke (1996) also suggest that tourism incorporates leisure. According to Collin (1994), leisure as a noun means 'free time to do what you want'. He also defines the leisure industry as 'companies which provide goods and services used during people's leisure time'. This includes holidays, cinema, theatres, visitor attractions, etc. This shows that like hospitality, not all leisure organizations are concerned with tourism.

The distinctions between tourism, leisure and hospitality is blurred. A number of examples of this were suggested by Horner and Swarbrooke (1996) and are shown in Figure 1.1.

The best example of the blurring of the distinction between tourism, hospitality and leisure is the American import, the resort complex concept.

The tourism market is very diverse and incorporates a diversity of market segments which each have their own demand characteristics. We will return

- The resort complexes such as Club Méditeranée and Center Parcs offer both hospitality services and leisure facilities on the same site, under the ownership of one organization. Furthermore, they offer this mixture to a market largely consisting of tourists; in other words, people who have travelled away from home and are spending at least one night away from their normal place of residence.
- Theme parks are increasingly offering on-site accommodation units to encourage visitors to spend more time, and thus more money, on site. A good example of this is the Futuroscope theme park in Western France which now has several hotels, of different grades, within the boundaries of the park.
- The trend amongst hotels in most European countries is to build in-house leisure facilities for their guests such as gymnasia and swimming pools. This is seen as necessary to attract two very different groups of clients, namely leisure visitors at weekends, and business customers on weekdays.
- Leisure shopping is being developed as a tourist activity. Shopping is now used as a way of motivating trips to destinations as diverse as Liverpool in the UK, with its Albert Dock complex, the craft centres of rural Norway and the gold shops of Dubai.
- Sophisticated catering operations are being developed at visitor attractions to boost income. These can range from fast-food outlets to themed restaurants. Interestingly many of these current developments in Europe are mirroring earlier ones in North America.

Figure 1.1   Examples of the blurring of tourism, leisure and hospitality organizations
Source: Horner and Swarbrooke (1996)

to this in Chapter 10 when we consider the nature of demand in different market segments of the tourism market. It is sufficient here to highlight some of the different market segments in tourism, notably:

- **Business Tourism** is a tourist trip that takes place as part of people's business occupational commitment, largely in work time, rather than for pleasure, in people's leisure time (Horner and Swarbrooke, 1996). It incorporates individual business trips, attendance at meetings, training courses and conferences; visiting and organizing trade fairs and exhibitions; undertaking product launches; and incentive travel. There is a blurring of business tourism with leisure tourism, particularly when a business person takes their family with them on business, or extends their business trip to incorporate a relaxing holiday after their work is finished (Davidson, 1994).
- **Hedonistic Tourism** involves the tourist in seeking pleasurable activities. The tourism experience is based on physical pleasure and social life. The hedonistic tourist is often younger and travels in a group with other like-minded people.
- **Educational Tourism** involves the tourist travelling for education. This form of tourism is not a new phenomenon, but is an important segment of the tourism business.
- **Religious Tourism** is one of the oldest forms of tourism and involves people travelling often as a sense of duty rather than for pleasure and leisure.

We will expand this analysis of different market segments in tourism further in Chapter 10.

Let us now turn our attention to defining consumer behaviour.

Horner and Swarbrooke (1996) have defined consumer behaviour in tourism as:

Consumer behaviour is the study of why people buy the product they do, and how they make their decision.

Before we consider definitions and models which have been adapted for the tourism sector, it is important for us to consider the general definitions which were developed by researches who were considering consumer behaviour as a general topic.

The process by which a consumer chooses to purchase or use a product or service is defined as the consumer behaviour process. Consumer behaviour has been defined by Engel, Blackwell and Miniard (1995) as:

Consumer behaviour is those activities directly involved in obtaining, consuming, and disposing of products and services including the decision processes that precedes and follows these actions.

This definition emphasizes the importance of the psychological process which the consumer goes through during the pre-purchase, and post purchase stages. Solomon (1996) incorporated the concept of consumer needs and wants into his definition as follows:

Consumer behaviour is the process involved when individuals or groups select, purchase, use, or dispose of products, services, ideas or experiences to satisfy needs and wants.

This definition introduces the idea that consumers may make purchase decisions in groups, and not just simply as individuals. The processes which are highlighted in these definitions are very complex and for this reason it has been more common to illustrate the consumer behaviour process with reference to models rather than definition. These will be reviewed later in this chapter.

Before we consider consumer behaviour models in more depth, however, it is important that we consider the role of consumer behaviour in the marketing process.

The understanding of consumer behaviour is vital if the marketing activity carried out by organizations is to be effective. Marketing is concerned with the relationship between consumer or buyer and seller. Marketing relies on the idea that organizations should put the central focus on the consumer for all their activities.

Organizations often consider their consumer's wants and needs, but also rely on persuading them to buy their products and services. This is often referred to as consumer persuasion, rather than putting the consumer at the centre of the organization in a process which is often referred to as consumer sovereignty.

The marketing concept does suggest however that the overriding inclination of the organization will be to serve the final consumer's wants and needs, as their main priority. This will mean that the organization constantly researches consumer demand and the reasons for this demand.

The organization will seek constantly to find out what the consumer wants both today and in the future, and will work hard to produce the products and services that are requested by the assembly of correctly designed marketing mixes.

The provision of these well-designed products and services will require an understanding of consumer behaviour and the ability to predict how this will change in the future.

The organization will also have to understand how and why a consumer makes a choice. This will enable them to persuade the consumer to choose their products and services, rather than those offered by the competition. It will also allow the organization to develop products and services that are correctly positioned for their target market.

The definitions of marketing demonstrates the different approaches which have been taken to the marketing philosophy. Kotler and Armstrong (1994a) defined marketing as follows:

A social and managerial process by which individuals and groups obtain what they need and want through creating and exchanging products and values with others.

This definition emphasizes the requirement for products and services to reflect consumer wants and needs.

Levitt (1986) emphasizes the fact that organizations must provide consumers with added value appeal in his definition:

a truly marketing minded firm tries to create value satisfying goods and services that consumers will want to buy.

This definition also highlights the importance of consumer needs and wants as being central to the marketing function. The UK-based Chartered Institute of Marketing definition also emphasizes the fact that the marketing philosophy involves putting the consumer or customer as the central focus for the organizational decision-making process:

Identifying, anticipating, and satisfying customer requirements profitably.

Piercy (1992) suggests that a market-led approach which considers consumer demand is essential for two reasons:

- ultimately all organizations are forced to follow the dictates of the market (i.e. the paying customer) or go out of business
- the organization can pursue organizational effectiveness by being 'market-led' and focusing on the customer's needs, wants and demands.

Piercy (1992) has also explained the reasons for organizations finding it difficult to adopt marketing. These have been summarized by Horner and Swarbrooke (1996). One of the main reasons here is the fact that there are considerable barriers to the introduction of marketing such as ignorance of customer characteristics, lack of information, inflexible technology and competitive threat. It can be suggested, however, that the most likely reason for organizations not adopting a truly marketing-led approach is the fact that they do not really understand consumer behaviour in depth. They have simply learnt how to persuade consumers to purchase by trial and error, rather than having a sophisticated understanding of these complex purchasing processes.

They have, however, become very sophisticated at persuading consumers to purchase, despite an apparent lack of understanding. As far back as 1957, Vance Packard in his book *The Hidden Persuaders* portrayed a frightening manipulative view of the marketing faction. He showed how organizations, even at that time, could manipulate consumers, including children, into buying products and services.

This work suggests that the ability to persuade consumers to purchase products may not necessitate a detailed understanding of their behaviour patterns and motives. It may be enough just to have the ability to persuade them to purchase. Despite the view, the authors suggest that a deeper understanding of the consumer behaviour process will help with the marketing of products and services.

Calantone and Mazanec (1991) outlined the value of consumer behaviour for the marketing management process in tourism. An understanding of consumer needs, attitudes and decision processes will allow the marketing manager to improve their decision-making process. It will allow the marketing manager to forecast behaviour in the future and therefore avoid over-optimism or underestimates of consumer demand (Calantone, di Benedetto and Bojanic, 1987, 1988). An understanding of consumer behaviour is also important for product development of new tourism products and facilities. It will allow the marketing manager to have a clearer view of the types of benefits that consumers are looking for, and enable these to be reflected in the development process. The development of effective and efficient advertising campaigns also requires an understanding of consumer behaviour. Benefit segmentation is often used here so that the manager can design the advertising campaign based on the particular benefits sought by the market segment.

Calantone, Schewe and Allen (1980), for example identified five benefit segments of consumers, which could be used to develop effective advertising campaigns. The use of benefit segmentation also allows the marketing manager to understand changes which may occur with time (Calantone and Sawyer, 1978) and from season to season (Calantone and Johar, 1984). This will allow the advertising copy to be amended to reflect the different benefits sought during different periods.

Benefit segmentation also allows the marketing manager to identify very well-defined groups of people and target them with well-designed products and services. Several tourist practitioners have recently developed promotions specifically for target groups. Saga, for example, targets the over-50 market exclusively with well-designed direct mail brochures. Savani (1986) also noted the rise in direct targeting of the lucrative over-50 market. Similarly, PGL, have targeted the child and young adult who are looking for an outward-bound type holiday away from their parents (see Case Study 1). We will return to the use of benefit segmentation in the marketing process in later chapters.

To finish this chapter, we will consider the marketing planning process and consider how an understanding of consumer behaviour helps with the marketing planning process in tourism marketing. Marketing Planning was developed as a systematic way of incorporating marketing into an organization. The marketing planning process is defined by McDonald (1989) as a series of steps which incorporates all aspects of the marketing process. This model is shown in Figure 1.2.

Figure 1.2   The marketing planning process
Source: McDonald (1989)

We can use this model of the marketing planning process to consider the usefulness of an understanding of consumer behaviour. This is considered in more depth in Figure 1.3.

It can be seen here that an understanding of consumer behaviour will allow a more effective marketing planning process. Some examples of where this understanding helps, are:

- understanding of why consumers currently choose products and services and the benefits they seek, including their USP (Unique Selling Proposition)
- forecasting of consumer demand which will bring efficiencies

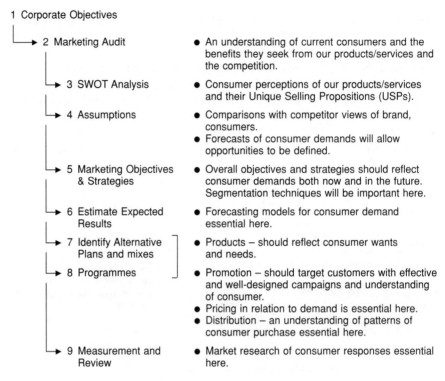

1 Corporate Objectives

2 Marketing Audit
- An understanding of current consumers and the benefits they seek from our products/services and the competition.

3 SWOT Analysis
- Consumer perceptions of our products/services and their Unique Selling Propositions (USPs).

4 Assumptions
- Comparisons with competitor views of brand, consumers.
- Forecasts of consumer demands will allow opportunities to be defined.

5 Marketing Objectives & Strategies
- Overall objectives and strategies should reflect consumer demands both now and in the future. Segmentation techniques will be important here.

6 Estimate Expected Results
- Forecasting models for consumer demand essential here.

7 Identify Alternative Plans and mixes
- Products – should reflect consumer wants and needs.

8 Programmes
- Promotion – should target customers with effective and well-designed campaigns and understanding of consumer.
- Pricing in relation to demand is essential here.
- Distribution – an understanding of patterns of consumer purchase essential here.

9 Measurement and Review
- Market research of consumer responses essential here.

Figure 1.3   The marketing planning process and the usefulness of an understanding of consumer behaviour
Adapted from McDonald (1989)

- targeting of particular market segments
- correct positioning of product
- design of effective marketing mixes and reflection of consumer behaviour in all elements of this – product, promotion, price, and place (distribution)
- review of how new products and services have been received and an exploration of this in relation to consumer behaviour.

The conclusion here therefore is that the marketing planning process will be helped immensely if the marketing manager has a thorough understanding of consumer behaviour. Whether this understanding is developed as a result of thorough and systematic research or as a result of 'gut feel' and past experience is a matter of opinion.

There are many examples of individuals who have spotted an opportunity and developed products to exploit them without much detailed research. These organizations are usually headed by entrepreneurs, who, we could argue, have an interest and inbound understanding of consumers and who do not require sophisticated research to confirm their ideas. Even these organizations, however, investigate consumer behaviour in more depth as the organization reaches maturity and more competitive products arrive on the market.

Conclusion

Now that we have considered the role of consumer behaviour in the marketing process, let us now consider in more detail the history of tourist behaviour.

Discussion points and essay questions

1 Discuss the reasons for tourism, leisure, and hospitality marketing becoming increasingly blurred.
2 Evaluate the importance of the fact that consumers may make purchase decisions for tourism products in groups, rather than as individuals.
3 'Tourism marketing relies entirely on the fact that consumers can be persuaded to buy by powerful communication techniques' (Horner and Swarbrooke, 1996).
    Critically evaluate this statement.

Exercise

Conduct a small-scale survey to investigate the importance of the high spend nature of tourism products on the purchase decision of consumers.

2 The history of tourist behaviour

Introduction

We do not know the name of the first tourist or the era in which the first holiday was taken. This may be because it is so difficult to define what is meant by the words *tourist* and *holiday*. Or does it reflect the fact that chroniclers did not believe that the phenomenon of tourism was significant enough to be worth recording? Perhaps, but we know that for centuries tourism has existed in one form or another and has given us a legacy of travel writing, dating back to Roman times. It has also stimulated some of the world's greatest literature, such as Chaucer's *Canterbury Tales*, for instance. Therefore, while we may talk of mass tourism as a twentieth-century phenomenon, tourism in the broadest sense of the word has existed for centuries.

In this chapter, the authors will endeavour to briefly address the chronological development of tourist behaviour. It is difficult to understand current tourist behaviour, or predict future behaviour, unless one understands a little about the past. As we shall see, the history of tourist behaviour is a complex subject. Furthermore, there is relatively little by way of empirical data or artefacts from which we can derive a history or chronology of early tourist behaviour.

Most historians of tourism have tended to focus on Europe, from the Greeks and Romans to the railway and Thomas Cook in the UK. However, it is important to recognize that tourism has existed in other continents for centuries. Furthermore, we need to remember that there are many different types of tourism, including: business tourism, health tourism, religious tourism, educational tourism and hedonistic tourism, for example.

Finally, there is a need to distinguish between domestic and international tourism, together with inbound and outbound tourist flows.

The first tourists

We do not know, for sure, who the first tourists were and where they lived. It is often thought that the beginnings of tourism date back to ancient Greece and Rome because we have evidence of tourism, from these eras, in terms of travel writing, for example. However, as archaeologists know, it is dangerous to be too dogmatic about history, based on current knowledge, and the artefacts we have found up until now. Who is to say that we will not find, in due course, evidence that tourism pre-dates the Greek and Roman times? This has already happened over the years in other areas of history, leading to historians having to re-think accepted ideas on everything from who discovered the USA to who built the so-called 'Roman roads' in England.

Future research may ultimately show us that tourism pre-dates the Greek era and may indeed have first developed outside Europe. To date, little research appears to have been undertaken on the development of tourism outside Europe. Furthermore, in countries like the USA which were settled by people from the 'Old World', the study of the history of tourism begins with the first holiday-making activities of these colonists. However, some forms of tourism, notably visiting friends and relatives, undoubtedly already existing amongst Native Americans long before the Europeans arrived.

Unfortunately, in this chapter, by and large, the authors must base their comments on existing knowledge rather than hypothesizing about what we may come to know in the future. Nevertheless, it is important that the reader reads what follows with the previous two paragraphs in mind.

Regions of the world

We will now look at the chronological development of tourist behaviour, in two respects, namely:

- the varied type and pace of development in the different regions of the world
- the way different types of tourism have developed including visiting friends and relatives, business tourism, religious tourism, health tourism, educational tourism and hedonistic tourism.

In the first instance, therefore, we will outline the historical development of tourism in the following regions of the world:

- Europe
- North America
- Central America, the Caribbean and South America
- Africa
- Middle East
- Asia
- Australasia and the Pacific Rim
- Antarctica.

The emphasis in this section will be on international rather than domestic tourism.

Europe

Today, Europe is the most popular continent as a destination for international tourists, although it is slowly losing its position in the world tourism market to other regions, such as the Pacific Rim. It is appropriate that Europe should continue to hold this pre-eminent position, for most commentators consider it to be the birthplace of modern tourism.

The development of tourism in Europe, as elsewhere, rested on two essential pre-requisites, namely:

- a desire to travel
- the removal of obstacles that prevented people from taking trips.

As we shall see, the desire to travel, until relatively recently, was predominantly based on religious devotion, concerns over health, and trade, rather than pleasure. The obstacles that needed to be overcome so that people could become tourists of whatever kind, were largely related to transport, both in terms of the lack of adequate roads and sea transport, and the risk of attack faced by travellers. Tourism could only begin to develop when these problems were removed or ameliorated.

The earliest recorded tourism in Europe dates back to the time of Ancient Greece. It tended to be specialist in nature and related to religious practice. People visited religious festivals and consulted oracles. They also visited sporting events like the Olympic Games which began in BC 776 – but even these had a religious significance.

The oldest recognized travel writing also dates from this millennium. For example, we have the writings of Herodotus, a historian who lived in the fifth century BC, who travelled by sea to Egypt, Persia, Sicily and Babylon. He recorded his experiences in ways which both informed and entertained the reader. Travel writing is thus an activity with a history that stretches back over two thousand years.

It was the Romans who were largely responsible for introducing the idea of tourism for pleasure, rather than for utilitarian purposes such as religious devotion, health or business. They started the hedonistic, sensual tradition in tourism which has perhaps reached its peak in our age.

The Romans were perhaps the first to create purpose-built tourism resorts, both at the coast and inland. These resorts often combined leisure pursuits such as bathing, or the arts, with health, in terms of thermal spas. Such resorts were not only found in Italy itself, but also in the Roman provinces. They also gained a reputation as being places where Romans could escape from the moral codes which constrained their everyday lives. This lead to 'loud parties, excessive drinking, and nude bathing' (Sharpley, 1994). So we can see that there is little that is new in the behaviour of today's tourists!

However, the Romans also developed tourism based on sightseeing within their Empire, utilizing the roads which had been built for the convenience of troops and trade. Romans visited famous buildings while young Romans were sent to Greece to be educated.

Yet, although the Romans pioneered the idea of hedonistic tourism, it was an elitist activity, beyond the means of most Romans. It is this fact which distinguishes it from today's mass tourism.

The steady march of tourism development in Europe was halted by the Dark Ages. With the end of the Roman Empire came the end of most tourism in Europe, although there was still some business tourism in the form of trade. Historians are, however, re-thinking the so-called Dark Ages and are questioning whether they were as dark as we have been led to believe.

However, one form of tourism, that was to become the earliest form of mass tourism, was born in Europe at this time, namely, the pilgrimage. This form of tourism reached its peak during the Middle Ages, and the numbers travelling were large given the population of Europe at the time. For example, by 1300 some 300 000 people visited Rome in that year alone (Sharpley, 1994). Other major destinations for European pilgrims included Jerusalem and Santiago de Compostella. There were also shorter pilgrimages such as those taken by the English to Canterbury.

The pilgrimages were supported by a well-developed infrastructure of accommodation, eating places and even guide books, and were thus the forerunners of the modern tourism industry.

Towards the end of the Middle Ages there was a growth in what might be termed educational tourism, where people travelled to see great paintings and buildings, meet famous artists, and learn more about language and culture. Italy was the favoured destination for such trips which were the origin of the 'Grand Tour'. However, in contrast to the pilgrimages which were more democratic, such trips were largely the preserve of the wealthy and well-educated.

Both pilgrimages and the Grand Tour originated the tradition of Northern Europeans travelling to Southern Europe as tourists, which continues to this day.

The Grand Tour reached its zenith in the seventeenth and eighteenth centuries, with the sons of aristocrats spending up to four years travelling around Europe. As many as 20 000 young English people alone could be on the continent at any one time (Sharpley, 1994). As well as Italy, the tour usually encompassed France, Holland, Germany, Austria and Switzerland.

In the latter decades of the eighteenth century the Grand Tour changed in nature with more people travelling but taking shorter trips. They tended to be older than previously and more middle class than aristocrats, and were more interested in sightseeing and hedonism than learning. The aristocracy began to desert the Grand Tour and look for more exclusive leisure activities elsewhere.

Nature and the scenic beauty of landscapes started to become a major attraction for some tourists, stimulated by the growth of the Romantic Movement in art. This movement created the perceptions which still determine the way we view rural landscapes and visit the countryside today.

Contemporary with the rise of the Grand Tour came the rediscovery of the spas which had been so popular with the Romans. The poor sanitary conditions of the burgeoning towns of Europe in the fifteenth and sixteenth centuries stimulated an interest in health amongst the upper classes. Doctors, such as Turner in 1562, extolled the medicinal virtues of spa waters. Bath in England was a pioneer in the European spa movement, but there were many others such as Royal Tunbridge Wells, also in England, and numerous examples in France, Germany and Italy. Many of those were not new spa resorts, but were old Roman resorts. In later years, in the nineteenth century, other spas were developed, most notably in Poland, Belgium and the Czech Republic, for instance.

The spas became major centres of fashion, social activities and gambling. Over time, like the Grand Tour, the spas became less exclusive as middle-class people began to visit them. This process led to their commercialization and to their becoming places to live as well as just visit.

In Britain the early seaside resorts, such as Scarborough, were developed on the premise that people would bathe in the sea to improve their health, rather than for pleasure.

In the nineteenth century we can see the real foundations being laid for the development of modern tourism, due most notably to the introduction of railways. This, and the results of the Industrial Revolution in Britain and some European countries, created the conditions for the growth of larger scale forms of tourism. The seaside resort was the main beneficiary of this change, particularly in Britain where the industrial revolution occurred first. Some of the newly urbanized and industrialized population had some leisure time and disposable income to enable it to travel for pleasure, while the squalor of many towns and cities created a desire to escape for a short time.

In Britain this new demand was met by resorts which served largely regional markets. Blackpool catered for Lancashire, Scarborough for Yorkshire, and Margate and Brighton accommodated the needs of London. This pattern of regional catchment areas for many resorts lasted well into the 1950s and 1960s, and has not yet disappeared.

However, as rail services improved and journey times were reduced, resorts grew up which were further from the major centres of population and industry, such as Torquay. These tended to attract more affluent tourists from all over Britain.

The rise of seaside resorts was also seen in continental Europe, where resorts developed to meet the needs of the urban dwellers of France, Belgium, Holland and Germany, from the North Sea to the Atlantic shores of Brittany.

Just as we have seen throughout history, as resorts developed by the upper classes became favoured by the middle classes, the former moved on in search of more exclusive destinations. Thus, wealthier Britons, for example, began to visit resorts in mainland Europe. Sir George Young has estimated that 100 000 Britons were crossing the English Channel in 1840, while the number had risen to 1 000 000 by the turn of the century (Sharpley, 1994). These Britons began to choose resorts in Southern France where the climate was better, as places to spend the winter, away from the cold of Britain. Here we see the forerunners, albeit a small elite, of today's flow of elderly Britons who travel to Benidorm for several months every winter for exactly the same reason.

It was sun-seeking affluent Britons who in the late nineteenth century stimulated the growth of resorts such as Nice and Biarritz. These resorts were also frequented by royalty from other European countries; they thus became fashionable places. Their image as glamorous risqué playgrounds for the rich was enhanced by the opening of casinos and the growth of gambling.

Another development in the nineteenth century that was to have a profound impact on the growth of tourism was the creation of the modern tour operator, which traditionally is thought to be the excursion business started by Thomas Cook in 1841, in Britain. This company, which has since become a byword for tourism, started by organizing local rail excursions in Leicestershire, but by the end of the nineteenth century it was taking British tourists to Egypt. It also dealt with the travel arrangements of travellers from many other countries. By taking responsibility for organizing trips for tourists, Thomas Cook made travel accessible to those who lacked the language skills or the confidence to travel independently. It thus laid the foundations for modern package tourism.

By the beginning of this century the seeds of long-haul international leisure tourism were taking root. Sharpley, writing in 1994, estimates that in the years leading up to World War I, up to 100 000 Americans visited Europe each year.

Other future tourism markets were also being pioneered in the early years of the twentieth century including skiing holidays which have now reached their zenith.

Tourism continued to develop after World War I. The 1920s were the heyday of the Trans-Atlantic cruise market. Sun-bathing also developed as a leisure activity in the hedonistic days of the same decade. A sun tan became fashionable rather than being associated with lower-class rural dwellers and manual labourers.

From the 1930s onwards, the growing availability of the motor car further stimulated tourism. It opened up areas that were beyond the public transport system. During the inter-war years the aeroplane began to play a small role in the tourism market as an option for the wealthier classes, particularly in Europe. These improvements in transport coincided in Europe with an increase in leisure time as a result of legislation on the length of the working week in many European countries. An example of this trend is the Holidays with Pay Act of 1938 in Britain.

This era also saw the growth of the holiday camp concept, particularly again in Britain, through the activities of entrepreneurs such as Billy Butlin. These camps reached their peak in the early years after World War II and were clearly the forerunners of modern inland complexes such as Center Parcs.

The rapid growth of mass tourism in Europe since the late 1940s has been well documented. It has been explained by the coincidence of a number of inter-related factors occurring at the same time, including:

- increases in disposable income
- advances in aircraft technology
- the greater availability of motor cars

- further increases in leisure time
- education
- the growth of tour operators and the package holiday.

The first wave of mass tourism in Europe consisted of annual migrations to the Mediterranean, in search of sun, by the residents of Northern Europe. Until recently this was largely a one-way flow although now there is a rapid growth in outbound tourism from these Mediterranean countries, notably Italy and Spain.

Not all Europeans have shown the same desire to visit other countries even though they can afford to, as we can see from the example of the French, who still show a preference for holidaying at home. This may reflect the variety of tourism opportunities that exist within their own country, as well as being the result of government initiatives designed to encourage people to holiday at home for economic reasons. These initiatives include the development of new purpose-built resorts on the Languedoc and Aquitaine coasts and in the French Alps, for instance.

These developments illustrate another major recent trend in the European tourism market, namely, the increasing role of governments as both attraction developers and destination marketers. Governments have also often been the catalyst for the growth of a modern form of tourism in Europe – social tourism, where holiday-taking is viewed as a right and may form part of the social security system. While never popular in Britain, it is an important element of the market in France and Germany, for example.

However, it would be wrong to suggest that the last four or five decades have been a period of growth for all forms of tourism. In the 1950s, 1960s and 1970s the opportunities offered by jet travel and new Mediterranean destinations considerably reduced demand for both Trans-Atlantic cruises and the seaside resorts of Northern Europe. Interestingly, in recent years, we have seen the renaissance of the European cruise market, but now it is more about mass appeal and budget prices than elegance and exclusivity. Nothing typifies better the march of mass tourism and the democratization of travel than this fact.

It would also be incorrect to imply that the growth of tourism has been a Pan-European phenomenon. Until the political change of the late 1980s and early 1990s in Eastern Europe, the countries of the East were locked in their own tourism world. Domestic tourism existed on a large-scale and cross-border tourism also existed although it largely took place wholly within the Eastern bloc. Visits to Western Europe were rare and reserved for the political elite. This process is now changing and new markets are opening up for Mediterranean resorts just as European tourists are starting to look further afield to the USA, Asia and the Caribbean for their holidays.

The final trend we should note in the historical development of tourism in Europe is the fact that Britain is no longer at the forefront of developments. Germany is the world's largest generator of international trips and the Dutch, Belgians, Swedes and Danes take more holidays per head than the British. Even the most successful tourism developments in the UK are now often imported, such as the Center Parcs concept from the Netherlands or the Waterfront developments that were based on experience in the USA. Perhaps the most significance example of this trend is the fact that Thomas Cook is now German-owned.

However, the future of tourism in Europe may in future not be about what happens in different European countries, but rather about events in the rest of the world. Tourism is increasingly a truly global market but it is a market in which Europe is losing its dominant position.

North America

Some histories of tourism in the USA and Canada begin in the nineteenth century, but clearly the first peoples, the Native Americans, had been travelling around the continent of North America for centuries before the colonists arrived. This travel, while not often recorded by historians, must have been motivated by religious devotion, the desire to keep in touch with relatives and the need to look for new hunting grounds.

We should also recognize the role played by these Native Americans in helping the early settlers find their way around their newly adopted homeland.

However, it is correct to say that the modern tourism industry in the USA only dates back to the mid-eighteenth century. It is not surprising that the earliest growth of tourism in the USA should have occurred in New England, one of the first areas of the country settled by Europeans.

In the latter half of the century, coaching inns and taverns began to develop to meet the needs of tourists. An early example is now part of the Old Deerfield Inn complex in Massachusetts. City centre hotels began to develop later, with the first recognized such hotel being the Tremont in Boston, which opened in 1829.

However it was the railway which really first stimulated tourism in the USA, both for pleasure and business. It particularly opened up the 'Wild West' to settlers, commercial travellers and curious tourists. In 1830 there were only 23 miles of railway track in the USA, but that by 1880 the figure was 93 267, and that by 1920 it had reached 240 293 (Lundberg, 1990).

The railway companies also contributed to the growth of tourism through the building of hotels and resort complexes in New England. Later they were heavily involved in the development of Florida from the turn of the century.

The next major phase of tourism growth in the USA was stimulated by the growth of car ownership. In 1914 there were already 2 million private cars on the roads but by the 1930s, at the height of the Depression, there were some 25 million (Lundberg, 1990).

Car ownership stimulated two new developments in US tourism, namely:

● the creation of the roadside motels, offering accommodation that was convenient for motorists. While the motel concept did not extend to Europe until the 1980s it dates back in the USA to the 1920s

- a growing number of visitors to remote national parks that were beyond the public transport network. This started what has become a major theme of US domestic tourism, namely, visiting wilderness areas in a private car or RV (recreational vehicle).

The development of US tourism was also stimulated by the creation of travel agency chains, beginning with 'Ask Foster' in 1888 and American Express three years later. Since World War II, both domestic and outbound tourism has increased in the USA. Indeed, for many Europeans the stereotype of a tourist is normally an American. Yet the truth is that, given the size of the population, Americans are not great world travellers. Relatively few possess a passport and the majority exhibit a preference for domestic holidays. This may well reflect the great size and diversity of their own country, but it may also be related to other issues such as the notably modest level of skill in foreign languages possessed by most Americans.

In recent decades, the USA has, however, pioneered a number of new forms of visitor attractions which have been adopted elsewhere in the world. These include:

- theme parks, beginning with Disneyland in California which opened over 40 years ago
- leisure shopping
- open air museums, with live interpretation, such as Old Sturbridge Village, the Plimoth Plantation, and Mystic Seaport in New England
- waterfront redevelopment projects, for example, those of Baltimore, Boston and San Francisco.

Furthermore, they have led the way in the development of some new tourism markets that have spread to Europe. For example, the 'Snowbirds', which travel to Florida and the South West from the North to escape the harsh winter, are now being imitated by the Britons who winter on the Spanish and Portuguese coasts.

The USA also provided the model for the development of destination marketing agencies around the world, based on the principle of public–private sector partnership, through the Visitor and Convention Bureaux, which are found in most US towns and cities.

If we now turn our attention to Canada, much tourism has traditionally been based on the beauty of the natural environment. In the late nineteenth and early twentieth centuries it was the railroad which stimulated the growth of Canadian tourism. Rail companies such as Canadian Pacific developed hotels as well as providing the transport for tourists.

In recent years, however, Canada has started to broaden its tourism appeal in a number of ways, notably:

- becoming a destination for skiers from Europe
- offering city breaks that explore the different linguistic cultures, such as English-speaking Toronto and French-speaking Montreal.

Central America

Tourism in Central America (including Mexico) has a relatively long history, but it has experienced rapid growth since the 1960s. In 1960 the region received 749 000 international arrivals, according to the World Tourism Organization, but this figure had risen to 2 919 000 in 1970 and more than 7 000 000 by 1989. According to the World Tourism Organization, there were major differences in the place of origin of tourists visiting different countries within the region. Mexico, for example, received 92 per cent of all its visitors from the USA and Canada, and only 3 per cent came from other Latin American countries. On the other hand, the equivalent figures for Guatemala were 26 per cent and 56 per cent respectively. Mexico's situation is clearly explained by its proximity to the USA. However, while Mexico has focused on beach and coach tour holidays, other countries in the region have pioneered new forms of tourism, notably eco-tourism. It is in this field that Belize and Costa Rica have built their fledgling tourist industries in the past decade.

The Caribbean

The Caribbean is a single name that covers hundreds of very different islands. It includes countries with different colonial histories, including Dutch, French, Spanish and British colonies, and countries with distinctly different modern political histories. Cuba is part of the same region as the American influenced capitalist 'tax havens' of the Virgin Islands and the Bahamas. So it is no surprise to learn that its tourism takes many different forms, but two factors we have already mentioned have determined the tourism history of the area, namely colonial history and modern politics.

The first point is evident in the markets for different Caribbean Islands. Former British colonies such as Jamaica and Barbados attract British visitors, whereas former French colonies and French 'Outre Mer Départements' such as Guadeloupe and Martinique attract mainly French tourists. At the same time a shared history and language draws Spanish tourists to the Dominican Republic.

However, this pattern is showing evidence of breaking down with up-market British tourists being attracted to the French-speaking Caribbean and those in search of value-for-money visiting the all-inclusive resorts of the Dominican Republic.

Cuba illustrates the second point about modern politics perfectly. Seaton (1996) tells us that, 'up to the 1958 revolution, Cuba was the most successful Caribbean destination with a thriving tourism industry primarily controlled by US interests and made up of US visitors'. Gambling was perhaps the major motivation for these tourists.

After the revolution, the US government introduced a trade blockade of Cuba and the flow of American tourists dried up. To some extent they were replaced by visitors from Europe who were sympathetic to the politics of the new regime of Fidel Castro.

The story continues today with Cuba trying to broaden its appeal and attract mass-market package tourists to offset its loss of financial support from the old Soviet Union.

Interestingly, though, while we have seen that the Caribbean is a very diverse region, its countries have a long tradition of working together in mutually beneficial destination marketing campaigns. This has been largely achieved through the Caribbean Tourism Organization, a governmental agency whose origins date back to 1951, which has an office in New York.

In recent years, the Caribbean has attracted, primarily, three types of tourism, namely cruises, beach holidays and visits from people who emigrated, or whose parents emigrated from the region.

South America

Tourism to South America has a history that dates back decades but it did not really grow dramatically until the 1960s. The World Tourism Organization, in 1990, reported that between 1950 and 1960 the number of international arrivals grew only from 410 000 to 426 000. However by 1970 the figure was 2 422 000 and by 1989 it was up to around 8 000 000 arrivals.

In the early days of tourism in South America, cruises were a major product and air travel developed rapidly in the region between the two World Wars, at a time when cities such as Buenos Aires were seen as sophisticated places to visit.

Business tourism has been present in the region for decades based on the exploitation of crops such as coffee and vital raw materials such as the nitrates required by the fertilizer industry, and the mining of tin, for example.

Recent decades have seen the rise of newer forms of tourism in South America such as visits to the cultural heritage sites of Peru and trips to the carnival in Rio de Janeiro, Brazil.

Political stability has always been an inhibiting factor for the development of tourism in some countries such as Bolivia and Paraguay. However this very instability has become quite a motivator for a small niche market of adventure travellers.

The market for South America has developed considerably in Spain and Portugal in recent years, due to the common shared language and the growth of foreign holiday-taking by Spanish and Portuguese tourists.

In 1990, the leading players in attracting international tourism in South America, according to the World Tourism Organization, were:

Argentina	1 951 000
Brazil	1 929 000
Venezuela	615 000
Colombia	541 000

However, we must not ignore the fact that some of these countries also have significant domestic tourism markets too, notably Argentina and Brazil.

Africa

The continent of Africa is so diverse that making generalizations about it is at best problematic, and at worst, meaningless. But we can say that tourism has existed in Africa for many centuries. We know, for instance, that the Greeks and Romans visited the sights of Egypt.

There has also been more outbound tourism from some parts of Africa, over the centuries than one might think, particularly in terms of business tourism and religious tourism. For example, Nigerians who are Muslims have made pilgrimages to the Middle East for a very long time.

However, Africa is undoubtedly largely a receiver rather than a generator of international trips, and has been since the last century. We should remember that Thomas Cook was offering tours to the historic treasures of Egypt at the end of the nineteenth century.

During the first half of the twentieth century, the British played a major role in opening up Africa as a tourist destination, particularly in the countries which were then still part of their Empire.

In the 1920s and 1930s, the two main regions which attracted foreign visitors, apart from Egypt, were:

● Kenya, where the appeal was big game hunting
● Morocco, which was a popular winter sun destination, favoured by, amongst others, Winston Churchill.

After gaining their independence, many African countries sought to attract tourists to help develop their economies. Between the 1960s and 1980s, a number of African countries began to attract foreign tourists. Tunisia and Morocco became popular summer sun destinations, and wildlife holidays were being offered in Tanzania and Botswana, for example. In the 1960s, Scandinavian tourists discovered Gambia, which in the 1980s was to become a popular winter sun destination for British tourists.

Africa also saw some early experiments in what is now termed sustainable tourism. For instance, there were experiments in small-scale rural tourism in the Casamance region of the former French colony of Senegal.

However, the growth of tourism in Africa has been constrained by political instability and the poverty of many countries. For instance, in the past three decades tourism has been disrupted by a range of problems, including:

● war in Uganda
● civil war in Nigeria
● a coup d'état in Gambia
● the threat of terrorism in Egypt and Algeria.

The link between politics and tourism is most clearly seen in regions of South Africa. After the country was ostracized by the international community because of its apartheid policies, relatively few international tourists visited South Africa and few residents of the country travelled abroad. Only the white minority could participate actively in the well-developed domestic tourism industry. At the same time, some whites travelled to the so-called 'tribal homelands' like Bophutatswana and resorts such as Sun City where mixed race relationships were tolerated.

With the end of apartheid and the election of a new government, South Africa has begun to attract large numbers of foreign tourists. Indeed buying property in the country has become popular amongst Europeans and Americans. There has also been a large growth in business tourism, with the resumption of normal trade relations between South Africa and the rest of the world.

Finally, as some African economies have developed, most notably that of Nigeria, outbound tourism from these countries has grown, both in terms of business and leisure tourism.

The Middle East

The countries of the Middle East have a long history of involvement in the tourism industry, most notably in terms of religious tourism. This region is the most important pilgrimage destination in the world for three major religions, namely:

● Muslims, for whom both Mecca and Jerusalem are very sacred places. The tourist flow to Mecca is probably the largest single annual movement of tourists in the world
● Christians, for whom the cities of Nazareth, Bethlehem, Jerusalem and Jericho are the most important religious cities
● Jews, for whom Jerusalem is the holiest city.

However, it is not only religion which has brought tourists to the region. The Middle East has also always been an important crossroads for business travellers. Some Silk Route caravans used to be routed through Syria and Jordan to the Mediterranean coast, for instance.

Until its civil war, the Lebanon, and Beirut specifically, was one of the world's most fashionable and sophisticated tourist destinations. This is clearly illustrated by an advert placed by the British airline BOAC in 1962 which described Beirut as an 'international playground'. It offered a return flight for £105 – a fortune in 1962 – and promised passengers, 'exotic night spots', great skiing, and 'fabulous beaches'.

The wars between Israel and her neighbours in 1967 and 1973, and the civil war in Lebanon in the 1970s and 1980s, greatly hindered the rise of tourism in the region. However, in recent years the Middle East peace process has helped stimulate a rejuvenation and growth of the industry. It has particularly stimulated the development of cross-border tours of the regions' heritage, typically featuring Jordan, Israel, Palestine and Egypt.

However, at the time of writing, tension has risen in Israel and the Palestinian territories, which is threatening the future of pilgrimage and cultural tourism in the region.

Nevertheless, Israel is still seeing its tourism arrivals growing on its Red Sea coast, in resorts like Eilat, particularly in relation to winter sun packages and watersports holidays.

Finally, Middle Eastern countries that have never before tried to attract tourists are either attempting to develop tourism or at least are starting to make it easier for tourists to enter them, including:

- Dubai, with its emphasis on shopping and desert safaris in four-wheel drive vehicles
- Iran, which is increasingly opening its borders to foreign tourists
- Lebanon, which is rebuilding its tourism industry and attempting to re-enter the international tourism market.

Asia

Clearly, Asia is a large continent which encompasses a wide variety of national tourism markets with very different characteristics.

In countries like Thailand and the Philippines inbound tourism began with visiting sailors, followed by the arrival of package tourism in the past two decades. For example, according to Richter, writing in 1989, Thailand's market grew as follows:

	Arrivals
1960	81 340
1970	628 671
1980	1 858 801
1986	2 818 292

Source: Richter in Hitchcock, King and Parnwell (1993)

Thailand's resorts are now a cheap, good quality destination for Europeans seeking a sun, sand and sea holiday, but Bangkok has still maintained its reputation for sex tourism which dates back to its days as a shore trip for sailors.

In India, there is a strong tradition of domestic tourism of two types, namely:

- trips to hill stations during the hot summer months
- visits to religious festivals.

Inbound tourism, on the other hand, has tended to focus on historic cities but coastal resorts such as Goa and Kerala have become major destinations for foreign package tourists looking for winter sun holidays.

While most Asian countries have been trying to attract foreign tourists, Japan has been trying to encourage its population to holiday abroad, 'as a way of alleviating trade friction with neighbouring countries' (Mackie in Harrison, 1992). Indeed in 1986 some 5.5 million were taking foreign holidays (Inove, 1991). However, the holiday market in recent decades in Japan has been constrained by the continued habit amongst Japanese people of working long hours and taking fewer holidays than other nationalities.

The tastes of Japanese tourists and their tendency to demand familiar food, drink and accommodation can be a controversial issue, as for example on the Gold Coast in Australia. They also show a preference for other Asian countries with cultures more similar to their own such as South Korea.

In recent years the newly industrialized nations of Asia such as South Korea and Singapore have started to become significant generators of international tourist trips.

In recent years, some countries in Asia have begun to attract foreign tourists in significant numbers, including China and Burma (Myanmar). One of the most spectacular growth rates in international arrivals has been seen in Vietnam. According to figures quoted in Hitchcock, King and Parnwell (1993), visitors to Vietnam rose from just 20 000 in 1986 to 187 000 in 1990 and with an estimate of 500 000 in 1995. This growth has been fuelled by political change in the country itself, a desire by foreigners to see its cultural and heritage attractions, and by a growing trade in visits by American Vietnam War veterans.

Across the region, special interest and beach-based tourism are taking over from the 'travellers' of yesterday.

Finally, the 'jet-age' has created important 'stop-over markets' for certain Asian countries such as Hong Kong and Singapore, on air routes between Europe and Australasia.

Australasia and the Pacific Rim

Australia and New Zealand, though they have relatively small populations, have a long tradition of outbound tourism, particularly amongst the younger population of both countries. Harcourt et al. (1991) offered figures on the growth of outbound tourism from Australia, as follows:

	Outbound trips
1965	161 692
1975	911 815
1985	1 512 018

These tourists have traditional taken relatively long trips to Europe and Northern America, but Asia is now also attracting large numbers too.

At the same time, the main market for inbound tourism to Australasia has traditionally been people from Europe primarily, visiting friends and relatives (VFR) who have emigrated to the region. In the early days, this market was largely English-speaking but it increasingly reflects the multicultural nature of Australian society. Many of the 'VFR' tourists are now equally likely to be Greek or Asian.

But Australia has also attracted considerable numbers of leisure tourists from Japan, who have shown a particular preference for the Gold Coast of Queensland. This has led to a growth of infrastructure geared to the tastes of Japanese visitors. Australasia is also attracting growing numbers of tourists from Europe and North America, who are lured by the natural beauty. For example, there are trips to the Kakadu National Park in Northern Australia and whale watching in New Zealand.

The islands of the South Pacific have long held an appeal for Western tourists as they are perceived to offer exotic 'paradise' experiences. They are also now attracting Japanese visitors making nostalgic trips to World War II battle sites on islands like Guam.

Antarctica

Antarctica is unique in the tourism world in that its lack of a permanent resident population means that the only tourism is inbound, rather than outbound or domestic.

The region did not begin to attract tourists until the 1950s. However, although numbers are still small, the growth rate has been dramatic. Statistics quoted by Hall and Johnston (1995), in an edited work on Polar tourism, present the following picture of the growth of arrivals in Antarctica:

1957–1958	194
1967–1968	147
1977–1978	845
1987–1988	2782
1992–1993	7037

The same text tells us that more than 90 per cent of visitors to the region arrive by sea, on cruise ships. These cruises originate from ports in Australasia, Argentina and Chile, principally. While the cruises may last for an average of 12 to 15 days, most cruise passengers spend only a few hours on land in the Antarctic.

Inter-regional comparisons across the world

There have clearly been considerable differences in the nature and volume of tourism demand between different countries and regions of the world. Some have been generators of international trips while others have generated very few such trips. On the other hand certain regions have traditionally been popular tourists destinations while others have until recently attracted relatively few tourists. There are also very different levels and patterns of domestic tourism between different countries, even within the same region of the world. For example, French people take far more domestic holidays that their neighbours in Germany.

The nature of tourism in different countries has been influenced by a myriad of factors including, for example:

● climate
● geographical location

- history
- language
- the development of transport systems
- levels of economic development
- the quality of landscapes and townscapes
- government policies towards tourism
- the degree of economic and political stability.

However, in recent years the picture of world tourism demand has begun to change dramatically. Newly industrialized countries such as Korea have started to become major generating countries for tourism trips. At the same time, countries renowned for receiving tourists, such as Spain, have also begun to generate tourist trips. Political change has created opportunities for Eastern Europeans to travel outside their own region.

At the same time, there has been a general growth in long-haul travel which has taken tourists to countries where they did not travel before, outside their own continent.

Table 2.1 shows how the regional shares of international tourist arrivals have changed over time.

Table 2.1   Regional shares of international tourist arrivals, 1950–1990 (%)

Date	Country					
	Africa	Americas	East Asia/ Pacific	Europe	Middle East	South Asia
1950	2.0	30.0	–	66.0	–	0.1
1960	1.5	24.0	–	72.0	–	0.3
1970	1.8	23.0	–	70.0	–	0.6
1980	2.5	19.0	7.0	69.0	2.0	0.8
1990	3.3	20.0	11.0	64.0	1.4	0.8

Source: World Tourism Organization (1991)

The most significant trends appear to be the relative decline in the Americas and the increase in the share of East Asia and the Pacific. However, we must put these percentage share figures in context. While the Americas show a reduction in their share of international tourist arrivals of a third, between 1980 and 1990, their number of visitors actually grew from 7 485 000 to 84 000 000 over the same period (World Tourism Organization, 1991). In other words, these figures have to be seen in the context of the phenomenal rise in international tourism which was experienced between 1980 and 1990.

Nevertheless, there is a clear trend towards the Pacific Rim and, to a lesser extent, Africa, which is evident in the history of international tourism over the past few decades, and particularly the last 10 to 15 years. As far as we can see this trend seems set to continue.

Different types of tourism

Having looked at the chronological development of tourism from a geographical perspective, it is now time to consider it in terms of different types of tourism. Dividing tourism up into sub-types is always subjective, but the authors believe that the way they have chosen allows interesting points to be made about the growth of tourism and the development of tourist behaviour.

This section, therefore, covers the following types of tourism:

- Visiting friends and relatives
- Business tourism
- Religious tourism
- Health tourism
- Social tourism
- Educational tourism
- Cultural tourism
- Scenic tourism
- Hedonistic tourism
- Activity tourism
- Special interest tourism.

Visiting friends and relatives (VFR)

This phenomenon clearly dates back to the earliest days in pre-history when migration first separated families. Notwithstanding the immense difficulties of travelling in ancient times, it is natural that, from time to time, family members would have wanted to see each other. The same is true of friends who were permanently or temporarily parted by migration and nomadic lifestyles. Weddings and religious festivals provided opportunities for the earliest form of 'VFR' tourism.

In recent centuries this form of tourism has been further stimulated by a range of factors, including:

- increased leisure time
- improved transport systems
- better housing so that people can now accommodate their friends and relatives more comfortably in their own homes.

The VFR market is notoriously difficult to measure, for two main reasons, namely:

- much of it is domestic and no national boundaries are crossed
- VFR tourists do not usually make use of commercial accommodation establishments, where visitor data could be collected.

However, the growth of economic migration in recent decades, around the world, has given a new impetus to this market. The families or individuals who migrate permanently or temporarily, to improve their economic well-being, create markets for VFR trips. While such trips bring little benefit for accommodation suppliers, they can bring considerable new business for transport operators and travel agents, as the following examples illustrate:

- so-called 'guest workers' in Germany returning home by air and rail to Turkey to visit friends and family
- trips to India, Pakistan and Bangladesh from the UK
- Moroccan and Algerian people, who live in France using ferries and flights to visit their families in North Africa
- expatriate British workers returning home for brief visits to the UK from Middle East countries such as Saudi Arabia and Kuwait.

Clearly, the demand for visiting families is potentially greater amongst those communities where the extended family, rather than the nuclear family, is the norm.

Business tourism

We are inclined to think of business tourism as a fundamentally modern phenomenon. In our minds it is means by purpose-built convention centres, business people jetting around the world, product launches, training seminars, and incentive travel packages. Yet, business tourism is one of the oldest forms of tourism, it is just that the type of business tourism has changed over time.

Until this century, business travel was largely related purely to trade, to selling and transporting goods to customers who resided outside the area of production. It thus involved:

- visits to potential customers by 'sales people', the so-called commercial travellers
- the transporting of goods to the customer.

This activity has been going on for longer than we often imagine and each new piece of archaeological research seems to indicate that its history extends even further back into the mists of time. Furthermore, early business tourism is not restricted to any one continent. Evidence of it has been found, in terms of artefacts discovered by archaeologists, that could only have been produced elsewhere, all over Africa, the Americas, Asia, the Middle East and Europe. There is evidence of trade taking place in all these countries.

There is a tendency to believe that, because of the poor state of transport systems until the modern era, most trade generally only involved short-distance movement. This is clearly not true. Not only were ships used widely for longer distance trade, but also well-developed, long-distance overland routes existed many centuries ago.

Perhaps the greatest example of this phenomenon is the former 'Silk Route' which brought silk from China to Europe by way of such magically named places as Samarkand and Constantinople. This route, or more accurately set of interconnecting routes, covered thousands of kilometres and was used for hundreds of years.

From its early days, business tourism developed its own infrastructure, reflecting the needs of the business traveller. In the case of the Silk Route this revolved around food, accommodation for the travellers, and the supply of water for their beasts of burden in the arid regions of Central Asia. Many of the buildings that served these travellers remain today as a memorial to early business tourism such as the caravanserai where caravans of merchants would stop for rest. Some of these are now being restored as tourist attractions, in Turkey, for example. Indeed, one of the authors recalls a meal taken in a fourteenth-century caravanserai in the Azerbaijani city of Baku, more than a decade ago!

The desire of merchants to travel together for safety led to the growth of caravans, and thus the development of a new type of professional, the caravan master. But early trade and business tourism also led to the growth of a range of professions over the years including sailors, carters and canal boat operators, all with their own unique lifestyles.

Alongside the individual business trips and the activities of those involved in transporting goods, the third major stream of business tourism has been the trade fair. Here people from a region or a specific industry would gather together to sell to each other and exchange professional news. Such trade fairs are not a recent invention, they date back hundreds of years. For example, in the Middle Ages, there was a famous annual fair at Beaucaire, on the banks of the Rhône, which was known all over the Western world.

In Europe, at least, the growth of business tourism was greatly stimulated by the Industrial Revolution, and throughout the world it was made easier by the introduction of the railway.

However, like leisure tourism, the real boom in business tourism did not occur until after World War II. Its rapid growth has been fuelled by a number of factors, including:

- improvements in transport technologies
- the rise of the global economy
- the growth of supra-national trading blocks such as the European Union and the trade agreement between the USA, Canada, and Mexico, NAFTA, for example
- the effort made by governments to attract high-spending business tourists to their country
- the development of new forms of business tourism such as incentive travel.

Business tourism is no longer just about sales trips and the transport of goods. It now involves conferences where information is exchanged, lavish events to launch new products, survival weekends to motivate or reward staff, and intensive training courses.

New forms of business tourist have appeared linked to these developments in business tourism. There is the company trouble-shooter, the trainer and the conference circuit traveller. However, certain traditional types of business traveller are declining in numbers, notably the 'commercial traveller' made increasingly obsolete by developments in communication technologies. Their passing has been the death knell for many small, privately owned 'commercial' hotels in the UK.

A whole new industry has arisen to serve these modern types of business tourists, as well as the 'traditional' individual on a business trip. It is an increasingly specialist field with major corporations seeking to achieve competitive advantage in this most lucrative of tourist markets.

It is important to recognize that throughout history there has been a strong link between leisure tourism and business tourism. The business tourist becomes a leisure tourist when the working day is over and is often accompanied by a partner who is a full-time leisure tourist. Furthermore, as they are often travelling at someone else's expense, business tourists can represent a particularly high-spending segment.

The way business tourists have chosen to spend their leisure time has, however, often been controversial. For example, it is business tourists who have often been the stimulus for the growth of red light districts and prostitution, from Amsterdam to Bangkok.

Religious tourism

We saw earlier in this chapter that, in Europe for example, religion was a major catalyst for early tourism. Religious tourism usually includes visiting places with religious significance, like shrines, or attending religious events such as saint's day festivals. However, it would be a mistake – though one which is often made by tourism historians – to talk about religious tourism mainly in terms of Christian pilgrimages in Europe.

Religious tourism undoubtedly existed long before Christianity. Devotion to a religion motivated trips by ancient peoples including the Egyptians, Greeks and Jews. Travel for religious reasons existed in India and Asia, for example, before Christ was born. Many early religions that motivated pilgrimages in ancient times are now much less influential, such as the fire-worshippers or Zoroastrians.

And at a time when Europe was in the so-called 'Dark Ages' the Islamic religion came into existence. We in the West often forget that the Islamic pilgrimage to Mecca is still perhaps the greatest single tourist flow in the world, eclipsing in size modern Christian pilgrimages.

Having made this important point, we would like to return to Christian tourism in Europe to make several, hopefully interesting, points.

Firstly, it is often said that the difference between tourism in the past and modern tourism is that the former was small-scale and elitist while the latter is on a mass scale and more democratic. Yet if we look at the European Christian pilgrimages we can see a very different pattern, as can be seen from Figure 2.1.

We can see that this form of religious tourism peaked in the Middle Ages and has since declined, as religious observance has declined, particularly in Northern Europe. It also reflects the rise of Protestantism in Europe which

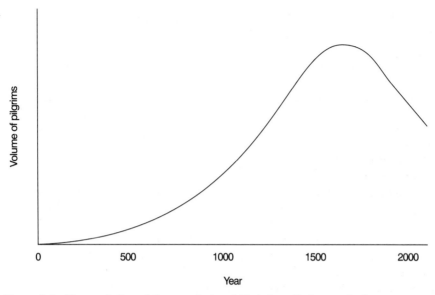

Figure 2.1 The evolution of the popularity of Christian pilgrimages in Europe

has never placed the same emphasis on pilgrimages as Catholicism. Where the latter religions are still practised by the majority of the population, such as Ireland, the pilgrimage is still popular.

For one market segment, there is a strong link between religious and health tourism. These are the people who visit more modern shrines such as Lourdes in the hope that they will be cured of their diseases.

Finally, the religious tourism in Europe is a good example of how infrastructure developed for one form of tourism can be used in the future for another type of tourism. The great cathedrals that were built as symbols of, and places for, religious devotion and pilgrimages, are now merely another sightseeing attraction for the package tourist. Events with great religious significance, such as processions parading the towns' patron saints through the streets, become entertainment for tourists. Pilgrimage routes, such as Santiago de Compostella have become themed tours for ordinary non-religious tourists, while accommodation built to shelter pilgrims has become a trendy stopover for tired cyclists.

However, this can only happen when the original fundamental purpose has largely become obsolete or of relatively minor significance. It is therefore not happening to Islamic infrastructure, for instance, in an era when the Islamic religion is growing and flourishing.

Health tourism

As we saw in the context of Europe, health tourism laid the foundations for the development of much of the modern tourism industry in Europe. Although pioneered by the Romans, it did not become popular again until the sixteenth and seventeenth centuries. It grew then as a response to the unsanitary conditions in many towns and cities.

At first, health tourism was simply about exploiting natural phenomena, such as mineral springs and sea water, for their medicinal benefits. However, as time went on, these resorts also became centres of fashion and social activity. The history of these spas and resorts is described in a little more detail earlier in the chapter, in the section on Europe. However, it would be wrong to suggest that this development was only confined to Europe. Spa resorts grew up in other continents such as those found in the USA in upstate New York.

It would be also incorrect to give the impression that seaside bathing and spa visiting were the only forms of health tourism. In the seventeenth and eighteenth centuries, many wealthy Europeans paid lengthy visits to reputed doctors at renowned medical schools such as Montpellier in France. These visits resulted in some of the most famous travel writing of the era.

Also, for centuries, climate has played a major part in health tourism. While in Northern Europe, this usually means the idea of travelling in search of the sun, it has motivated very different types of tourism flow. Particularly during the age of colonial expansion, European colonists often sought to escape summer heat by moving up to the cooler hills. An excellent example was the practice in India of spending the summer at hill stations like Simla. In doing this, they were however only continuing a much earlier tradition established by the Maharajas.

Health tourism, in Europe at least, is an excellent example of fashion cycles in tourist behaviour. Many of the spas which were so popular between the sixteenth and nineteenth centuries in Europe went into decline in the first half of the twentieth century. They ceased to be socially fashionable while improvements in health-care standards made them less necessary. In some resorts political instability and the onset of war made them less accessible to their former markets. While this is generally true, there are exceptions, like Germany, where the involvement of trade unions and social tourism organizations in spa tourism has meant that some have maintained their position.

However, in France, though not in the UK, spas have enjoyed a renaissance in recent years with the growing interest in health. They have again become smart places where health care is combined with leisure facilities and entertainment. The Auvergne region of France, in particular, is exploiting this new interest in spas to develop high-spending forms of health tourism.

In recent years the interest in health has even led to a rediscovery of sea-water bathing as a health-enhancing activity. Thalassotherapy is very popular in France, for example, where companies such as Accor have invested heavily in the necessary facilities.

We have also seen the rise of the 'health farms' in Europe and the USA where many women and some men take a short break to lose weight and improve their fitness.

The most sophisticated modern form of health tourism is that where people travel abroad for medical treatment, to institutions which are perceived to be world leaders in their field.

Two case studies later in the book offer more detail on the 'health farm' market and the international spa market respectively (see Case Studies 13 and 14).

Social tourism

In general, the holiday market is a commercial market where consumers are asked to pay a full market price for their vacation. However, in a number of countries, tourism and holiday-taking is also encompassed within the realms of welfare policy. Here, holidays are subsidized in some way, either by government or voluntary sector agencies such as non-profit making organizations or trade unions. This may be termed social tourism.

This form of tourism is largely absent from the UK where its only manifestation is in the area of subsidized holidays for carers, offered by some charities and local authorities. However, it is much more prevalent in other countries, notably Germany, Spain and France.

In the latter country, social tourism is well developed and its 'infra-structure' includes:

- 'Chéques-Vacances' which can be exchanged for tourism services
- social tourism holiday villages and centres, operated by non-profit-making associations.

This provision is subsidized by employers, trade unions and the government. However, pressures on public spending are currently casting a shadow over the future of social tourism in France.

Although not strictly speaking social tourism, we have seen in recent years, attempts being made by the tourism industry to provide a better service for groups in society who have been largely ignored, or even discriminated against, by the industry. These groups include two in particular, namely:

- consumers with disabilities, including those with mobility problems, impaired sight or hearing difficulties
- single-parent families who are often unable to take advantage of the usual 'family' offers stipulating that a family means *two* adults and a number of children. This is clearly discriminatory in a world where, due to divorce, an increasing number of families have a single parent.

As yet, however, little effort appears to be being made, overall, by the tourism industry, in Europe at least, to encourage people from ethnic minority communities to participate in the mainstream tourism market. Yet, in many European countries these communities represent markets that run into hundreds of thousands of consumers.

Perhaps, however, the situation reflects the feeling that many ethnic communities have their own established patterns of tourism demand, such as visiting friends and relatives in the country from which their parents and grandparents came. This market is often serviced by specialists suppliers, drawn from the communities themselves.

However, the USA shows that in due course such communities do develop a demand for mainstream travel services, but these may still be met by specialist operators drawn from these communities. This is true, for instance, of the Black American market.

Educational tourism

Educational tourism, or travelling to learn, has a long history, from the days when wealthy members of the Greek and Roman elites travelled to increase their understanding of the world. Centuries later came one of the greatest manifestations ever of education tourism, in Europe at least, the 'Grand Tour'.

In recent decades, educational tourism has developed in a number of ways, of which two are perhaps particularly worthy of note. They are:

1 **Student exchanges**, where young people travel to other countries to study and learn more about the culture and language of other people. Such exchanges have developed strongly between educational institutions in North America and Europe. For example, many Americans travel to Aix-en-Provence in France to attend special courses put on for them by the local university. Sometimes the relationship goes even deeper, as in the case of the Université Canadienne Française which operates a campus for inbound Canadian students, at Villefranche-sur-Mer on the French Riviera. Exchanges are also well developed between member states of the European Union, thanks to the ERASMUS programme, now being superseded by the SOCRATES scheme.
2 **Special Interest Holidays**, where people's main motivation for taking a trip is to learn something new. This market has grown rapidly in recent years and now encompasses everything from painting holidays to cookery classes, gardening-themed cruises to language classes. This market is particularly strong amongst early retired people, the so-called 'empty-nesters'.

Cultural tourism

Cultural tourism is clearly linked to the special interest tourism we have just been discussing. However, it is broader in scope. The desire to experience other current cultures and view the artefacts of previous cultures has been a motivator in the tourism market since Greek and Roman times. Today, it is extremely popular and is often viewed positively by tourism policy makers, as a 'good' form of tourism, as 'intelligent tourism'.

Cultural tourism encompasses many elements of the tourism market, including:

● visits to heritage attractions and destinations, and attendance at traditional festivals

- holidays motivated by a desire to sample national, regional or local food and wine
- watching traditional sporting events and taking part in local leisure activities
- visiting workplaces whether they be farms, craft centres or factories.

Clearly, cultural tourism is the core of the tourism product in many countries and is the main reason why tourists visit these countries.

However, concern is often expressed at the impact tourists can have on the cultures they wish to experience, making this a very sensitive sector of the tourism market.

Scenic tourism

The desire to view spectacular natural scenery has stimulated tourists since time immemorial. However, it perhaps really 'came of age' in the nineteenth century, through the influence of the 'Romantic Movement' in the arts. Artists and writers drew inspiration from the natural environment and created popular interest in landscapes. Tourists then began to come to view these same landscapes for themselves, and to follow in the footsteps of the artists.

An example of this phenomenon in the UK is the way in which Wordsworth stimulated tourism to the Lake District, through his poetry. Today, his houses in the heart of the area, Dove Cottage and Rydal Mount, attract tens of thousands of tourists in their own right.

Scenic tourism grew dramatically in the last century in both Europe, particularly in the Alps, and in the USA, where the steady growth of tourism was one of the factors that led to the creation of the world's first national park there in 1872.

As well as mountains, water-related scenery also became a draw for tourists in the nineteenth century. The Lakes region of Italy, for instance, and the dramatic coastal scenery of Brittany and Cornwall, became popular during this era.

We must remember that in seaside resorts that we now see as urban areas, their original appeal to their first visitors was often their natural scenery.

Hedonistic tourism

We tend to believe that hedonistic tourism, motivated by a desire for sensual pleasure, is a modern creation, encapsulated in the now classic four 'S's' of sea, sand, sun and sex. However, hedonistic holiday-making has a much longer history. We saw earlier that the Romans practised this form of tourism in their resorts. In the UK such tourism has given rise to the term, the 'dirty weekend', usually associated with the south coast resort of Brighton. Here Londoners in the strict Victorian era took their 'partners', or someone else's partner, off to Brighton where they could behave in ways that were not acceptable in London!

Paris, from the nineteenth century onwards, developed as Europe's first capital of hedonistic tourism. Young men from affluent families were sent there to complete their 'education' in the ways of the world. This often involved visiting brothels, going to risqué shows and gambling.

However, other cities too based much of their appeal on hedonism and pleasure-seeking. Writing about Vienna, Steward (1996) says 'By far the strongest component of the city's place image was its reputation for frivolity [and] the pleasure-loving nature of its inhabitants.'

Hedonistic tourism has reached new peaks though in the current era with the rise of the 'sea, sun, sand and sex' package holiday, from the 1960s onwards. The promise of hedonistic experiences is now the core offer of some operators such as Club 18–30, in the UK market. We have also seen the rise of distinct hedonistic market segments in recent years, such as the so-called 'Shirley Valentines', Northern European married older women who travel to the Mediterranean resorts in search of romance with local men.

Though often harmless fun, hedonistic tourism is often seen to have a negative impact on both the tourists themselves and the host community. Both are at risk from diseases such as AIDS, while the latter is often offended by the tourists' behaviour.

Finally, there is currently considerable international debate about sex tourism, particularly involving Europeans travelling to developing countries, for sex with children. This is clearly far from harmless and represents the morally unacceptable face of hedonistic tourism.

Activity tourism

Activity holidays are a more recent development but are a rapidly growing market. They are based upon the desire for new experiences on the part of the ever more sophisticated tourist, and are also a reflection of growing social concerns such as health and fitness.

Activity tourism is a broad field that encompasses, for example:

- using modes of transport to tour areas which require effort on the part of the tourist such as walking, cycling and riding
- participating in land-based sports such as golf and tennis
- taking part in water-based activities like diving and wind-surfing.

Some forms of activity holidays can be criticized in terms of their impact on the physical environment. Golf courses take up valuable green field sites, while walking and riding cause erosion. On the other hand, activity tourism is often viewed positively because it is seen as a phenomenon which improves people's health.

Special interest tourism

In recent years we have seen the growth of special interest tourism, where the motivation is a desire to either:

1 indulge in an existing interest in a new or familiar location, or
2 develop a new interest in a new or familiar location.

Like activity-based tourism, special interest tourism can be either:

● the focus of the whole holiday, or
● a way of spending one or two days during a holiday.

Special interest tourism is a niche market acting like activity-tourism, but it differs in that it involves little or no physical exertion. The types of interest are, nevertheless, very diverse with some of the most popular being:

● painting
● gastronomy, both learning to cook and enjoying gourmet meals in restaurants
● military history and visiting battlefields
● visiting gardens
● attending music festivals.

Summary

The list of types of tourism we have just examined is clearly subjective but, hopefully, it does show the breadth of the tourism market. It illustrates too that the different types of tourism are linked. For example, religious tourism can also be seen as cultural tourism. At the same time the brief preceding section has shown that few forms of tourism are new.

But what about the future? Perhaps the next major development in tourism will be the rise of techno-tourism, tourism based on new technologies such as Virtual Reality. This could be a revolutionary change where tourism no longer involves travel, and tourism experiences of a kind can be enjoyed from the comfort of the tourist's own home.

Conclusion

To understand present and future tourist behaviour it is essential that we have an appreciation of the history of consumer behaviour in tourism. For that reason we have spent a relatively large number of pages discussing the history of tourism demand. However, it is important to recognize that it has still only been an outline, full of generalizations, where countries have been reduced to a paragraph or less. Nevertheless, hopefully, the reader will have identified a number of key points, notably the following:

1 tourism is older than we often appreciate
2 tourists have existed for centuries in many countries, not just in Europe and the USA.

The emphasis in this chapter has been on international tourist flows, but we must also recognize that domestic tourism has, perhaps, a longer history, and is certainly much greater in volume. However, it is harder to measure and it is the growth of mass international tourism which has been at the forefront of the rise of modern tourism.

Discussion points and essay questions

1 Discuss the ways in which Britain played a major role in the growth of modern tourism.
2 Critically evaluate the suggestion that tourism history was born in Europe but its future lies in Asia and the Pacific.
3 Discuss the ways in which business tourism demand has changed over the past two thousand years in terms of both the types of business tourism and business tourism destinations.
4 Using examples, evaluate the suggestion that few, if any, tourism markets are new.

Exercise

Choose a country from *each* of the following regions of the world:

- Europe
- the Americas
- Africa
- Asia.

For each country, produce a summary of its history as a destination for inbound foreign tourists, using statistics wherever possible.

Finally, compare and contrast the situation in each country and suggest reasons for the similarities and differences.

3 Main concepts in consumer behaviour, including models of consumer behaviour which have been adapted for tourism

The purpose of consumer behaviour models is to attempt to give a simplified version of the relationship of the various factors that influence consumer behaviour. The models were developed and describe consumer behaviour with the intention of trying to control the behaviour patterns. The models, however, fall short of these objectives and at best give the reader an appreciation of interactive factors that influence behaviour patterns.

It is only possible to review some of the general consumer behaviour models here. One of the earliest models of consumer behaviour was proposed by Andreason (1965). This model is shown in Figure 3.1.

The model recognizes the importance of information in the consumer decision-making process. It also emphasizes the importance of consumer attitudes although it fails to consider attitudes in relation to repeat purchase behaviour.

A second model, which concentrates on the buying decision for a new product, was proposed by Nicosia (1966). This model is shown in Figure 3.2. The model concentrates on the firm's attempts to communicate with the consumer, and the consumers' predisposition to act in a certain way. These two features are referred to as Field One. The second stage involves the consumer in a search evaluation process which is influenced by attitudes. This stage is referred to as Field Two. The actual purchase process is referred to as Field Three, and the post-purchase feedback process is referred to as Field Four. This model was criticized by commentators because it was not empirically tested (Zaltman, Pinson and Angelman, 1973), and because of the fact that many of the variables were not defined (Lunn, 1974).

The most frequently quoted of all consumer behaviour models is the Howard–Sheth model of buyer behaviour which was developed in 1969. This model is shown in Figure 3.3. The model is important because it highlights the importance of inputs to the consumer buying process, and suggests ways in which the consumer orders these inputs before making a final decision.

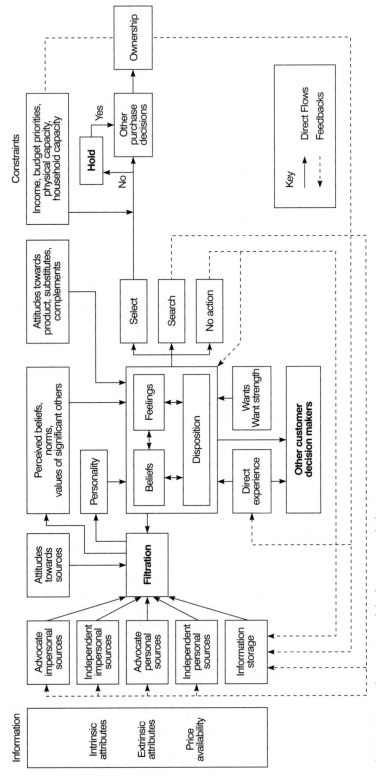

Figure 3.1 Andreason's model of consumer behaviour

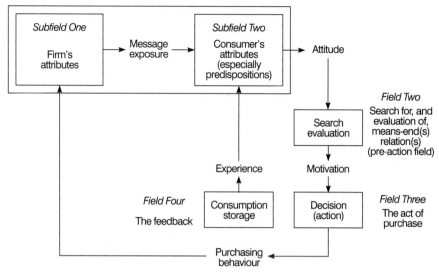

Figure 3.2   A summary description of the Nicosia model
Source: Nicosia (1966)

The Howard–Sheth model does have limitations, and does not explain all buyer behaviour. It is however, a comprehensive theory of buyer behaviour that has been developed as a result of empirical research (Horton, 1984). More recent research on consumer behaviour has concentrated more on the exchange processes and has attempted to look at the marketer's perspective on the process. One example of such an approach is shown in Figure 3:4. This model was developed by Solomon (1996). He also suggested that consumer behaviour involves many different actors. The purchaser and user of a product might not be the same person. People may also act as influences on the buying processes. Organizations can also be involved in the buying process. One example of an organization which may make purchase decisions is the family.

The models which have been considered so far are useful in academic research.

Foxall and Goldsmith (1994) suggested that these models mean little in the absence of a general understanding of how consumers act. They suggest that consumer behaviour is a sequence of problem-solving stages as follows:

● the development and perception of a want or need
● pre-purchase planning and decision making
● the purchase act itself
● post-purchase behaviour which may lead to repeat buying, repeat sales and disposition of the product after consumption.

Much of marketing activity, they suggest, concentrates on adapting product offerings to particular circumstances of target segment needs and wants. It

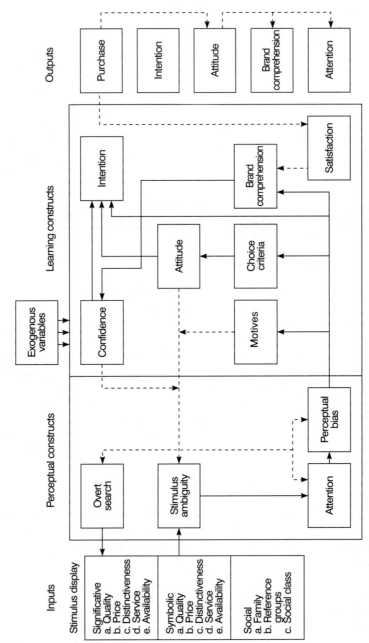

Figure 3.3 The Howard–Sheth model of buyer behaviour
Source: Howard and Sheth (1969)

	Consumer's perspective	**Marketer's perspective**
Pre-purchase issues	How does a consumer decide that he/she needs a product? What are the best sources of information to learn more about alternative choices?	How are consumer attitudes toward products formed and/or changed? What cues do consumers use to infer which products are superior to others?
Purchase issues	Is acquiring a product a stressful or pleasant experience? What does the purchase say about the consumer?	How do situational factors, such as time pressure or store displays, affect the consumer's purchase decision?
Post-purchase issues	Does the product provide pleasure or perform its intended function? How is the product eventually disposed of, and what are the environmental consequences of this act?	What determines whether a consumer will be satisfied with a product and whether he/she will buy it again? Does this person tell others about his/her experiences with the product and affect their purchase decisions?

Figure 3.4 Some issues that arise during stages in the consumption process
Source: Solomon (1996)

is also common to stimulate an already existing want through advertising and sales promotion, rather than creating wants.

The definitions and models which have been presented so far have been from general marketing theory. Tourism is, by its very nature, a service rather than a product which may have a considerable effect on consumer behaviour. Services have been defined by Kotler and Armstrong (1994a) as:

Any activity or benefit that one party can offer to another that is essentially intangible and does not result in the ownership of anything. Its production may or may not be tied to a physical product.

The intangible nature of the service offering will have a considerable effect on the consumer during the decision-making process involved with purchase. This, coupled with the high spend aspect of tourism, will mean that tourism involves the consumer in a high risk decision-making process. This will mean that the consumer will be highly interested and involved in the decision-making process, since there is a considerable amount of risk associated with the purchase decision. This has been recognized by Seaton (1994) as follows:

They involve committing large sums of money to something which cannot be seen or evaluated before purchase. The opportunity cost of a failed holiday is irreversible. If a holiday goes wrong that is it for another year. Most people do not have the additional vacation time or money to make good the holiday that went wrong.

There is a philosophical question as to whether service marketing is substantially different to product marketing (Horner and Swarbrooke, 1996). It is clear, however, that tourism products have many distinctive features which mean that consumer behaviour will be fundamentally different. To cope with these differences, academics have developed definitions and models of consumer behaviour, specifically for tourism. These range from the more general definitions to more detailed models.

Middleton (1994) presented an adapted model of consumer behaviour for tourism which was termed the stimulus-response model of buyer behaviour. The model is shown in Figure 3.5. This model is based on the four interactive components with the central component identified as 'buyer characteristics and decision process'.

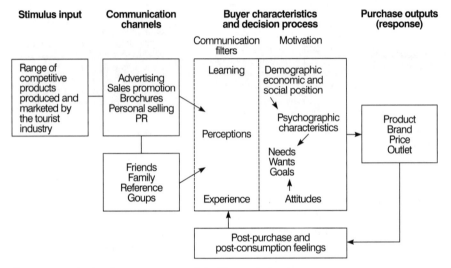

Figure 3.5   A stimulus-response model of buyer behaviour
Source: Middleton (1994)

The model separates out motivators and determinants in consumer buying behaviour and also emphasizes the important effects that an organization can have on the consumer buying process by the use of communication channels.

Other models which attempt to explain consumer buying behaviour in tourism have been advanced. Wahab, Crompton and Rothfield (1976) have suggested a linear model of the decision-making process in tourism. This is shown in Figure 3.6.

Initial framework   Conceptual alternatives   Fact gathering

Definition of assumptions   Design of stimulus   Forecast of consequences

Cost benefits of alternatives   Decision   Outcome

Figure 3.6   Linear decision-making process in tourism
Source: Wahab, Crompton and Rothfield (1976)

All of these models which have been adopted for tourism offer some insights into the consumer behaviour process involved during the purchase and post-purchase decision. The problems with the models is that little empirical research has been conducted to test these models against actual consumer behaviour. This is obviously an area which necessitates further detailed research. We will return to this discussion later in the book, when we consider models of consumer behaviour in tourism in more depth.

Schmöll (1977) quoted in Cooper *et al.* (1993), developed a model which hypothesized that consumer decisions were a result of four elements as follows:

- travel stimuli, including guide books, reports from other travellers and advertising and promotion
- personal and social determinants of travel behaviour including motivators, desires and expectations
- external variables, including destination images, confidence in travel trade intermediaries and constraints such as cost and time
- characteristics and features of the service destination such as the perceived link between cost and value and the range of attractions and amenities offered.

Mathieson and Wall (1982) suggested a linear five-stage model of travel buying behaviour, which is shown in Figure 3.7.

| Felt need/ travel desire | Information collection and evaluation image | Travel decision (choice between alternatives) | Travel preparation and travel experiences | Travel satisfaction outcome and evaluation |

Figure 3.7 Travel-buying behaviour
Source: Mathieson and Wall (1982)

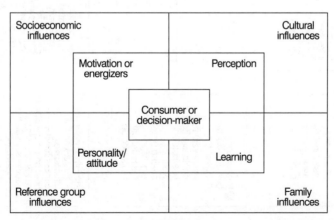

Figure 3.8 Consumer decision-making framework
Source: Gilbert (1991). Copyright John Wiley & Sons Limited. Reproduced with permission

48

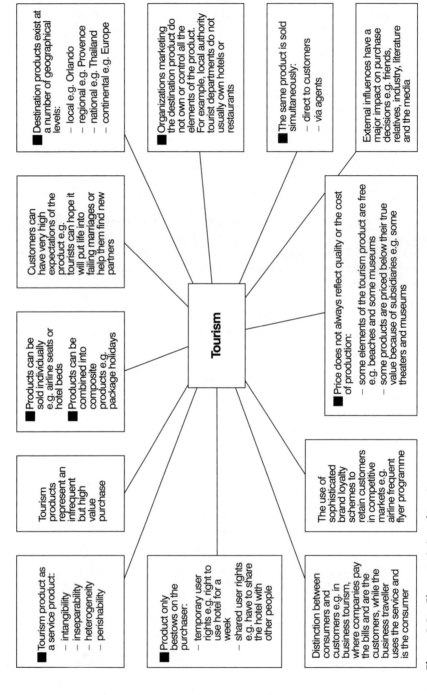

Figure 3.9 Characteristics of tourism

Gilbert (1991) suggested a model for consumer decision-making in tourism, which is shown in Figure 3.8. This model suggests that there are two levels of factors which have an effect on the consumer. The first level of influences are close to the person and include psychological influence such as perception and learning. The second level of influences include those which have been developed during the socialization process and include reference groups and family influences.

All of these models which have been adapted for tourism offer some insights into the consumer behaviour process involved during the purchase and post-purchase decision stages. The problems with the models is that little empirical research has been conducted to test these models against actual consumer behaviour. This is obviously an area which requires further detailed research. We will return to this discussion later in the book, when we consider models of consumer behaviour in tourism in more depth.

Conclusion

Most consumer behaviour models in tourism seem to be linear and rather simplistic, compared to general consumer behaviour models. Yet, as Figure 3.9 illustrates, the diverse characteristics of tourism mean that consumer behaviour in tourism will inevitably be very complex. The inadequacy of models of tourist behaviour is a subject we will return to in Chapter 6.

Discussion points and essay questions

1 The purchase of a holiday does not result in the consumer owning any physical product. Discuss the effect of this on consumer behaviour.
2 Evaluate the reasons for a consumer choosing to buy a composite tourism product, rather than the individual components.
3 The media can have a major influence on consumer choice in tourism. Evaluate the ways in which a tour operator can use this feature to boost sales.

Exercise

Design a small-scale consumer panel which could be used to evaluate the reasons for consumers choosing a particular tourism product.

Part Two
The Purchase-decision Process

In this part, we will look at the factors which influence the tourist to purchase a particular tourism product. Part Three will then go on to consider the ways in which we can model how these factors are translated into the final purchase decision.

As far as the factors are concerned, we will divide these into:

1 the motivators, the factors which motivate the tourist to wish to purchase a particular product
2 the determinants, the factors which determine to what extent the tourist is able to purchase the product they desire.

However, before we move on to the two chapters that cover these issues, perhaps we should begin with a few words about the tourism product itself.

1 The product is complex and multi-layered in that:
   - it has both tangible elements (hotel beds, food, etc.) and intangible elements (service delivery)
   - it can range from a simple one-night stay in a hotel or a day trip to a theme park to a tailor-made eight-week round-the-world itinerary.
2 The tourist buys an overall experience rather than a clearly defined product. The experience has several clear phases, namely:
   - the anticipation phase, before the trip commences
   - the consumption phase during the trip
   - the memory phase after the trip has ended.
3 The tourist is part of the production process in tourism which means that their:
   - attitudes, mood and expectations affect their evaluation of their tourist experience rather than just the quality of the product they are offered by the industry
   - behaviour directly impacts on the experience of their fellow tourists with whom they share a resort, aircraft or hotel.
4 The tourist experience is heavily influenced by external factors, which are beyond the control of the tourist or the company that sells them a product.

These external influences include weather, strikes, war and outbreaks of disease.

In this part of the book, we are going to restrict ourselves to a consideration of one type of tourist product, the package holiday. This is the most complex tourism product and it is the one which distinctly separates tourism products from those of other industries such as hospitality and transport.

By necessity, we will have to generalize about the subject and about the motivators and determinants that affect tourists. But we must recognize that, as Ryan (1997) says:

The context, meanings, and experiences of tourism can vary from holiday to holiday, from tourist to tourist. To talk of the 'tourist experience' seems to imply a homogeneity which, in reality, is not always present.

4 Motivators

Introduction

A wide range of factors motivate consumers to buy tourism products. In this chapter, we will examine the motivators which encourage tourists to make particular purchase decisions. The authors will begin by outlining the range of motivators that are thought to influence tourists. There will then be a discussion of how motivators vary between different types of tourism product and different groups of people.

It is important to recognize that there is still a dearth of detailed, reliable, research on this subject, across the whole breadth of tourism. Some of the comments in this chapter, therefore, represent subjective observations on the part of the authors. However, in most cases these observations are ones with which many other academics and practitioners would concur.

The number and range of motivators

Motivating factors in tourism can be split into two groups, namely:

- those which motivate a person to take a holiday
- those which motivate a person to take a particular holiday to a specific destination at a particular time.

There are many potential motivators that could relate to either or both of these. Furthermore, there are a number of potential 'variations on a theme' for each individual motivator, and a myriad of ways in which they can be combined.

No widely recognized way exists of categorizing the main motivating factors in tourism. However, some of the major ones are outlined in Figure 4.1.

However, there are other ways of classifying motivators in tourism and the wider field of leisure. We will now go on to outline some of these.

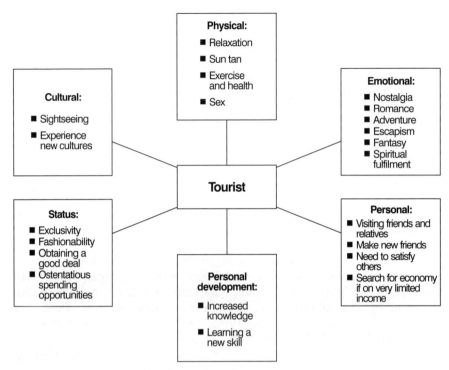

Figure 4.1   A typology of motivators in tourism

The leisure motivation scale

In 1983, Beach and Ragheb developed a model called the Leisure Motivation Scale, which sought to clarify motivators into four types, based on the work of Maslow. The four types were as follows:

(a) *The intellectual component, which assesses the extent to which individuals are motivated to engage in leisure activities which involve . . . mental activities such as learning, exploring, discovery, thought or imagery.*

(b) *The social component which assesses the extent to which individuals engage in leisure activities for social reasons. This component includes two basic needs . . . the need for friendship and inter-personal relationships, while the second is the need for the esteem of others.*

(c) *The competence-mastery component which assesses the extent to which individuals engage in leisure activities in order to achieve, master, challenge, and compete. The activities are usually physical in nature.*

(d) *The stimulus-avoidance component which assesses the desire to escape and get away from over-stimulating life situations. It is the need for some individuals to avoid social contact, to seek solitude and calm conditions; and for others it is to seek to rest and to unwind themselves.*

We have to recognize that the motivators that make people wish to take a holiday are not universally present. Some people appear to have little or no desire to take a holiday, for whatever reason.

Motivators and the individual tourist

Every tourist is different and so are the factors they are motivated by. The main factors determining an individual tourist's motivations are probably:

1 **personality**, in other words, are they:
   ● gregarious or a loner?
   ● adventurous or cautious?
   ● confident or timid?
2 **lifestyle**, which provides the context for their purchase decision. The motivations are likely to be different for people who are very concerned with being fashionable, are preoccupied with their health, live alone and want to make new friends, or enjoy partying.
3 **past experience** as a tourist and particular types of holiday, both positive and negative.
4 **past life** – motivations such as most notably nostalgia are a direct result of people's life to date. This may include where they took their honeymoon or military battles they have taken part in.
5 **perceptions** of their own strengths and weaknesses, whether these relate to their wealth or their skills.
6 **image** – how they wish to be viewed by other people.

We must also recognize that motivators change over time for each individual in response to changes in their personal circumstances. These circumstances might include:

● having a child, or meeting a new partner
● an increase or reduction in income
● worsening health
● changing expectations or experiences as a tourist.

Multiple motivations

No tourist is likely to be influenced by just one motivator. They are more likely to be affected by a number of them at any one time. The office worker staring out of an office window in suburban London today may be motivated by a desire to take any holiday, anywhere to escape the monotony of their daily working life. However, they may have a number of other motivators that would influence the type of holiday they would like to take. They may, for example:

- want to escape a wet spell at home, and enjoy some sun and get a suntan
- desire a chance to take some physical exercise as a contrast with their sedentary lifestyle and to improve their health
- wish to pursue a hobby, whether it be surfing or eating Italian food
- want to widen their circle of friends or find a new partner
- wish see a particular church or museum
- want to relax.

Most people's holidays represent a compromise between their multiple motivators. Either one motivation becomes dominant or a holiday is purchased which ensures all of the motivators can be at least partly satisfied.

Shared motivators

We rarely take holidays alone, and who we take them with has an influence over the factors which influence our decisions. Imagine a women who is married and is the mother of two young children, is a member of a women's football team, and a church-goer. Her motivations may be different depending on which group she is intending to holiday with. If she is taking a trip with her children, then meeting their needs and keeping them happy may be her main motivation. On the other hand, she and her husband may be taking a trip on their own, to celebrate their wedding anniversary, in which case romance may be the main motivator. When she takes a trip to play football with her team, it may be seen as escapism or a chance to indulge her passion for playing football. Finally, with her fellow church-goers, she may be seeking spiritual fulfilment from a trip.

It is rare, perhaps, for every member of a holiday party to share exactly the same motivators. Differences in this respect undoubtedly account for much of the stressful side of holiday-making.

Many trips represent a compromise between those in a group travelling together where:

- the views of a dominant member may prevail
- each member will go their own way for at least part of the time
- the group will stay together but each member will be allowed to choose what they will all do on one or two days.

Expressed and real motivators

We do not always express our true motivations because we:

- do not feel they will be seen by others as being acceptable. It can be difficult to admit that you are only going on holiday to party and enjoy casual sex. It is far easier to talk about a more general desire to relax, unwind and 'have a good time'

- may not always recognize our motivations – they may be subconscious or unconscious
- may recognize that they are apparently conflicting. For example, we may want to relax by dancing and partying all night!
- can be aware of contradictions between our motivating factors and our actual behaviour. We may claim to want to improve our French when we go to France and meet French people. Then, because of our circumstances, or budget or perhaps fear, we book a stay in an English-owned villa, in a village in the Dordogne where there seem to be few French people and everyone speaks English! This could be the result of an unfortunate chain of events or the outcome of the triumph of a subconscious motivator not to be humiliated in public, on holiday, because of one's lack of current ability to speak French.

The following hypothetical case study illustrates the complexity of the subject of motivators in the tourist behaviour field.

Case study: The Brown family

Perhaps we can best describe the points made in the last few sections of this chapter through a mini case study of a hypothetical family, the Browns.

In 1988, Mr and Mrs Brown married and took their honeymoon on the French Riviera. Both were keen sailors and chose this destination because they wanted to be able to go sailing together every day. They were besotted with each other, and every evening they sought the most romantic places they could for late candlelit dinners. Dancing and making love were high on their list of priorities and they did not care if they never spoke to another person during the whole of their holiday. Both were young and adventurous and took part in a range of other activities like rock-climbing and ballooning. Mrs Brown would have also liked to look around the art museums but her husband was not interested, so she gave in because she did not want her husband to be unhappy.

By 1998 things have changed. The Browns now have two young daughters, and their relationship has deteriorated. Mr Brown is still obsessed with sailing but Mrs Brown has given it up. This year they are on holiday with friends at an old farmhouse on a Greek island. They say this is because they have not seen these friends for many years. However, their real motive is to minimize the need for them to have to talk to each other and to give them an opportunity to share the child care and go off separately from time to time. The whole holiday has been planned around keeping the children happy for they know that if the children are miserable, everyone in the group will have an awful holiday. Mrs Brown secretly hopes to meet a new lover on the beach, while her husband is out sailing. Mr Brown wants to sail to help him relax. However, one evening they go together for a candlelit dinner, at their friends' suggestion, to a romantic restaurant that they went to years ago, overlooking the harbour. The evening is a disaster – there is an icy atmosphere and they barely speak to each other.

Mrs Brown spends much of her holiday time taking part in her new interest of horse-riding which she took up following the previous year's holiday in Majorca, when she tried it for the first time. Mrs Brown chose the farmhouse because it has a swimming pool to keep the children happy, and all mod cons in the kitchen, to minimize the work involved in preparing meals and doing the dishes. This matters a lot because these days, as Mr Brown rarely helps out in the kitchen.

> Before coming away they told their neighbours they were taking a holiday to relax. The truth is, it was a last attempt to see if they could rescue their ailing marriage.
>
> Hopefully, this case has illustrated some of the points we have made so far in this chapter. It also shows the close link that exists between motivators and determinants. The latter subject will be taken up in Chapter 5 but let us now return to the question of motivators.

Motivators and different market segments

Not only are motivators different for each individual tourist but perhaps they also vary between different market segments. For example, the tourism industry seems convinced that segments are based on demographic criteria. They seem to assume that:

1 young people want to party, relax, drink heavily, have sex, dance, and make lots of new friends
2 elderly people are presumed to have a preference for sedate activities like bowls and bingo, and to be almost obsessed by nostalgia
3 parents are thought to be preoccupied with the need to keep their children happy. They are also thought to want to escape from their parental responsibilities from time to time to spend time together.

There has been some research to test the motivating factors for different demographic groups. In 1996, Kaynok et al. published a study of Irish travellers' perceptions of salient attributes that led to their travel preferences of major foreign holiday destinations. This study found significant differences between tourists of different ages, sexes, educational attainment, income and marital status.

Young people preferred vacations which gave opportunities for activity-based holidays while older travellers sought restful destinations with sightseeing opportunities. The more highly educated respondents showed a preference for destinations offering opportunities for nature-based or cultural activities. One the other hand, those people with a lower level of educational attainment stressed the importance of a vacation where they could try new and unfamiliar activities that were very different from their everyday life. Those on lower incomes saw their holiday as a chance to get away from the monotony of everyday life, and indulge in activities that built up their self-confidence. On the other hand, higher income earners wanted an intellectually stimulating holiday with excitement, and the chance to increase their knowledge of the destination area.

Motivators and gender

One aspect of demographics which the tourism industry seems to believe determines personal motivators is gender. Different products such as golf trips or shopping trips seem to be based solely on a desire to match the perceived motivators of men and women respectively.

However, when one looks at a range of personal motivators, there is some evidence to suggest that there is in fact relatively little difference between the sexes.

Research quoted by Ryan (1997) noted that with fourteen motivators there were significant differences in the weighting given to them by men and women in three cases. Women placed rather more value on trying to use a holiday to:

- avoid daily hustle and bustle
- relax physically
- relax emotionally.

National and cultural differences

As yet, relatively little work appears to have been done on national and cultural differences in relation to motivators. This is rather surprising at a time when more and more tourism organizations are seeking to sell their products to people in other countries.

We know that in some instances there are great similarities between groups of countries in terms of motivators. People in Northern European countries and the Northern states of the USA are often motivated by the desire to develop a suntan. However, in hot countries like India and Saudi Arabia, the intention is to take trips to the cooler hilly areas to escape the intense heat at lower altitudes.

Some motivators are universal, such as nostalgia and romance, and the desire to see sights, although the actual behaviour will be influenced by the nationality and culture of the tourist.

Many people around the world seek some form of spiritual fulfilment. However, the desire for such fulfilment, and the wish to embark on a pilgrimage to gain it, is more common generally amongst Muslims than Christians these days.

Motivators and different types of tourism product

Marketers clearly try to link the products they develop to the factors which motivate their target markets. Conventional wisdom certainly seems to indicate a belief that some motivators are closely associated with different types of tourism product. This is perhaps best illustrated in the visitor attractions sector. Figure 4.2 suggests some possible links between motivators and different types of visitor attraction.

We can see that there are some different motivators for different types of products, but there are also common ones such as status. Most of us are

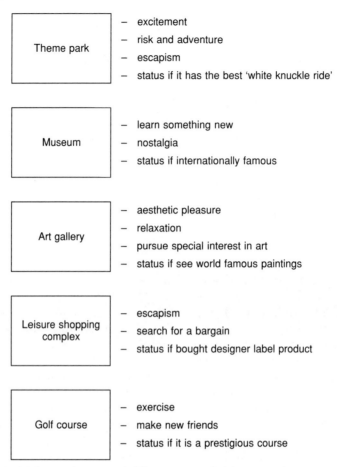

Figure 4.2   Major motivators and different types of visitor attractions

interested in status, but its meaning varies from one type of attraction to another.

It is also important to recognize that the motivators listed in Figure 4.2 are highly generalized. They ignore the fact that attractions serve many markets, which each have their own different motivators. Young people at a theme park may want excitement for themselves, but grandparents may go there with their grandchildren to please the children. Families may search out the gentler rides, while parents may want the nostalgic pleasure of revisiting a park they visited as children.

Motivators and the timing of purchase decisions

Motivators can also vary depending on when the decision to purchase a holiday is made. A last-minute booking may reflect a desire to obtain a discounted bargain or a wish to surprise a partner, or be a response to stress at work. On the other hand, a vacation booked many months in advance may be a result of a desire to:

- visit a famous annual event where early booking is essential to secure accommodation and flights
- enjoy the pleasure of looking forward in anticipation to the holiday.

Conclusion

It appears that the issue of motivation is highly complex and depends on a range of factors, including:

- the personality and lifestyle of the potential tourist
- their past experiences
- who they are planning to take a vacation with
- their demographic characteristics
- how far in advance they book their trip.

As you read Chapter 5, it will become clear that there are great similarities between motivators and determinants. There is a thin line, a grey area, between our desires and the factors which determine our actual behaviour.

Discussion points and essay questions

1 Examine the ways in which an individual's personality may affect their motivators in relation to taking a holiday.
2 Discuss those changes involved in suggesting that people with certain demographic characteristics will be motivated by particular factors.
3 Compare and contrast the likely motivators of people taking a 'sun, sea, sand and sex' holiday to a Greek island, with those on an upmarket holiday cruise around the Caribbean.

Exercise

Design and implement a questionnaire survey of a small number of adults to try to ascertain the main motivating factors that influence their choice of holiday. You should then produce a critical evaluation of your survey to highlight and account for its weaknesses.

5 Determinants

Types of determinants

There are two types of determinants, namely:

1 those factors which determine whether or not someone will be able to take a holiday
2 those factors which determine the type of trip, if the first set of determinants allow a holiday to be taken.

In this chapter we will generally be considering the latter set of factors.

The type of trip taken can encompass a huge range of variables, including:

- the destination for the trip
- when the trip will be taken
- the mode of travel to be used
- the duration of the trip
- who will comprise the holiday party or group
- the type of accommodation that will be used
- the activities undertaken by the tourist during the holiday
- how much will be spent on the trip.

We can further subdivide determinants into:

- those which are personal to the tourist
- those which are external to the tourist.

These two types of factors are illustrated in Figure 5.1 and 5.2 respectively. Both are generalized pictures but they serve to illustrate the variety of determinants that exist.

Some of these determinants can preclude the individual from taking any trip. Health problems could be the best example of this phenomenon. Others will simply affect the type of trip that is taken.

It is clear that the determinants listed in Figure 5.1 will not carry equal weight with all tourists at all times. Different individuals will perceive

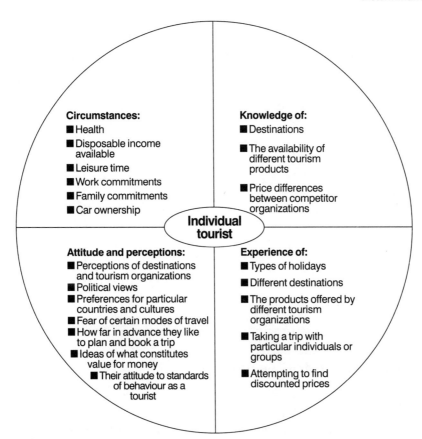

Figure 5.1   Personal determinants of tourist behaviour

certain determinants to be more important than others, based on their attitudes, personalities, principles, fears and past experiences. Even for the same individual the weighting given to each determinant will vary over time with changes in age, family situation and experience as a tourist.

Where some personal determinants are shared by a large proportion of the population, they may represent a market opportunity for the tourist industry.

As economies grow in the Pacific Rim, and European and American companies fight to compete in world markets, there are pressures on leisure time; managers feel they need to be at work as much of the time as possible. This has been one of the reasons for the growth of intense short duration forms of vacation such as themed weekend breaks. These meet the needs of tourists looking for a short break from work that will stimulate them.

At the same time, many airlines have seized upon the determinant which can stop some people taking any form of foreign holiday, namely, the fear of flying. This determinant clearly reduces their potential market. Therefore, they have begun to offer courses to help people overcome their fear of flying.

Figure 5.2   External determinants of tourist behaviour

It is clear from these two brief examples that the tourism industry can exploit certain determinants for their own benefit, or seek to influence them, again for their own benefit.

Perhaps the best example of the industry influencing and exploiting a determinant is the issue of price. Many tourists like to feel they have found a holiday at a discounted price. There is considerable status value potentially in being seen to have 'negotiated' a good deal for a tourism product. Therefore, the industry emphasizes the bargain dimension in its selling with banner headlines in travel agents and offers such as 'free child places', '20% off' and 'free insurance'.

The factors in Figure 5.2 can clearly be broken down into 'subfactors', as the following examples demonstrate:

- Political factors:
  - government legislation and policy
  - immigration restrictions and visa requirements
  - civil disorder and terrorism
  - the nature of the political system
  - taxation policy, e.g. airport taxes and tourist taxes.
- The media:
  - travel media, e.g. holiday features on television, in newspapers and guidebooks
  - non-travel media, e.g. news programmes and wildlife programmes on television.

- Tourism organization marketing:
  - foreign destinations' advertising campaigns
  - tour operators' brochures
  - travel agents' special promotions.

The extent to which the tourists' behaviour is determined by their own personal determinants or external determinants varies between tourists in relation to factors such as their personality and their lifestyle.

Extrovert people may be more inclined to take account of external determinants, such as the views of their many friends and relatives. Introverts, on the other hand, may rely more on their own experiences. Well-educated people who watch news programmes regularly and take an interest in world-wide social or environmental issues may be influenced by external factors such as the human rights record of a particular country's government. Those who either do not worry about such things, or do not even know of the situation in that country, may not even consider this factor.

It is also important to note that most determinants can be either facilitators, or constraints upon, tourists who wish to turn their motivations and desires into reality or not.

For instance, high disposable income will be a facilitator while limited and low disposable income would be a constraint. Likewise, a guidebook which painted a rosy picture of a resort would be likely to persuade a potential tourist to visit it, in contrast to a negative portrayal which would normally have the opposite effect.

The determinants of group travel

In the case of group travel, whether it be a family or a party of friends, the issue of determinants is particularly complex.

Each individual has their own determinants but the group has a set of determinants of its own. Each individual's determinants must be satisfied in a way that keeps the group as a whole content. This means compromise on behalf of every group member.

Alternatively, a strong group member may impose their determinants, such as a fear of flying, on every other group member. The others would have preferred to fly to their holiday destination, but find themselves taking a ferry instead to meet the needs of the dominant group member.

The myth of rational decision making

Tourists do not make wholly rational decisions based on perfect information. They may be ignorant of many of the determinants listed in Figures 5.1 and 5.2.

On the other hand, they may be well aware of them but choose to ignore them. For example, a young couple with two small children and stressful jobs may know they cannot afford a holiday, but they feel so desperate for a break from the daily routine that they decide to take a trip anyway. This is not rational behaviour although, to anyone in a similar situation, it is wholly understandable! As in other aspects of life, pressure and emotion often overwhelm logic.

The role of unforeseen circumstances and opportunism

Following on from the issue of rational decision making, are the twin matters of unforeseen circumstances and opportunism. Plans based on a tourist's current situation may become obsolete literally overnight due to unforeseen changes in their personal circumstances. An obvious example relates to the tourist's health where a decision to take a skiing holiday based on good previous experiences of such holidays would need to be rethought if the prospective tourist breaks one of his or her legs!

On the other hand, unforeseen circumstances can have a positive effect on tourist behaviour. A family may have decided that they cannot afford to take a trip from the UK to France, this year. Then the value of the pound against the franc rises dramatically and newspapers start offering cheap ferry tickets. This persuades the family to change their mind and take a short trip to Northern France.

The last-minute discounted purchase phenomenon

The concept of determinants is geared to the idea of a relatively long period spent by the tourist planning their vacation, gathering information and evaluating alternatives. However, one of the growing phenomena of the tourist industry today is the 'last-minute purchase' decision. Here the determinant is a desire to escape at short notice and a willingness to accept a less than ideal product if the price is low enough.

The role of the tourism industry

The tourism industry plays a major role in affecting the determinants of tourist behaviour. For example, it:

- develops products specifically to match the determinants of some tourist behaviour. For example, it can offer packages designed for tourists who have particular health problems such as mobility difficulties
- provides information to prospective tourists on everything from health problems to visa requirements, destination climate data to information on the destination's cultural attractions

- designs its promotional messages to fit the key determinants of the behaviour of different groups of tourists. This might include emphasis on discount deals for those with limited incomes or those who like to search for bargains, reassurance about the safety of a destination, or selling the resort as one that has good facilities for children
- influences determinants such as offering people with limited budgets the opportunity to purchase tourism products on credit with repayments over a period of time.

A key role is played in this respect by the travel agent, who is the intermediary between producers in the tourism industry and their clients.
As Ryan (1997) says:

The information provided becomes part of the information that determines a holiday-maker's expectations. The travel agent possesses the means to create the antecedents of success or failure of the holiday.

Poor, or inappropriate advice from an agent that leads to the tourist having an unsatisfactory holiday may well determine their future behaviour in a number of ways. It may make them:

- avoid using the same agent in the future
- decide not to buy the products of the same tourism organization again
- give a negative view of their holiday destination to friends and relatives.

Time lapses and determinants

Many tourists probably make purchasing decisions under the influence of determinants, or perceptions of determinants, which are outdated. They may have perceptions of destinations and tourism organizations which are no longer accurate. For example, someone may still have an image of a quiet unspoilt Greek island as it was 20 years ago, when they last visited it. This may persuade them to make a return trip to the island, which is now highly developed and crowded. Or a business traveller may avoid booking with an airline because of its reputation gained a few years ago for being unreliable and having old aircraft. However, in the intervening period, this problem may have been eliminated by the purchase of new aircraft.

Tourism organizations must be aware of these time lapses and outdated determinants of tourist behaviour when planning their marketing activities.

One-off experiences of determinants of tourism behaviour

The industry should also not underestimate the impact of one-off bad experiences as determinants of future tourist behaviour. A delayed flight or a failure of the airline to deliver a pre-ordered special diet meal on one flight can result in tourists:

- boycotting the airline in future
- giving negative views about the airline to friends and relatives.

Conclusion

The determinants of tourist behaviour are complex and diverse. They include personal determinants which are different for each tourist. There are also external determinants which will be interpreted in different ways by individual tourists. Finally, we have also seen that the issue of determinants is linked to other matters, such as the actions of the tourism industry, the idea of rational decision making, last-minute purchases and the composition of holiday parties.

In the next chapter, we will see how motivators and determinants combine in the purchase–decision process.

Discussion points and essay questions

1 Describe the ways in which personal circumstances such as health, family commitments and work commitments could influence the type of trip taken by tourists.
2 Discuss the range of media that might influence tourist behaviour and the ways in which these might affect purchase decisions.
3 Explore the reasons why tourists' perceptions may not accurately reflect the main determinants that are, in reality, affecting them at a particular time.

Exercise

Carry out a survey amongst a small group of your friends/ colleagues/fellow students to try to identify which of the determinants in Figures 5.1 and 5.2 were the most influential when they last booked a holiday. You should then produce a report, outlining your results, and noting any difficulties you experienced in collecting and interpreting the data.

6 Models of the purchase decision-making process

Introduction

Having considered the motivators and determinants of tourist behaviour in the previous two chapters, it is now time for us to look at the purchase decision-making process as a whole. Before that we need to spend a little time looking at the characteristics of the product purchased by tourists.

Tourism products are complex because they exist at two different levels, namely:

- the package holiday, which is a combination of the products of individual sectors such as accommodation, transport, destinations and visitor attractions
- the products of these individual sectors, which can be sold as stand-alone products such as an air ticket or a theme park visit as part of a day trip.

In this chapter, we will focus on the former, as it is the product which distinguishes the tourism industry from other industries such as transport and the hotel industry.

Tourism product and services

Tourism products are largely services. Marketing theorists, such as Kotler and Armstrong (1994a), have attempted to define services in relation to their intangibility and the fact that purchase of a service never results in the ownership of anything. They have attempted to clarify the differences between products and services by stating the characteristics of services as being:

- **Intangibility**. Services have the characteristics of being intangible in that they cannot be seen, or tasted or smelled before purchase. Tourism companies have tried to overcome this problem by offering the consumer videos of the holiday locations to make the experience seem more 'real'.

The use of advanced technology such as Virtual Reality is also predicted to overcome the problem. Despite these advances, the consumer still has to take considerable risks when choosing their tourism product because of the intangible nature.

- **Inseparability**. Services have the characteristic of overlap between the production and performance of the service and the consumption of it. A service in its purest sense has the provider and customer face to face. This will influence consumer buying behaviour and means that consumers may change their behaviour patterns, according to their experiences.
- **Heterogeneity**. It is very difficult for the tourism provider to give the same level of service at every consumption time. The mood that the consumer is in will also affect his or her appraisal of the service – it will never be the same twice. This means that it is very difficult for the consumer to judge the potential quality of experience they will gain when they purchase the tourism product. It also means that it is dangerous for them, when they are considering repeat purchase, to rely on past experiences. What was a happy experience in the past for them, may turn out to be the complete opposite. They may have changed and have different perceptions and expectations. Similarly, the service may have changed over time.
- **Lack of ownership**. The consumer only has access to the activity or facility when he or she buys the service. The consumer never owns anything at the end of the transaction. Service often lead to feelings of satisfaction rather than the ownership of a tangible item. This means that the purchase of a service will have a considerable emotional significance for the consumer.

Convenience vs shopping goods

The characteristics of the services is only one aspect in relation to tourism products. General marketing theorists have also separated out convenience and shopping goods as having different characteristics (Middleton, 1994).

- A convenience good is a manufactured item that has a typically low price and is bought more frequently.
- A shopping good has a typically high price and is bought less frequently.

Shopping goods generally satisfy higher order needs in Maslow's hierarchy of needs. Howard and Sheth (1969) noted that the purchase of convenience-type goods involved the consumer in routinized problem-solving behaviour, whereas the purchase of shopping goods involved the consumer in extensive problem solving.

The spectrum of buyer behaviour for these two types of goods or services is explored in more depth in Figure 6.1.

This figure shows that the characteristics of services that fit into the shopping products category has a considerable effect on the consumer buying

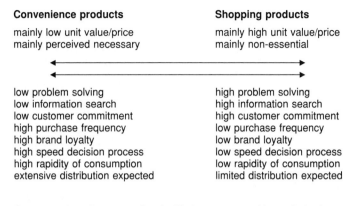

Convenience products

mainly low unit value/price
mainly perceived necessary

Shopping products

mainly high unit value/price
mainly non-essential

Convenience products	Shopping products
low problem solving	high problem solving
low information search	high information search
low customer commitment	high customer commitment
high purchase frequency	low purchase frequency
high brand loyalty	low brand loyalty
high speed decision process	low speed decision process
high rapidity of consumption	low rapidity of consumption
extensive distribution expected	limited distribution expected

Spectrum of products associated with the spectrum of buyer behaviour:

Convenience products

Shopping products

Convenience products	Shopping products
urban bus transport	holidays
commuter train transport	hotel accommodation
bank services	air transport
post office services	private education
take-away foods	motor cars
washing powder	freezers
cigarettes	carpets
branded chocolate bar	furniture

Figure 6.1 Spectrum of buyer behaviour characteristics – goods or services
Source: Middleton (1994)

behaviour. From this it can be seen that a much more complex set of issues is involved in the purchase process for tourism products, than for fmcg (fast-moving consumer goods) products. The process involves the consumer in a more difficult set of decisions, a lengthier decision time and a higher level of commitment. Middleton (1994) suggests that this results in a lower brand loyalty and the expectation of a more limited distribution chain.

Let us now consider some of the other complexities in consumer behaviour involved in the purchase of tourism products. These complexities are shown in Figure 6.2 and are summarized below.

High involvement in purchase decision and high consumer commitment

The behaviour of consumers when they are purchasing tourism products and services demonstrates a high involvement in the process and high levels of commitment because of the nature of the products and services. This means that the behaviour patterns during purchase are not routinized and every purchase occasion will show different approaches. The consumer will be actively involved in the buying process and will 'shop around' before coming to a decision. This will mean that the decision process will involve longer periods of time.

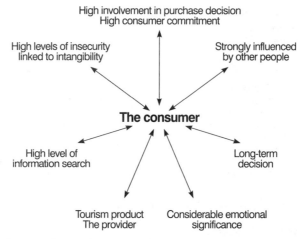

Figure 6.2   The complexity of consumer behaviour in tourism – the demand side

The consumer will also change their behaviour patterns according to the type of holiday to be taken, their motives for the particular purchase occasion, and their position in the family life cycle.

High levels of insecurity linked to intangibility

The intangible nature of tourism products and services means that the consumer can often have high levels of insecurity during purchase. They cannot try out the product or service before purchase and will therefore be looking round for reassurance about their choices. This will mean that their behaviour patterns will be very complex and will probably involve many people and agencies. The individual may take advice from their friends, family, travel agent and TV holiday programmes, for example, before making their choice of annual holiday.

Considerable emotional significance

The purchase of a holiday will be a major event in an individual's life. A holiday will let the individual escape from their work environment and grey skies to renew their flagging spirits. The choice of holiday may also affect other close members of the family and there may have to be compromises made during the decision-making process. The consumer may also be considering other substitute products and services in place of a holiday. They may, for example, be thinking about the purchase of other major items such as a car or home, rather than spending money on a holiday. This type of decision has particular emotional significance for the individual and their close associates.

Strongly influenced by other people

The individual is likely to be strongly influenced by other people during their decision-making process for tourism products. If we take an example of an individual choosing a holiday product, they are likely to be influenced by other members of their family, and members of other reference groups. This makes their behaviour patterns very complex and difficult to study. The people who influence their decision will also change their views over time.

Long-term decision

Despite the growth in the last-minute holiday bargain, most decisions that individuals make about tourism products are made a long time in advance. This means that the individual may be in a completely different frame of mind when they make their purchase decision, from when they actually go on holiday. It also means that the individual will be trying to predict what they want to do in the future. This means that the decision itself may have an immediate effect on the individual. We all know the feeling of hope and anticipation felt when, in the depths of winter, we book a holiday in sunny climes!

High level of information search

We have already seen that the choice of tourism products usually has considerable emotional significance for the individual. This will mean that individuals will usually carry out an extensive information search before they make their final choice. This will involve consultation with individuals, groups, organizations and media reports, before a decision is made. This process of research and reflection means that the behaviour patterns are very complex.

From the above, we can see that the purchase of tourism products and services does not involve the consumer in routinized behaviour patterns. This is completely different from their behaviour patterns when they are purchasing fast-moving consumer goods (fmcg), which are more mechanized and predictable.

The tourist decision-making process

The decision to purchase a tourism product is the outcome of a complex process. This is the result of a number of factors which we will consider in this chapter, which relate to the consumer and to the external influences that act upon them.

However, it is also true that the diverse and interdependent characteristics of many tourism products make the purchase decision in tourism a complex phenomenon in its own right.

- Which destination (country, region, resort)?
- Which mode of travel (scheduled air, charter air, ferry, rail, coach, car, bus)?
- Which type of accommodation (serviced or non-serviced)?
- How long will the holiday be (days/weeks)?
- At which time of the year will the holiday be taken (season, month, specific date)?
- Package holiday or independent travel?
- Which tour operator (if package holiday)?

Figure 6.3   Decisions involved in choosing a holiday

This fact can be illustrated by thinking about the range of decisions a tourist has to make when choosing a holiday. These can be seen in Figure 6.3.

A myriad of factors affect the holiday purchase decision, some of which are illustrated in Figure 6.4. Clearly these relate strongly to the motivators and determinants outlined in Chapters 4 and 5 respectively.

While Figure 6.4 shows only a selective line of the relevant factors, it does give a good idea of both the number and scope of such factors. These factors make up what might be termed the 'Consumer Decision-Making Framework' (Gilbert, 1991). Figure 6.5 illustrates the model put forward by Gilbert to explain the framework within which tourists make their decisions.

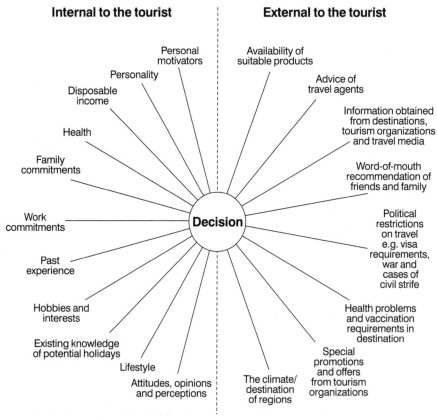

Figure 6.4   Factors influencing the holiday decision
Source: Adapted from Horner and Swarbrooke (1996)

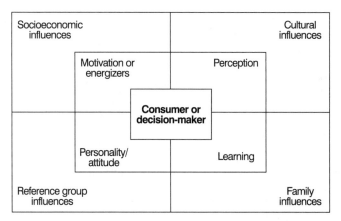

Figure 6.5   The consumer decision-making framework
Source: Gilbert (1991). Copyright John Wiley & Sons Limited. Reproduced with permission

It is also important to recognize that the complexity of tourist decision making is heightened by the fact that choosing their holiday is not the last decision a tourist has to make. Once on holiday they have to make a further set of decisions about what to do once they arrive at their holiday destination. They have to decide how to spend each day in terms of excursions and leisure activities as well as where to eat and drink, and so on.

Each of these apparently simple decisions is therefore the result of a complex decision-making process.

Models of purchase decision making in tourism

Cooper et al. (1993) have identified three stages in the development of general consumer behaviour theory in relation to purchase behaviour as follows:

The three phases of consumer behaviour theory

1 The early empiricist phase covered the years between 1930 and the late 1940s. It was dominated by empirical commercial research and industry attempted to identify the effects of distribution advertising and promotion decisions.
2 The motivational research phase of the 1950s placed a greater emphasis upon in-depth interviews, focus groups themselves as a perception tests and other projective techniques. There was a great deal of activity directed at uncovering real motives for actions which were perceived to lie in the deeper recesses of the consumer's mind.
3 The formative phase from the 1960s provided the first general consumer behaviour textbook (Engel, Kollat and Blackwell, 1968) and other influential books (such as Howard and Sheth, 1969) followed soon after.

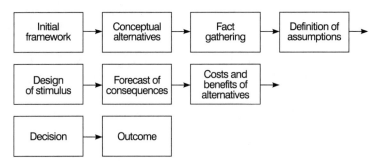

Figure 6.6   The Wahab, Crompton, and Rothfield model of consumer behaviour in tourism
Source: Wahab, Crompton, and Rothfield (1976)

However, the early interest in consumer behaviour tended to focus on manufacturing industries, and later on general service industries. It was only in the 1970s that academics began to develop purchase decision models in tourism. It is important to recognize that these purchase decision models were being developed simultaneously with the work of writers like Cohen and Plog on the related subject of tourist typologies. One of the earliest attempts to devise a model of the purchase decision process in tourism is that published in 1976 by Wahab, Crompton and Rothfield. This is illustrated in Figure 6.6.

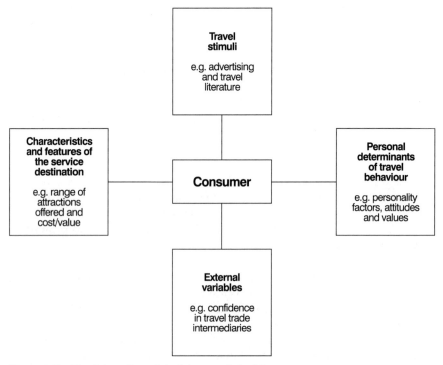

Figure 6.7   The Schmöll model of the travel decision process

This model sees the tourist purchase as an activity involving conscious planning and a logical thought process. It excluded the possibility of purchases made on a whim or spontaneous decision to take a trip. Yet we know that in the 1990s, the tour operation sector offers heavy discounted 'last minute' holidays to ensure full load factors on charter airlines and fully utilized hotel room allocations. These are proving so popular with a section of the market that they are leading to people not even worrying about the destination or accommodation provided that the price is low enough. This seems at odds with the model developed by Wahab, Crompton and Rothfield.

Figure 6.7 illustrates the model of the travel decision process put forward by Schmöll in 1977 (quoted in Cooper et al., 1993).

The Schmöll model suggests that purchase decisions are the result of the interaction of four fields of influence, which are both internal and external to the tourist. It also stresses the important effect that the tourist's own perceptions have on the final purchase decision.

The third frequently quoted market is that put forward by Mathieson and Wall in 1982. This is illustrated in Figure 6.8 in its basic form.

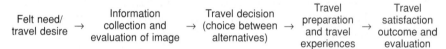

Figure 6.8   The Mathieson and Wall travel-buying behaviour model
Source: Mathieson and Wall (1982). Reprinted by permission of Addison Wesley Longman Ltd

The same authors also offer a framework for understanding the purchase decisions that involves four factors. According to Cooper et al. (1993), these are as shown in Figure 6.9.

Cooper et al. (1993) comment that:

the model is based on a geographers product-based perspective rather than that of a consumer behaviourist

The models we have briefly discussed all seem to see the decision as a linear process, and no distinctions are made about which factors may weigh heavier than others when decisions are being made.

- Tourist profile (age, education, income, attitudes, previous experience and motivators)
- Travel awareness (image of a destination's facilities and services, which is based upon the credibility of the source)
- Destination resources and characteristics (attractions and features of a destination)
- Trip features (distance, trip duration and perceived risk of the area visited)

Figure 6.9   The Mathieson and Wall purchase decision framework
Source: Cooper et al. (1993)

In 1987, Moutinho published a 'Vacation tourist behaviour model' which differed from most previous markets in two respects, namely:

1 It recognized that there are three distinctly different stages in the decision-making process, as follows: pre-decision stage and decision process; post-purchase evaluation; future decision making. The model recognized that the last of these stages would feed back to the first, through a loop in the system.
2 It explicitly noted that purchase decisions are a result of three behavioural concepts: motivation, cognition and learning.

There are many other models, although this brief section has highlighted most of the most widely discussed 'classic' models.

A critique of purchase-decision models in tourism

Most of the models we have discussed to date have some common weaknesses that both: limit their value in explaining the complex way in which purchase decisions are made in tourism, and make it difficult for tourism marketers to make use of them when developing their marketing strategies. The main weaknesses are as follows:

1 In general they are based on little or no empirical research, and there is little evidence that they represent the reality of how decisions are actually made.
2 A large number of the best-known models are now at least 15 years old. This is a significant weakness in an industry where consumer behaviour is believed to be constantly evolving. Thus most of the major models pre-date recent developments in tourist behaviour, including:
   ● the rise of the all-inclusive resort holiday
   ● the growth of direct marketing
   ● the increasing popularity of last-minute spontaneous purchases of tourism products
   ● the growing use of the Internet and multi-media systems that can be accessed from the tourists own home.
3 Most of the models developed to date have originated from work carried out by academics in North America, Australia and Northern Europe. Few, therefore, reflect the nature of consumer behaviour in the major emerging markets of South East Asia and Eastern Europe.

Another major criticism is that they tend to view tourists as a homogenous group. Clearly, this is not the case. Every tourist is different and it is possible to segment tourists on the basis of a range of factors that will influence their own individual process of making a purchase decision. Some of these factors have been explored in Chapters 4 and 5, and include, for example:

- whether tourists are travelling alone or if they are members of a family group or party
- how experienced tourists are and their past experiences as tourists
- their personality, in that some tourists make spontaneous last-minute decisions about their holiday plans, while others may enjoy spending months planning their trip.

Many models also fail to recognize the impact of motivators and determinants on the purchase decision. Some motivators and determinants may be so powerful that they totally dominate the purchase decision, to the exclusion of all other factors. These could be as diverse as an obsessive hobby such as steam railways or rock climbing to a health problem.

The majority of models also presume a high degree of rationality in the decision-making process which is not always evident. Rational decision making in tourism is limited both by the imperfect information which is available to most tourists, and by the fact that many consumers will be influenced by their own opinions and prejudices which may be irrational.

Most models also seem to assume that purchase behaviour and the process of making a decision remains constant regardless of the nature of the holiday being purchased. This is very questionable, as the following contrasting examples show.

1 The purchase of a 28-night tailor-made round-the-world package by a couple, valued at £5000, which includes stopovers with pre-booked airport transfers and accommodation in Dubai, Hong Kong, Tahiti, Sydney, Los Angeles and New York. A range of alternative airline offers have to be studied and bookings made to ensure seats on all the relevant flights. Pre-planning is also required in terms of pre-trip vaccinations. The consumer has a definite start and finish date for the tour, dictated by their annual leave from their job, so that there is no flexibility about departure and return dates.
2 The purchase of a heavily discounted last-minute 14-night holiday by a young student, who simply wants the cheapest summer sun holiday available. The destination is irrelevant and departure dates are fairly flexible, as the tourist has seven weeks off college in which to take the two-week long trip. However, they cannot make a decision until they have found out whether or not they will be required to re-sit any exams. Once they know they are able to travel, they want to be on the beach, as soon as possible!

Clearly, in these cases, the nature of the purchase decision and the effort put into making it will vary significantly. Similar differences would exist if we were to examine other types of holiday.

Purchase decision-making and marketing in tourism

Marketing professionals in tourism are increasingly aware of the need to understand how their consumers make their decisions to purchase a particular product. Currently, the research conducted by tourism organizations about consumer behaviour is only just beginning to tackle this subject seriously. It would therefore be fortuitous if the academic models could be used by marketers. An appreciation of how consumers make decisions would help them develop their marketing plans in relation to the following, for example:

- when to attempt to influence consumers, in other ways, focusing marketing activities at the time when most consumers are making decisions to buy a particular product
- the choice of advertising media based on which media the majority of consumers use to gain information about tourism products
- the selection of appropriate distribution channels or marketing intermediaries.

Therefore, we have to ask ourselves, are the models reliable enough to be used in this way. Perhaps not, for, as we noted previously, we must remember that many of them are at least 15 years old.

Marketing professionals who want to see if they can put these models into practice to guide their activities need to see if there is any link between them and the technique of market segmentation. For in a sense, these techniques represent an attempt to explain purchase decisions by reference to various characteristics of the tourist.

In other words, segmentation splits the population into subgroups who share the same purchase characteristics. It suggests that the decision of everyone in the subgroup is primarily determined by one set of influences. These influences are, in classic marketing theory, divided into four, as follows:

1 Demographic, e.g. age, sex, race, stage in the family life cycle
2 Geographical, e.g. where the tourist lives
3 Psychographical, e.g. the personality and lifestyle of the tourist
4 Behaviouristic, i.e. the relationship of the tourist to the product, e.g. the benefits they expect to receive from the purchase and whether or not they are first-time or regular purchasers of the product.

Tourism marketing traditionally relies heavily on segmentation, yet of these four sets of characteristics, only the psychographic plays a significant role in current purchase decision models in tourism. Yet marketers are also aware of the limitations of the four segmentation criteria outlined above. It is widely recognized that purchase behaviour is a result of the combination of two or more of these criteria, not just one.

The models do not help us to identify or predict the behaviour of individual tourists. It is very difficult to operationalize such general models at a time when marketing is increasingly a matter of targeting individual tourists, using computer databases.

Nevertheless, there seems little doubt that, in spite of their weaknesses, these models have a role to play in tourism marketing.

Conclusion

We have looked at the process by which tourists make their purchase decisions, to buy a vacation, and how this process has been modelled by academics. These models appear to have some significant weaknesses in terms of describing, let alone explaining, the process by which tourists decide to buy a holiday. This chapter has also briefly highlighted the potential links that exist between purchase decision models and market segmentation techniques. The last thought on this subject must be that we still have a long way to go before we understand the way in which tourists choose their vacations.

Discussion points and essay questions

1 Outline the factors that make the study of the purchase decision making in tourism such a complex activity.
2 Evaluate the main strengths and weaknesses of the Wahab et al. and Schmöll models, as ways of explaining how tourists make purchase decisions.
3 Discuss the problems which marketing professionals might experience in trying to put into practice the models of purchase decision behaviour outlined in this chapter.

Exercise

Think about the last holiday you purchased, and produce a simple model to illustrate the process you followed to make the decision and the factors which you took into account. You should then ask a group of friends, fellow students or colleagues to do the same, independently, without talking to each other. Then, compare the models and identify and try to explain both the similarities and the differences.

Finally, you should note the difficulties experienced in carrying out this task. What do they tell you about the problems of studying purchase decision behaviour in tourism?

Part Three
Typologies of Tourist Behaviour

In Part Two we looked at how individual tourists make their purchasing decisions. It is now time to look at ways in which academics and marketers have sought to group tourists together on the basis of shared characteristics. This has resulted in both typologies of tourists and methods of segmentation. Part Three of the book will consider both of these.

These typologies are important for a number of reasons. They:

● represent an attempt to increase our knowledge of consumer behaviour in tourism
● can help marketers make important decisions on product development, pricing, promotional media and distribution channels
● may form the basis of market segmentation techniques
● might potentially help to predict future trends in tourist behaviour.

In the following chapter, the authors will consider both the typologies which academics have produced as well as the application of classic segmentation techniques to tourism.

7 Typologies of tourist behaviour and segmentation of the tourism market

For over two decades, academics have sought to produce meaningful typologies of tourists and their behaviour. At the same time, practitioners have tried to apply and adapt classic market segmentation techniques to the tourism industry. In this chapter, we will consider both of these approaches separately, although clearly there are links between them.

Academic typologies

The most fundamental debate, perhaps, is that about whether people are tourists or travellers. Although the term 'tourist' dates back two centuries, it has only become a word in popular usage in recent decades. Sharpley (1994) suggested that the terms tourist and traveller were, until recently, used interchangeably, to describe 'a person who was touring'. However, nowadays, the two words means different things when they are used.

There is the idea that a tourist is someone who buys a package from a tour operator, while the traveller is the person who makes their own independent arrangements for their vacation. The idea has grown up that somehow the latter type of behaviour is somehow superior or better than the former. Therefore, many people who buy tourist packages want to still see themselves as travellers.

Horner and Swarbrooke (1996)

As Sharpley (1994) noted, the term traveller,

is usually applied to someone who is travelling/touring for an extended period of time, particularly back-packing on a limited budget. It contains a spirit of freedom, adventure, and individuality. The word tourist on the other hand, is frequently used in a rather derogatory sense to describe those who participate in mass produced, package tourism.

Boorstin, more than 30 years ago, illustrated well that the debate over this issue is full of subjective judgements when he wrote about the 'lost art of travel' in the following terms:

The traveller, then, was working at something; the tourist was a pleasure seeker. The traveller was active; he went strenuously in search of people, of adventure, of experience. The tourist is passive; he expects interesting things to happen to him . . . he expects everything to be done to him and for him.

Boorstin (1964)

As this quote shows, the debate is not new but it has come back into focus in recent years as status conscious tourists have sought to differentiate themselves from other tourists and their experiences. As Sharpley (1994) has noted:

disliking and trying to avoid other tourists at the same time as trying to convince oneself that one is not a tourist is, in fact, all part of being a tourist.

Culler (1981) put it succinctly when he wrote that,

all tourists can always find someone more touristy than themselves to sneer at.

The tourism industry has, in recent years, recognized the implications of this whole debate and has begun to emphasize more and more the 'non-touristy', 'unspoilt' nature of destinations. It has also sought to massage the egos of customers by convincing them that the product they are buying means they are travellers not tourists.

Having discussed this general issue about the classification of tourists, it is now time for us to turn our attention to a consideration of some well-known academic typologies of tourists. It will be interesting if we look at these typologies in a chronological order to see if we can see any trends in the classification of tourists.

Cohen (1972)

The influential sociologist, Cohen, identified four types of tourists, in 1972, as follows:

- The organized mass tourist buys a package holiday to a popular destination and largely prefers to travel around with a large group of other tourists, following an inflexible predetermined itinerary. In general such tourists tend not to stray far from the beach or their hotel.
- The individual mass tourist buys a looser package that allows them more freedom, for example, a fly-drive holiday. They are more likely than the organized mass tourist to look for the occasional novel experience. However, they still tend to stay on the beaten track and rely on the formal tourist industry.
- The explorer makes their own travel arrangements and sets out, consciously, to avoid contact with other tourists. They set out to meet local people but they will expect a certain level of comfort and security.

- The drifter tries to become accepted, albeit temporarily, as part of the local community. They have no planned itinerary and choose their destinations and accommodation on a whim. As far as possible, the drifter shuns all contact with the formal tourism industry.

Cohen described the former two types of tourist as institutionalized tourists, and the latter two as non-institutionalized. The latter are, Cohen agreed, the people who are the pioneers who explore new destinations. The institutionalized travellers then follow on later when it has become less adventurous and more comfortable to travel there because of the development of a tourist industry and infrastructure. Sharpley (1994) quotes Goa in India as an example of this phenomena.

The same author, Richard Sharpley, criticizes Cohen's typology on the grounds that the institutionalized and non-institutionalized types are not entirely distinct from each other. He argues that even 'explorers' make use of specialist guidebooks to choose their transport routes and accommodation.

Plog (1977)

In 1977, Plog sought to link personality traits directly with tourist behaviour, and divided people up into psychocentrics, and allocentrics. He argued that the former were less adventurous, inward-looking people. They tend to prefer the familiar and have a preference for resorts which are already popular. Allocentrics, on the other hand, are outward-looking people who like to take risks and seek more adventurous holidays. Plog believed such people would prefer exotic destinations and individual travel. Between these two extremes, Plog suggested a number of intermediate categories such as near-psychocentrics, mod-centrics, and near allocentrics. He suggested that psychocentric American tourists would holiday at Coney Island while allocentrics would take their vacation in Africa, for example.

Sharpley quite rightly criticizes this idea of linking types of tourists with specific destinations. He wrote in 1994:

Destinations change and develop over time; as a resort is discovered and attracts growing numbers of visitors, it will evolve from an allocentric to a psychocentric destination.

Perreault, Dorden and Dorden (1979)

Based on a survey of 2000 householders, Perreault, Dorden and Dorden produced a five-group classification of tourists, as follows:

- budget travellers who had medium incomes, but sought low-cost vacations

- adventurous tourists who were well educated and affluent and showed a preference for adventurous holidays
- homebody tourists were cautious people who took holidays but did not discuss their vacation with other people, and spent relatively little time planning it
- vacationers were a small group who spent lots of time thinking about their next holiday. They tended to be active people in lower paid jobs
- moderates had a high predisposition to travel but were not interested in weekend breaks or sports.

Cohen (1979)

Cohen, in 1979, suggested a five group classification of tourists, based on the type of experience they were seeking, as follows:

- the recreational tourist for whom the emphasis is on physical recreation
- the diversionary tourist who seeks ways of forgetting their everyday life at home
- the experiential tourist who looks for authentic experiences
- the experimental tourist where the main desire is to be in contact with local people
- the existential tourist who wants to totally immerse themselves in the culture and lifestyles of their vacation destination.

Sharpley (1994) noted that this classification was not 'based on any empirical research: it is a mechanical categorisation'.

Westvlaams Ekonomisch Studiebureau (1986)

A survey of 3000 Belgians produced the following typology which identified seven types of tourists:

- active sea lovers who want to take a holiday by the sea, with a beach close by
- contact-minded holiday makers value making new friends on holiday, and being hospitably received by local people
- nature viewers want to be well received by the host population while enjoying very beautiful landscapes
- rest-seekers want a chance to relax and rest while on holiday
- discovers like cultural holidays and some adventure, but they also like to meet new people
- family-orientated sun and sea lovers, who were the largest group, like to do things together as a family and seek 'child-friendly' activities
- traditionalists value safety and security and try to avoid surprises by sticking with familiar destinations and types of holiday.

Dalen (1989)

A Norwegian survey of 3000 activities led to a four group classification, as follows:

- Modern materialists want to get a tan to impress people when they get home. They like partying and are more concerned with drink than food. Hedonism is their main motivation.
- Modern idealists also seek excitement and entertainment but want both to be more intellectual than the last group. They do not, however, want mass tourism or fixed itineraries.
- Traditional idealists demand quality, culture, heritage, famous places, peace, and security.
- Traditional materialists always look for special offers and low prices and have a strong concern with personal security.

American Express (1989)

American Express commissioned a survey by Gallup of 6500 people in the USA, UK, West Germany and Japan, which resulted in the following five type classification:

- adventurous, who are independent and confident and like to try new activities
- worriers, who worry about the stress of travel and their safety and security while on holiday
- dreamers, who are fascinated by the idea of travel and they read and talk a lot about their travel experiences and different destinations
- economizers, who simply see travel as a routine opportunity for relaxation rather than as a special part of their life. As such they want to enjoy holidays at the lowest possible price
- indulgers, who want to be pampered when they are on holiday.

Smith (1989)

Smith identified seven types of tourists, as follows:

- explorers are a small group who travel almost as anthropologists
- elite tourists are experienced frequent travellers who like expensive tailor-made tours
- off-beat tourists aim to get away from other tourists
- unusual tourists make side trips from organized tours to experience local culture
- incipient mass tourists travel to established destinations where tourism is not yet totally dominant
- mass tourists expect the same things they are used to at home

- charter tourists have little or no interest in the destination itself providing that the holiday gives them the entertainment and standards of food and accommodation they expect.

Urry (1990)

Urry, in the UK at least, popularized the term the 'post-tourist' that had earlier been mentioned by writers like Feifer. This tourist is a product of the so-called 'post-modern' age. They recognize that there is no such thing as an authentic tourism product or experience and accept pseudo events for what they are. To the post-tourist, tourism is just a game and they feel free to move between different types of holiday. Today they may take an eco-tourism trip to Belize, while next year they may lie on a beach in Benidorm.

As Feifer (1985) said, the post-tourist is conscious of being a tourist, an outsider, 'not a time traveller when he goes somewhere historic; not an instant noble savage when he stays on a tropical beach; not an invisible observer when he visits a native compound'.

If such a tourist is now a reality, then as Sharpley suggested in 1994:

For the post-tourist, then, the traveller/tourist dichotomy is irrelevant. The traveller has matured and evolved into an individual who experiences and enjoys all kinds of tourism, who takes each at face value and who is in control at all times. In effect, the post-tourist renders tourist typologies meaningless!

Wood and House (1991)

The debate about sustainable tourism has, in recent years, led to some moralistic and judgemental approaches to the classification of tourists. For example, there is the idea of the Good Tourist, put forward by Wood and House in 1991. Such a tourist is one who behaves in a responsible manner towards the environment and the host community in their holiday destination. It is argued that all tourists can aspire to join this group if they modify their behaviour in particular ways. Horner and Swarbrooke (1996) have suggested that, for tourism organizations, 'this group may represent a potentially lucrative niche market, which must be sold products it can feel good about buying'.

Wickens (1994) (in Seaton et al., 1994)

Relatively few writers have attempted to produce typologies of tourists visiting a particular destination. One recent exception to this situation is that produced by Wickens in 1994 in relation to a resort on the Chalkidiki peninsula in Greece. She based her research on Cohen's typology of 1972, and produced a five group typology, as follows:

- Cultural heritage tourists, who are interested in the natural beauty, history and culture of Greece. They long to experience the 'traditional Greek village life' portrayed in the holiday brochures. They use the seaside resort as a basis to tour the attractions in the region. This group tends to be made up of family groups and older holiday makers.
- Ravers, who are attracted by the nightlife and the cheapness and availability of alcohol and nightlife. They also enjoy the sun and the beach. They tend to swim and sunbathe in the day and go 'clubbing' at night. These are mostly young people with males in the majority.
- 'Shirley Valentines', who are women on holiday with other women who hope for romance and sexual encounters with Greek men. For these women their holiday represents an opportunity to get away from their everyday lives of domesticity.
- 'Heliolatrous' tourists, who are sun-worshippers whose main aim is to get a tan. They spend much of their holiday in the open air.
- 'Lord Byrons', who tend to return year after year to the same destination and even hotel or accommodation unit. They are in love with Greece, particularly its perceived relaxed, 'laid back' lifestyle. They want to be treated as a guest not as a tourist. They are after nostalgia and lament the impact of mass tourism on their favourite destination.

We have just looked at a brief selection of typologies which have been produced over the last 25 or so years. Many others have been omitted because of limitations of space. However, we have tried to offer a range of influential and less well-known typologies from authors of different nationalities. It is now time to see if we can identify some common threads in those we have discussed.

A comparison of typologies

Most of the typologies attempt to group tourists together on the basis of their preference for particular vacation experiences in terms of:

- destinations
- activities while on holiday
- independent travel vs package holidays.

Some recognize that the motivations of tourists are tempered in reality by the determinants that contribute to their choice of vacation such as disposable income, for example.

A number of influential early typologies were not based on empirical research but as we have seen, many of the recent typologists – Perreault, Dorden and Dorden, Dalen and American Express, for example – have arisen out of empirical studies.

In 1987 Plog attempted to produce a typology of typologies. He wrote:

researchers may actually come up with fairly similar dimensions but may label them differently. As it turns out, there possibly are a very limited number of psychographic/personality dimensions . . . These dimensions may be more clearly defined, or combined in various ways, but they are covered by about eight broad categories.

These categories were; 'venturesomeness', 'pleasure-seeking', 'impassivity', 'self-confidence', 'playfulness', 'masculinity', 'intellectualism', and 'people orientation' (Plog, 1987).

A critique of typologies

Not surprising, the attempts to classify tourists which we have discussed, and others, have attracted criticism, on a number of fronts, as follows:

1 'Broad brush' typologies based on simplistic, stereotypes cannot hope to encompass the complex patterns of behaviour we see in the real world.
2 Almost all the typologies do not allow for the fact that individual consumers can move between types in response to the impact of different determinants over time, including changes in health, income, leisure time, and family and work commitments.
3 They also tend not to recognize that many holidaymakers do not have autonomy over their choice of holiday destination and vacation activities. The decision is often the result of a compromise between the tourist and the other members of the holiday party whether they be friends or relatives. Therefore what someone does on holiday may not reflect their true desires or personality.
4 Many of the most influential typologies are at least ten years old and therefore cannot represent the many changes in consumer behaviour which have taken place in recent years. They often pre-date newer developments such as mass long-haul holiday markets, budget cruises and the Internet, for example.
5 There is still a bias towards Europe and the USA in the vast majority of typologies. Far less has been published on the types of tourist found in Asia, Africa and the Middle East, for example, which might yield very different results.
6 On the other hand, some typologies are generally used as if they can be applied to people in all countries. They appear to ignore national and cultural differences, which surely weakens their validity.
7 Researchers have sometimes attempted to develop generally applicable typologies from surveys with small samples, which is at best questionable.
8 Many typologies are descriptive and, as such, do not greatly help us to increase our understanding of tourist behaviour.

9 They often ignore the fact that people may mature as tourists as they become more experienced as travellers. As Lowyck, Van Langenhave and Bollaert (1992) argue, it must be debatable 'whether it makes sense at all to divide people into different types without taking into account their full life spans'.

10 Too many typologies ignore the gap between professed preferences and actual behaviour, which is an important phenomenon in the tourism market. The gap can be caused by a number of factors ranging from social conventions, ego and even self-delusion.

11 There are methodological criticisms of the typologies too. For example, some commentators argue that some researchers have allowed their own value judgements to influence their work.

12 There are still many gaps in the typology literature. For example, little has been written about the business tourist.

These criticisms are not intended to decry the idea of typologies but rather to illustrate how difficult it is to develop convincing typologies. Perhaps it also proves that there will never be one typology that reflects the behaviour of all tourists. Instead we may need as many typologies as there are tourism products, tourism markets, countries and cultures!

The marketing applications of typologies

Notwithstanding their considerable limitations, these typologies, although not developed with marketing in mind, have a potential role to play in tourism marketing. This could clearly contribute to decisions over product development, price and distribution. However, their main role could well be in the field of promotion, particularly in the design of the messages which tourism organizations attach to their products, for different groups of potential customers. For example.

- 'travellers' want to be convinced that the holiday they may buy is not the type of 'package' bought by 'tourists'
- Perreault's 'budget travellers' need to be told that their prospective holiday package represents good value for money
- Plog's 'allocentrics' need to have the adventurous aspect of a product highlighted for them
- Dalen's 'traditional idealists' must be persuaded that their desired destination is safe.

On the other hand, practitioners would find it difficult to do these things as current methodologies would make it very difficult and expensive for them to identify each of these groups and target different messages to different groups.

It is perhaps, therefore, time for us to move on to consider ways of classifying tourists that are devised specifically to make marketing more effective.

Market segmentation

Market segmentation has been well defined by Dibb et al. (1994) as:

The process of dividing a total market into groups of people with relatively similar product needs, for the purpose of designing a marketing mix that precisely matches the needs of individuals in a segment.

This clearly illustrates the fact that market segmentation is a form of consumer classification designed specifically to serve the marketing function. This is one difference between segmentation and the typologies which we discussed earlier, which were largely developed by academics who were generally not concerned with their potential role in marketing. The second key difference is that whereas the typologies have been devised specifically in relation to tourism, segmentation is a concept derived from general marketing across all industries.

Classic segmentation criteria and their application in tourism

There are five classic ways of segmenting markets, in other words, the consumer population can be subdivided on the basis of five different criteria, into groups which share similar characteristics as buyers. We will now discuss each of these in turn, in terms of their use in the tourism industry.

Geographical segmentation

This method categorizes market groups on the basis of geographical factors, and is widely used in tourism as the following examples illustrate.

1 Theme park markets are often described in terms of catchment areas, expressed in geographical terms. In other words, Disneyland Paris is said to have an international catchment area and Alton Towers a national market, while most others in the UK have a regional catchment area
2 Tour operators consider where their clients live when deciding which departure airports to offer flights from
3 Airlines which develop their routes on the basis of geographical patterns of demand
4 An assumption that people from cool Northern climates will often show a preference for warmer Southern climates when selecting their holiday destinations
5 The desire of urban dwellers to visit rural locations for leisure, as a contrast with their everyday environment.

Socio-economic segmentation

This technique seeks to subdivide markets on the basis of socio-economic variables. In the UK this is really another term for socio-economic class as the British approach to socio-economic segmentation is largely based on the

JICNAR's classification. This splits society into six groups, based on occupation, represented the letters A, B, C1, C2, D and E. Although this is an apparently crude approach to segmentation it is widely used with tourism organizations describing their markets in terms of classes A and B or C2D. For example, the case of the UK theme park market is an example of the latter with museums and opera performances being typical of the former.

Demographic segmentation

This form of segmentation, based on subdividing the population on the basis of demographic factors, has proved particularly popular in tourism, as the following examples illustrate.

1 Age, with some tour operators, notably SAGA and Club 18–30 in the UK, who segment their potential market purely in terms of age.
2 Sex, with many weekend break packages and conference partner programmes, based on stereotypes in relation to gender. For instance, golf is usually seen as a male activity while it is argued that women will prefer shopping.
3 Religion. This is clearly at the heart of the pilgrimage market for example.

One demographic factor that has always been heavily used in tourism is the idea of family status. The assumption is that a consumers' behaviour is determined by where they are in the family life cycle. Figure 7.1 illustrates the way this model might be used in relation to the market for visitor attractions.

This family life-cycle model is based on the approach used by the tourism industry. However, there are other forms of the life-cycle model.

This approach is also used by tour operators, including:

● Holidays for teenagers holidaying separately from their parents and wanting independence and an active holiday, for example, PGL in the UK.
● So-called family holidays where free child places are offered to make holidays more affordable for growing families.
● Products which have been traditionally aimed at 'empty nesters' to take advantage of their disposable income and leisure time, such as cruises and painting holidays.

Other demographic factors have also been used by tourism organizations including language. Destination marketing agencies have to produce literature in the different languages spoken by their key markets, for instance.

Two criteria which have rarely been used are race and nationality. The former is very sensitive but perhaps it will become increasingly utilized as Europe becomes more of a multicultural society. Already race is a very

Stage in family life cycle	Likely preferences and needs of consumers
Child	Stimulation. Other children to play with. Parental guidance and support.
Teenagers	New experiences. Excitement. Status. More independence from parents. Opportunities for active participation. Social interaction with other teenagers.
Young adult	New experiences. Freedom of action. Opportunities for active participation. Social interaction with other young adults.
Young couple	New experiences. Romance.
Young couple with baby	Facilities for babies. Economy. Ease of access for pushchairs and prams.
Growing families	Economy, e.g. a family ticket. Something for all the family to do.
'Empty nesters'	Chance to learn something new. Passive rather than active participant most of the time.
Elderly	Watching rather than doing. Economy. Company of other older people. Easy accessibility for people with mobility problems.

Figure 7.1   The family life cycle and visitor attractions
Source: Adapted from Swarbrooke (1995a)

relevant criteria in the USA, with the rise of the African American market. At the same time, the rise of trans-national companies in tourism, like Accor and TUI, may make national differences an ever more important way of segmenting the market for an organization's product.

The three methods we have discussed so far are rather crude, but they are relatively easy to measure. The next approach is more sophisticated but is also more difficult to identify and measure.

Psychographic segmentation

This technique is based on the idea that the lifestyle, attitudes, opinions, and personality of people determine their behaviour as consumers. This is a more modern approach than the other three we have considered, and it has already begun to influence a wide range of industries including clothing, food, drink, perfume and cars. It is also beginning to be seen in tourism as the following examples show.

1 Health farms and spas target their marketing at consumers who aspire to lead a healthy lifestyle.

2 People who are environmentally aware and whose lifestyle is influenced by environmental concerns are a good target market for conservation holidays.
3 Hedonistic sun, sand, sea, and sex holidays are usually targeted at extrovert people.
4 People who seek thrills are the target market for bungee-jumping or 'white-knuckle rides' at theme parks.

This method of segmentation is, as we said, the most modern and it is also the most fashionable with marketers at the moment.

Behaviouristic segmentation

This technique groups consumers according to their relationship with a particular product. The range of variations on this approach is illustrated in Figure 7.2. This diagram is clearly selective but it shows both the number of approaches and the links between them.

Behaviouristic segmentation is used widely in tourism as we can see from the following examples.

1 Airline Frequent Flyer Programmes (FFPs) are aimed at regular users to increase loyalty to the product and make people more enthusiastic purchasers of the product.

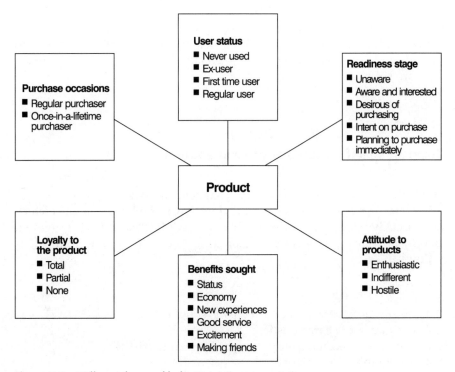

Figure 7.2   Different forms of behaviouristic segmentation

2 Hotels and airlines stress the quality of their service.
3 Budget tour operators, airlines and hotel chains promote services to consumers whose main 'benefit sought' is economy.

A critique of the classic methods of segmentation

There are three major criticisms of the application of the classic segmentation techniques to tourism, as follows:

1 Some of them are dated and have not kept pace with changes in society. For example, the traditional family life cycle looks increasingly inappropriate, with the rise of divorce and single parent families, non-related group households and couples who choose not have children, for instance.
2 It can be argued, too, that some techniques fail to recognize that tourist behaviour changes over time in response to changes in the circumstances of each tourist. Therefore, they will move between segments from time to time, as their income grows, their health deteriorates, or they start using the Internet to gain tourist information, for example.
3 The fact that much market research in tourism is too poor and unreliable to allow us to accurately implement any of these methods.

In general, therefore, all we can do, perhaps, is segment general behaviour or motivations, rather than individual people. Marketers must then try to identify and target who is in their particular segment at a specific time when they are seeking to sell a certain product.

Tourism-specific methods of segmentation

While the five classic methods come from general marketing, some tourism academics and practitioners have sought to suggest other techniques which are specially relevant to tourism. For example, Middleton (1994) suggested that there were six ways of segmenting markets in travel and tourism, as follows:

1 Purpose of travel
2 Buyer needs, motivations and benefits sought
3 Buyer and user characteristics
4 Demographic, economic and geographic characteristics
5 Psychographic characteristics
6 Price.

While four of these are similar to the classic methods they are worded differently. More fundamentally, Middleton adds two others, namely Purpose of travel and Price.

Other authors have suggested different methods of segmentation for individual sectors within tourism. Swarbrooke (1995) has suggested three extra criteria in relation to the visitor attraction market, namely:

- visitor party composition including individual, family group or groups of friends
- visit type and purpose such as educational trips and corporate hospitality
- method of travel to attractions for instance, private car or public transport.

Likewise, Shaw (1990) has offered a range of appropriate ways of segmenting the airline market, including:

- journey purpose – business, holiday, visiting friends or relatives
- length of journey – short-haul or long-haul traveller.

Shaw believed that these were important criteria in determining the kinds of product a consumer would wish to purchase.

The special case of business tourism

Business tourism is unusual in terms of segmentation in that the market can be segmented into two types of buyer or user, namely:

- the business traveller, who is the consumer of the product, the user of the service, but who usually does not pay the bill
- their employer, who is the customer, the purchaser who pays the bill.

This distinction becomes important when one considers Airline Frequent Flyer Programmes (FFPs) for example. Traditionally the employer (customer) has paid the bill but it has been the business traveller (consumer) who has enjoyed the benefits of the FFP, such as free flights for partners. Now airlines are realizing that it is the customers, the employers, who really need to be wooed and are trying to appeal to them with discounted fares.

Marketing applications and segmentation in tourism

We noted earlier that segmentation is designed to serve the needs of marketers. It is not surprising therefore, that writers such as Middleton

(1994) believe that: 'Market segmentation and product formulation, are mirror images if they are correctly matched'.

Indeed segmentation is designed to help with all 4 'P's' of the Marketing Mix, namely Product, Price, Place and Promotion. This link is discussed in more detail in Chapter 13, so at this stage we simply need to make two brief points.

Firstly, successful marketing is not based just on one method of segmentation alone; instead it makes use of a blend of different techniques, that will be different on every occasion. We might link personality with geographical place of residence, or we might focus on benefits sought in relation to different demographic factors.

A combination of socio-economic geographical and demographic factors underpins the use of the ACORN residential neighbourhood classification system in tourism marketing.

Secondly, tourism organizations have to deal with, what Middleton (1994) has called, 'multiple segments'. For example he says that hotels serve at least five segments, namely: corporate/business clients, group tours, independent vacationers, weekend/midweek package clients, and conference delegates. As he says, 'most [tourism] businesses deal with not one but several segments'.

Conclusion

While we have considered the so-called 'academic typologies' separately from segmentation techniques, there are clearly links between them. According to Horner and Swarbrooke (1996):

The typology of Plog (1977) is based firmly on the principles of psychographic segmentation in that it is based on the personality of the tourist ... Concepts such as the 'Post-Tourist' are closely linked to another element of psychographic segmentation, namely lifestyles. For the post-tourist, tourism is just another aspect of their post-modern lifestyle.

We have seen how difficult it is to produce convincing typologies and segmentation methods and how all the existing approaches have attracted criticism.

Hopefully, the reader appreciates the importance of continually up-dating both the typologies and our approaches to segmentation to reflect changes in society and consumer behaviour. Finally, perhaps, we should not focus on how academics or marketers see tourist behaviour, but rather we should try to find out how the tourists themselves evaluate their own behaviour. It is, after all, the perceptions that consumers hold that shape their real behaviour.

Discussion points and essay questions

1 Discuss the potential application of the following typologies of tourists behaviour to the marketing of tourism products:
   ● Cohen (1972)
   ● Dalen (1989).
2 Evaluate the concept of the 'post-tourist' and examine its potential impact on the tourism market.
3 Develop your own typology of tourists for a destination of your choice, such as that produced by Wickens in 1994 (in Seaton et al., 1994), for a resort in the Chalkidiki region of Greece.

Exercise

Write a report examining the application of the five classic methods of market segmentation to *one* of the following markets:

● mass package tours
● scheduled airlines
● theme parks
● country house hotels
● cruises
● health spas.

You should suggest which method or methods are most relevant and which combination of methods would be most appropriate.

Part Four
Tourism Demand and Markets

Having looked at the theoretical dimension of tourist behaviour in Parts Two and Three, we now turn our attention to the current facts and figures relating to tourism demand and markets, world-wide.

In four chapters, we will explore:

- the global pattern of tourism demand
- national differences in demand in relation to domestic, outbound and inbound tourist flow
- the nature of demand in different market segments
- the markets for different sectors of tourism.

8 The global pattern of tourism demand

Introduction

In this chapter, we will consider the patterns of tourism demand, divided by global regions. We will start our analysis by considering the factors that influence tourism demand.

We shall continue our analysis by considering some of the key factors that influence tourism demand in more detail. These include the economic position of the regions or countries, the degree of urbanization and the overall quality of life.

The chapter will finish with an analysis of tourism demand for regions of the world and we will draw comparisons between the different regions.

Factors that influence tourism demand

The factors that influence the levels of global tourism were explored by the World Tourism Organization in 1995 and are shown in Figure 8.1.

Exogenous factors affecting tourism include:

- Economic and financial developments
- Demographic and social changes
- Technological innovations and improvements
- Infrastructural, equipment and facility investment
- Political/legislative/regulatory factors
- Environmental planning and impact issues
- Trading developments
- The safety of travel

Key market forces directly affecting the demand for, and supply and distribution of, tourism products and services, include:

- Consumer knowledge of tourism possibilities, and tourist requirements
- Destination product development, and products/services development by the private sector operators
- Trends in the structure of the travel and tourism operating sector
- Marketing
- Supply of skilled and experienced human resources

Figure 8.1 Factors shaping the development of tourism
Source: World Tourism Organization (1995)

It can be seen from Figure 8.1 that consumer issues have an effect on the levels of tourism demand. Demographic and social changes affect the patterns of tourism demand. One example of this is the ageing demographic profile of Europe, which is allowing the development of tourism products for 'third age' groups. The second important factor which affects tourism demand is consumer knowledge of tourism possibilities. This is particularly relevant in developed economies, where individuals will generally be eager to learn about the opportunities for travel, particularly where political or economic factors have affected their decision in the past. The growth of tourism programmes on television, for example, has widened consumer knowledge on the opportunities available to them.

Tourism arrivals and receipts

There has been a growth in the movement of international tourists of more than 7.2 per cent per annum in the period 1950 to 1992 (World Tourism Organization, 1995). This growth has been faster than for any other commercial sector and constitutes a higher proportion of the value of exports than any other sector.

The World Tourism Organization have also explored the influences and determinants that affect the choices that individuals make when choosing a tourism product. These are shown in Figure 8.2.

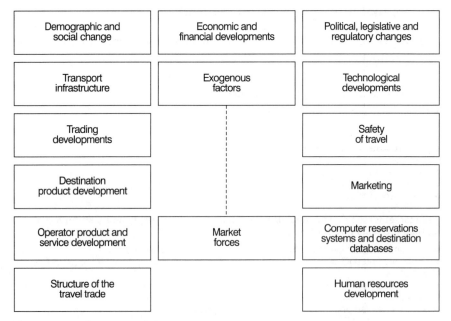

Figure 8.2   Influences and determinants
Source: World Tourism Organization (1995)

It can be seen from Figures 8.1 and 8.2 that many issues have an effect on levels of tourism demand. Demographic and social changes affect the patterns of tourism demand. One example of this is the ageing demographic profile of Europe, which is having an effect on the development of tourism products specifically aimed at third age sections of the population.

Consumer knowledge of available tourism products also influences tourism demand. This is particularly important in developed countries, where individuals will generally be eager to learn about the opportunities for travel, particularly where political or economic factors have affected their decisions in the past. The growth of television programmes and specialist magazines on tourism has also been a reflection of the growing interest in tourism. These programmes have also fuelled tourism demand.

The growth and development of tourism companies offering more choice to consumers has also fuelled tourism demand. The development of large aircraft that can travel long distances and carry large numbers of passengers has helped in the development of new long-haul destinations, for example. Computer reservation systems and destination databases has made it easier for consumers to book travel packages.

The reduction in prices for tourism holidays has also increased the demand for tourism products. The development of value for money holiday packages by the UK package holiday operators, for example, was the main reason for the large numbers of British people travelling overseas on holiday packages, resulting in strong outbound tourism from the UK.

Key determining factors influencing tourism demand

We can now consider some of the factors that influence tourism demand in more detail.

The economic position of the region or country has a direct effect on the levels of tourism demand. There are various ways in measuring economic activity of individual countries or regions. It can be anticipated that the world's biggest economies will provide a large proportion of tourism demand. The economic position for major regions of the world is shown in Table 8.1.

It can be seen from Table 8.1 that certain regions of the world, such as the European countries have considerable GDP per head. Other regions have shown considerable growth of GDP over the ten-year period 1985–1995. This is particularly marked in Asia where GDP per head has grown considerably during this period. This suggests that an increase in tourism demand in this region could be anticipated over the same period.

Global economic conditions have improved during 1997, with an output growth estimated to be about 3 per cent during the year (Morgan, Pain and Hubert, 1998). Growth has been particularly buoyant in North America and economic prospects in Europe have also improved. The growth of the German and French economies has been particularly marked.

Table 8.1 Economic data for the world region

Regional GDP	$bn, 1995	Growth, 1985–1995
World	27 657	3.2
Industrial countries	21 605	2.5
G7	18 524	2.5
EU12	7 980	2.4
EU15	7 449	
Asia a	2 424	7.8
Latin America	997	2.6
Eastern Europe	756	−3.8
Middle East and Europe	699	3.4
Africa	389	2.3
Regional GDP per head	*$, 1995*	*Growth, 1985–1995*
World	4 855	
Industrial countries	24 351	1.8
G7	27 379	1.8
EU12	21 302	2.0
EU15	21 475	
Asia a	808	6.0
Latin America	3 162	0.6
Eastern Europe	2 022	−4.5
Middle East and Europe b	2 421	0.3
Africa	612	−0.5
Regional trade: value	*Exports, $bn, 1995*	*Imports, $bn, 1995*
World	4 950	
Industrial countries	3 359	3 261
G7	2 462	2 377
EU12	1 811	1 701
EU15	2 003	1 869
Asia	909	938
Latin America	195	198
Middle East and Europe b	180	179
Africa	95	97
Regional trade: volume growth %	*Exports, 1985–1995*	*Imports, 1985–1995*
World	6.4	
Industrial countries	5.5	6.1
G7	5.9	6.1
EU12	5.3	5.6
Asia a	12.9	12.1
Latin America	5.8	8.0
Middle East and Europe b	6.1	1.3
Africa	2.9	1.0

Source: *The Economist Pocket World in Figures 1998 Edition*; a excludes Japan, b includes Turkey

Growth of domestic demand in Japan, in contrast, has been particularly weak. The outlook for the whole of the East Asian economy depends on the recent events which have occurred in the economic markets of this region, and the effects on the wider world economy. The five economies which have been most affected by the Asian currency crisis of 1997, include Korea, Indonesia, Malaysia, the Philippines and Thailand. These countries represent a smaller proportion of world trade, however, in comparison to neighbouring countries such as China and Hong Kong.

We can consider different regions of the world in relation to GDP growth and consumer price inflation to be the areas of the world with the most potential in relation to tourism demand. Figures 8.3 and 8.4 show the GDP growth trends and consumer price inflation for different OECD regions.

These charts show that there was considerable growth of GDP in Asia during 1996, but this has collapsed in 1997 and 1998. There has been a

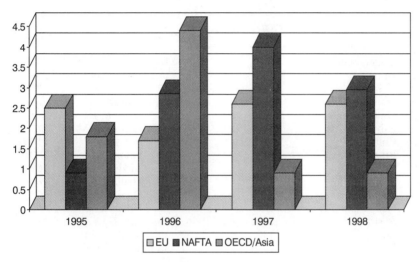

Figure 8.3   OECD GDP growth
Source: Morgan, Pain and Hubert (1998)

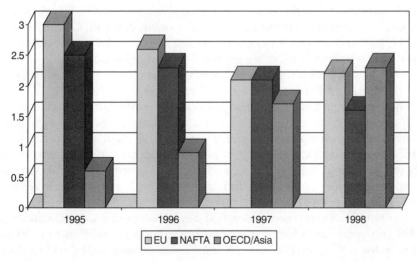

Figure 8.4   OECD consumer price inflation
Source: Morgan, Pain and Hubert (1998)

gradual growth in GDP for Europe during the same period. Consumer price inflation has slowed in the EU, during the period 1995–1998, whereas it has increased for the Asian regions. These changes in the economic position for different regions will have a considerable effect on tourism demand.

The regions of the world with the countries that have the biggest economies in relation to GDP will have a major contribution to the world tourism demand. The world's biggest economies for 1997 are shown in Table 8.2.

Table 8.2   The world economy

		GDP ($bn)			GDP ($bn)
1	United States	7 100	16	Mexico	305
2	Japan	4 964	17	Switzerland	286
3	Germany	2 252	18	Argentina	278
4	France	1 451	19	Taiwan	260
5	United Kingdom	1 095	20	Belgium	251
6	Italy	1 088	21	Austria	217
7	China	745	22	Sweden	210
8	Brazil	580	23	Indonesia	190
9	Canada	574	24	Turkey	169
10	Spain	532	25	Thailand	160
11	South Korea	435	26	Denmark	156
12	Netherlands	371	27	Hong Kong	142
13	Australia	338	28	Norway	136
14	Russia	332	29	Saudi Arabia	134
15	India	320	30	South Africa	131

Source: *The Economist Pocket World in Figures 1998 Edition*

We can expect that the world's major economies shown in this chart will make a substantial contribution to world tourism demand. Countries such as the United States of America, Japan and Germany for example, will be very influential in contributing to world tourism demand.

Table 8.2 also shows the importance of the Asian economies such as Japan, South Korea and Indonesia in terms of economic strength.

The purchasing power of the population of a particular region or country will also contribute to the tourism demand figures, particularly as tourism demand relies heavily on discretionary income. We can look at the countries of the world that have the highest purchasing power. These countries are shown in Table 8.3. It can be seen that many European countries such as Switzerland, Norway, Belgium and Austria are high in this table in relation to purchasing power.

The human development index was developed by the United Nations in 1990 and combines adult literacy and life expectancy with income levels. This index is designed to give an impression of how well developed the quality of life is for individuals in the countries studied. The figures for the top 30 countries in the world are shown in Table 8.4.

Table 8.3 Highest purchasing power

GDP per head in PPP (USA = 100)

1	Luxembourg	140.6	14	Iceland	75.8
2	United States	100.0	15	Germany	74.4
3	Switzerland	95.8	16	Netherlands	73.9
4	Kuwait	88.2	17	Italy	73.6
5	Hong Kong	85.1	18	United Kingdom	71.4
6	Singapore	84.4	19	Australia	70.2
7	Japan	81.9	20	Sweden	68.7
8	Norway	81.3	21	Finland	65.8
9	Belgium	80.3	22	Qatar	65.6
10	Austria	78.8	23	Israel	61.1
11	Denmark	78.7	24	United Arab Emirates	61.0
12	Canada	78.3	25	New Zealand	60.6
13	France	77.9			

Source: *The Economist Pocket World in Figures 1998 Edition*

Many European countries feature high in the list, including the Netherlands, and all the Scandinavian countries. Asian countries such as Japan and South Korea also feature in the top 30 countries in the human development index, which shows their potential in relation to tourism demand.

The final factor which we will consider in relation to tourism demand is population data.

The growth of a population may lead to an increase in tourism demand, according to the economic position of individuals in the country. The

Table 8.4 The quality of life

Human development index

1	Canada	95.1	16	Denmark	92.4
2	United States	94.0		United Kingdom	92.4
3	Japan	93.8	18	Germany	92.0
	Netherlands	93.8	19	Ireland	91.9
5	Norway	93.7	20	Italy	91.4
6	Finland	93.5	21	Cyprus	90.9
	France	93.5		Greece	90.9
8	Iceland	93.4		Hong Kong	90.9
9	Spain	93.3	24	Israel	90.8
	Sweden	93.3	25	Barbados	90.6
11	Australia	92.9	26	Bahamas	89.5
	Belgium	92.9		Luxembourg	89.5
13	Austria	92.8	28	Malta	88.6
14	New Zealand	92.7		South Korea	88.6
15	Switzerland	92.6	30	Argentina	88.5

Source: *The Economist Pocket World in Figures 1998 Edition*

Table 8.5   Fastest growing populations, 1985–1995

Average annual growth (%)

1	Oman	4.5	11	Macao	3.5
	Yemen	4.5	12	Iran	3.4
3	Qatar	4.3		Jordan	3.4
4	West Bank and Gaza	4.2		Madagascar	3.4
5	Gambia, The	4.1	15	Côte d'Ivoire	3.3
6	Guinea	4.0		Niger	3.3
7	Saudi Arabia	3.7	17	Ethiopia	3.2
	Zaire	3.7		Kenya	3.2
9	Libya	3.6		Mali	3.2
	United Arab Emirates	3.6		Syria	3.2

Source: *The Economist Pocket World in Figures 1998 Edition*

countries which have experienced the fastest growing population during the period 1985–1995 are shown in Table 8.5. However, as these are generally countries with less developed economies, their impact on global tourism demand is slight, in spite of their rate of population growth.

Countries that have a high percentage of their population in work are likely to show substantial levels of tourism demand – these countries are illustrated in Table 8.6.

Table 8.6   Workers of the world

Highest % of population in labour force, 1995–1996 or latest

1	Singapore	57.0	12	United States	51.3
2	Denmark	55.8	13	Hong Kong	50.8
3	Iceland	55.6		Lithuania	50.8
4	Latvia	55.1		Ukraine	50.8
5	Switzerland	55.0	16	Bahamas	50.7
6	Romania	53.4	17	Canada	50.1
7	Japan	53.2	18	Sweden	49.6
8	Burundi	52.9	19	Finland	49.4
9	Czech Republic	52.6		Norway	49.4
	Thailand	52.6		United Kingdom	49.4
11	Belarus	52.5	22	Germany	49.1

Source: *The Economist Pocket World in Figures 1998 Edition*

It is clear again that the general level of economic development in these countries is also an important factor. Romania and Burundi have high percentages of their population in work but they generate few outbound tourist trips.

The degree of urbanization for a country over a period of time also indicates that substantial economic development has occurred. The degree of urbanization for a range of countries for the period 1970–1994 is shown in Table 8.7.

It can be seen from Table 8.7 that many European countries such as France, Germany and the UK have seen a gradual increase in urbanization during the period 1970–1994. Other countries such as Brazil, The Dominican Republic, Gambia and South Korea have shown considerable increases of urbanization over the same period.

Table 8.7 Urbanization in a range of countries 1970–1994 expressed as a percentage of the total population residing in urban areas

Country	1970	1975	1980	1985	1990	1994
Australia	85.6 (1971)	–	85.7 (1981)	85.4	85.4 (1986)	85.2
Brazil	55.9	59.6	67.6	72.0	75.6	78.7
Bulgaria	52.3	58.7	62.1	64.8	67.8	70.7
China	–	–	20.6 (1982)	–	26.2	30.2
Dominican Republic	39.8	45.7	51.2	54.5	58.7	64.6
France	70.0 (1968)	–	73.3 (1982)	–	74.0	–
Gambia	14.2 (1972)	15.9 (1973)	18.2	–	–	25.5
Germany	73.6	75.4	76.2	76.6	76.3	–
Israel	85.3 (1972)	81.9 (1974)	86.7	89.2	90.0	92.6
Singapore	100.0	100.0	100.0	100.0	100.0	100.0
South Korea	41.2	48.4	57.3	65.4	74.4	76.6
United Kingdom	78.4	–	87.7 (1981)	–	–	89.5
United States of America	73.5	–	73.7	–	75.2	76.2

Source: United Nations

We have now considered many of the factors that contribute to tourism demand. We have seen that some regions of the world have remained fairly static, in relation to economic development and urbanization of the population. Many European countries fit into this category. It would not be expected that these countries would be showing a considerable growth in tourism demand. Other areas of the world such as Asia, however, are showing a rapidly increasing economic position and increasing levels of urbanization. This position, however, changed in 1997 when many of the Asian economies suffered a setback. We can now turn our attention to the actual figures for international tourism to see how these factors have affected tourism demand in reality.

International tourism demand

International tourism is dominated by Europe and the Americas which in total attracted 83 per cent of all world-wide arrivals in 1990 (inbound) and residents of these two regions accounted for 84 per cent of all international tourist arrivals in the same period (outbound), according to the World Tourism Organization.

The trends of international travel arrivals and receipts by regions for the period 1990–1995 is shown in Tables 8.8 and 8.9.

It can be seen from Tables 8.8 and 8.9 that arrivals to Europe and the Americas are declining, whereas arrivals to East Asia and Pacific, South East Asia and the Middle East are on the increase. The increase in tourism receipts has been particularly dramatic in the East Asia and Pacific region.

Table 8.8   International travel – arrivals by region, 1990–1995

	1990 ('000)	1992 ('000)	1993 ('000)	1994 ('000)	1995 ('000)	Average annual growth 1990–1995 (%)	Market share 1990 (%)	1995 (%)
Europe	286 700	307 300	313 700	329 800	337 200	3.3	62.4	59.5
Americas	93 600	103 400	103 700	107 000	11 900	3.6	20.4	19.7
East Asia and Pacific	53 100	62 700	69 600	77 000	83 600	9.5	11.6	14.7
South Asia	3 200	3 600	3 600	3 900	4 400	6.6	0.7	0.8
Middle East	7 600	8 000	9 000	9 900	11 000	7.7	1.7	1.9
Africa	15 100	17 600	18 100	18 300	18 800	4.5	3.3	3.3
World	459 200	503 600	517 600	545 900	567 000	4.3	100.0	100.0

Source: World Tourism Organization; 1 totals figures for 1993 and 1994 do not match with Table 8.1 because the regional revised details figures are not available, 2 totals may not add up because of rounding

Table 8.9   International travel – receipts by region, 1990–1995

	US$ millions					Average annual growth 1990–1995 (%)	Market share 1990 (%)	1995 (%)
	1990 ('000)	1992 ('000)	1993 ('000)	1994 ('000)	1995 ('000)			
Europe	144 000	162 600	158 000	173 200	189 800	5.7	54.4	51.1
Americas	69 500	84 700	90 300	95 700	95 200	6.5	26.3	25.6
East Asia and Pacific	38 800	47 200	52 300	61 900	69 300	12.3	14.7	18.6
South Asia	2 100	2 800	2 800	3 200	3 700	12.0	0.8	1.0
Middle East	5 100	5 400	4 800	5 100	6 700	5.6	1.9	1.8
Africa	5 200	5 900	6 000	6 400	6 900	5.8	2.0	1.9
World	264 700	308 600	314 000	346 700	371 700	7.0	100.0	100.0

Source: World Tourism Organization; totals may not add up because of rounding

The trend in international tourist arrivals divided by region can be seen much more clearly if the period 1980–1995 is considered. Figures for market share for this period, divided by region, are shown in Table 8.10.

It can be seen that during the period 1980–1995, there has been a reduction in the market share for Europe, the Americas, the Middle East and South Asia. This is particularly marked for Europe. There has been an increase in market share for East Asia and the Pacific region, and Africa.

Table 8.10   International tourist arrivals – trends in regional market share, 1980–1995

Region	(%)		Change	
	1980	*1995*		
Europe	65.80	59.41	−6.39	↓
Americas	21.43	19.72	−1.72	↓
Middle East	2.09	1.98	−0.11	↓
South Asia	0.80	0.76	−0.04	↓
East Asia/Pacific	7.31	14.80	+7.49	↑
Africa	2.56	3.33	+0.77	↑

Source: World Tourism Organization

The World Tourism Organization have made forecasts for annual growth rates in international tourist arrivals for major regions of the world. They have forecast that international tourist arrivals will grow from 456 million in 1990 to 600 million in 2000 and to 937 million in 2010 (World Tourism Organization, 1995). This represents a doubling of arrivals in two decades. A more detailed forecast for individual regions of the world is shown in Table 8.11. This forecast shows the particular importance of the growth in tourist arrivals which is predicted for the East Asia and Pacific, and South Asia regions. Growth in tourist arrivals in other areas such as Europe and the Americas, will be more steady during the same period.

The number of people who engage in tourist activity grows every year. It is predicted that alternative forms of holidays, such as those related to active pursuits, and exposure to local society will grow at the expense of resort-based tourism (World Tourism Organization, 1995). The Asian, African and Middle Eastern outbound markets are in their introductory or growth stages and there will be a great potential for these in the future. The Asian tourist has traditionally visited cities, but there is growing interest in beach-based tourism. The Japanese tourist, for example, is showing an interest in beach-type holidays.

The World Tourism Organization predicts that there will be an increasing interest in environmental issues by consumers from western industrialized markets. Tourism organizations will also increase their targeted marketing

Table 8.11   Forecasts of tourist arrivals by region

Africa

Growth rate:	1990–1995	4.5 per cent a year
	1995–2000	5.5 per cent a year
	2000–2010	4.0 per cent a year

International tourist arrivals: 2000 – 24.3 million
                                        2010 – 36 million

Intraregional arrivals' share will rise from 38 per cent in 1990 to nearly 42 per cent in 2010

Americas

Growth rate:	1990–1995	4.2 per cent a year
	1995–2000	5.5 per cent a year
	2000–2010	3.5 per cent a year

International tourist arrivals: 2000 – 146.7 million
                                        2010 – 206.9 million

Intraregional arrivals' share will decline from 78 per cent in 1990 to 68 per cent in 2010

East Asia and the Pacific

Growth rate:	1990–1995	6.1 per cent a year
	1995–2000	7.6 per cent a year
	2000–2010	6.5 per cent a year

International tourist arrivals: 2000 – 101 million
                                        2010 – 190 million

Intraregional arrivals' share will rise from 73 per cent in 1990 to 80 per cent in 2010

Europe

Growth rate:	1990–1995	2.2 per cent a year
	1995–2000	3.2 per cent a year
	2000–2010	2.5 per cent a year

International tourist arrivals: 2000 – 372 million
                                        2010 – 476 million

Intraregional arrivals' share will show little change, i.e. 88 per cent in 1990, to 87 per cent in 2010

Middle East

Growth rate:	1990–1995	3.4 per cent a year
	1995–2000	4.6 per cent a year
	2000–2010	2.5 per cent a year

International tourist arrivals: 2000 – 11 million
                                        2010 – 18 million

Intraregional arrivals' share will rise from 34 per cent in 1990 to nearly 38 per cent in 2010

South East Asia

Growth rate:	1990–1995	5.1 per cent a year
	1995–2000	7.2 per cent a year
	2000–2010	6.5 per cent a year

International tourist arrivals: 2000 – 5.8 million
                                        2010 – 10.4 million

Intraregional arrivals' share will rise from 30 per cent in 1990 to 32 per cent in 2010

Source: World Tourism Organization (1995)

to particular market segments such as those related to demographic or lifestyle factors.

We can see that the regions of the world that the World Tourism Organization has predicted to grow in terms of tourism demand are the regions that we identified in the first section of this chapter as those that have experienced rapid periods of economic growth, increased standards of living, and increased urbanization. These changes are particularly marked in the East Asia and the Pacific region.

Table 8.12 Top countries in terms of highest expenditure per trip abroad

Rank		Country	Average expenditure per trip abroad (US$)	
1985	*1994*		*1985*	*1994*
8	1	Japan	972.9	2261.9
3	2	Australia	1268.5	1843.2
18	3	Thailand	513.8	1728.7
1	4	Taiwan (Prov. of China)	1687.1	1605.8
5	5	Singapore	1165.4	1603.2
2	6	Indonesia	1559.4	1600.7
10	7	Norway	817.7	1587.0
7	8	Israel	992.8	1523.1
25	9	Belgium	323.5	1453.8
33	10	Brazil	203.1	1395.7
6	11	New Zealand	1029.1	1337.8
4	12	Korea Rep.	1252.1	1296.1
17	13	Netherlands	515.8	1019.5
11	14	South Africa	809.8	950.2
12	15	United States	707.4	937.8
23	16	Finland	425.3	849.1
19	17	Sweden	494.8	838.3
15	18	China	532.2	813.1
31	19	Colombia	258.8	796.6
16	20	France	516.2	777.7
22	21	Denmark	436.0	770.9
32	22	Italy	247.4	732.4
14	23	Austria	547.0	711.2
13	24	Puerto Rico	564.6	668.6
30	25	Ireland	273.8	665.1
20	26	Chile	485.6	652.0
29	27	Switzerland	283.6	630.0
21	28	Argentina	455.8	588.8
28	29	Germany	284.9	565.0
27	30	United Kingdom	294.7	556.1
26	31	Canada	312.9	514.6
9	32	Mexico	827.1	452.5
35	33	Egypt	63.1	391.6
24	34	Portugal	368.3	355.8
34	35	Spain	178.1	326.4

Source: World Tourism Organization (1996)

Table 8.13 Outbound tourism – regions of the world, 1994 – arrivals at destination

Region	Outbound destinations						
	Africa	Americas	East Asia/Pacific	Europe	Middle East	South Asia	Total
Africa	8 202 610	257 437	380 427	4 242 476	1 982 146	92 048	15 157 144
East Asia/Pacific	299 950	7 492 805	102 078 829	10 139 461	2 989 900	625 414	123 626 359
Europe	6 090 541	15 293 365	9 261 192	283 044 919	2 809 940	1 812 507	318 312 464
South Asia	47 466	210 370	1 185 833	1 215 217	705 662	964 007	4 328 555
Americas	546 364	79 247 633	5 616 037	21 783 645	481 674	376 866	108 052 219
Middle East	866 656	191 786	279 561	2 147 823	7 626 128	194 424	11 660 509

Source: World Tourism Organization (1996)

Tourism departures and expenditures

Tourism arrivals and receipts are an important part of the picture of tourism demand. This book, however, is about consumer behaviour and we should therefore be particularly interested in departures and expenditures. The World Tourism Organization has classified countries of the world according to their average expenditure per trip abroad. This data, which is shown in Table 8.12, shows a comparison between 1985 and 1994.

It is interesting to note that certain countries have changed their ranking during this period. Many countries have changed their position in the ranking, and this is particularly marked for the countries that have already been identified as having growing economies and improving standards of living. Of particular note here is Japan (8th to 1st), Thailand (18th to 3rd), Belgium (25th to 9th), Brazil (33rd to 10th) and Columbia (31st to 19th).

We can now finally look at the outbound tourism statistics for the major regions of the world to draw some comparisons. The outbound tourism statistics are shown in Table 8.13.

It can be seen from Table 8.13 that tourists from Africa travel extensively to Europe and the Middle East. Tourists from East Asia and Pacific travel particularly in their own region although they also travel to Europe and the Americas. Europeans also travel extensively within their own region, but also travel to the Americas and the East Asia/Pacific region. Europeans also form the largest regional group of outbound tourists.

Tourists from South Asia show a particular preference for the East Asia/Pacific region, whereas those from the Americas show a particular preference for the Americas and Europe. Tourists from the Middle East show a particular preference for the Middle East and Europe region.

Conclusion

We have considered the factors that affect world tourism demand figures. Inbound and outbound tourism is predicted to grow in importance over the next decade. Outbound tourism is predicted to grow rapidly from countries within the Asian regions. The Asian, African and Middle Eastern outbound markets are in their introductory or growth stages and there will be a great potential for developments from these regions in the future.

The nature of demand may alter as increasing numbers of outbound tourists travel from these regions. Increasing interest in beach holidays and environmental issues are examples of trends which are predicted for outbound tourists from Japan and Asia, in general.

We now need to turn our attention to the national differences in tourism demand. This will be explored in Chapter 9.

Discussion points and essay questions

1 Explain the reasons for the development in the levels of inbound and outbound tourism from East Asia and the Pacific regions of the world.
2 Explore the relationship between consumer knowledge of tourism opportunities and demand for tourism products. Discuss the ways in which a consumer can gain knowledge about tourism opportunities.
3 Evaluate the reasons for the Japanese tourists showing a growing interest in a beach-type holiday, rather than a city-based holiday.

Exercise

Design and conduct a small-scale survey of tourists to discover their interest in visiting the East Asia and Pacific area of the world. Do they envisage any problems involved in visiting areas such as these?

9 *National differences – domestic, outbound, inbound*

Introduction

In the previous chapter, we looked at the pattern of world demand divided by regions of the world. It has been shown that certain areas of the world such as the Asia Pacific and Far East are growing in their levels of tourism. In this chapter, we will consider the differences between individual countries in more depth. We will start by considering the outbound and inbound tourism figures for a range of countries, and then we will consider individual countries in more depth. This will enable us to look at particular issues related to tourism demand on a country by country basis. The chapter will conclude with a discussion on the similarities and differences between individual countries in relation to their tourism figures.

Inbound and outbound tourism receipts

Table 9.1 illustrates outbound tourist expenditure for 60 centres, in 1994. On the basis of this data, a number of points can be made, as follows:

1 The range of expenditure varies from $203 million for Ecuador to $43 562 million for the USA. This reflects both differences in economic development and population size. Even in countries with a similar population, the figures can vary dramatically. For example, France and the UK have similar sized populations but the figures are $13 773 million and $22 185 million respectively. Other factors are clearly involved in accounting for differences in overall expenditure ranges.
2 The average current rate of growth of outbound tourist expenditure between 1980 and 1994 varies dramatically too, from –5.6 per cent for Libya and –0.87 per cent for Poland, to 19.55 per cent for Singapore and 20.19 per cent for Bangladesh.
3 The change in the share of worldwide expenditure between 1980 and 1994 also shows significant differences. Over this period the following

Table 9.1 Outbound tourism receipts – the top 60 countries, 1994

Rank 1994	Country	Tourism Expenditure (US$ Million)		Rank 1980	Average Annual Growth Rate (%)	% Share of Expenditure Worldwide	
		1994	1980		1980/1984	1994	1980
1	United States	43 562	10 385	2	10.78	14.62	10.12
2	Germany	41 419	20 599	1	5.12	13.90	20.08
3	Japan	30 715	4 593	6	14.54	10.31	4.48
4	United Kingdom	22 185	6 893	3	8.71	7.45	6.72
5	France	13 773	6 027	4	6.08	4.62	5.88
6	Italy	12 181	1 907	13	14.16	4.09	1.86
7	Netherlands	10 983	4 664	5	6.31	3.69	4.55
8	Canada	9 439	3 122	9	8.22	3.17	3.04
9	Austria	9 330	2 847	10	8.85	3.13	2.78
10	Belgium	7 782	3 272	8	6.38	2.61	3.19
11	Taiwan	7 618	818	24	17.28	2.56	0.80
12	Switzerland	6 325	2 357	12	7.31	2.12	2.30
13	Mexico	5 338	4 174	7	1.77	1.79	4.07
14	Sweden	4 864	1 235	21	10.29	1.63	1.20
15	Australia	4 339	1 749	16	6.71	1.46	1.70
16	Spain	4 188	1 229	22	9.15	1.41	1.20
17	Korea. Rep	4 088	350	36	19.19	1.37	0.34
18	Singapore	3 923	322	38	19.55	1.32	0.31
19	Norway	3 712	1 310	20	7.72	1.25	1.28
20	Denmark	3 583	1 560	18	6.12	1.20	1.52
21	China	3 036	–	–	–	1.02	–
22	Brazil	2 931	1 160	23	6.84	0.98	1.13
23	Thailand	2 906	244	44	19.36	0.98	0.24
24	Israel	2 600	533	31	11.99	0.87	0.52
25	Argentina	2 576	1 791	15	2.63	0.86	1.75
26	Kuwait	2 146	1 339	19	3.43	0.72	1.31
27	Indonesia	1 900	375	34	12.29	0.64	0.37
28	Venezuela	1 861	1 880	14	−0.07	0.62	1.83
29	Malaysia	1 737	470	32	9.79	0.58	0.46
30	Portugal	1 698	290	40	13.46	0.57	0.28
31	South Africa	1 678	756	26	5.86	0.56	0.74
32	Finland	1 665	544	29	8.32	0.56	0.53
33	Ireland	1 575	742	27	5.52	0.53	0.72
34	Greece	1 125	190	48	13.55	0.38	0.19
35	New Zealand	1 101	534	30	5.30	0.37	0.52
36	Czech Republic	1 076	–	–	–	0.36	–
37	Egypt	1 067	573	28	4.54	0.36	0.56
38	Hungary	925	88	63	18.30	0.31	0.09
39	Turkey	866	115	54	15.51	0.29	0.11
40	Puerto Rico	797	400	33	5.05	0.27	0.39
41	Columbia	756	250	43	8.22	0.25	0.24
42	Chile	639	195	47	8.85	0.21	0.19
43	Iran	570	1 700	17	−7.51	0.19	1.66
44	Croatia	552	–	–	–	0.19	–
45	Romania	449	73	65	13.85	0.15	0.07
46	India	408	113	55	9.60	0.14	0.11
47	Syria	400	177	50	6.00	0.13	0.17
48	Pakistan	398	90	62	11.20	0.13	0.09
49	Jordan	394	301	39	1.94	0.13	0.29

Table 9.1 *(Continued)*

Rank 1994	Country	Tourism Expenditure (US$ Million)		Rank 1980	Average Annual Growth Rate (%)	% Share of Expenditure Worldwide	
		1994	1980		1980/1984	1994	1980
50	Peru	323	107	57	8.21	0.11	0.10
51	Slovenia	316	–	–	–	0.11	–
51	Poland	316	357	35	–0.87	0.11	0.35
52	Morocco	302	98	60	8.37	0.10	0.10
53	Costa Rica	300	62	67	11.92	0.10	0.06
54	Slovakia	284	–	–	–	0.10	–
55	Iceland	249	42	76	13.56	0.08	0.04
56	Bulgaria	242	–	–	–	0.08	–
57	Tunisia	216	55	70	10.26	0.07	0.05
58	Cameroon	212	82	64	7.02	0.07	0.08
59	Bangladesh	210	16	93	20.19	0.07	0.02
59	Libya	210	470	32	–5.59	0.07	0.46
60	Ecuador	203	228	45	–0.83	0.07	0.22
	World Total	297 894	102 586		7.91	100.00	100.00

Source: World Tourism Organization

countries saw significant increases in their share of outbound tourist expenditure:

- USA – 10.12 per cent to 14.62 per cent
- Japan – 4.48 per cent to 10.31 per cent
- UK – 6.72 per cent to 7.45 per cent
- Taiwan – 0.80 per cent to 2.56 per cent
- Hungary – 0.09 per cent to 0.31 per cent.

Over the same period some countries saw a decline in their share of the worldwide outbound expenditure, as follows:

- Germany – 20.08 per cent to 13.90 per cent
- France – 5.88 per cent to 4.62 per cent
- Mexico – 4.07 per cent to 1.79 per cent
- Argentina – 1.75 per cent to 0.86 per cent
- Kuwait – 1.31 per cent to 0.72 per cent
- Iran – 1.66 per cent to 0.19 per cent.

Both sets of figures are clearly accounted for by political, social and economic factors peculiar to each of them.

Table 9.2 shows inbound tourism receipts for 1994. It is clear from this list that there are great variations again. The receipts of the USA are nearly 30 times greater than those of Norway. Major destination countries like Greece and Portugal earned less from foreign tourists than countries like Germany and Belgium which are less renowned as destination countries. Part of the

Table 9.2 Inbound and tourism receipts – a range of countries, 1994

Country	International Travel Receipts US $m
United States	60 406
France	24 845
Italy	23 754
Spain	21 491
United Kingdom	15 176
Austria	13 152
Germany	10 817
Switzerland	7 630
Mexico	6 318
Canada	6 309
Australia	5 903
Netherlands	4 743
Belgium	4 667
Turkey	4 359
Greece	3 858
Portugal	3 826
Japan	3 464
Denmark	3 175
Sweden	2 838
Norway	2 169

Source: OECD (1996). Copyright OECD 1996

reason for this is the different cost of being a tourist in the higher cost, more developed economies of Germany and Belgium.

A comparison of data in Tables 9.1 and 9.2 also shows major differences in the balance of payments in respect of tourism in 1997. For example:

- The USA earned nearly 50 per cent more from foreign tourists visiting the country than its own nationals spent abroad.
- German tourists spent four times more abroad than foreign tourists did in Germany.
- Foreign tourists in France spent nearly twice as much as French people did when they travelled abroad.
- Foreign tourists in Spain spent five times more than Spanish people did travelling to other countries.

Table 9.3 looks at trends in inbound visitor figures in 16 countries between 1986 and 1994. This data shows some interesting national differences as follows:

1 Between 1986 and 1994 visitors to South Korea more than doubled while those to the USA increased by around 80 per cent over the same period.

Table 9.3   Inbound tourism for a range of countries, 1986–1994

	1986	*1990*	*1992*	*1994*
Australia	1 429 400	2 215 300	2 603 260	3 362 240
Brazil	1 934 091*	1 091 067*	1 687 945*	1 700 464*
Bulgaria	7 567 062	10 329 537	6 123 844	10 068 181
Dominican Republic		1 305 361	1 415 147	1 716 789
Germany		17 045 000	15 147 000	14 492 000
Israel	1 102 264	1 063 406*	1 509 520*	1 838 703*
Italy	53 314 906	60 295 921	50 088 720	51 814 449
Japan	2 061 526	3 235 860	3 581 540	3 468 055
Nigeria		226 242	271 854	327 189
Russian Federation	4 308 900 (USSR)		3 009 488	4 642 899
South Korea	1 659 972	2 958 839	3 231 081	3 580 024
Taiwan		1 934 084	1 873 327	2 127 249
UK	13 897 000	18 013 000	18 535 000	21 034 000
United States	25 358 501*	39 539 010*	47 261 029*	45 504 325*
Vietnam			440 000*	940 707*

Source: World Tourism Organization; figures from WTO refer to *visitors* arriving at frontiers, apart from those marked * which are specifically numbers of *tourists* arriving at frontiers

2 The number of foreign visitors to Brazil actually fell from 1 934 091 in 1986 to 1 700 464 in 1994. Likewise Italian visitors fell from 53 314 906 in 1986 to 51 814 449 in 1994.

3 Nigeria welcomed less than 1 per cent of the number of tourists visiting Italy in 1994.

4 In Vietnam, where data has only been available since 1992, tourist arrivals more than doubled in just two years, between 1992 and 1994.

Having looked at the data in Tables 9.1, 9.2 and 9.3, we can now consider some of the major tourism generating countries in more depth.

United States

The United States is one of the most important countries in the world in relation to inbound and outbound tourism receipts. The market for outbound tourism from the US has the greatest potential for growth. International travel has never been appealing to Americans, and less than 20 per cent of Americans currently own a passport (Euromonitor, 1996a). Economic growth and competitive prices, however, have fuelled the growth in tourism over the period 1990–1995. There was a growth in outbound tourism during 1993 despite the fact that there were unfavourable currency values. The growth in inbound tourism has grown slowly over the period 1990–1995 because of the well-developed market and problems with the economy in some adjoining countries such as Mexico.

Table 9.4 The market for travel and tourism in the United States by volume, 1991–1995

	Volume '000				
	1991	*1992*	*1993*	*1994*	*1995*
Incoming tourism	42 987	47 261	45 779	45 714	43 779
Outgoing tourism	42 206	44 726	45 446	49 975	49 772
Domestic tourism*	980	1 063	1 137	1 216	1 317

Source: Euromonitor (1996a); * actual number of person trips

The overall volumes of travel and tourism in the United States for the period 1991–1995 is shown in Table 9.4.

The market for outgoing tourism is growing steadily and has the greatest potential for growth. The value of the tourism is shown in Table 9.5. If this is converted into figures by value at constant prices, as shown in Table 9.6, it can be seen that domestic tourism has remained static, whereas outgoing tourism is showing a gradual increase in value terms.

Table 9.5 The market for travel and tourism in the United States by value, 1991–1995

	$ million				
	1991	*1992*	*1993*	*1994*	*1995*
Incoming tourism*	64 238	71 257	74 171	75 060	74 010
Outgoing tourism*	45 344	49 615	51 980	53 085	58 445
Domestic tourism**	44 804	49 173	52 593	53 215	53 934

Source: Euromonitor (1996a); * calculated as payments/receipts on travel and transport, ** travel payments only

Table 9.6 The market for travel and tourism in the United States by value at constant prices, 1991–1995

	$ million				
	1991	*1992*	*1993*	*1994*	*1995*
Incoming tourism*	64 238	69 182	69 907	68 926	66 977
Outgoing tourism*	45 344	48 170	48 992	48 747	52 891
Domestic tourism**	44 804	47 740	49 569	48 866	48 809

Source: Euromonitor (1996a); * calculated as payments/receipts on travel and transport, ** travel payments only

The largest share of visitors to the United States come from Europe. The greatest regional increases in visitors came from both Asia/Middle East and South America. The number of travellers from Asia and the Middle East increased by more than 39 per cent in the period 1991–1993, and travellers from South America increased by 47 per cent in the same period (Euromonitor, 1996a).

Outgoing tourist growth has been fuelled by a steady economic growth in the United States during 1994 and 1995. This has encouraged business travel, although there has been a decline in the business purchase of Business Class travel by companies.

Germany

Germany is an important country in relation to inbound and outbound tourism receipts.

The market for incoming tourist has experienced a general downturn with expenditure by international tourists in Germany down by 0.2 per cent to approximately DM17.15 billion in 1995 (Euromonitor, 1996a). This decline is likely to continue and is likely to rise at a slower rate than the expenditure of German tourists abroad. The figures for the incoming tourism market are shown in Table 9.7.

Table 9.7 The incoming tourism market (overseas residents) by value, 1991–1995

	Expenditure (DM million)	
	Current rsp	*Constant 1991 rsp*
1991	17 686	17 686
1992	17 747	17 064
1993	18 000	16 729
1994	17 180	15 576
1995	17 146	15 268

Source: Euromonitor (1996a)

The expenditure by German residents abroad rose by 8 per cent to reach DM73 billion in 1995. Expenditure by Germans on outbound travel has grown by 40 per cent in the period 1991–1993 to DM73 billion in 1995, an increase of approximately 40 per cent over the period 1991–1995. The growth in the outbound tourism market for the period 1991–1995 is shown in Table 9.8. The Germans spend substantial amounts of money when they travel abroad, only exceeded by the French and the Greeks.

Table 9.8   The outbound tourism market
(German residents) departures, 1991–1995

	Departures (million)
1991	31.8
1992	33.7
1993	31.8
1994	44.0
1995	49.5

Source: Euromonitor (1996a)

The expenditure of the outbound tourism market in millions of DM is shown in Table 9.9.

The expenditure by Germans on trips within Germany has grown in recent years to DM147 million in 1995. The large expenditure on domestic tourism, shown in Table 9.10, can be explained by the large amount of

Table 9.9   Expenditure of the outbound
tourism market (German residents),
1991–1995

	Expenditure (DM million)	
	Current prices	*Constant rsp*
1991	51 923	51 923
1992	57 623	55 407
1993	62 731	58 300
1994	67 223	60 946
1995	72 601	64 649

Source: Euromonitor (1996a)

Table 9.10   Expenditure of the domestic
tourism market, 1991–1995*

	Expenditure (DM million)	
	Current prices	*Constant rsp*
1991	123 930	123 930
1992	136 443	131 195
1993	149 429	138 874
1994	143 208	129 835
1995	147 442	131 293

Source: Euromonitor (1996a); * includes a
high proportion of business travel

Table 9.11 The incoming and outbound tourism market in Germany in millions, 1991–1995

	1991	*1992*	*1993*	*1994*	*1995*
Incoming Tourism Market	14 294	14 514	13 209	13 364	13 538
Outbound Tourism Market	31 800	33 700	31 800	44 000	49 500

Source: Euromonitor (1996a)

expenditure on business trips taken by Germans within their own country, and the fact that Germans often take domestic holidays in preference to holidays abroad.

A summary of the incoming and outbound tourism market in Germany is shown in Table 9.11.

Japan

The appreciating value of the yen in the early 1990s encouraged overseas travel by the Japanese but had a negative effect on the numbers of incoming visitors. Declining visitor numbers have also been accompanied by a reduction in the spending of foreign tourists. The market for incoming tourism in Japan for the period 1991–1995 in terms of visitor numbers is shown in Table 9.12 and the market for incoming tourism in Japan by expenditure for the same period is shown in Table 9.13.

Outgoing tourism has grown steadily over the period 1991–1995. This can be seen in Table 9.14. The number of Japanese tourists travelling abroad has continued to grow to an estimated 13 million in 1995, representing a growth of almost 50 per cent since 1991 (Euromonitor, 1996a). The strength of the yen against the dollar during this period made international travel attractive

Table 9.12 The market for incoming tourism in Japan by number of visits, 1991–1995

	Visits '000	
	Total visitors	Tourists
1991	3533	2104
1992	3582	2103
1993	3410	1925
1994	3468	1916
1995	3490	1890

Source: Euromonitor (1996a)

Table 9.13   The market for incoming tourism in Japan by expenditure, 1991–1995

	Value (Y billion)	
	Current rsp	Constant 1991 rsp
1991	461.1	461.1
1992	455.7	448.5
1993	394.8	383.3
1994	348.0	333.6
1995	328.1	314.0

Source: Euromonitor (1996a)

Table 9.14   The market for outgoing tourism in Japan by number of visits, 1991–1995

	Visits '000	
	Total visitors	Tourists
1991	10 634	8 699
1992	11 791	9 839
1993	11 934	9 954
1994	13 580	11 340
1995	15 520	13 000

Source: Euromonitor (1996a)

to the Japanese. The sale of package tours has grown, as prices have fallen. The Japanese consumer has been looking for cheaper prices for international travel which has fuelled widespread discounting in the Japanese travel market. This situation looks set to continue if the current downturn in the Japanese economy persists.

United Kingdom

The United Kingdom has a considerable tourism market in world terms. The major growth sectors within the UK travel market for the period 1991–1995 are shown in Table 9.15.

It can be seen that the outbound travel market has grown at a quicker rate than the inbound market in both volume and value terms over the five-year period. The number of trips taken by visitors to the UK has risen at a lower

Table 9.15 Major Growth Sectors within the Travel Market, 1991–1995, 1994–1995

	% value growth	
	1991–1995	*1994–1995*
Incoming tourism:		
Traffic (million trips)	+24.3	+4.4
Expenditure (current £ million)	+43.9	+6.4
Constant 1991 rsp	+29.7	+3.6
Outbound tourism:		
Traffic (million trips)	+31.2	+6.0
Expenditure (current £ million)	+60.6	+11.9
Constant 1991 rsp	+44.8	+9.0
Domestic tourism:		
Traffic (million trips)	+26.3	+8.6
Expenditure (current £ million)	+55.0	+12.0
Constant 1991 rsp	+39.8	+9.1

Source: Euromonitor (1996a)

rate than the number of trips taken by UK residents at home (Euromonitor, 1996a).

Inbound tourism has steadily increased to the UK over the last few years. Volumes rose 4 per cent during 1995 and expenditure from incoming tourism in real terms has increased by 30 per cent over the five-year period to 1995. The incoming tourism market by value and volume is shown in Tables 9.16 and 9.17 respectively.

Outbound tourism has also increased 31 per cent over the five years to 1995. UK holidaymakers are very determined to have their holidays abroad, despite the recession which occurred in the 1980s and 1990s. The discounting which has occurred in the UK package holiday market has

Table 9.16 The incoming tourism market (overseas residents) by value, 1991–1995

	Value (£ billion)	
	Current rsp	*Constant 1991 rsp*
1991	7 386	7 386
1992	7 891	7 609
1993	9 376	8 896
1994	9 989	9 249
1995	10 628	9 583

Source: Euromonitor (1996a)

Table 9.17   The incoming tourism market (overseas residents) by volume, 1991–1995

	Traffic visits to the UK ('000)
1991	17 126
1992	18 535
1993	19 488
1994	20 385
1995	21 282

Source: Euromonitor (1996a)

fuelled the growth of sales, particularly to long-haul destinations. The outgoing tourism market by volume and value for the period 1991–1995 is shown in Tables 9.18 and 9.19 respectively.

The levels of domestic tourism in the UK have also grown over the past few years with the value of domestic tourism market increasing by 55 per cent over the period 1991–1995 (Euromonitor, 1996a). The domestic tourism

Table 9.18   The outgoing tourism market (UK residents) by volume, 1991–1995

	Traffic visits abroad ('000)
1991	30 808
1992	33 835
1993	35 842
1994	38 136
1995	40 424

Source: Euromonitor (1996a)

Table 9.19   The outgoing tourism market (UK residents) by value, 1991–1995

	Value (£ billion)	
	Current rsp	*Constant 1991 rsp*
1991	9 951	9 951
1992	11 243	10 842
1993	12 707	12 056
1994	14 283	13 225
1995	15 983	14 412

Source: Euromonitor (1996a)

Table 9.20   The domestic tourism market by volume, 1991–1995

	Traffic trips taken (million)
1991	94.4
1992	95.6
1993	90.9
1994	109.8
1995	119.2

Source: Euromonitor (1996a)

Table 9.21   The domestic tourism market by value, 1991–1995

	Value (£ billion)	
	Current rsp	*Constant 1991 rsp*
1991	10 470	10 470
1992	10 665	10 284
1993	12 430	11 793
1994	14 495	13 421
1995	16 234	14 638

Source: Euromonitor (1996a)

market by volume and value are shown in Tables 9.20 and 9.21 respectively.

The reasons for the increase in domestic tourism can be partly explained by several summers with good weather, together with the growth of all-weather holiday centres and short breaks.

France

France has always been a major destination for foreign tourists, largely due to the range of scenery and attractions which the country can offer the foreign visitor. The country also has an excellent climate for tourism ranging from the sunny Mediterranean climate of the south to the snowy climate of the French Alps. This has led to the development of tourism both in the summer and winter months. Revenue from inbound tourism has more than doubled in the last decade despite the world-wide recession and a strong French currency.

France did, however, experience problems in their tourism market during 1995 when there was a sharp decline in both the size of foreign receipts from tourism as well as the number of visitors going to France because of the combination of political and economic factors.

The devaluation of other European currencies such as the Italian lira and Spanish peseta have made these countries more attractive to the budget-conscious traveller. Paris, the capital of France, has also experienced terrorist bombing. The French government has continued to carry out nuclear tests in the South Pacific which has proved unpopular with foreign holidaymakers. This decline in 1995 can be seen in Tables 9.22 and 9.23.

Table 9.22   The market for incoming tourism in France by number of arrivals*, 1991–1995

	Millions	
	Arrivals	*Bed nights*
1991	55.0	396.0
1992	59.6	428.4
1993	60.1	430.1
1994	63.1	443.0
1995	52.0	394.2

Source: Euromonitor (1996a); * stays of four days or more

Table 9.23   The market for incoming tourism in France by expenditure, 1991–1995

	FF billion	
	Current rsp	*Constant 1991 rsp*
1991	138.7	138.7
1992	133.3	130.2
1993	137.0	130.9
1994	142.1	133.4
1995	123.7	113.7

Source: Euromonitor (1996a)

There has been a steady increase in the market of outbound tourism from France, despite the many holiday opportunities which France offers to the French. The market for outgoing tourism from France is shown in Table 9.24.

The French have easy access to bordering European countries such as Spain, Switzerland, Italy and Germany. Despite this, 70 per cent of the French

Table 9.24 The market for outgoing
tourism from France by number of
departures, 1991–1995

	Millions	
	Departures	*Bed nights*
1991	10.1	170.0
1992	10.7	180.6
1993	10.4	174.7
1994	10.5	176.5
1995	10.8	178.2

Source: Euromonitor (1996a)

Table 9.25 The market for domestic
tourism in France by number of holidays,
1991–1995

	Millions	
	Number of holidays	*Bed nights*
1991	53.7	727.1
1992	56.4	741.8
1993	50.1	744.3
1994	54.5	745.6
1995	55.1	746.2

Source: Euromonitor (1996a)

Table 9.26 The market for domestic
tourism in France by expenditure,
1991–1995

	FF billions	
	Current rsp	*Constant 1991 rsp*
1991	325.1	325.1
1992	341.0	333.0
1993	335.4	320.3
1994	356.2	334.4
1995	364.3	334.8

Source: Euromonitor (1996a)

still prefer to remain at home for their holidays, creating the largest domestic tourism market in Europe (Euromonitor, 1996a). The numbers of holidays taken by the French in France, coupled with the expenditure, continues to rise year on year. This is shown in more detail in Tables 9.25 and 9.26.

Spain

Spain is a major European holiday destination. It offers a wide range of scenery and an excellent climate, which have allowed the country to develop substantial tourism receipts particularly in the package holiday business. The market for incoming tourism to Spain is shown in Tables 9.27 and 9.28.

Table 9.27   The market for outgoing tourism in Spain by number of journeys, 1991–1995

	'000
1991*	2552
1992*	2081
1993	5967
1994**	3577
1995***	3634

Source: Euromonitor (1996a); * figures refer to number of persons; ** new methodology to ascertain the number of journeys was employed in 1994 which gave rise to an apparent difference in number compared with 1993 figures; *** estimate

Table 9.28   The market for outgoing tourism in Spain by expenditure, 1991–1995

	Billions	
	Current rsp	Constant 1991 rsp
1991	473	473
1992	482	455
1993	464	419
1994	274	236
1995*	312	257

Source: Euromonitor (1996a); * estimate

It can be seen that Spain has experienced a steady increase in arrivals and receipts during the 1991–1995 period. There is an increasing number of East German visitors to Spain. The numbers of bookings by Russian tour operators such as Intourist and Sputnik has doubled during 1995 (Euromonitor, 1996a).

The market for outgoing tourism from Spain is still a young market which offers substantial potential for growth. In 1990, the number of journeys that Spaniards took abroad accounted for only 9 per cent of total holidays taken by Spaniards. The figure had declined even further by 1995 when journeys abroad represented only 7.7 per cent of total holidays taken (Euromonitor, 1996a).

The market for outgoing tourism in Spain is shown in Tables 9.29 and 9.30. The Spanish like to go to other European countries and France is the most popular destination. Other cheaper destinations such as Turkey, Tunisia and Morocco are also becoming popular with Spaniards.

Table 9.29   The market for incoming tourism in Spain by number of arrivals (overseas residents), 1991–1995

	Millions	
	Total arrivals	*% change*
1991	53.5	–
1992	55.3	3.4
1993	57.3	3.3
1994	61.4	7.5
1995*	63.6	3.6

Source: Euromonitor (1996a); * estimate

Table 9.30   The market for incoming tourism in Spain by expenditure, 1991–1995

	Ptas billion	
	Current rsp	*Constant 1991 rsp*
1991	1991	1991
1992	2265	2005
1993	2514	2269
1994	2868	2470
1995*	3100	2549

Source: Euromonitor (1996a); * estimate

Table 9.31   The market for domestic tourism in Spain by number of trips taken, 1991–1995

	Journeys ('000)
1991*	13.1
1992*	12.8
1993	85.8
1994**	51.7
1995***	43.0

Source: Euromonitor (1996a); * figures refer to number of persons; ** new methodology to ascertain the number of journeys was employed in 1994 which gave rise to an apparent difference in number compared with 1993 figures; *** estimate

Table 9.32   The market for domestic tourism in Spain by expenditure, 1991–1995

	Ptas billion	
	Current rsp	Constant 1991 rsp
1991*	890	890
1992	911	860
1993	1639	1479
1994**	1034	891
1995*	1084	891

Source: Euromonitor (1996a); * estimates; ** new methodology

The levels of domestic tourism in Spain is fairly stagnant. The period 1991–1995 was overshadowed by recession, with Spaniards tending to take higher volume, lower value domestic holidays. The market for domestic tourism in Spain is shown in Tables 9.31 and 9.32. The Spaniards showed an increasing trend in choosing to stay in private accommodation and travelling in groups in private cars to save money. Cost saving is a priority for Spaniards when they are touring their own country (Euromonitor, 1996a).

Newly emerging generating countries

We have already considered the increasing importance of countries that are experiencing a dynamic growth of the outbound market. Two countries at a dynamic stage of their development are South Korea and Taiwan. Many destinations have experienced a strong increase in visitor numbers from these two countries, particularly in long-haul markets. However, this phenomenon has been greatly reduced in 1998 due to the effects of recession in both countries.

Other countries experiencing a strong growth in outbound travel during the late 1990s are Singapore and Hong Kong. China is also a country which is expected to show a considerable growth in outbound tourism statistics (Economist Intelligence Unit, 1995b).

The growth in Europe continues to emanate from Eastern Europe, with Poland and Hungary showing strong growth. Russian tourists have also started to appear in larger and larger numbers in many destinations. However, the economic crisis experienced in Russia in 1998 threatens the future of this market.

National differences in tourism markets

Table 9.33 illustrates the relative scale of domestic, inbound and outbound tourism in ten selected countries. The allocation of 'high', 'medium' and 'low' takes into account the geographical size of the country and its resident population, for example.

Table 9.33   Relativity levels of domestic, inbound and outbound tourism in ten selected countries

Country	Domestic	Inbound	Outbound
Australia	Medium	Medium	High
Dominican Republic	Low	High	Low
France	High	High	Medium
Germany	Medium	Low	High
Japan	Medium	Low	Low
Netherlands	Medium	Medium	High
Nigeria	Medium	Low	Low
Russia	Medium	Low	Low
Spain	High	High	Medium
USA	High	Medium	Low

A deeper investigation of the factors behind these differences shows that:

1 there are many different factors that account for different scales of domestic, inbound and outbound tourism
2 even where the scale of the market is relatively similar, the markets themselves can be very different.

Let us now illustrate this by considering each country in turn.

Australia

Australia, as a developed economy where people have relatively high amounts of leisure time, has a reasonably highly developed domestic tourism market. Its inbound market has been traditionally related to migration from Europe but has now grown to include leisure tourists from Asia and Europeans who do not have relations in the country. However, its geographical isolation ensures that it will never be a mass-market destination for people from other continents. A large proportion of Australians travel abroad for holidays, again reflecting both the geographical isolation of this country which creates a desire to see other places, together with the availability of time and disposable income. However, the isolation influences the market in that the major outbound segment is young people who travel abroad for from one month up to a year. If you live thousands of miles from most potential destinations, a short trip hardly seems worthwhile. The young people and their parents often see a journey to Asia, Europe or North America almost as completing their education, and opening their eyes to the wider world. It could thus almost be seen as the modern version of the 'Grand Tour'.

The Dominican Republic

The Dominican Republic, on the other hand, is a poor developing country with low levels of both domestic and outbound tourism as a result. However, it has become a major destination in recent years for:

- Europeans looking for inexpensive, all-inclusive, sun, sand and sea holidays in an exotic location
- gamblers from Caribbean countries and South America who come to play the casinos.

In the latter case, the local language of Spanish is the 'Lingua franca' of many of the visitors so there is no language problem.

France

France is the world's top tourist destination because of:

- its generally attractive climate
- its diversity of attractions, from the culture and romance of Paris to the chic of the Riviera, from the friendly villages of Brittany to the vineyards of Burgundy, from the beaches of the West Coast to the Alpine ski resorts
- government investment in the tourism product from the 1960s such as new resorts of the Languedoc-Rousillon coast
- its strong image for food and wine

- its accommodation establishments and restaurants offer relatively good value (outside Paris!)
- effective marketing of the product by the government.

These factors also help to explain the country's high level of domestic tourism and the medium level of outbound tourism. However, there are other reasons. A high proportion of French people own second homes in their own country which encourages them to take trips in their own country. Furthermore, the outbound tourism sector is not highly developed which means foreign holidays remain quite expensive for French people. Language problems further constrain their ability to take holidays abroad.

Germany

Conversely, in Germany, outbound tourism is very high, reflecting both the highly developed state of the economy and the statutory holiday entitlement enjoyed by employees, together with a lack of domestic attractions. The climate is not good for summer sun holidays and there is a relative lack of stylish coastal resorts and picturesque cities. The same reasons also explain the only medium level of domestic tourism and the low inbound demand. For foreign tourists, Germany is also an expensive destination, again reflecting the highly developed state of its economy.

Japan

Japan, perhaps surprisingly in view of the stereotypes of the Japanese tourist, generates, in reality, relatively low levels of outbound demand. This is largely experienced by the high cost of living in Japan and the long hours worked. Indeed, the Japanese government is so worried about this fact that they are now encouraging their citizens to take more holidays! The main segment who do travel from Japan are young women travelling together, the so-called 'office ladies' and other segments rarely found elsewhere such as the 'working soldiers'. As a developed economy, Japan has medium levels of domestic tourism but receives only a low level of inbound tourism. This may be due to its high cost of living, language difficulties or its isolation from traditional tourist trip generating countries. With the help of Asian tourist markets, which are actually closer to Japan in some cases, it might become more widely visited in the future.

The Netherlands

As an affluent country, the Netherlands generates large numbers of outbound tourist trips. Outbound tourism is also stimulated by the small size and lack of diversity of the Netherlands itself, which limits domestic tourism opportunities too. The highly unbalanced nature of the Netherlands and its flat terrain leads Dutch people to seek foreign destinations which are more rural and hilly. They are major players in both the camping and caravanning and eco-tourism markets. The lack of diversity and hills also reduces inbound tourism to the Netherlands, which is restricted to the city of Amsterdam and the bulbfields in Spring.

Nigeria

As a developing country with a large population Nigeria has a medium level of domestic tourism, largely related to visiting friends and relatives. Its relatively low level of economic development also resists outbound tourism although there is an annual inflow of Muslim pilgrims to Mecca and business tourists. Because of its unstable political history and poor infrastructure, it also attract relatively few tourists.

Russia

Domestic tourism in Russia is at the medium level reflecting the well-developed domestic tourism industry which grew up under Communism. Subsidized social tourism at Black Sea resorts created a large domestic market but this has shrunk since the end of Communism. Domestic tourism is probably lower than it was ten years ago because of the reduction in subsidies and the drastic reduction in the living standards of most Russians. Inbound tourism was always low because of political restrictions on inbound tourism, but it is now being constrained by political instability, crime and the weakening of the transport infra-structure. Outbound tourism is growing but is still restricted to a small wealthy elite. However, this small market is high spending and attracts shopping tourists and even second-home owners to a variety of destina-tions from Benidorm to Cyprus and Greece.

Spain

Spain has a well-developed domestic tourism market based on the variety of attractions in the industry, both in the countryside and coast. Family-owned second homes in the country also stimulate domestic tourism as does the large-scale provision of social tourism schemes in the country. The breadth of attractions also account for the high inbound tourism situation, albeit most of it gravitating to the coast. In recent years, the emphasis has switched to other aspects of the product, notably the cities. This began in 1992 with the Olympics in Barcelona, Madrid designated as the European City of Culture, and Expo '92 in Seville. Spanish outbound tourism is still only on a medium level but is growing, particularly amongst young people who are travelling abroad for education and culture in ever greater millions.

USA

Finally, we turn to the USA, where domestic tourism is high due to:

- the range of attractions available and the diversity of landscapes
- the well-developed transport infrastructure
- the highly developed tourism industry, which is a world leader in theme parks, for example.

These same reasons attract a growing number of inbound tourists, from Europe and Asia, as well as Canada. At the same time, outbound tourism from the USA is lower than one might expect, partly because of the attractions of holidaying at home.

However, the lack of outbound trips taken by American tourists also reflect other factors such as:

- their general lack of skills in speaking foreign languages
- their fear of terrorist attacks
- the fact that many people in the USA are too poor to afford the cost of travelling outside the USA.

We can see therefore that the scale of domestic inbound and outbound tourism reflects a range of different factors, some general, some specific to particular countries.

Conclusion

It was expected that 1995 would signal a period of recovery for many of the world's leading economies, which in turn would lead to an increase in tourism. The recessionary tendencies have however persisted and increased levels of unemployment in many OECD countries has meant that consumer confidence and spending on leisure travel has been slow to recover. The purchasing power of individual countries' currencies abroad also has a considerable effect on leisure travel. Germany and Japan both have disappointing economic performances, but the strength of their currencies mean that they will continue to experience large travel markets.

The largest growth in tourism in the 1990s has come from Asia, however, this trend is threatened by the economic crisis experienced in this region in 1998.

A comparison of the outbound and inbound levels of tourism for major countries of the world is shown in Table 9.34. It can be seen from this table that, even in the mature industrialized countries, there are distinct differences between the patterns of inbound and outbound tourism in relation to population. These differences can be attributed to the influences and determinants which affect the choices of individuals in a particular market.

If we use these factors to explore comparisons of different countries we can begin to understand the reasons for the differences. The French, for example, have a beautiful country with a favourable climate and well-developed infrastructure for tourism. They also have considerable variations in geographic and climatic conditions, so that it is possible to both ski and worship the sun in beautiful surroundings at different times of the year. These factors have encouraged the French to stay at home for holidays which has meant that figures for outbound tourism are smaller than for other industrialized countries.

The United Kingdom, in comparison, has experienced a long-term trend of high outbound tourism figures. Many factors have contributed to this trend – not least the poor summer weather that the UK traditionally experiences. The most important influence however on the growth of outbound travel, has been the development of the package holiday companies in the UK, over a long period of time. This has made the package holiday to sunny climes accessible to people from all social backgrounds.

This theme will be considered again in Chapter 15 when we consider whether there is a rise of the global/Euro tourist in the post-modern world.

Table 9.34   Comparisons of different types of tourism for a cross section of countries

Volumes '000 1995 Country	Level of outbound tourism	Level of inbound tourism	Population 1995 '000	Comments
United States	49 772	43 779	262 890	Levels of inbound and outbound fairly well balanced
Germany	49 500	13 538	81 540	Levels of outbound tourism exceed smaller inbound figures
Japan	15 520	3 490	125 568	A growing inbound and outbound market
United Kingdom	40 424	21 282	58 576	Large numbers of outbound tourism
France	10 800	52 000	58 030	The French tend to stay at home for holidays. Large inbound business
Italy	16 400	30 500	57 316	Large volumes of inbound and domestic tourism
Spain	3 634	63 600	39 190	Low levels of outbound tourism. Large business for inbound tourism. Package holidays an important part of the market

Source: Euromonitor (1996a, 1997); *The Europa World Year Book* (1997); *The Statesman's Year Book* (1997–98)

Discussion points and essay questions

1 'The development of inbound tourism by a country is much more dependent on natural features than marketing activity' (Horner and Swarbrooke, 1996). Discuss this statement, with reference to individual countries.
2 'The inclusive tour (IT) sector was valued at $34 bn in Europe in 1992, when 400 mn air based IT's were taken by European residents' (World Tourism Organization, 1995). Discuss the importance of the inclusive tour in the development of international tourism.
3 Explore the reasons for industrialized countries having different levels of inbound and outbound tourism.

Exercise

Select one of the countries of the world that is experiencing a growth in inbound and outbound tourism. Quantify the growth figures over the last ten years and suggest reasons for this trend.

10 *The nature of demand in different segments of the tourism market*

Introduction

Until now, we have tended to focus upon the traditional vacation as the core tourism product and the conventional holidaymaker as the tourist. However, we know that the tourism market is very diverse and the product far from homogenous. Therefore, in this chapter, we will look at the nature of demand in a number of the different segments of the tourism market. This is not an attempt to produce a comprehensive typology of market segments in tourism but rather is meant to illustrate the diversity of market segments in tourism, each of which have their own demand characteristics:

- family market
- hedonistic tourists
- the 'backpacker' market
- VFR – visiting friends and relatives
- excursionists or day trippers
- educational tourists
- religious tourists
- the 'snowbird' market
- ethnic minority tourists
- tourists with disabilities
- social tourism
- the short break market.

The family market

The first point to make is that the nature of the family varies dramatically from one country to another. In the USA and Northern Europe, the family usually means the 'nuclear family' with two parents and between one and three children. However, in Southern Europe, the Middle East and many Asian countries, there is the phenomenon of the 'extended family', with a higher number of children and the inclusion of other relatives in the holiday party and/or their involvement in the purchase decision.

At the same time we must note that, in the so-called developed world, there is also the growing phenomenon of the 'single-parent family', where, due primarily to divorce, the family unit consists of one parent and the children.

However, in this section we will focus upon the nuclear family of Northern Europe. This segment represents the core market for many tour operators and types of products, including camping and caravanning trips, self-catering holidays and theme parks, for example.

The core determinant in the family market is the existence of children. Many families choose holidays that meet the needs of the children. These needs will vary depending on the age of the children, as follows:

- Babies. Here the need is to choose a holiday where the baby's safety and comfort will be the primary concern. This could mean avoiding countries with poor hygiene standards and choosing airlines and hotels offering special services for babies such as free baby food.
- Infants, from say two to five years old, where a short journey to the destination can be a priority as the child may get bored on long journeys. Safety in this case may mean ensuring that young children who are keen to practise their walking cannot get into danger on balconies or near swimming pools.
- Early school-age children, from around five to twelve years, often want to play with children of a similar age and may be content with the simple pleasures of play areas and swimming pools.
- Teenagers, aged 13 to 18, will usually want to be increasingly independent and enjoy more and more adult activities.

The point comes at which the young person wants to take a holiday separately from their parents. This could take the form of:

- an educational trip organized by their school
- an organized children's camp like BUNAC or Camp America
- an activity-based trip such as a PGL canoeing holiday in the UK or a farm-based vacation, for example, the 'Gîtes d'Enfants' in France
- a single-sex group holiday with a group of friends.

On the other hand, many children may continue to take at least some holidays with their parents into early adult life, particularly if they cannot afford a holiday because they are on a low income.

The number of children in a family also has an impact on demand. Families with several children may need to look for an economically priced holiday due to the high cost of raising children. This explains why they are a major component of the market for camping and caravanning holidays, for example.

The preference of many families for self-catering holidays is partly explained by the desire to minimize holiday costs. However, it is also a result of the desire of some families not to be bound by the formality and etiquette involved in staying in a hotel and eating at particular times.

Children tend not to fit well into such rigid regimes and self-catering has the advantage of being less regimented.

The tourism industry works hard to attract the lucrative family market, particularly through discounts for children and free child places. However, often, such offers are of little value to single-parent families as they are usually based on the stereotypical nuclear family of two adults and several children. Thus, the industry is failing to fully come to terms with a rapidly growing variation in the traditional family market.

Hedonistic tourists

A very different market is that of the hedonistic tourist, the pleasure-seeker. This market is traditionally associated with younger people and brand names such as Club 18–30 in the UK. It is a development of the original 4 'P's' concept of sun, sand, sea and sex tourism, with perhaps the addition of the fifth 'S' of Sangria to represent the consumption of alcohol.

Increasingly the hedonistic tourist in recent years has also driven the growth of a distinctive style of nightlife and partying in destinations such as Ibiza.

For the hedonistic tourist, the main motivator is the desire for physical pleasure and social life. At the same time there is a fashion dimension with different resorts moving in and out of fashion, depending on the perceived quality of the local nightlife.

The hedonistic tourist's day often looks very different to that of the family on holiday we have just been considering. They tend to wake late and then spend their time round the swimming pool or on the beach. They will then usually go out partying and not get to bed until the following morning.

Hedonistic tourists often travel in single-sex groups of friends and prefer the freedom and economy offered by simple, self-catering accommodation.

This phenomenon of hedonistic tourism is particularly associated with Northern Europe and has been criticized on two main grounds, namely:

- that the heavy drinking can lead to fights and problematic relations with the local host community, the so-called 'lager lout' phenomena
- the fear that much of the casual sex on such holidays is unprotected and therefore carries the risk of spreading HIV or AIDS.

However, we should note that hedonistic tourism is not a new phenomenon in tourism. As we saw in Chapter 3 the Romans visited spas for largely hedonistic reasons, and in the late nineteenth century and early twentieth century, young men travelled to Paris to gamble and visit brothels. The only difference, really, is that modern hedonistic tourism is a mass market and the tourism industry promotes this form of tourism overtly, as in the Club 18–30 advertising campaigns of the mid-1990s.

There are some forms of 'hedonistic' tourism, on the other hand, which are either illicit or illegal, notably the phenomenon of sex tourism in destinations such as Bangkok and the Philippines. Increasingly children are being drawn into this activity. The key difference of course with the hedonistic tourism we discussed earlier is that in this case payment may be involved and one of the partners may well be an unwilling participant. The main sex tourism client tends to be male and older than the 'sun, sea, sand, sex and Sangria' tourist we discussed above. They can be of any nationality but this market appears to be well developed in Japan and Northern Europe. However, in countries such as Australia and Sweden it is illegal for residents to take sex tourism trips. This is an example of governments regulating tourist behaviour and it also demonstrates that the old marketing cliché, 'the customer is always right', is wrong!

The 'backpacker' market

Another form of tourism which appears to appeal mainly to a younger market is 'backpacking', where tourists use a 'rucksack' or 'backpack' rather than a suitcase to carry all they need for their trip. However, the term has come to signify more than simply the type of luggage used by this tourist. It also implies:

● independent rather than packaged travel
● a desire to keep expenditure to a minimum
● a tendency to try to get off the beaten tourist track
● a trip that might extend beyond the usual duration of one to two weeks for a normal holiday.

This latter point is very important because it is linked to the fact that most backpackers are usually students, who have long vacations. Or it can involve people taking a year out from education before they begin college or taking a year out after completing a college course. It is therefore a form of travel based on the idea of spending a longer period over a vacation than is the norm for most people.

'Backpacking' is a truly international market that is popular with young people from every developed country, particularly the USA, UK, Netherlands, Germany, Australia and Japan. It could be argued that this is an early example of the truly global tourist, for the behaviour of backpackers tends to be similar regardless of their nationality. This is partly because backpacking has its own parallel travel media consisting of guides like the 'Lonely Planet' and 'Rough Guide' series. These tourists read the same guides and therefore often stay in the same accommodation and visit the same attractions.

Backpacking is very popular currently in long-haul destinations such as South-East Asia and South America. Within Europe there is the well-known phenomenon of the 'Inter-Railer', backpackers who travel across Europe by rail, utilizing discounted rail fare packages offered to young people.

Backpacking is likely to grow as the number of students around the world grows. However, it is unlikely to become popular with other groups in society because there seems no prospect of most people in employment gaining much more paid holiday time. However, it could begin to appeal more to early retired people who have the time and want to be a little more adventurous in their holidaymaking activities.

VFR – visiting friends and relatives

The 'VFR' market is one for which there is little reliable data. As such people do not stay in commercial accommodation and are usually domestic tourists, they are rarely recorded by tourism statisticians. Although this market is of no real interest to the accommodation sector it is very important for the visitor attraction market. Friends and relatives usually feel obliged to take their visitors out during their stay which brings business for local attractions.

For some people, particularly those on lower incomes, visiting friends and relatives can be an inexpensive alternative to a normal holiday.

The VFR market clearly involves a strong social motivation or it can be driven by a sense of family duty. VFR tourism can also be related to more formal occasions such as weddings and funerals.

Students tend to be heavily involved in the VFR market in two main ways, namely:

1 They make many new friends at college who they may visit during their vacation and/or after their course has ended.
2 They are visited by their parents in most cases and feel obliged to show them around the area.

Whilst most VFR tourism is domestic there is an international dimension. This is particularly the case in relation to people whose relatives have emigrated to another country. Some notable tourist flows as a result of this phenomenon are:

● Turkish workers travelling home from Germany to Turkey and their relatives visiting them in Turkey.
● Relatives travelling between the UK and India and Pakistan.
● British people travelling to visit relatives in Australia and New Zealand.
● Tourist flows between North African countries and France.

Visiting friends and family, notably the latter, is particularly highly developed in those countries, such as those of the Middle East and Asia, where the extended family is the norm.

Excursionists or day trippers

The day tripper or excursionist is generally a domestic tourist and is the core market for most visitor attractions, many seaside resorts and some rural areas.

In general, the excursionist does not wish to travel too far given that they only have one day or less available for their leisure activities. This often results in the day-trip market for an attraction being limited to those who live within up to one-and-a-half hours driving time, although in larger countries like the USA, excursionists may be willing to travel further than this for a day trip. While the duration of the trip is generally the whole day, they can be as short as three to four hours.

Some day trips require pre-planning and booking but the majority do not. They can therefore be a spontaneous decision. The day tripper has a spare day and will decide in the morning where to go. Their decision may well be influenced by the weather. If it is sunny a theme park trip might be selected, while rain could well result in the alternative selection of an indoor attraction such as a museum.

The day-trip market is largely a car-based market, although coach excursions also play a significant role in the market, particularly amongst other day trippers.

Day trippers are also major consumers of food and drink services and also tend to make considerable use of leisure shopping facilities.

While day trips are normally domestic they can be international. For example, shopping trips by Britons to France, and Malaysian people to Singapore. At the same time, there has been a growth in longer distance trips. For example, UK tour operators currently offer winter season day trips by air from UK airports to destinations like Paris, Prague and Reykjavik, from £99 upwards. Tourists can even take a 10-hour trip to Tromso, beyond the Arctic Circle, from Heathrow airport, for around £200.

Educational tourists

There has been a massive growth in the broad field of educational tourism in recent years. This has been fuelled by both the growth in higher and further education world-wide and the desire of many older tourists to learn something new during their annual vacation.

Travelling for education is not a new phenomenon. In the UK in the seventeenth and eighteenth centuries, the sons of the aristocracy undertook the 'Grand Tour' to complete their education. Since the 1980s, in Europe, there has also been a growth in school student exchange schemes.

Educational tourism today has a number of dimensions including:

1 Student exchanges between universities where students may travel for periods ranging from two or three months to a year. In some cases, in Europe, these have been subsidized by European Union initiatives such as the ERASMUS and SOCRATES programmes.
2 Young people attending language classes in a foreign country, which can last from a week to several months. Part of these courses may be trips to see local attractions and students may well live with local families for the duration of their course.

3 Themed holidays where tourists travel with like-minded people to pursue a common interest which could be archaeology, a foreign culture, painting or cooking.

In the first two cases the consumer, i.e. the tourist themselves, may not be the actual customer who makes the decision or pays the bill. In these cases, the customer might be the college or the parents respectively.

Religious tourists

Religious tourism is one of the oldest forms of tourism. It is unique, perhaps, in that it is driven by a sense of duty and obligation rather than a search for pleasure and leisure.

The 'Haj' pilgrimage by Moslems to Mecca in Saudi Arabia is undoubtedly the greatest single flow of religious tourists in the world today. It is estimated that in 1996, around 200 000 Moslems made this pilgrimage from Indonesia alone! Every able-bodied Moslem with the financial means is expected to make this pilgrimage at least once. The Haj takes place during a set period each year, namely the twelfth month of the Islamic calendar. However, there are pilgrimages which can take place at any time of the year such as Umroh.

The Christian pilgrimage phenomenon inspired classic literature such as Chaucer's *Canterbury Tales*. However, it is now much less important than it once was due to the decline in the number of active worshippers, in Europe particularly. Pilgrimages still take place to Rome, Jerusalem, Santiago to Compstella and Lourdes. Pilgrimages and visits to holy sites are also a major motivator of religious tourism trips for Hindus and other religions.

In general, the phenomenon of the pilgrimage is a highly restricted market, being only available to believers in a particular faith.

The traditional infrastructure of religious tourism has also become an attraction for the non-religious tourist, most notably cathedrals and churches. At the same time, due to the growing pressures of life, many non-believers are taking short trips to religious establishments for relaxation and spiritual enlightenment. For instance, men (only) can visit Orthodox monasteries in Mount Athos in Greece, for a short period, free of charge, providing they abide by the regime of the Monastery.

The 'snowbird' market

The first international mass tourism market was based on the 'summer sun' holiday, where Northern Europeans travelled to Southern Europe in the summer to get a suntan. One of the latest major growth markets in the USA and Northern Europe is also inspired by climatic motivators. In the USA this involves 'snowbirds' from the cold, snowy Northern States of the USA travelling to southern states like Florida and California with their mild winter climates. In Northern Europe it involves people travelling to Southern European destinations to escape the winter climate at home. On both continents this phenomena has two interrelated characteristics, namely:

● the trips are of long duration, from between four weeks and four months
● they are normally taken by retired people who have the time to take such a long vacation.

The motivations of older people to take such trips are not so much related to the desire to get a tan but rather by a wish to:

● escape the cold weather in their own country
● reduce their expenditure on heating at home
● improve their health given that they may suffer from illnesses like arthritis which may be exacerbated by the damp, cold weather in their home country
● make new friends and have a less lonely life than they might in their own community.

Ethnic minority tourists

Many countries contain ethnic minority communities, many of which may have been present in the country for generations. Often these will have maintained contact with their original country, and will have their own patterns of tourism and tourism infrastructure.

In many developed countries few people from ethnic minorities are regular purchasers of the product of the mainstream tourism industry. Few of the customers of the major UK tour operators, for example, come from the Asian, Afro-Caribbean and Chinese communities.

However, that is not to say that many people from ethnic minority groups are not making leisure trips; as we saw in the section on VFR tourists. In some cases though, lack of disposable income in ethnic minority groups, which suffer above-average rates of unemployment, is probably a factor in the low take-up of the holidays offered by tour operators.

Nevertheless, although as yet only really in the USA, in the case of the Black American market an outbound and domestic distinctive ethnic market has developed, served by specialist travel agents. What is more, this parallel market relates to both leisure tourism and business tourism. In the latter case there is, for instance, an organization of Black convention organizers.

It remains to be seen whether, as ethnic minority communities grow in various countries, become more integrated and gain greater economic power, they will enter the mainstream market or represent a parallel market place.

Tourists with disabilities

One of the most controversial areas within tourism is the issue of tourists with disabilities and their opportunities to take tourist trips. In many cases tourists with disabilities are denied equal access to tourist products. However, we need to recognize that there are many kinds of disability and degrees of disability, including:

1 Mobility problems, ranging from elderly people who may have difficulty climbing stairs to people who are confined to a wheelchair.
2 Sight difficulties ranging from minor impairment to a complete lack of vision.
3 Hearing difficulties, ranging from minor impairment to complete hearing loss.

These are the most widely recognized disabilities which affect travel but there are many others.

Clearly, the needs of such tourists may dictate every aspect of their holiday choice and may even determine whether they are able to take a holiday at all. The situation is further complicated if their condition is such that they need someone to accompany them, for this person may not be easy to find, and will normally have to pay as much as the traveller with disabilities.

It has to be recognized that the situation for travellers with disabilities varies from country to country, being more sympathetic in the USA and Scandinavia than in most other countries. An American person with disabilities wishing to travel to Scandinavia, for example, should be able to do so with the minimum of inconvenience. However, a Greek or Turkish traveller with disabilities wishing to visit South America may find it is an impossible dream.

Social tourism

Social tourism is a largely European phenomenon that is based on the idea that tourism is a social right of the citizen and/or tourism brings social benefits to the individual, so that some form of subsidy or state support is justified.

In the current climate of deregulation, privatization and reduced public expenditure in Europe, social tourism is under threat. Nevertheless, it is still significant in countries like Germany, France and Spain. It takes a number of forms, including:

1 Subsidized visits to health spas for people with particular illnesses, in France.
2 The State and employer supported 'Chéques Vacances' scheme in France which helps workers on lower incomes to be able to afford to take a holiday.

3 Non profit-making holiday centres owned and operated by trade unions or voluntary sector organizations in a wide range of European countries, notably Germany, France or Spain.

Social tourism reached its peak, perhaps, in the former Soviet Union, where it encompassed every worker and was the core of the Soviet domestic tourism industry. It also had an international dimension within the old 'Eastern bloc' nations where tourists used subsidized resort facilities and accommodation, in other Eastern European countries.

The short break market

The growth of the five-day week with a full two-day weekend, and the rise of car ownership, as well as faster aircraft, have all helped stimulate the development of the short weekend break market since the 1960s in the developed world. It is also now a growing phenomenon in the recently developing economies of Asia.

In most cases, the short break is an additional holiday rather than a substitute for the main annual holiday.

Short breaks exist in a number of forms, including:

- romantic weekends for a couple in a city like Rome or Paris, or for an American couple in an old New England inn
- shopping trips, for example, a group of women friends in the UK going to London or a party of Russian tourists flying to Paris to buy luxury goods or a visit to Indonesia by a group of Singaporean tourists who want to buy authentic craft products
- visiting friends and relatives (VFR) trips
- health farm or health spa breaks, designed to relieve stress or improve the health of the tourist
- special interest and activity breaks such as fishing trips, painting, horse-riding, or golf
- breaks built around a special event whether it be a theatre performance or a football match
- unwinding, relaxing breaks in country house hotels in the UK or 'Gîtes d'Interludes' in France, for example.

While not comprehensive, this selection of types of break illustrates that they are both domestic and international. One of the fastest growing sectors in tourism is the international city break market. Furthermore, tourists are prepared to travel further and further for a short break. In 1997–1998, breaks of four and five nights were being offered by UK tour operators to Montreal, Dubai, Cape Town and even Hong Kong! Although it is difficult to generalize, short breaks tend to be either:

1 planned and booked well in advance, to heighten the sense of anticipation, or

2 purchased at the last minute as a reaction to stress or a particularly difficult week at work, or alternatively, as a spontaneous celebration of a happy event or good news.

In the developed world, the short break is likely to grow in importance as work pressures arising from the increasingly competitive situation in all industries increase.

Conclusion

We have seen that there are a number of different submarkets within tourism, some of which are interrelated. For example, the VFR phenomenon is a submarket but it is often also a form of short break market. Furthermore, it is a significant element of the day-trip market when the VFR tourist is taken to visitor attractions by their hosts. It would have been possible to identify a number of other such submarkets.

For tourism marketers it is important to realize that the tourism market is not a homogenous whole but rather a collection of overlapping submarkets each with their own characteristics.

Discussion points and essay questions

1 Discuss the likely problems that might arise from the presence at the same time in a resort, of *both* hedonistic tourists and families.
2 Evaluate which sectors of tourism benefit *most* and *least* from *both* VFR tourists and 'backpackers'.
3 Explore the possible motivators and determinants of a day trip to an art gallery *and* a seaside resort *and* a craft workshop.

Exercise

You should make contact with a local or national group which represent people with any type of disability. Ask them what difficulties their people experience, as a result of their disability, when they are choosing and taking a holiday. Finally, you should suggest what the tourism industry could do to make it easier and more enjoyable for such people to take a holiday.

11 Consumer behaviour and markets in the different sectors of tourism

Introduction

One of the problems of writing a book on consumer behaviour in tourism is that tourism is not a single homogenous activity or market. It is a complex web of interrelated sectors each of which has its own characteristics in terms of consumer behaviour.

In this chapter we will endeavour to demonstrate the diversity of forms of consumer behaviour and markets found within tourism.

Before we go any further we must stress that in this chapter we will be concerned with the behaviour of the tourists who are the final consumers of the various markets and consumer organizations. However, within the complex structure outlined in Figure 11.1, it is clear that there are other producer/customer relationships, namely those between suppliers and producers and producers and intermediaries. This is true, for example, of the vitally important relationship between hoteliers (supplier) and tour operators (customer) and between airlines (customer) and travel agents (intermediary).

We should also point out that most of this chapter is concerned with leisure tourism, but we should not ignore the massively important 'parallel world' of business tourism. Later in this chapter, therefore, we will devote some space to discussing the unique nature of consumer behaviour in business tourism.

Finally, by way of introductory comments, it is clear that, in addition to differences between behaviour in different sectors, there are also significant differences within sectors. Towards the end of this chapter we will illustrate this point through examples drawn from the tour operations and accommodation sectors.

We will now look at some of the different sectors of tourism in terms of differences and similarities in relation to several key demand characteristics.

Factors taken into account when making a purchase decision

Price, in almost all cases, seems to be a constant factor regardless of which sector of tourism we consider. Location is another standard factor whether we are talking about the area of a city in which a hotel is located, the

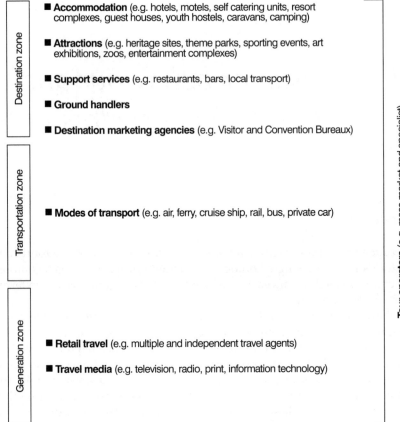

Figure 11.1   The sectors of tourism

departure airport offered by a tour operator, or how far an attraction is from the visitor's home. We can also assume that the tourist's previous experience of an organization's services and the reputation of the organization will also be relevant to purchase decisions in all sectors of tourism.

By contrast, there are also some differences too, for example:

● safety is a major issue for choosing airlines in some parts of the world, or selecting a holiday destination, but would rarely be an explicit factor taken into account when choosing a hotel
● fashionability can be a major consideration when choosing a holiday destination, but is rarely relevant to the choosing of airlines or accommodation units.

Seasonality

Most sectors have peak and off-peak seasons although these differ from one country to another. Often peak seasons will be the same for different sectors in any particular country. School holidays will usually be the peak time of demand for tour operators, charter airlines and visitor attractions. However, for city centre hotels, and scheduled airlines, school holidays are their off-peak season, because that is when business people usually take their holidays, with their families.

Distance travelled to use tourism products and services

Due to the nature of the tourism product, tourists always have to travel to the location where the tourism product or service is delivered. This distance can vary from a few hundred metres in the case of travel agent to hundreds of kilometres in the case of a hotel bed.

Frequency of purchase

We might find that in the UK, for instance, the average person makes the following number of purchases of different tourism products in a typical year:

Visitor attractions	12	(2 museums, a zoo, 2 theme parks, 2 historic houses, a factory shop, an art gallery, 2 festivals or special events, and a waterfront development like the Albert Dock, in Liverpool)
Inclusive tour offered by a Tour Operator	2	(a summer sun two-week package and an off-peak weekend city break)
Airline seat purchased independently, not as part of a package holiday	1	(a flight to visit a relative in the USA)
Accommodation purchased independently, not as part of a package holiday	1	(hotel stopover on the way to a family wedding in another part of the country)
Retail travel outlet	4	(to book the holidays, plus an air ticket, and a hotel)

Methods of segmenting the market

In most sections of tourism there are some common methods of segmenting the market which appear to work well. These include:

- geographical (where consumers live)
- demographic (age, sex and family status)

- business vs leisure travellers
- frequent travellers vs infrequent travellers
- independent tourists vs organized groups.

On the other hand, there seem to be a few approaches to segmentation which appear to largely be applicable to one sector only. For example, in the visitor attraction sector, the tourists' personality can be an important way of segmenting the market. Introvert, studious people may prefer to visit museums whilst extrovert adventurous risk-takers may form the core of the market for theme parks where 'white knuckle rides' are the main attraction.

Price paid for the product or service

The products offered by tourism organizations vary dramatically in price. The typical range of prices for the products of different sectors is as follows:

- Destinations – usually no direct fee or price is paid by the tourist to enter a destination
- Retail travel – no direct price is charged to the customer although the retail travel outlet receives a proportion of the price paid by the tourist, from the tour operator as commission
- Visitor attractions – many are free but even the most expensive rarely charge more than £20 for admission
- Restaurants – meals can vary in price, from £1 to over £100
- Accommodation – can be free (e.g. monasteries) or around £10 per night (youth hostels) at one extreme. At the other end of the spectrum, a luxury hotel or resort could charge several thousand pounds per night
- Transport – coach fares can cost five to ten pounds, while long-distance journeys on Concorde will cost thousands of pounds
- Tour operators – weekend breaks, self-catering holidays, and last-minute discounted holidays can cost less than £100 per person, while a fully inclusive escorted tour around the world may cost over £10 000.

Clearly the price charged also varies dramatically between countries. A hotel room in a good quality hotel may cost more than £150 in Hong Kong, £75 in Paris and £50 in Bangkok.

Methods of booking or reserving

In the visitor attraction sector, pre-booking is rare, whereas in sectors like airlines, hardly anyone would consider not pre-booking, and turning up at an airport in the hope that a seat will be available to their chosen destination. The accommodation sector falls somewhere between these two extremes, in that some people pre-book while others wait until they arrive in a place and then walk around to find a suitable hotel.

Where pre-booking is the norm, the choice is between using inter-mediaries or agents, and booking directly with the producer. Most of the products of tour operators are sold via intermediaries as are the majority of flights and ferry trips. However, the trend in all sectors seems to be towards direct booking.

So as we can see, there are both similarities and significant differences between the sectors of tourism in terms of aspects of consumer behaviour.

Special cases

The picture presented so far is very generalized and there are three special cases which we will now discuss. These are:

- retail travel
- destinations
- business tourism.

Retail travel

Retail travel is a unique sector in tourism in that it does not have a product of its own. Instead it exists to provide a service, namely giving consumers access to the products of the other sectors of tourism.

Its different function in the tourism system means that it differs from the demand for other sectors in a number of respects. For example, the peak season is not when people travel but rather when they book their trips. In the UK, for example, this can mean the period immediately after Christmas when many people book their summer holidays.

Destinations

From the consumer's point of view, it is perhaps better to see the destination as a 'do-it-yourself' (DIY) kit, rather than as a finished product. It offers the tourist a range of opportunities from which the consumer can produce their own product or experience. The choice of possible permutations are virtually limitless, subject only to constraints like money, and information, tourists can use the destination in many different ways. This is illustrated in Figure 11.2, where we look at how different tourists might use the destination of Crete.

The varying ways in which different tourists will use the same destination will depend on the characteristics of these tourists such as their age, sex, past experience, hobbies and interests, lifestyle and personality.

Finally, as we noted earlier, destinations are also unique amongst the sectors of tourism, in that no direct charge is made for using them. It is

Tourist A   Stays in a large modern resort hotel, in a quiet resort, eats in the hotel, and spends most of the day sunbathing by the hotel pool, and then drinking in the hotel bar at night.

Tourist B   Stays in a simple apartment complex on the coast, wakes late, sunbathes and then goes partying in the nightclubs of Aghios Nikolaos in the evening.

Tourist C   Makes their base in a small traditional pension, relaxes over long meals in local tavernas and attempts to make contact with Cretan people.

Tourist D   Uses a modern resort hotel as a base, but spends all day visiting cultural sites including the Temple at Knossos and the archaeological museum in Heraklion.

Tourist E   Stays in the cheapest accommodation they can find because they want to spend all their time and money indulging their interest in watersports such as diving and windsurfing.

Tourist F   Tours Crete by hire car, staying a few nights in each place they like the look of; they have no pre-planned itinerary.

Tourist G   Takes a cruise around the Mediterranean which includes a one-day port call to Heraklion and an optional excursion to the Samarian Gorge.

Figure 11.2   Different potential uses of Crete as a destination

possible for tourists to use a range of services, for example, beaches, parties and free museums, without incurring any expenditure. They can also 'window shop' and enjoy walking around historic streets absolutely free of charge.

Business tourism

Business tourism is a very different activity to leisure tourism and the business traveller is a fundamentally different consumer to the leisure traveller. The world of business tourism exists in parallel to that of leisure tourism. Sometimes business tourists use similar services to leisure tourists such as hotel bedrooms and airline seats. Other times they use services which are uniquely offered to them such as convention centres. Even where they use the same hotels and airlines as leisure tourists, special provision may be made to meet their needs such as in-bedroom computer access points, and on-board fax machines on aircraft. They also have their own infrastructure of business travel agents and incentive travel organizations for example.

Figure 11.3 illustrates the differences between consumer behaviour in business tourism and leisure tourism.

The first point in this figure is particularly important because in recent years there has been tension in the relationship between the employers (customers) business travellers (consumers) and the tourism industry, most notably airlines.

Companies looking to reduce their travel budgets and arrange them more effectively have often been irritated to see airlines offering their employees who travel on business 'perks' such as Air Miles. The companies believe that as the customer who pays the bill, it is they who should receive any benefit that may be offered by airlines. Many of them would prefer lower fares instead of 'perks' for their employees.

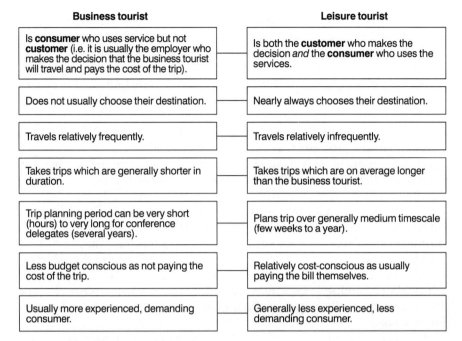

Figure 11.3   Differences in consumer behaviour between business tourists and leisure tourists

Taking the final element in Figure 11.3 further, the expectations of business tourists tend to be higher than the average leisure traveller. This may be because:

- They are more experienced travellers and therefore have a more comprehensive understanding of general standards in the tourism industry, against which to judge the performance of an individual tourism organization.
- They are often travelling on a higher daily budget than the average leisure traveller.
- The airlines and hotel sectors have recognized the lucrative nature of the business tourist and have therefore focused their promotional efforts on impressing the business tourist, thus raising their expectations.

However, before we take these points too far let us remember that many leisure tourists today are also business tourists in their working lives.

This brings us to a further interesting point, namely the links that do exist between business tourism and leisure tourism, in terms of consumer behaviour. These include the following four examples:

1 When the working day is over the business tourist becomes a leisure tourist, eating out in restaurants, drinking in bars and watching entertainment performances.

2 Conference programmes often have social programmes for delegates which will probably feature attractions predominantly aimed at leisure tourists such as folklore shows, and museums for example.

3 When a business tourist has finished the business they have to conduct, they may choose to stay on for a few days as a leisure tourist. This is more likely to be the case if the destination is a long way from their home or is a well-known leisure tourism destination. They may well use this extra time to take 'add-on' trips. For instance, a trip to mainland China could be added on to a business trip to Hong Kong Island.

4 Business tourists may take their partner with them; while they are working, their partner will be behaving as a leisure tourist.

Finally, we should note that in the longer term the demand for business travel may decline as the need for trips is substituted by the use of communication technologies such as video-conferencing. The market for training courses that involve students or tutors travelling to meet the other could also be reduced by the development of Virtual Reality simulations, which allow training to be conducted at the trainee's usual place of work. This is already playing a part in the training of surgeons in new techniques, for instance.

However, it seems likely that there will be business tourism for the foreseeable future, for as long as personal face-to-face contact is either thought to be essential or desirable.

Differences within individual sectors of tourism

In this chapter, we have focused upon similarities and differences in consumer behaviour between the different sectors of tourism. However, it would be wrong not to look at the differences in behaviour that can exist within the same sector. We will illustrate this point through four examples drawn from the accommodation and tour operation sectors respectively.

Luxury hotels and budget motels

There are clearly different motivators for guests at five-star hotels than would be the case for budget motels. The luxury hotel client seeks a special experience, status and a high level of personal service. On the other hand, the budget motel user is motivated by a desire for a functional experience, a convenient location and economy.

Serviced and non-serviced accommodation units

The consumers who may prefer to use non-serviced, or self-catering accommodation for their holidays may well make this choice because they:

- have children and find self-catering more flexible than staying in hotels
- may be on a limited budget and, by taking food with them, or buying cheaply from local supermarkets, they should be able to enjoy a holiday in the same destination at a lower cost than would be the case if they were to stay in a hotel
- may prefer to buy and cook fresh local food products than eat hotel meals, based on imported ingredients and international menus
- could be suspicious of hygiene standards in the local hospitality industry.

Mass market and specialist tour operators

Tourists who buy mass-market package tours and those buying the products offered by specialist operators are often seeking different benefits from their purchase.

The mass-market customer may well be motivated by a desire for:

- a low-cost product
- visiting destinations which are clearly popular and have a well-developed infrastructure for tourists
- the company of other tourists
- a more passive, resort-based holiday.

Conversely, the tourist who buys a specialist tour operator's package may well be motivated by their wish to:

- appear to be a sophisticated consumer
- pursue a particular personal interest whether it be a sport like diving or a hobby like bird-watching
- visit less popular destinations that are 'off the beaten track'
- mix with relatively few other tourists.

Long-term plans and 'last minute' purchases

The tour operating field also sees significant differences in consumer behaviour in terms of when people plan and book their holidays.

Some customers like to plan and book their holiday months before they travel. This may be because they fear that if they do not they may not find the exact product or be able to arrange the itinerary, they want. Therefore this type of behaviour is more commonly found amongst tourists who wish to take more unusual or exotic holidays or have definite views on which accommodation establishment they wish to use.

On the other hand, some tourists prefer not to plan or book their vacation trip until very late, maybe within a few days of their departure. This could be for a number of reasons including the following:

- a belief that they may be able to take advantage of last-minute discounting by tour operators

- the excitement of making a late decision in that one does not know ones destination until the last minute
- a late unforeseen opportunity to take time off work.

In general, 'last minute purchase' is associated with consumers who are less concerned with where they go or specific hotels, than with price and departure dates.

Conclusion

We have seen that there are similarities and differences in demand characteristics between the different sectors of tourism. However, as we have just seen, there are also significant differences within individual sectors of tourism.

Finally, it is important to recognize that there are differences in the structure and nature of the tourism industries between countries, so that some of the points made in this chapter would vary in their application in different countries.

Discussion points and essay questions

1 Discuss the marketing implications of the differences between business tourism and leisure tourism, for airlines and hotel chains.
2 Compare and contrast the main ways of segmenting the market in the different sectors of tourism.
3 Examine the differences in consumer behaviour within an individual sector of tourism of your choice.

Exercise

Design and conduct a small survey of tourists to identify similarities and differences in the way they purchase:

- accommodation services
- package holidays
- visits to attractions.

Part Five
Consumer Behaviour and Marketing

Clearly, consumer behaviour in tourism is a subject worthy of academic study in its own right. However, it is also a matter of growing interest to tourism practitioners as organizations seek to keep ahead of changes in consumer tastes so that they can ensure that they offer what the customer wants. Modern tourism marketing we are told, must be customer-centred if it is to be successful.

In this part, therefore, we will briefly explore two of the most important areas where consumer behaviour and marketing are linked together, namely:

- Chapter 12 will discuss the applied side of consumer behaviour research, in other words, marketing research.
- Chapter 13 will cover the relationship between the marketing mix or 4 'P's' and consumer behaviour in tourism. This means looking at how tourism organizations might manipulate their product, price, place and promotion to reflect the characteristics and desires of their customers.

12 Researching tourist behaviour – marketing research

Most tourism practitioners and students will be aware of the lack of reliable, up-to-date statistics for tourism in most countries of the world. We seem to know even less about why tourists do what they do or, alternatively, do not do what the industry would like them to do. Yet, we are talking about arguably the world's largest industry and the mainstay of many national economies across the globe.

At the same time, modern marketing is predicated on the idea that knowing your customer, and then anticipating and meeting their needs, is the key to success.

There seems to be an apparent contradiction here in that we know how important consumer behaviour research is for the tourism industry but we are not doing as much of it as we should. Is this because we are ignoring this issue or is it a reflection of how difficult it is to carry out consumer research in the tourism field?

In this chapter, we will look at the following:

- the data on consumer behaviour which tourism marketers require, both qualitative and quantitative
- the problems involved in collecting and interpreting this data.

In this chapter, we are focusing upon marketing research rather than market research. Marketing research is the collection of data with the single intention of using it to make an organization's marketing activities more effective. In other words, in contrast to market research, it is applied action-based research.

The tourism industry needs research data for a variety of purposes. It helps to:

- identify opportunities for product development
- set prices in relation to those of competitors and to what consumers are willing to pay
- ensure that the distribution network is working effectively
- select the best combination of promotional techniques and the most appropriate advertising media

- subdivide the total market into segments which can be targeted by the organization
- make adjustments to customer service in the light of customer comments
- review and change brands and logos
- make decisions about investment in new facilities
- choose locations for new hotels and theme parks, for instance
- suggest opportunities for diversification.

Tourism organizations require a wide variety of data on tourist behaviour, both qualitative and quantitative including the following:

- Statistical profiles of tourists. Many research projects collect information on the profile of tourists visiting everything from a country to a visitor attraction, over a particular period. This data might typically include:
  - the age and sex of tourists
  - their stage in the family life cycle
  - where they live
  - their occupation and income.
- Statistical records of tourist behaviour. Here we are concerned with data about:
  - where tourists like their holidays
  - what time of the year people take their main vacation
  - how much they spend on their holiday
  - how many trips they take each year.
- How tourists make purchasing decisions. We saw in Chapter 6 that the process by which tourists make purchase decisions is very complex. It is clear that the process is different for each tourist, as are the motivators and determinants which shape the final decision.
- Who makes the purchase decision. Within a family or group who are travelling together marketers need to know who makes the decision so that they know who to target with their promotional messages.
- When the purchase decision is made. This too is important because it should influence when a tourism organization plans its promotional campaigns. An organization needs to know at what time of the year most decisions about the main holiday are taken, and how far ahead of the taking of the holiday, purchase decisions are made.
- Consumer perceptions. It is the tourist's perceptions that really matter because it is these perceptions which determine their actual behaviour. Organizations, therefore, need to understand consumer's perceptions about individual products, destinations, types of holiday and particular tourism organizations. When interpreting these perceptions it is important to recognize that perceptions are often based on factors which are beyond the control of tourism organizations. At the same time, the perceptions can often be based on an old experience which is no longer relevant to the reality of the current situation.
- Tourist satisfaction. Chapter 17 explores the complexities of measuring tourist satisfaction. However, it is clear that the industry must understand

Table 12.1 International travellers to Las Vegas

	1990	Percent change	Int'l market share	1991	Percent change	Int'l market share	1992	Percent change	Int'l market share	1993	Percent change	Int'l market share	1994 (r)	Percent change	Int'l market share	1995	Percent change	Int'l market share	Percent change '90 to '95
1 Canada (1)	983 000	31.2%	43.9%	1 152 000	17.2%	46.6%	1 248 000	8.3%	47.2%	1 294 000	3.7%	46.3%	1 636 000	26.4%	47.6%	1 334 000	-18.5%	42.4%	35.7%
2 Germany	147 000	44.1%	6.6%	182 000	23.8%	7.4%	213 000	17.0%	8.0%	245 000	15.0%	8.8%	237 000	-3.3%	6.9%	274 000	15.6%	8.7%	86.4%
3 Japan	226 000	46.8%	10.1%	163 000	-27.9%	6.6%	157 000	-3.7%	5.9%	149 000	-5.1%	5.3%	221 000	48.3%	6.4%	235 000	6.3%	7.5%	4.0%
4 United Kingdom	180 000	65.1%	8.0%	137 000	-23.9%	5.5%	138 000	0.7%	5.2%	156 000	13.0%	5.6%	208 000	33.3%	6.1%	194 000	-6.7%	6.2%	7.8%
5 China (2)	54 000	–	2.4%	72 000	33.3%	2.9%	57 000	-20.8%	2.2%	75 000	31.6%	2.7%	130 000	73.3%	3.8%	117 000	-10.0%	3.7%	116.7%
6 France	39 000	-26.4%	1.7%	77 000	97.4%	3.1%	69 000	-10.4%	2.6%	105 000	52.2%	3.8%	86 000	-18.1%	2.5%	116 000	34.9%	3.7%	197.4%
7 South Korea	23 000	–	1.0%	21 000	-8.7%	0.8%	28 000	33.3%	1.1%	62 000	121.4%	2.2%	98 000	58.1%	2.9%	79 000	-19.4%	2.5%	243.5%
8 Benelux (3)	22 000	-31.3%	1.0%	41 000	86.4%	1.7%	57 000	39.0%	2.2%	58 000	1.8%	2.1%	67 000	15.5%	1.9%	77 000	14.9%	2.4%	250.0%
9 Switzerland	32 000	–	1.4%	28 000	-12.5%	1.1%	53 000	89.3%	2.0%	43 000	-18.9%	1.5%	50 000	16.3%	1.5%	70 000	40.0%	2.2%	118.8%
10 Australia	48 000	6.7%	2.1%	50 000	4.2%	2.0%	68 000	36.0%	2.6%	61 000	-10.3%	2.2%	77 000	26.2%	2.2%	69 000	-10.4%	2.2%	43.8%
11 Italy	48 000	37.1%	2.1%	62 000	29.2%	2.5%	81 000	30.6%	3.1%	56 000	-30.9%	2.0%	68 000	21.4%	2.0%	65 000	-4.4%	2.1%	35.4%
12 Mexico (4)	98 000	-10.1%	4.4%	107 000	9.2%	4.3%	117 000	9.3%	4.4%	100 000	-14.5%	3.6%	104 000	4.0%	3.0%	60 000	-42.3%	1.9%	-38.8%
13 Brazil	18 000	–	0.8%	22 000	22.2%	0.9%	20 000	-9.1%	0.8%	33 000	65.0%	1.2%	38 000	15.3%	1.1%	56 000	47.4%	1.8%	211.1%
14 Hong Kong	34 000	–	1.5%	31 000	-8.8%	1.3%	32 000	3.2%	1.2%	34 000	6.3%	1.2%	37 000	8.8%	1.1%	37 000	0.0%	1.2%	8.8%
15 Spain	12 000	-33.3%	0.5%	19 000	58.3%	0.8%	18 000	-5.3%	0.7%	15 000	-16.7%	0.5%	29 000	93.3%	0.8%	32 000	10.3%	1.0%	166.7%
16 Argentina	9 000	–	0.4%	12 000	33.3%	0.5%	28 000	133.3%	1.1%	12 000	-57.1%	0.4%	27 000	125.0%	0.8%	21 000	-22.2%	0.7%	133.3%
17 Other Nordic (5)	13 000	–	0.6%	14 000	7.7%	0.6%	10 000	-28.6%	0.4%	17 000	70.0%	0.6%	19 000	11.8%	0.6%	20 000	5.3%	0.6%	53.8%
18 Philippines	17 000	–	0.8%	21 000	23.5%	0.8%	15 000	-28.6%	0.6%	19 000	26.7%	0.7%	16 000	-15.8%	0.5%	20 000	25.0%	0.6%	17.6%
19 New Zealand	14 000	–	0.6%	11 000	-21.4%	0.4%	7 000	-36.4%	0.3%	12 000	71.4%	0.4%	14 000	16.7%	0.4%	16 000	14.3%	0.5%	14.3%
20 Sweden	24 000	–	1.1%	13 000	-45.8%	0.5%	29 000	123.1%	1.1%	17 000	-41.4%	0.6%	11 000	-35.3%	0.3%	16 000	45.5%	0.5%	-33.3%
21 Columbia	4 000	–	0.2%	6 000	50.0%	0.2%	4 000	-33.3%	0.2%	5 000	25.0%	0.2%	9 000	80.0%	0.3%	8 000	-11.1%	0.3%	100.0%
22 Venezuela	3 000	–	0.1%	1 000	-66.7%	0.0%	6 000	500.0%	0.2%	3 000	-50%	0.1%	8 000	166.7%	0.2%	1 000	-87.5%	0.0%	-66.7%
23 All other	193 000	–	8.6%	229 000	18.7%	9.3%	191 000	-16.6%	7.2%	223 000	16.8%	8.0%	248 000	11.2%	7.2%	231 000	-6.9%	7.3%	19.7%
Grand total	2 241 000	24.8%	100.0%	2 471 000	10.3%	100.0%	2 646 000	7.1%	100.0%	2 794 000	5.6%	100.0%	3 438 000	23.0%	100.0%	3 148 000	-8.4%	100.0%	40.5%

(1) Canadian visitor estimates based on Las Vegas Visitor Profile Study.
(2) China includes People's Republic of China and Republic of China/Taiwan.
(3) Benelux includes Belgium, Netherlands and Luxembourg.
(4) Mexico includes 'In-flight Survey' data only for visitors filling out a INS I-94 form. (Beyond the 40 kilometer US Border Zone.)
   Mexican arrivals visiting the US with border crossing permits (INS form SW-444) are not included in these tabulations.
   (The methodology for collecting Mexico data was changed in 1992, comparison to years prior to 1992 are not relevant.)
(5) Other Nordic includes Norway and Denmark.

(r) 1994 International statistics were revised 9/96

Sources: US Dept of Commerce, ITA 'In-flight Survey' and 'Summary and Analysis of International Travel to the United States', Las Vegas Convention and Visitors Authority

what determines whether or not customers will be satisfied with the products which it offers. We need longitudinal research which helps us to see how the expectations of tourists rise over time so that we can keep ahead of those expectations.

- The identification of trends in tourist behaviour. We need to be able to identify trends in tourist demands so that tourism organizations can anticipate them and develop new products accordingly.
- Segmentation criteria. As more and more organizations adopt the technique of segmentation there is a great need for research which identifies the characteristics of different segments, and allows organizations to place individual tourists into the appropriate segments.
- Product positioning in relation to competitors. We need to know how tourists perceive the similar product of different organizations and how they decide which one to purchase.
- The attitude of non-users. It is important, if an organization is to gain new customers, that it knows why tourists are not currently purchasing its products. It can then try to attract some of these people by modifying its product range.
- Cultural and national differences in tourist behaviour. At a time when more and more tourism organizations are seeking to sell their products internationally, it is vital that we understand cultural and national differences in marketing and tourist behaviour. There are two types of differences as follows:
  - 'hard' differences such as variations in the main holiday season dates
  - 'soft' differences such as attitudes towards service and the desire for particular types of facility.

Table 12.2 1995 top ten overseas markets for Las Vegas: country comparisons

	Gender of traveller (Percentage of adult travellers)	
	Male	*Female*
All to Las Vegas	59%	41%
Switzerland	69%	31%
Germany	60%	40%
South Korea	60%	40%
Japan	59%	41%
Republic of China	57%	43%
Italy	54%	46%
United Kingdom	53%	47%
Australia	52%	48%
France	52%	48%
Benelux	48%	52%

Source: Las Vegas Convention and Visitors Authority (1996)

- The link between the consumer behaviour of tourists and their purchase of other products. People do not buy vacations in isolation from how they purchase other products. They are an extension of people's everyday lifestyles. A knowledge of this link helps tourism organizations to plan joint promotions such as those between a supermarket and an airline, for instance.

There are clearly many different types of data required by tourist organizations.

Case study 5, Cathay Pacific Airways, shows a fine example of a tourism organization collecting data on the perceptions of its service held by its customers. This data will help it improve every aspect of its marketing activities.

Table 12.3   South Korea – historical visitation to Las Vegas

Year	Travellers	% Change
1990	23 000	–
1991	21 000	–8.7%
1992	28 000	33.3%
1993	62 000	121.4%
1994	98 000	58.1%
1995	79 000	–19.4%
% change from 1990–1995		243.5%

Source: Las Vegas Convention and Visitors Authority (1996)

On the other hand, Tables 12.1, 12.2, 12.3, 12.4 and Figure 12.1, taken from a 1996 report by the Las Vegas Convention and Visitors Authority, illustrate the statistical reporting of tourist profiles and behaviour, discussed earlier in this chapter.

Current weaknesses in consumer behaviour research in tourism

While there have been improvements in recent years, there are still some general weaknesses in consumer behaviour research in tourism. Some of the major weaknesses are illustrated in Figure 12.2.

Perhaps some of these weaknesses are avoidable given the inherent problems involved in the collection and interpretation of research data in tourism.

Table 12.4   South Korean tourists – statistical facts

	S. Korean travellers	All overseas travellers	Unit of measurement
1 Number of visitors to Las Vegas 1995	79 000	1 754 000	–
2 Advance trip decision	35	79	Average number of days
3 Advance airline reservation	21	52	Average number of days
4 Information sources			
Airlines	7%	18%	Percentage of travellers
Friends/relatives	29%	38%	Percentage of travellers
Tour operator/company	3%	16%	Percentage of travellers
Travel agent	80%	71%	Percentage of travellers
5 Used a prepaid package	69%	46%	Percentage of travellers
6 Travelled with a tour group	40%	13%	Percentage of travellers
7 Size of travelling party	2.7	2.0	Average no. of people
8 Purpose of trip			
Vacation/holiday	43%	69%	Percentage of travellers
Visiting friends/relatives	19%	9%	Percentage of travellers
Business/Convention	14%	14%	Percentage of travellers
Other	24%	8%	Percentage of travellers
9 Nights stayed/destinations			
Nights stayed in each destination	2.1	3.3	Average no. of nights
Number of States visited	3.1	3.0	Average no. of States
Total nights stayed in US	26.3	21.5	Average no. of nights
10 Port of Entry to the US (a)			
Most common port of entry	LA (39%)	LA (45%)	–
Next most common port of entry	SF (32%)	SF (14%)	–
11 Main US destination is Las Vegas	24%	22%	Percentage of travellers
12 Top leisure activities			
Casinos/gambling	75%	76%	Percentage of travellers
Shopping	80%	88%	Percentage of travellers
Sightseeing of city	76%	82%	Percentage of travellers
Dining in restaurants	56%	75%	Percentage of travellers
Visiting national parks	67%	61%	Percentage of travellers
13 US expenditures per day			
Transportation within US (b)	$6.50	$11.86	Spent per person per day
Lodging (c)	$6.12	$17.72	Spent per person per day
Food/beverage	$5.78	$16.56	Spent per person per day
Shopping	$20.80	$20.74	Spent per person per day
Entertainment (d)	$5.44	$12.33	Spent per person per day
Other spending	$9.09	$6.28	Spent per person per day
Average US daily expenditures	$53.69	$85.53	Spent per person per day
14 Gender of travellers			
Male	60%	59%	Percentage of travellers
Female	40%	41%	Percentage of travellers
15 Age of travellers	40.7	39.0	Average age
16 Annual household income (e)	$60 300	$76 800	Average

Source: Las Vegas Convention and Visitors Authority (1996). (a) Port of Entry Codes: LA = Los Angeles, SF = San Francisco. (b) Does not include airfare to US. (c) Does not include package price paid before arrival to US. (d) Includes gaming expenditures. (e) Converted to US$ for comparison purposes

Gender of travellers

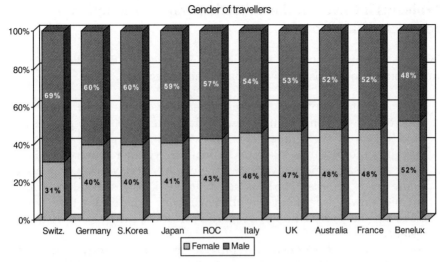

'All to Las Vegas' category includes all overseas visitors as well as Mexican visitors who arrive by air
Does not include Canadian visitors
ROC=Republic of China (Taiwan)
Benelux includes Belgium, Netherlands & Luxemburg

Figure 12.1   Gender of travellers to Las Vegas.
Source: Las Vegas Convention and Visitors Authority (1996)

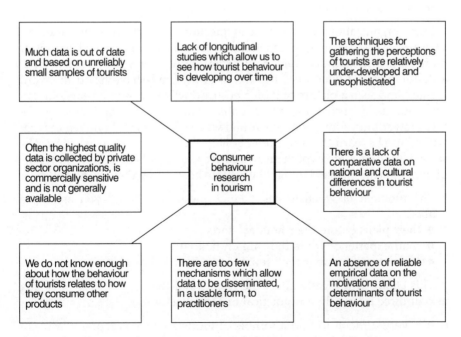

Figure 12.2   Main weaknesses in consumer behaviour research in tourism

Problems involved in the collection and interpretation of research data in tourism

We can identify a number of problems involved in the collection and interpretation of tourism research data. These include:

1 Difficulties in identifying and measuring tourism where the tourists do not cross any national boundaries, i.e. domestic tourism. No records are usually kept of such movements even though they may represent the majority of tourist trips taken to destinations within a country.
2 There are disagreements over how long one has to stay away from home before one is a tourist. The standard definition involves spending at least one night away from home. In other words it excludes day trips which make up the overwhelming proportion of most theme park visits for instance.
3 Tourists when questioned can provide inaccurate information either deliberately or accidentally. They may, for example:
   ● mislead the interviewer because they do not wish to offend them by saying they have not enjoyed the company's product
   ● lie about their activities on holiday because they are ashamed of them
   ● genuinely not remember how much they spent on holiday or they may exaggerate the amount they spent to give the impression that they are wealthier than they are in reality.
4 It is also very difficult for tourists to answer some of the standard questions they are often asked, such as:
   ● where and when did you first hear about this destination?
   ● are you likely to use this airline again in the future?

Many organizations ask this type of question but could you answer them? They first ask you to analyse something which may have happened up to 50 or more years earlier. In any event, how do you know when you first heard about a destination and what does it mean anyway. I may have heard the word 'Venice' and seen a picture of it on a postcard when I was five years old, but may not have visited the place until I was fifty. When I answer the interviewer's question about where and when I first heard about Venice what will he or she learn that can possibly help them with their marketing. The second question is too hypothetical to elicit a useful reply or it could lead to me giving them the answer I think they want to hear, rather than the real one!

5 The problem of when to ask people questions. Should you ask them about:
   ● their plans before their holiday starts
   ● their experience while they are on holiday
   ● their memories after they return from their holiday?

This choice will greatly affect the results and the easy answer of saying ask all three is usually not practical or cost-effective.

6 It is very difficult to find a sample of tourists which is representative of tourists as a whole, for a variety of reasons including the following.

- The problem of seasonality of demand in tourism means that different types of tourists and nationalities will use tourism products at different times of the year, so surveys conducted at one time of the year may miss whole market segments.
- Tourists are all individual and so are the decisions they make so how can any sample be representative?
- Interviewers will often prefer to interview people they think look friendly or they find sexually attractive, or who speak the same language. All of these can lead to a biased sample.

If we move on to consider the more sophisticated fields of qualitative research, the problems become even greater. One needs to be a trained psychologist perhaps to effectively elicit answers to complex questions such as 'Why did you choose this holiday?'

Usually such a question simply receives a reply which reflects the conscious thinking only, e.g. price. However, there may be many deep-seated subconscious reasons for the choice of a holiday that are very important but are likely to be missed.

There are a range of other problems involved in marketing research in tourism including:

1 The fact that perhaps the most valuable marketing data is never made public. It is collected by organizations, for their own purposes, and is kept secret due to its commercial value to the organization.
2 Some public sector research, while publicly available, is flawed perhaps because it has often been collected for 'political' purposes such as to justify an increase in departmental budgets.
3 Where marketing professionals carry out research they may be inclined to either:
   - have it worded so that the results cannot imply that they have not been doing their job questions well, or to prove that they have been doing a good job
   - suppress the results or discredit the research if the outcome is critical of current marketing practices.
4 Good marketing research is expensive and when budgets are under pressure it is often the first item to be cut. While this may have little short-term impact its long-term effects may be, literally, immeasurable.

We can see therefore that marketing research is a vital aspect of tourism marketing but it is one which is fraught with problems.

The future of consumer behaviour research in tourism

More and more academics and practitioners are working to improve the quality and quantity of consumer behaviour research in tourism. Perhaps this is an indication that tourism is at last maturing as an industry.

The authors believe that, over the coming years, consumer behaviour research in tourism will need to develop in the following ways if it is to become more effective.

- The development of more sophisticated techniques for collecting qualitative data in tourism. These might include:
  - Focus Groups, groups of consumes who are similar in terms of age, sex and income, for example. These groups are then used to elicit new attitudes and perceptions. They could be shown a draft brochure, for example, or asked their opinion of a destination which a tour operator is intending to offer to its customers.
  - Observation, to overcome the problem where tourists prefer to do one thing but in reality do another.
  - User Diaries, where consumers are asked to recount their activities and impressions as they go through their holiday.
  - Informal Conversations, with tourists. Chris Ryan has advocated the use of informal conversations with tourists as a way of gauging their views and perceptions, in spite of the subjectivity of the technique. Ryan (1995) argues that:

Conversations are an excellent research methodology for revealing the confines and ambiguities involved in holiday-taking, and illustrates this with a discussion about the importance of [the] friendliness [of the people towards the tourists] . . . Free-ranging conversations are an important resource for researchers. They confirm the nature of the tourist experience, and whether the concerns identified by researchers [involved in the] project are indeed the concerns of those questioned . . . Research that denies the opportunity for holidaymakers to speak of their own experience in their own words is itself limited.

- Making greater use of secondary and individual sources. More use should be made of a range of indirect and secondary sources including:
  - Wider dissemination of the work of academic researchers and the report produced by organizations such as MINTEL and the Economist Intelligence Unit. There is a clear role here for state-owned tourist boards. The English Tourist Board Marketing Intelligence journal, *Insights*, is a good example of such a dissemination mechanism.
  - Using feedback on consumer behaviour and perceptions from intermediaries such as travel agents.
  - Organizations undertaking more systematic scanning of their business environment in terms of those political, economic, social and technological factors which influence tourist behaviour.
- Satisfaction – related research. In this era of buzz words like quality and customer-led marketing, more and more attention will be focused upon the issue of tourist satisfaction. This issue is dealt with in more depth in Chapter 17. In terms of marketing research, the implications of this concern with tourist satisfaction means a greater role for:

- research which helps us identify where 'critical incidents' occur in tourism and consumers' responses to them. These incidents might include employers responding when the service delivery system fails, employee responses to complaints or special requests from customers, and spontaneous unsolicited employer actions. The results of this research would help organizations enhance their service delivery
- interviews with consumers before, during and after their consumption of the product. These interviews would highlight how the product measured up to the customers' expectations, and how their experience is likely to affect their future purchase behaviour.

Conclusion

We have seen that tourist behaviour research is a complex field. However, it is a vital activity if the industry is to satisfy its customers and flourish. Consumer research needs to cease to be the 'Cinderella' of the tourism industry and to become, instead, the cornerstone of decision making in the industry.

In the next chapter we will see how the marketing mix is manipulated by tourism organizations in response to patterns of consumer behaviour. Research has a vital role to play in determining the appropriate marketing mix at a particular time.

Discussion points and essay questions

1 Discuss some of the main problems involved in carrying out customer questionnaire surveys.
2 Evaluate the ways in which tourism organizations can use the results of marketing research to improve their marketing.
3 Discuss the advantages and disadvantages of qualitative and quantitative research in tourism.

Exercise

Think about a tourism organization of your choice. Imagine that the organization has decided that it needs to know more about its existing customers to help it improve the effectiveness of its marketing activities. However, it can only afford a survey with ten questions. You should therefore devise a questionnaire that contains the ten best questions you can think of to gain valuable information that will help the organization to improve its marketing.

13 The marketing mix and tourist behaviour

Once they have obtained their research data on consumer behaviour, tourism organizations have to manipulate their marketing mix or 4 'P's', to reflect the nature of their target markets. In this chapter, we will explore the ways in which tourist behaviour influences the 4 'P's' and the ways in which tourism organizations seek to exploit market trends through the use of the marketing mix variables.

This will mean covering a range of issues relating to the 4 'P's', including, for example:

- Product – tangible aspects, service element, branding
- Price – discounting, value-for-money
- Place – the role of intermediaries, direct sell
- Promotion – advertising, brochures, sales promotions.

Introduction

Once the tourism organization has identified its target customers, it must try to understand their behaviour and try and reflect this in their marketing programmes. The marketing mix is the set of variables that the organization can alter in the short term and the long term, in order to satisfy their customer requirements. The marketing mix is composed of the product, the price, the place and the promotion. These four components of the marketing mix can be amended separately or in combination with one or more of the other components. The marketing mix is therefore like a set of levers which the organization can adjust to meet their aims.

This chapter will look at each of the elements of the marketing mix and discuss the important aspects of each in relation to consumer behaviour for tourism organizations. This book does not contain a comprehensive review of the marketing itself. (Readers who are seeking this type of analysis should refer to Horner and Swarbrooke, 1996.)

We will commence our analysis with reference to the product.

The product

The tourism product must be designed or amended to reflect consumer needs and wants. One of the key objectives for any tourism organization is product positioning which was defined by Kotler and Armstrong (1994b) as:

The way in which the product is defined by consumers on important attributes – the place the product occupies in the consumers' minds.

The correct positioning of a product will mean that the consumer can recognize it as being distinct from the competitor's product because theirs will be unique; often intangible elements are associated with the product which will allow the organization to differentiate their offerings.

The organization must understand their consumer's needs and wants before they can correctly position their products and services in relation to their competitor's products. They will also have to study the market and the competition before they can effectively spot a gap in the market place which they can exploit. Organizations often use positioning maps to help them spot an opportunity in a particular market place. An example of a positioning map for the hospitality industry prior to the development of budget hotels is shown below in Figure 13.1.

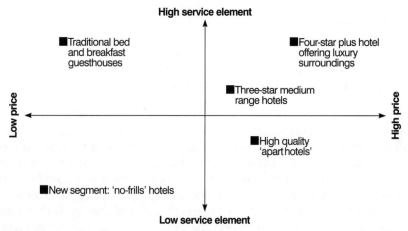

Figure 13.1 Positioning map of the UK hospitality industry prior to the development of the budget market
Source: Adapted from Horner and Swarbrooke (1996)

Consumer preferences were moving towards being more budget conscious as a result of the recession that gripped the country during the early 1990s. Consumers were wanting better value for money products and were prepared to sacrifice high levels of service to achieve this. The hospitality organizations developed their ranges of budget hotels under various brand names to reflect this demand (Horner and Swarbrooke, 1996). The correct positioning of the product to reflect consumer behaviour is therefore vital for the organization.

The position of the product in the product life cycle will also mean that a particular type of consumer will be attracted to the product, and that the marketing programme will have to reflect their needs and wants. The product life cycle incorporates four main stages, which are shown in Figure 13.2.

The product life cycle model has been criticized as a forecasting model (Dhalla and Yuspeh, 1976). It does, however, allow the organization to identify different types of consumer which are attracted to their products, according to where they are in the life cycle.

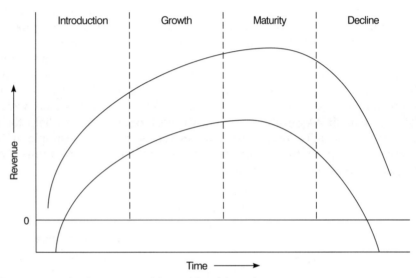

Figure 13.2   The four stages of the product life cycle

The tourism organization will probably have products and services in different parts of the product life cycle. They will be attracting different types of consumers to each of their products, and the marketing mix will have to be designed around their needs. This concept is illustrated in Table 13.1, which refers to a tour operator that markets products at three different stages in the product life cycle. The marketing programme for each product is different because it has to reflect the needs and wants of the particular group of consumer in the market segment.

It can be seen here that each product requires a particular marketing strategy to reflect the target group's needs and wants.

Branding

One of the key aspects of differentiation for a product or service is branding. Kotler and Armstrong (1994b) defined branding as:

a name, term, symbol or design or combination of them, intended to identify goods or services of one seller or group of sellers and to differentiate them from those of their competitors.

Table 13.1 The tour operator's product portfolio, the target consumer, and the marketing programme

Product	Plc stage	Consumer	Marketing programme
Summer Sun holidays or FITs	Maturity	Middle majority – family clientele	Reassuring promotion emphasizing brand. Relaunching activity with new destination
Long-haul holidays or FITs	Introduction	Innovators – outer directed individual	Promotion to build awareness. Sales promotion (with distributors). Emphasis on product excitement
Flydrive holidays to the USA	Growth	Families in middle income bracket seeking new experiences	Brand building promotion. Work on distribution. Reassurance on safety in brochure

Source: Adapted from Horner and Swarbrooke (1996)

Brand names, logos or trade marks encourage consumers to buy products and services because they give them the benefits that they are seeking. These benefits range from familiarity and safety, to status and self-esteem (Horner and Swarbrooke, 1996).

Tourism organizations find branding particularly useful because a brand adds on tangible cues to a service which is largely intangible in nature. This idea is explored in more depth in Figure 13.3. This figure explores the

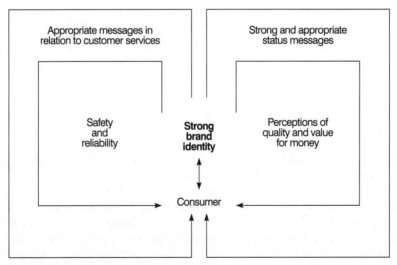

Figure 13.3 The importance of a strong brand name on consumer choice for a fully inclusive tour

benefits that a strong brand name brings to an organization which is marketing a fully inclusive tour (FIT) product.

The strong brand identity allows the organization to give the right type of messages to their target consumer. A powerful brand will also allow the organization to develop their product or service on an international basis since a strong brand will give messages of quality (Henley Centre, 1991/2). The major airlines have used powerful brands to develop their business, appealing to international consumers. The British Airways brand-building activity of 'The World's Favourite Airline' is one example of such an activity. The use of branding to appeal to an international tourism consumer and reflect their needs and wants is explored in Table 13.2.

Table 13.2 The use of branding to appeal to international consumers in tourism

Sector	Example	Comments
1 *Destinations*	Spain – 'España Passion for Life'	To attract new up-market customer seeking cultural experience
2 *Transport*	British Airways 'The World's Favourite Airline'	To attract international customer seeking reliability and customer service
3 *Attractions*	Disneyland Paris The Magic Kingdom	To attract children interested in the Magic of Disney
4 *Tour Operator*	TUI – Sustainable Programme	To attract environmentally conscious tourist
5 *Accommodation*	MGM – Las Vegas	To attract the customer interested in combining entertainment and gambling

We have now considered some of the important aspects of the product in relation to consumer behaviour. We will now turn or attention to the price.

The price

Pricing is a key principle for any organization when it is marketing products and services. The price that an organization charges for its products and services must strike a balance between what the organization is trying to achieve in financial terms, and most importantly, the needs and wants of consumers from the target group. The pricing decisions of organizations will be affected by a number of factors including the pricing objectives, legal and regulatory issues, the competition, and costs. The most important factor in terms of this book, however, is the perception of the consumer of price in relation to quality and value for money.

For non profit-making organizations, the objectives are often to encourage new users. This is often achieved by using differential pricing strategies, where different prices are charged for different market segments.

The consumer must see a link between the price charged and the product quality. Many tourism organizations charge a high price, which is a reflection of the special features of the product in terms of design or service delivery. A small tourism operator such as Cycling for Softies, for example (see Case Study 21), can charge relatively high pries for the special features of the holiday on offer, their attention to detail and their high levels of personal service.

The airlines charge different prices for different levels of service. This relationship is explored in Table 13.3.

Table 13.3 The relationship of price to consumer perception of quality for a major airline

Product	Customer	Customer expectations
First class – highest price	High socio economic group – customers with high status	● High levels of personal service ● Rapid check-in ● Large amount of space on board
Business class – medium price	Business traveller – medium/high socio-economic class	● Some personal service ● Reliable and quick check-in ● Good space allocation on board ● Business services on board
Economy class – lower prices	Families – low/medium socio-economic class – students/single people	● Little personal service ● Limited menus ● Little space on board ● Services for children

It can be seen from Table 13.3 that the price of each particular product in the airline industry links to the perceptions of the market segments, and is reflected in the levels of service and product offerings. The most important issue here, for the airline, is whether the customer perceives that the price they are paying represents good value for money in relation to the service delivery.

Tourism is a service industry, which means that it sells products which are perishable by their very nature. This means that organizations must work hard to obtain maximum usage or occupancy. If an airline or train departs when it is only half full it will be losing valuable revenue. The tour operator that is relying on high volumes to maximize profits will have to work hard to gain sales. Pricing is often used as a competitive advantage tool in tourism in a number of ways to try and influence consumers in their purchasing patterns. A summary of some of the ways that the industry uses price to influence consumer behaviour is shown in Table 13.4.

Table 13.4   The ways in which price is used in tourism to influence consumer behaviour

Technique	Example	Effects on consumer behaviour
Low introductory pricing	FIT – tour operator	Lures consumer in to new market
Low prices across the board	Economy air travel	Encourages consumer who is interested primarily in economy
Last-minute discounting	Middle range hotel	Encourages consumer to impulse purchase at last minute
Discounting to particular market segments	Museums	Encourages underprivileged groups to visit
Premium pricing	Luxury hotels	Encourages consumer who is looking for status, value and exclusivity

It can be seen from Table 13.4 that different pricing strategies will encourage consumers to enter the market or, in certain circumstances, to remain loyal to an organization. Pricing strategies can also encourage consumers to enter a market; it may also be used to discourage consumers from abusing natural resources or facilities.

We have now considered some of the important aspects of price. We will now turn our attention to place, or distribution.

Place (or distribution)

A distribution channel (or place) has been defined by Kotler and Armstrong (1994b) as:

the set of firms and individuals that take title or assist in transferring title, to the particular good or service as it moves from the producer to the final consumer.

Place is of great significance to consumers because they may like the product, and be able and willing to pay the price asked, but if they are unable to gain access to it, no sale will result. Consumers are affected by the intermediaries in the distribution chain. It is often the retailer who has the most powerful effect on the consumer when they are making their purchase decisions. The retail travel agent, for example, has a primary function in the relationship with the consumer on behalf of the package holiday operator. This function was summarized by Horner and Swarbrooke (1996), and is shown in Figure 13.4.

It can be seen from Figure 13.4 that the travel agent performs an important function in relation to the consumer. They can act as a powerful persuader in relation to consumer choice. They also act as a point of contact for customer complaints if a problem occurs with the holiday.

The special nature of tourism has led organizations to develop special distribution systems including consortia, central reservation systems, affiliations and specialist operators such as tour operators and travel agents.

The tourism industry has been very active in the development of direct sell operations. Computerized reservation systems have allowed service organizations such as airlines and hotels to communicate directly with the customer and cut out the intermediaries. This brings the organization distinct advantages with regards to the consumer because they are able to negotiate a sale directly with the consumer. It also allows the development of a relationship between the supplier and the consumer and facilitates sales promotion activity.

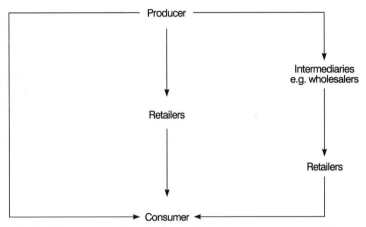

Figure 13.4 The function of the retail travel agent
Source: Horner and Swarbrooke (1996)

Tourism organizations do, however, tend to use direct sell encouraged by the development of multi-media systems which will be increasingly used by the industry.

POI (point of information) systems are multi-media computers which stand alone and provide the customer with interactive services. POS (point of sale) systems allow the customer to buy their tickets directly and pay by electronic fund transfer (EFT POS) systems for direct payments. These systems will be increasingly linked to POI systems and will mean that the customer can purchase tickets in shops, departure points or even from home. Innovations such as multi-media systems and CD-ROM will allow tourism organizations to develop a more sophisticated direct marketing business and travel agents will become increasingly redundant.

All of these developments will, however, depend on the attitude of the consumer. Consumers may resist the new technology and still feel happier being sold tourism products in a face-to-face experience within a retail shop. Their attitudes may well be determined by the market segment in which they fit.

A good example of organizations that use a combination of different sorts of distribution systems are the international airlines. This is explored in Figure 13.5.

The airlines sell directly to the customer using telephone or interactive systems such as Minitel in France. They also rely on their own retail outlets, and other intermediaries such as travel agents. The airlines are able to build different relationships with customers using the different distribution systems.

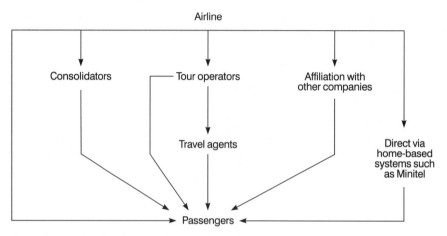

Figure 13.5   The distribution channels for airline seats

The airlines may negotiate discounts by using their direct sell network whereas they offer a full-cost business service to business people via a travel agent.

The distribution of tourism products is being revolutionized by the development of new electronic databases which can be incorporated into telecommunication systems. These include Computer Reservation Systems (CRS), global distribution systems (GDS) and Viewdata.

Many tourism organizations see the development of global sales and distribution systems as a key strategic objective. These systems will allow organizations to communicate directly with customers on a world-wide basis. These developments have allowed many tourism organizations the opportunity to develop direct marketing distribution channels.

We have now considered the major aspects of distribution in relation to consumer behaviour for tourism organizations. We must now consider the final part of the marketing mix – promotion.

Promotion

The final part of the marketing mix – promotion – is the way in which the tourism organization communicates in an effective way with its target customers.

Promotion is used by organizations to affect the way in which consumers behave and it is therefore a vital motivator for any tourism organization. Tourism organizations use a variety of methods for marketing communication, which are summarized in Figure 13.6.

The methods of marketing communication that a tourist origination uses depends on the type of product, the aims of the campaign and the market characteristics.

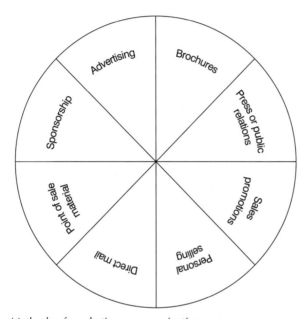

Figure 13.6 Methods of marketing communication

The definition and aims of the main types of promotion are explored in Table 13.5.

It can be seen from Table 13.5 that there is a variety of marketing communication techniques which will have different effects on consumer behaviour.

- Press or public relation techniques – the tourism organization will use these when it wants to create a favourable impression of the organization in the consumer's mind. An example of this type of activity is the long-running public relations campaign for British Airways as the 'World's Favourite Airline'.
- A brochure is used by tourism organizations when they are trying to initiate sales. The brochure should be used to reassure consumers about the product offering which is particularly important in a market where there is a high spend feature. A very good example of a tourism organization using a brochure to inform and reassure potential customers of their products is the technique used by Thomson, the tour operator in

Table 13.5   The definitions and aims of the main types of marketing communication in relation to consumer behaviour

Type of marketing communication	Definition	Comments on consumer behaviour
Advertising	Any paid form of non-personal communication and promotion of ideas about goods or services by an identified sponsor (Kotler and Armstrong, 1994b)	• Targets large consumer groups with strong visual images • Effective for mass-market high volume products • The consumer and potential consumer can be targeted with repeat message
Brochures	A catalogue or video to show the images of the holiday destination or hotel (Horner and Swarbrooke, 1996)	• Reassures consumer of what to expect • Allows the consumer to differentiate and discriminate between different offering
Press or Public Relations	Non-personal stimulation of demand for a product, service or business unit by planting commercially significant news about it in a published medium or obtaining favourable presentation of it on radio, television or stage, that is not paid for by the sponsor (Kotler and Armstrong, 1994b)	• Gives consumers or stakeholders favourable impression of the organization or product • A high profile image is lodged in the consumer's mind • Raises awareness of new products and services in potential consumer's minds
Sales Promotion	Short-term incentives to encourage purchase or sale of a product or service (Kotler and Armstrong, 1994b)	• Encourages the consumer to try the product/service for the first time • Encourages consumer loyalty
Personal Selling	Oral presentation in a conversation with one or more prospective purchases for the purpose of making sales (Kotler and Armstrong, 1994b)	• Persuades or coerces potential consumers, or existing consumers, to buy more • Give consumers favourable impression linked to customer services
Direct Mail	Communicating directly with customers without the aid of marketing intermediaries such as retailer or agents (Horner and Swarbrooke, 1996)	• To bring potential consumers into the market • To encourage past consumers to repeat purchase • To appeal to consumers using customized offering
Point of Sale Material	A sales promotion method that uses items such as outside signs, window displays and display rails to attract attention to inform customers, and to encourage retailers to carry particular products (Dibb, Simkin, Pride and Ferrell, 1997)	• To encourage consumers to purchase a product/service • To encourage the consumer to purchase more within a particular setting • To raise awareness in the consumer's mind of product/services

Table 13.5 *(Continued)*

Type of marketing communication	Definition	Comments on consumer behaviour
Sponsorship	The financial or materials support of an event, activity, person, organization or product, by an unrelated organization or donor. Generally funds will be made available to the recipient of the sponsorship deal in return for the prominent exposure of the sponsor's name or brand (Dibb, Simkin, Pride and Ferrell, 1997)	• To gain positive images of an organization in potential consumer's minds • To raise awareness of a product in consumer's mind when restrictions apply elsewhere • To associate products with popular individuals in the consumer's mind

the UK, where they show customer ratings for every aspect of the holiday, e.g. food, accommodation and location, based on market research with returning customers from the previous year.

• Advertising is used by tourism organizations when they want to reach large audiences in an efficient manner. Television advertising is often used by tourism companies at the beginning of the booking season to encourage early interest and bookings. Advertising is often used to repeat the marketing communication messages in an attractive and appealing manner. The logic here is that repetition of messages will have a greater positive effect on the consumer.

• Sales promotion is often used by tourism organizations to try to encourage the potential consumer to try the product for the first time, or to attract repeat purchases. The package holiday companies in the UK have used sales promotion techniques extensively in their marketing programmes to influence consumer behaviour. Sales promotions such as 'free child places' target certain market segments at the beginning of the season and produce frenzied purchasing behaviour because places are strictly limited.

• Personal selling is very important in tourism because services by their very nature involve a high degree of face-to-face selling activity. Personal selling is used by tourism organizations either directly or indirectly to initiate sales or encourage consumers to buy more. The large exclusive hotels, for example, use personal selling at reception and throughout the hotel to sell the guest more products and services during their stay.

• Point of sale material will help the tourism organization to encourage consumers to enter the market or buy more of the particular product or service. It is very important that the point of sale material and merchandising material in general meets consumer expectations. Styling and colouring of the material should be attractive to the consumer and should reflect the organization's image and brand identity. It is very important that the styling of materials should be updated with new themes and colours according to customer perceptions. The theming of public houses in the UK by the big breweries on a 'Irish' theme is one example of point of sale and merchandising activity. It is likely that the 'Irish' theme will become unfashionable with time, and re-styling along another theme will be necessary.

● Direct mail is the final technique which organizations can use to communicate with consumers. This is being developed extensively by tourism organizations because the use of sophisticated databases will allow the development of customized promotional offerings. The large hotel chains, for example, can talk directly to their corporate clients. They may even communicate directly with individual business clients to inform them of new products and services on offer within their operation.

The intangibility of services means that the promotional techniques which tourism organizations use often have special characteristics. Tourism organizations often use symbols to stress the nature of the service to the consumer. This makes it easier for the consumer to identify with the organization and to recognize their products and services. The symbols which are developed by organizations are often linked to strong brand identities. The holiday company Thomson, for example, uses the brand name and the bird in flight symbol to help the consumer to identify with feelings of freedom associate with their holiday products.

The link of promotion to lifestyle has been extensively developed in such markets as alcoholic drinks and the car industry. There are signs that the tourism industry is beginning to develop similar styles of advertising to reflect consumer lifestyles. The tour operator brochures for example, are becoming more like designer lifestyle magazines. It is predicted by the authors that this type of development will continue in the future. The development of niche tourism products designed to appeal to distinct market segments will mean that these types of selective promotional literature based on consumer lifestyle will become increasingly popular.

Conclusion

In this chapter we have looked at the key issues involved in the development of each part of the marketing mix in relation to consumer behaviour. It is important to remember that there are some general points which can be made about the design and subsequent manipulation of the marketing mix:

● tourism organizations should consider each element of the marketing mix separately and evaluate the relationship of each part to consumer behaviour

- the tourism organization should ensure that the different components of the marketing mix interact effectively to produce the desired effect on the target consumers and their behaviour patterns
- the tourism organization should consider how their total portfolio of products have an effect on their consumers' behaviour patterns. Construction and manipulation of an effective marketing mix to reflect consumer behaviour patterns is vital for tourism organizations.

Discussion points and essay questions

1 'Customers purchase benefits not products.' Discuss this statement in relation to the design and implementation of effective marketing mixes for tourism organizations.
2 Outline the role of promotion within tourism marketing, particularly in relation to consumer behaviour.

Exercise

Choose one tourism product or service. Consider how each element of the marketing mix for the chosen product or service has been designed to reflect consumer wants and needs. Are there any improvements which could be made to any element of the marketing mix, in your opinion?

Part Six
Topical Issues in Consumer Behaviour

In this part the authors want to highlight four issues in consumer behaviour in the tourism field which are very topical. All of these subjects are currently exercising the minds of academics and practitioners alike. They are as follows:

1. the debate about the 'green tourist' and the extent to which such a market segment exists
2. the concepts of the 'Euro-tourist' and the 'global tourist', in other words, types of tourists and tourist behaviour that are relatively homogeneous, with few national differences. We will examine whether or not this phenomenon exists currently or may develop in the future
3. the emergence of new markets and types of demand, and the reasons underpinning their growth
4. the whole issue of quality and tourist satisfaction, given that we are always being told that only organizations that satisfy tourists with quality products and services will flourish in the future.

In all four cases we will endeavour to present the reader with a balanced discussion that makes the key issues clear.

At a time when the tourism industry and tourist behaviour is changing so rapidly, it is vital that all those involved in tourism are aware of these topical issues.

14 The green tourist – myth or reality?

Much has been said and written about 'green consumers' in general, and 'green tourists' specifically, yet there is little empirical evidence of their existence, in the tourism field at least. It could be argued, therefore, that much of the discussion to date has been based on wishful thinking, on behalf of either pressure groups and partisan observers on the one hand, or marketers keen to sell products by trying to give customers a 'feel-good' motivation for buying them.

What do we mean by green?

In a debate where terms are used frequently, but are rarely defined, we should perhaps begin by talking briefly about what we mean by the term 'green'.

Most definitions of the term focus on the natural physical environment and emphasize the importance of issues that are current today. This is in contrast to the now more fashionable term, 'sustainable', which tends to be concerned with the future and with the balance between the environment, society and the economic system. In recent years, environmental or 'green' issues have come to the forefront of public debate in many countries. These have included: 'global warming', animal welfare and wildlife conservation, organic food, pollution, and the recycling of waste products.

In the late 1980s and early 1990s a view has grown that there is now a green consumer, who considers environmental issues when deciding which product to buy or not to buy. One of the first illustrations of this was a consumer boycott of aerosol-based products that contained chloro-fluoro carbons or CFCs in the late 1980s, after the media and pressure groups alerted consumers to the environmental impact of these CFCs. This led to companies replacing CFCs with other ingredients.

Another example of the so-called 'green consumer' has been the growing concern with food safety and quality and an increase in demand for organic food.

Politicians too, recognized the rise of the 'green consumer' in the late 1980s and early 1990s, and rushed to endorse policies that were seen to be environmental friendly. In its most extreme manifestation, this development in public opinion led to the growth of 'green' political parties in the UK and France, for example.

Since the 1990s, however, it is true to say that in the UK at least, public concern with environmental issues appears to have lessened. Perhaps the recent recession has given people other, more pressing, concerns to worry about. If so, then consumer interest may return as the economy recovers.

It is important to recognize that most of what we have been discussing has been largely viewed from a UK perspective. Consumers have been interested in a range of environmental issues for many years in Germany, for instance, and the general level of public concern with these issues is consistently higher. We will see how they have had an impact on the German tourism industry later in the chapter, and in Case Study 12.

Tourism, green issues and sustainability

Although there has been relatively little explicit evidence of concern over green issues on the part of tourists, that is not to say that there has been no interest in the subject from anyone.

Since the early 1980s, there has been considerable debate, world-wide, on the environmental impacts of tourism, and on the links between green issues and tourism. It has become a high profile subject in recent years because of a number of factors, as follows:

- the writings of academics about the impacts of tourism, including the highly influential book by Mathieson and Wall, *Tourism: Economic, Physical and Social Impacts*, published in 1982
- popular, if rather subjective, books that have set out to influence the behaviour of tourists themselves, including:
  - Wood and House, *The Good Tourist* (1991)
  - Elkington and Hailes, *Holidays that Don't Cost the Earth* (1992).
- proactive action on behalf of North American hospitality organizations such as Intercontinental and Canadian Pacific, designed to make their activities more environmentally friendly
- the work of pressure groups, notably 'Tourism Concern'
- high-profile policy statements and initiatives by government agencies such as those taken in the UK in the early 1990s.

One thing is clear – as the debate has developed, the term 'green tourist' has not achieved the acceptance that the phrase 'green consumer' has in general. The whole debate has become complex, with a series of different terms being used.

Figure 14.1 shows some of the other words and phrases that are often used instead of the term 'green' in relation to both tourists and tourism.

Although these words are used, apparently, interchangeably with the term 'green', some of them are different in subtle ways, namely:

- ethical tourists will be concerned with a broader range of issues than the archetypal green tourist. For example, they may be interested in human resource policies in the tourism industry like pay levels and the employment of local labour, as well as the way in which the economic benefits of tourism are distributed throughout the economy
- eco-tourists are largely motivated by a desire to see the natural history of a destination. In addition they may or may not be interested in protecting the environment of the area, but it is certainly not their main concern
- alternative tourism usually means tourism that is less packaged and is smaller-scale. It is assumed that this will mean it is 'greener' than mass-market package tourism, but this is not necessarily the case
- intelligent tourism is related to the growing desire of some tourists to learn something new while they are on vacation. It is thus associated with particular forms of tourism which might be seen as educational including cultural tourism and study holidays. Again there is nothing inherently green about such holidays
- sustainable tourism is concerned with social justice and economic viability as well as the physical environment and is also about the future. Both of these differentiate it from mainstream green issues, and green concerns.

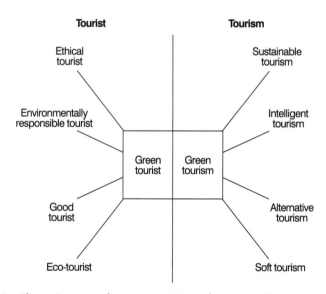

Figure 14.1   Alternative terms for green tourists and green tourism

We will return to some of these issues later in the chapter. They will also be discussed, albeit from a different point of view, in Chapter 16 when we look at emerging markets in tourism.

Of all these terms, the one most favoured by academics and practitioners is sustainable tourism. However, amongst the public this is still a relatively unknown term, while words like 'green' and 'environmentally friendly' are far more understood.

This gap between professionals and public in terms of terminology is undoubtedly an obstacle to the growth of public interest in the subject.

Whatever the term which is used, however, there are clearly a number of factors that can influence tourists and make them take an interest in green issues in tourism.

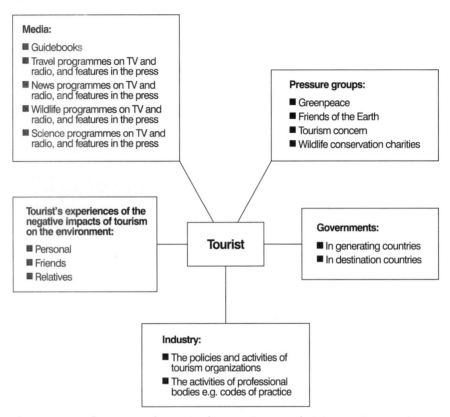

Figure 14.2   Influences on the tourist that may increase their interest in green issues

Figure 14.2 shows some of the influences which inform and interest tourists about green issues.

There is clearly a range of issues that might be of interest to a tourist who is interested in green issues.

Issues of concern to green tourists

The following diagram, Figure 14.3, attempts to identify a selection of issues that might be expected to be of concern to green tourists.

Clearly, many of these are interrelated, e.g. transport and pollution, and wildlife and conservation. However, it is important to recognize that they can be seen from different perspectives and that they can exist in more than one 'box' at a time.

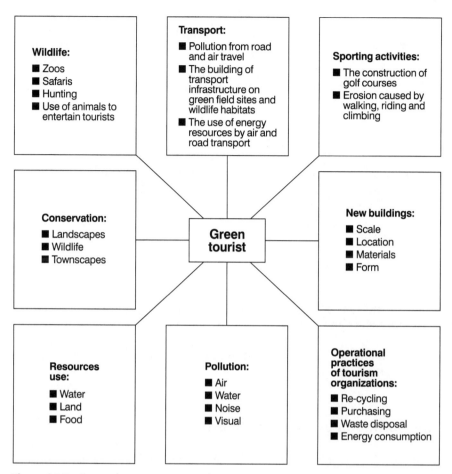

Figure 14.3   Issues that may concern the green tourist

'Shades of green tourists'?

As in any complex market, one cannot really talk about the 'green tourist' as if they were a homogenous group. Each individual tourist will have their own views that will determine their behaviour, and differentiate them from other tourists. It is therefore perhaps better to talk in terms of 'shades of green tourist', from dark green tourists to those with no hint of green whatsoever!

Figure 14.4 offers a representation of this concept and suggests some hypothetical examples of what it might mean in practice, in relation to tourist behaviour.

The different shades of green may reflect differences between consumers in terms of their:

● awareness and knowledge of the issues
● attitudes towards the environment in general

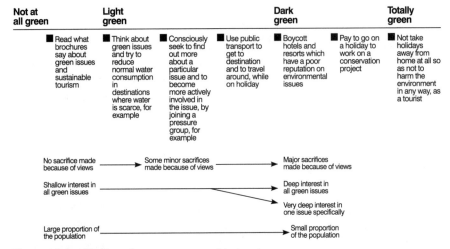

Figure 14.4 'Shades of green consumer' in tourism

- other priorities in life such as making a living, their health, family commitments and housing.

At the same time, we might wish to consider the possible factors which might motivate the 'green tourist'.

The motivation of the green tourist

Green tourists might be motivated by a number of motivations, including:

- an altruistic belief in the need to protect the environment
- a desire to 'feel good' about their behaviour as tourists
- a wish to improve their image amongst friends and relatives by being seen to be concerned with environmental issues.

Whatever, the motivation to be a 'green tourist' it may not always be converted into actual behaviour, because of the influence of a range of determinants.

Key determinants of behaviour

The main determinants that may prevent tourists from being able to behave in a greener manner include:

- information obtained from the media and pressure groups
- amount of disposable income and other concerns such as poor housing or unemployment

- personal previous experience or that of friends and relatives
- ownership or non-ownership of a private car
- interest in particular issues such as animal welfare or activities like riding and climbing
- preferences for particular types of holiday – beach, sightseeing, touring – and different destinations
- membership of particular environmental pressure groups and conservation organizations such as Greenpeace and the National Trust
- advice received from the industry, notably tour operators.

It is now time to see how these motivators and determinants are, or are not, reflected in actual tourism demand.

Evidence of the existence of the green tourist

Although much has been written about the 'green tourist', there has, to date, been relatively little empirical research to establish the existence of this market segment, and its main characteristics.

However, there seems little doubt that tourists are interested in the environmental quality of the destination areas where they spend their holidays. A report by BAT-Leisure Research Institute in 1993 claimed that, 'of ten criteria for a quality holiday listed by consumers, seven related to the environment' (Horner and Swarbrooke, 1996).

Guest surveys, conducted by the German tour operator TUI, also show that for German tourists at least, environmental quality does affect their satisfaction with their holiday. Figures 14.5 and 14.6 clearly demonstrate this fact in relation to five 'ecological' criteria, which have been identified by TUI, in relation to Cyprus.

However, this is more about consumers' vested interest in the environment as a key determinant of the quality of their holiday experience, than about tourist's concerns with the impact of tourism on destinations in general. The 'green tourist' should surely be interested in tourism in all destinations, not just where they are holidaying that year.

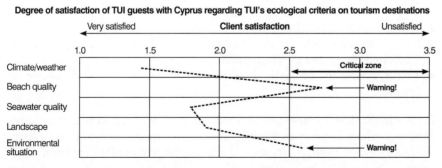

Figure 14.5   Guests' views on the environmental quality of their resort in Cyprus, 1992 TUI Guest Survey, summer 1992. Reproduced by kind permission of TUI

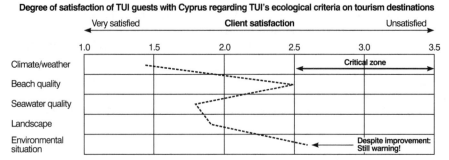

Figure 14.6 Guests' views on the environmental quality of their resort in Cyprus, 1995 TUI Guest Survey, summer 1995. Reproduced by kind permission of TUI

If this latter definition is used then there would appear to be relatively little explicit evidence of the existence of the green tourist today. In most cases, tourists either seem unaware of the issues, or have some awareness but do not seem to modify their behaviour or demands as a result. In general, there appears little evidence of consumers boycotting certain pursuits in tourism, because of their concerns over environmental issues. Few visitors to Spain, Greece or Turkey appear willing to forgo the pleasure of a swimming pool, for instance, to reduce pressure on scarce local water resources.

Likewise, relatively few tourists seem to make decisions based on environmental concerns. For example, very few tourists appear to:

● choose an airline based on the effectiveness of its environmental management practices
● boycott hotels which do not recycle waste or which provide complementary toiletries in their bathrooms, which have been tested on animals
● campaign against the building of new theme parks and accommodation units that destroy wildlife habitats.

To date, the only real examples of tourists' concern with environmental issues, amongst British tourists, at least, has related to wildlife. Tourists have responded, to some extent, to appeals not to:

● buy souvenirs made from parts of animals
● be photographed with monkeys and bears which are kept in captivity and 'exploited' by resort photographers
● attend bullfights or festivals that are alleged to involve cruelty to animals.

Interestingly, these issues to which tourists have responded to some degree are ones which have been highlighted by the media and animal welfare pressure groups. Perhaps, the lack of explicit interest in other environmental impacts of tourism on the part of the media and pressure groups may account for the relative lack of consumer interest in these other issues.

However, at the other extreme, we can recognize the growth of a small distinct niche of 'dark green tourists'. One manifestation of this development is the growth of 'conservation holidays' where tourists spend their holiday doing voluntary work on environmental projects.

Writing in 1996, the well-known guidebook publisher, Arthur Frommer, identified a number of such holidays including:

- the Sierra Club in the USA, and its projects to protect wilderness areas in areas like the Adirondack Forest Preserve in New York State
- the American-based La Sabranenque Restoration Project organization which operates in Europe to restore decaying villages
- Earthwatch, based in Massachusetts, USA, which organizes holidays whose volunteers work on environmental research projects.

Such projects also exist in the UK, for both adults and children, run by organizations such as the British Tourist for Conservation Volunteers and the National Trust.

The 'norm' is for volunteers on these projects to be unpaid but in some cases they even pay for the privilege of working on the project. Clearly, involvement in such schemes demonstrates a real commitment to environmental issues and a willingness to take environmentally friendly holidays.

Some commentators also seem to view the growth of eco-tourism as evidence of the rise of the 'green tourist'. However, while there is no doubt that eco-tourism is growing rapidly, it is very questionable whether those who take such trips can be viewed as 'green tourists'. They are motivated, mainly, by a desire to experience the ecology of destinations at close quarters and to get 'off the beaten track'. This is different, in the view of the author, from being committed to taking holidays that are environmentally friendly. In some ways, one could argue that, by going off the normal tourist routes, eco-tourists are responsible for spreading the negative environmental impacts of tourism to new areas. Therefore their activities may be harmful even though their intentions are good.

It appears that we can say there seems to be little interest in green tourism amongst most tourists, but that there is a small niche market of dark green tourists.

National differences in tourist attitudes towards environmental issues

We must, however, be careful not to generalize about this subject in ways that ignore national differences in attitudes. Concern with environmental issues in tourism appears to be at a very low level in the UK with little explicit consumer demand for greener holidays.

On the other hand, as we saw earlier, German tourists seem to be far more interested in environmental issues, if only because of their concern with the quality of their own holiday. At an anecdotal level, one of the authors can recall attending a conference in Vienna in 1992, where the manager was quizzed about the environmental practices of the hotel by the largely German and Austrian audience. The same author has never seen such a quizzing at any of the conferences he has attended in the UK. The other anecdotal evidence is that many German students who visit the UK on student exchanges appear appalled at the lack of recycling that occurs in the UK.

This is important because the authors believe that green tourists can only exist where there are already green consumers. In other words, being a green tourist is just an extension of the idea of the green consumer. In countries such as Germany, Sweden and the Netherlands, for example, there is a longer and deeper tradition of green consumerism, ranging from using recycled products to buying food with no additives. In these countries, environmental concern is an accepted part of social behaviour, in contrast to the UK, where it is still a relatively low priority for most people.

Maybe, as some people have suggested, green consumerism is a function of affluence, so that people become interested in environmental issues when their basic needs – housing, food and employment – have been satisfied. Perhaps, therefore, green consumerism will be at its highest level in affluent countries. This certainly seems to explain the situation in Sweden and Germany vis-à-vis the UK. It could also explain why countries which are currently striving to develop rapidly economically, like those of the Pacific Rim, appear to give a relatively low priority to environmental quality.

However, such an explanation seems over-simplistic and ignores cultural issues that influence national differences in consumer behaviour such as religious beliefs.

The role of the tourism industry: proaction or reaction?

It is interesting that, while there is little evidence of widespread environmental concern amongst tourists, the tourism industry has sought to take initiatives on the environment in recent years. This interest dates in most cases from the late 1980s or early 1990s when the general debate on the environment reached its zenith with the consumer boycott of CFC-based aerosols and the highly publicized concerns over global warming.

Governments, keen to appear responsible to the concerns of voters, sought to show they too were concerned about the environment. This is the context in which many tourism organizations began to take an active interest in the environment. They were responding to two perceived pressures, namely:

● consumer demand for greener tourism
● the threat of government regulation.

In the event, neither has generally occurred.

However, the industry's activities have continued and now it could be argued that the tourism industry is now leading public opinion rather than reflecting it, albeit often on a rather superficial level. Several examples will serve to illustrate this point, as follows.

1 Tour operators have begun to include information for their clients on environmental issues and have started to encourage them to become more concerned about the environment. For instance, the UK's leading tour operator now has a section on the environment in every one of its brochures, and has introduced the 'Thomson Holiday Code'.
2 Hotel chains such as Grecotel are adopting environmental management policies and devising campaigns to raise tourist awareness of environmental issues in destinations in Greece.
3 Sponsoring award schemes for environmentally friendly tourism are being created, such as the sponsorship of the 'Tourism for Tomorrow' awards by British Airways.

Many people have criticized the tokenistic approach to the environment taken by many tourism organizations. For example, the planting of a new tree for every guest who stays at a hotel or giving a few pennies to an environmental charity for each tourist who books a holiday, can certainly be viewed as cosmetic.

However, perhaps it could be argued that in taking such action the industry is just reflecting the general lack of in-depth interest in environmental issues held by most tourists.

At the other end of the spectrum, new organizations have sprung up which have targeted the 'dark green tourist' and have tried to sell them 'green holidays', such as eco-tourism packages. As we noted earlier, though, at a time when we are not sure what green or sustainable tourism really is, how can we be sure that these holidays really are greener than conventional holidays?

Conclusion

The debate on the existence or otherwise of the 'green tourist' is complicated by the lack of empirical data and the lack of a universally agreed definition of 'green' or sustainable tourism. We can still not be sure if sustainable tourism is about the kind of tourism we find in Belize or Benidorm. There is also too much subjectivity and too many value judgements are being made on the subject to make it easy to answer the question we set in the title of this chapter.

In general, the authors, however, suggest that most tourists do not appear to have a real concern with the environment that determines their behaviour as tourists. However, there are differences in the level of concern between different countries. At the same time there is a small, rather affluent niche market of people who either are, or at least wish to be seen as, 'dark green tourists'.

Perhaps the number of green tourists will grow in the future as more and more people around the world manage to satisfy basic human needs so that they can afford the time to consider environmental issues. It may also happen as we learn more about tourism's impact on the world environment, as the number of tourists grows world-wide.

On the other hand, it may prove to be a passing fashion. One day we may look back and say the 'green tourist' debate was an ego-trip for affluent middle-class tourists or an impossible dream.

Discussion points and essay questions

1 Discuss the implications of the concept of 'shades of green' in relation to tourist behaviour for *either* the tour operation sector *or* the hotel industry.
2 Critically evaluate the idea that eco-tourists are practising a form of 'green tourism'.
3 Discuss whether the tourism industry is leading tourist opinion on environmental issues, or vice versa.

Exercise

Devise and carry out a survey of *either* tourists in a destination *or* people in your local area who take holidays to establish the extent to which the 'green tourist' is a reality.

Your survey must be methodologically sound and your report will cover the following:

● how you selected the sample of people you surveyed
● how you selected the questions you asked
● the results
● your interpretation of the results
● any problems you experienced that you feel made your results less reliable than they might otherwise have been
● advice for researchers who may want to carry out similar projects in the future.

15 The rise of the global/Euro tourist?

Introduction

This chapter will consider whether there has been the emergence of a global or Euro tourist. The implications of this would be that organizations could target groups of consumers which have similar wants and needs on a global or European basis, without the need to refer to national differences. This would open up new opportunities for the marketing of tourism products and would bring potential economies. The chapter will also consider the emergence of the post-modern tourist and the implications of this for tourism organizations.

Definition of the global/Euro tourist

The globalization of markets has been driven by a combination of political, socio-cultural, technological, and economic factors which has been shown diagrammatically by Douglas and Craig (1995) as illustrated in Figure 15.1.

Economic factors influence people at a micro and macro level. They open up the opportunities for global marketing development and they have an

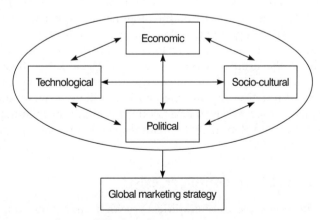

Figure 15.1 Forces shaping global marketing strategy
Source: Douglas and Craig (1995)

impact on individual spending patterns. Technological developments have had a tremendous impact on the development of global products. Computerized reservation systems, for example, have allowed hospitality organizations to develop hotel chains across national boundaries. Political forces influence the development of global business. Government policy can either encourage or discourage the growth of international trade. It can protect national competition and national markets by the introduction of barriers to entry or it can take a more open approach and encourage free competition on an international basis.

This book is more concerned with the final section of this model – socio-cultural developments. Social and cultural forces underline the emergence of interests and tastes and shape patterns of market demands (Douglas and Craig, 1995).

The global consumer, it is argued, is becoming more standardized in their lifestyle and approach, particularly as they are increasingly exposed to the international mass media.

The emergence of the Euro consumer or the global consumer has been explored by Halliburton and Hünerberg (1993), in their discussion of the factors on the supply side and the demand side that had fostered the development of this new type of consumer. These factors were termed 'global efficiency' and 'customer convergence'.

- Global efficiency – organizations will try to exploit the common characteristics of consumers to achieve efficiencies in production marketing and distribution.
- Customer convergence – customers from different countries of the world are becoming increasingly similar in their habits and purchase patterns. If customers are converging in their habits and buying patterns then the Euro consumer or global consumer could exist.

There have been conflicting ideas expressed by academics on the idea of globalization of products and services. Levitt (1983) was one of the first academics to support the move to globalization. A number of academics and commentators have supported this view (Guido, 1991; Ohmae, 1982).

Kotler and Armstrong (1994b), on the other hand, argued against the logic of globalization and suggested that it would only be relevant for large multi-national organizations such as McDonald's and Coca-Cola. Other commentators have also argued against the logic of globalization (Douglas and Wind, 1987; Kashani, 1989). It has been argued that there will be a continued relevance of cultural diversity and that markets will move increasingly from the mass-market approach to markets offering highly differentiated products to meet highly differentiated consumer needs in a variety of cultural settings (Homma, 1991).

Does the global/Euro consumer exist?

There have been few pieces of empirical research carried out to investigate whether the global or Euro consumer exists. Most of the commentary made on the subject has come from anecdotal evidence (Usinier, 1993).

Eshghi and Sheth (1985) have investigated the globalization of consumption patterns with data provided by the Leo Burnett Advertising Agency. This research compared lifestyle variables across four countries (France, Brazil, Japan and the United States). Their conclusion was that lifestyle influences were significant in explaining consumption behaviour but that their effect was not strong. Their data suggested that national and cultural differences continued to determine the consumption patterns of the sample in all four countries studied.

Woods, Chéron and Kim (1985) looked at differences in consumer purpose for purchasing in three markets – the United States, Canada and South Korea. The results of this research indicated that there were considerable differences in the purchasing patterns for consumers in the countries studied. The cultural and psychological differences between the consumers from different countries indicated that universal marketing was not appropriate.

Zaichkowsky and Sood (1988) looked at consumer involvement in 15 countries Argentina, Barbados, Canada, the United States, Finland, Yugoslavia, Sweden, China, Austria, Columbia, Australia, Chile, England, Mexico and France), towards eight products and services which they considered to have potential global appeal (air travel, beer, jeans, eating at a restaurant, hair shampoo, going to the cinema, soft drinks and stereo sets). This research showed that the level of consumer globalization was different according to the product category.

It is interesting to look at the characteristics shared by people of different nationalities. The inference is that if people have common characteristics, then the global consumer, or at the least the Euro consumer, might emerge. If we consider Europe, it can be seen that the populations of different countries are remaining fairly constant. This can be seen in Figure 15.2.

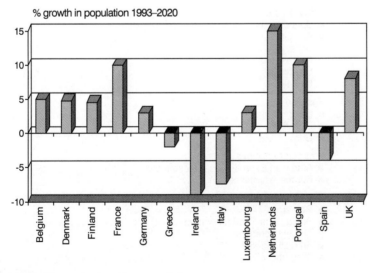

Figure 15.2 Europe's changing population
Source: Euromonitor (1995)

Academics such as Toop (1992) have considered the similarities in interests between Europeans and have suggested that there are common interests which many Europeans share. These common interests are shown in Figure 15.3.

It can be seen that some of the common interests mentioned in Figure 15.3 relate to tourism products. The common interest and recognition of Disney-branded products, for example, across Europe is not surprising given the development of the theme park on the outskirts of Paris.

Academics have taken the general concept of the Euro consumer and tried to suggest European-wide market segments. The multinational target groups are shown in Figure 15.4.

Sporting Events
- The European Cup and World Cup soccer competitions
- The Olympic Games
- Wimbledon and other 'Grand Slam' tennis tournaments
- Grand Prix motor racing

Music
- Leading pop groups
- The Eurovision Song Contest
- Festivals in Salzburg and Bayreuth

Travel and Transport
- Vacations in other European countries
- Concorde
- New York, San Francisco and Hollywood
- Luxury cars like Mercedes, BMWs and Jaguars
- Avis, Hertz and other car rentals

Television
- *Dallas*
- *Dynasty*
- *Kojak*

Children's interests
- Space travel
- Animals
- Dolls
- Pirates and buried treasure
- Lego toys
- Disney

Fashion
- Levis
- Benetton
- Gucci

Financial services
- American Express, Visa, Mastercard
- Europe Assistance

Social Concern
- Red cross
- World Wide Fund for Nature
- The environment
- Starvation relief
- Drug abuse

Figure 15.3   Common European interests
Source: Toop (1992)

	France	Germany	UK	Italy	Spain
Traditional	**Upper Bourgeois**				
	Bonne Bourgeoisie Traditionnelle	Konservativ-Technokratisches Milieu	Upper Middle Class Milieu	Neo-Conservatori	Pudientes
	Petty-Bourgeois				
	Petite Bourgeoisie Vertueuse	Kleinbürgerliches Milieu	Traditional Middle Class Milieu	Piccola Borghesia	Integrados
	Proletarian				
	Milieu Populaire Rigide	Traditionelles Arbeitermilieu	Traditional Working Class Milieu	Cultura Operaia	Modestos
	Archaic				
				Cultura Rurale Tradizionale	Tradicionales
Modern	**Well established**				
	Bourgeoisie Moderne	Liberal-intellektuelles Milieu	Progressive Middle Class Milieu	Borghesia Illuminata	Burguesia Moderna
	Mainstream				
	Milieu de l'Escalade Sociale	Aufstiegs-orientiertes Milieu	Social Climbers	Rampanti	Escaladores
		Modernes Bürgerliches Milieu			
		Modernes Arbeitnehmermilieu	Progressive Working Class Milieu	Crisalidi	
	Underpriviledged				
	Milieu Populaire Ecrasé	Traditionsloses Arbeitermilieu	British Poor	Sotto-proletariato Urbano	
	Milieu des Rebelles Frustrés	Hedonistisches Milieu			
Pro-active	**Post-modern**				
	Modernistes Pionniers	Postmodernes Milieu	Thatcher's Children	Edonisti	Postmodernos
Change	**Intellectual**				
	Héritiers de la Gauche Idéaliste	(Liberal-intellektuelles Milieu)	Socially Concerned	Critica Sociale	Progresistas

Figure 15.4 Multinational target groups
Source: Sinus GmbH and Socioconsult (1996)

This model, developed by Sinus GmbH and Socioconsult, tried to develop an international approach to consumer research, describing the so-called social milieus in France, Germany, UK, Italy and Spain. A comparison was made between the values, attitudes and beliefs in each social milieu across the five countries. The research showed that the certain segments of the population had a similar structure and attitudes in the five countries studied. This seemed to indicate that certain segments of the population could be selected and targeted by organizations without reference to national characteristics.

A longer debate about the Euro consumer and whether they are visitors or not can be found in Horner and Swarbrooke (1996).

The global consumer

There is evidence to suggest that an increasing number of global products are beginning to emerge. These have been developed primarily by large multinational enterprises. The debate still rages about whether the global consumer does in fact exist. Advertising agencies which design campaigns for products that are sold in more than one country are well aware of the subtle changes in message that have to be made so that the advertisements are acceptable to individual nationalities. Clark (1987) of J. Walter Thomson, for example, argues that consumers exhibit significant national and cultural variances. Usinier (1993) suggests that consumers always 'construct' the identity of brands when the brand represent a global product. It appears that the global product is pushed on to consumers rather than them demanding it for themselves. There has been some discussion about the false 'global' consumer and the fact that their resistance to global products will be hidden from global marketers (Clark, 1987). One important issue is knowing whether there are intellectual, ethical and practical reasons for protecting local cultures and consumers from globalization (Usinier, 1993). It was suggested quite early on, however, that organizations would find difficulties in creating global standardized approaches in marketing programmes due to natural entry barriers related to culture (Buzzell, 1968).

Since this time there have been a number of texts that have sought to advise the practitioner on how to gauge the decisions regarding standardization and globalization (Ghoshal, 1987; Hampton and Buske, 1987). The levels of standardization that can be achieved will depend on the nature of the product and the links of the product to the individual's national culture.

It could be assumed that tourism products are eminently suitable for globalization because tourism, in itself, has been described as 'the single largest peaceful movement of people across cultural boundaries' (Lett, 1989). It is arguably one of the most visible global and influential factors in global, social and economic development (Vellas and Bécheral, 1995). The movement of individuals across cultural boundaries widens their experiences and makes them become more aware of other cultural influences and products. The student traveller, for example, has had an educational experience which has widened their perspective and developed their attitudes. The international business traveller has similarly experienced the world and bought global brands from a wide range of duty-free shops in the increasingly standardized world of international air travel. These two groups, alone, represent an opportunity to organizations that are seeking to standardize their products in global offerings.

It is the very young, however, that are the most likely to become the global customer of tomorrow. The desire to be associated with global products, whether they be McDonald's or Disney, has never been better developed. Young children, who have been sensitized to global products from an early age, are exposed to multinational satellite channels such as MTV, the satellite music channel. It will be interesting to see whether these children will continue in their global desires when they become older or whether they will start to show renewed interest in their local national environment, and demand products that are strongly linked to their national identity.

We have considered the general philosophical question of whether there is such a thing as a global consumer or Euro consumer in the general sense. We have also suggested that the nature of tourism could lend itself to a global approach in marketing programmes. In Chapter 9, we saw that consumers from different countries of the world exhibit different patterns of spending on tourism. We can now turn our attention to consumer behaviour in relation to tourism in more depth to investigate whether any common patterns emerge.

Behaviour patterns and tourism

The purchase of tourism products by consumers is inherently linked to the economy. Many developed economies are reaching maturity in terms of the free time and personal income which consumers spend on tourism. The number of people in the world that are able to engage in tourist activity grows as the economic situation of countries improve and become integrated into the international economic networks. Tourist activity is therefore growing in areas such as Asia, Latin America and Eastern Europe (World Tourism Organization, 1995).

Very little research has been carried out to look at consumer behaviour in tourism in relation to nationality. The only clear link that has been established on a global basis is that as an individual's income rises, so their spending on tourism increases.

The average expenditure per trip abroad for individuals gives some indication of behaviour patterns in relation to tourism. These figures for a range of countries in 1994 are shown in Table 15.1.

It can be seen from this table that certain countries which are experiencing a growth in tourism, such as Japan, Thailand, Taiwan, Singapore and Indonesia, also have a high average spend for people travelling abroad. European countries, which are in a more mature stage of development, such as Germany, and the United Kingdom, have a much lower average expenditure per trip abroad.

Some comparative work has been carried out to consider the behaviour patterns of holidaymakers in different European countries. This work has been brought together by Euromonitor (1992), in its research on Germany, the United Kingdom, Italy and France. This data is shown in Tables 15.2, 15.3, 15.4 and 15.5.

Table 15.1   Top countries with highest expenditure per trip abroad

Rank 1985	Rank 1994	Country	Average expenditure per trip abroad (US$) 1985	Average expenditure per trip abroad (US$) 1994
8	1	Japan	972.9	2261.9
3	2	Australia	1268.5	1843.2
18	3	Thailand	513.8	1728.7
1	4	Taiwan (Prov. of China)	1687.1	1605.8
5	5	Singapore	1165.4	1603.2
2	6	Indonesia	1559.4	1600.7
10	7	Norway	817.7	1587.0
7	8	Israel	992.8	1523.1
25	9	Belgium	323.5	1453.8
33	10	Brazil	203.1	1395.7
6	11	New Zealand	1029.1	1337.8
4	12	Korea Rep.	1252.1	1296.1
17	13	Netherlands	515.8	1019.5
11	14	South Africa	809.8	950.2
12	15	United States	707.4	937.8
23	16	Finland	425.3	849.1
19	17	Sweden	494.8	838.3
15	18	China	532.2	813.1
31	19	Colombia	258.8	796.6
16	20	France	516.2	777.7
22	21	Denmark	436.0	770.9
32	22	Italy	247.4	732.4
14	23	Austria	547.0	711.2
13	24	Puerto Rico	564.6	668.6
30	25	Ireland	273.8	665.1
20	26	Chile	485.6	652.0
29	27	Switzerland	283.6	630.0
21	28	Argentina	455.8	588.8
28	29	Germany	284.9	565.0
27	30	United Kingdom	294.7	556.1
26	31	Canada	312.9	514.6
9	32	Mexico	827.1	452.5
35	33	Egypt	63.1	391.6
24	34	Portugal	368.3	355.8
34	35	Spain	178.1	326.4

Source: World Tourism Organization (1995)

It can be seen from Tables 15.2–15.5 that, in 1991, there is a direct relationship between social group and holiday choices. In general, the higher income and social group an individual is in, the more likely they are to take holidays. Differences in behaviour do start to appear, however, if a more detailed study is carried out. In Germany, for example, a high proportion of senior citizens holiday in Bavaria and Norway, whereas younger generations tend to favour North Germany. A large proportion of Germans also holiday within their home region (Euromonitor, 1992).

Italians are noted for taking their main holidays in the month of July and August, despite the fact that the government has been trying to persuade people to take their leave more evenly throughout the year (Euromonitor, 1992).

The leisure concept in Europe has been researched by Fitzpatrick Associates (Panama, 1993, quoted in INSEAD, 1996). This report proposed that there were common factors influencing consumers' holiday decisions across Europe, and summarized these as being:

- income, particularly the amount not already earmarked for other commitment

Table 15.2 Germany – socio-economic patterns of holidaying in the past 12 months, 1991

% adults	Total	Domestic	Abroad
All adults	59.2	44.5	29.5
Men	60.4	45.9	29.1
Women	58.1	43.3	29.9
Age group			
14–19 years	61.5	50.7	25.4
20–29 years	62.5	53.2	22.8
30–39 years	65.0	50.3	31.1
40–49 years	67.7	52.5	31.6
50–59 years	61.9	44.2	34.0
60–69 years	56.2	37.3	35.9
70 years plus	36.8	19.7	26.5
Marital Status			
Single	63.3	54.6	24.7
Married	61.8	43.7	33.3
Divorced	57.2	44.5	27.6
Widowed	36.5	22.1	23.8
Profession			
Schoolchild	69.4	57.4	30.1
Student	74.6	68.6	27.6
In job training	58.9	49.2	22.5
Employed	65.1	51.6	28.8
Unemployed	44.9	34.1	19.6
Housewife/husband	57.4	39.1	33.7
Retired	45.4	27.7	30.6
Income			
Below DM1500	35.9	23.4	20.3
DM1500–DM1999	42.6	28.9	22.3
DM2000–DM2999	55.7	39.5	28.4
DM3000–DM3999	63.0	47.1	32.7
DM4000–DM4999	68.3	53.5	31.0
DM5000+	72.3	60.1	33.8

Source: Euromonitor (1992)

Table 15.3   United Kingdom – profile of holidaytakers and non-holidaytakers, 1991

% adults	Taking no holiday*	Taking holiday* in GB	Taking holiday** abroad
Age			
16–24	21	13	21
25–34	18	17	18
34–44	14	19	19
45–54	12	13	17
55–64	12	16	15
65+	24	21	10
Social group			
AB	8	20	32
C1	20	22	26
C2	30	29	26
DE	43	29	17

Source: British National Travel Survey (British Tourist Authority) quoted in Euromonitor (1992); * four or more nights, ** one night or more

Table 15.4   Italy – socio-economic profile of holiday takers, 1990

% adults taking holiday in last three years	59
Life stage	
Pre–family	80
18–24	79
25–34	81
Family	57
children under 5	61
children 5–15	57
children 6–17	52
Late Stage	46
35–49	63
50–64	47
over 65	39
Social group	
AB	87
C1	74
C2	59
DE	38

Source: Euromonitor (1992)

Table 15.5 Type of holiday taker in France, 1990

% population taking holidays in last year	71
Life stage	
Pre-family	16
18–24	10
25–34	6
Family stage	27
Late stage	28
35–49	6
50–64	13
65+	9
Social group	
AB	28
C1	19
C2	9
D	8
Unclassified	7

Source: Euromonitor (1992)

- available free time
- age and family status
- price scales relating to destinations
- attractiveness relative to other destinations
- job sector (particularly farmers and self employed)
- owners of second homes.

They found that the proportion of Europeans taking a vacation or business trip abroad is around 26 per cent on average. Northern European holidaymakers are most likely to travel outside of their countries whereas Southern Europeans are more likely to stay at home. People are less likely to travel across borders when incomes are low. Second-home ownership is a very important factor. In Greece, Spain, Italy, the Netherlands, Denmark and France, over 10 per cent of holidaymakers spend their holidays in their second homes, which relieves their spending on travel abroad.

There is a general decrease in Europeans taking beach vacations and a rising interest in sporting and cultural vacations.

The report also found that Europeans who are over 55 are less likely to travel abroad compared to other age groups. This age group is currently being targeted with specifically designed holiday brands.

The World Tourism Organization (1995) has recognized that there will be a growing interest in people looking for specifically targeted tourism products linked to demographic factors (e.g. older persons, youth market).

- strong development of three-star standard hotels both in business centres and in resorts
- significant development of leisure oriented-hotel developments in destinations which are easy to reach by air, providing a 'seamless' tourist experience (e.g. linked with a Disney theme park
- the growing popularity of 'all-inclusive resorts', another manifestation of the growing demand for making holidays easier to organize
- minimal new development of high cost, fully serviced five-star hotels
- strong growth in no (or minimal) service accommodation
- increased provision of in-room facilities in serviced accommodation

Figure 15.5 Developments for more value-for-money oriented tourist accommodation customers
Source: World Tourism Organization (1995)

It is also recognized that consumers from westernized industrialized markets are becoming increasingly interested in environmental issues linked to tourism destinations. This will lead to the development of endemic tourism, i.e. based on cultural and national features of destinations. It is also predicted that the tourist will become more sensitive to value for money issues when purchasing tourism products. This will lead the industry to make a number of strategic moves – these are shown in Figure 15.5.

The Asian tourist will become a very important and growing part of the international tourism field. The Asian tourist has traditionally chosen city-based tourism as part of a tour. There has been a growth in beach-based Japanese segments, and it is probable that the 'adoption' of the beach resort type of holiday will spread and overtake the growth in traditional holidays (World Tourism Organization, 1995).

We have now considered some of the similarities between individuals' behaviour in different settings. The conclusions are that there are some common behaviour patterns which occur in particular market segments that transcend national boundaries. A division, however, can be drawn between the highly developed western-type economies such as the USA and many European countries and the developing economies such as the Asian countries.

Tourist behaviour in western economies has been shown to be very different from that in eastern economies. Research by Reisinger and Turner (1996) compared and contrasted the cultures of Asian tourists who were visiting the Australian Gold Coast. They found that there were considerable differences between the two groups and identified certain cultural features where the differences were most noticeable. These included their inter-actions, communication and display of feelings.

The research implied that variables in cultural dimensions should be used in the development of Australian tourism products for Asian tourists, and that organizations should try to develop culture-oriented marketing strategies. This illustrated that there are great differences between individuals from western and eastern cultures and implied that the global consumer does not exist.

To conclude this chapter, we will now consider the phenomenon of post-modernism and discuss how this may affect the development of the Euro tourist or the global tourist.

Post-modernism and tourist behaviour

The traditional view of the relationship between consumer and producer was that of the consumer demanding mass-produced goods and services at a low price. This led the producers into mass production of products and services that had universal appeal. This has been described at a process of McDonaldization (Ritzer, 1996). The closest the tourism industry has come to this phenomenon has been in the development of mass-market package holiday companies, which have developed products based on the premise that the transportation of large numbers of tourists would produce economies of scale. These companies developed fairly standardized good value products, and quality was often sacrificed to price (Sharpley, 1996).

The emergence of the post-modern consumer is predicted to have a major affect on the tourism industry (Sharpley, 1996). Post-modernism represents the end of the structured and ordered state of society and signifies the replacement of the belief in progress based on scientific rationality by an emphasis on choice, a plurality of ideas and viewpoints and 'the eclectic borrowing and mixing of images from other cultures' (Voase, 1995).

It is a replacement of modernism, which emerged from scientific and technological advances that occurred in the eighteenth and nineteenth centuries and led to mass production and the belief in the development of homogenous mass markets, where everybody would have similar attitudes and tastes. Post-modernist consumers, however, are showing different behaviour patterns. They find it difficult to separate reality from image, particularly as simulated experiences are increasingly developed. The post-modern tourist will seek out new experiences. The heritage tourism industry, for example, has been described largely as a post-modern phenomenon (Walsh, 1992).

The development of green or eco-tourism has also been attributed to the post-modern phenomenon (Sharpley, 1996). Concern for the environment and sustainability are, according to Munt (1994), the 'highest order discourse of post-modernization'.

The post-modern consumer may well remove the impetus from the standardization and globalization of tourism products. They will require more individualistic and highly developed products. It is likely that greater choice and variety of tourism products will be demanded. The desire for perceived quality and good value for money will, however, still force the tourism organization to still seek economies of scale.

There is evidence to suggest that the mass-market and standardized approach to tourism will become increasingly out of date over the next few years. The post-modern tourist will require much more individualist approaches with more variety and quality. One group that has emerged is the 'petit-bourgeois', a new group of consumers who are seeking experiences previously on offer to the upper classes, at a more affordable price (Sharpley, 1996). This phenomenon is clearly visible in the cruise sector, which has undergone a renaissance in recent years. In line with the concept of post-modernism, this renaissance has been based on making cruises less elitist and highbrow, putting more emphasis on fun and hedonism, and the rise of themed cruising. Some of these issues are discussed in Case Study 7, which features Carnival Cruises.

It is likely that if post-modernism is a reality that will lead to the rise of the 'post-tourist', it will be seen first in the major traditional generating countries of Northern Europe, Japan and the USA. However, finally, it is important to recognise that post-modernism is not a proven fact and perhaps it is simply part of broader trends in consumer behaviour. Furthermore, it is as yet too early to say if these changes will make it more or less likely that we will see the rise of the global or Euro tourist.

Conclusion

In this chapter we have discussed whether the Euro tourist or global tourist does in fact exist. We have seen that there is much evidence to suggest that these do not exist, although we have recognized that the very nature of tourism could allow tourist organizations to target groups of consumers on a European or world-wide basis.

Very different people live in different countries of the world. They have different cultures and different behaviour patterns. We only have to look at the contrast between the Australians and Asians, which has been discussed in this chapter, to see the differences which do exist.

It is possible, however, to select particular market segments on a European or world-wide basis for tourism products. Consumers who fit into these market segments can then be targeted with products of a similar nature. The airlines developed brands to target business travellers on an international basis. They do, however, have to subtly change particular aspects of the marketing mix to suit the national characteristics of the consumer.

Table 15.6 explores four market segments which could be targeted on a world-wide or European basis. It can be seen that these segments have very similar behaviour patterns and therefore seek similar benefits.

The business travellers want a good quality and reliable service with flexible booking arrangements and good quality products and services. British Airways has tried to target this market segment, by developing a strong brand image in association with a long-term public relation campaign using the logo 'The World's Favourite Airline'. They have also added extra features to their products to appeal to the business traveller. One example of such a development has been the introduction of more roomy seats in the business class, which recline fully, for long-haul flights.

The major international airlines have started to target the international business traveller directly by the use of in-flight

Table 15.6 Possible global consumers or Euro consumers of the future

Market segment	Benefits sought
The European or international business traveller	• Reliable service • Good quality surroundings • Flexible booking opportunities • Reliable connecting services
The young student traveller	• Good value for money products • Discounts • Flexible co-ordinated packages, e.g. round Europe, round the world • Educational experiences
The environmentally conscious tourist	• Sustainable tourism products • The opportunity to travel to remote and underdeveloped areas of the world • Reassurance of environmental features of the products
The middle-class family group tourist	• Good value for money • Discounted products • Reliability of service • Safety features

magazines which are often printed in different languages. These magazines carry features to appeal to the business traveller and carry advertisements for other organizations such as prestigious hotels and car hire companies, which also target this group.

The young student traveller represents another group that has similar behaviour patterns on a European or world-wide basis. This group have often experienced an advanced level of education and have the ability to understand and converse in foreign languages. They are increasingly exposed to satellite advertising, such as MTV – the satellite music channel. They are looking for good value holiday packages that take them to new out-of-the way destinations for new and exciting experiences.

The environmentally conscious traveller is a market segment that has been growing in size during the post-modern period. The group is generally still restricted to a small minority, and there are differences in numbers depending on the country (see Case Study 11 on British Airways, for more detail). The World Tourism Organization (1996) predict that this group of consumers will continue to grow in the foreseeable future. It is likely that new tourism organizations will develop products targeted at this group.

Existing tourism organizations will try to adapt their products to incorporate more environmentally friendly features (see TUI, Case

Study 12, as an example of this).

We have seen in this chapter that models are being developed to suggest that it is the development of the middle class that causes national boundaries to be crossed. The post-modern period has seen the development of the petit bourgeois. This has meant that there is the emergence of the middle-class family group tourist. This group is looking for new tourism experiences that mimic their bourgeois predecessors. They are wanting to see new places and allow their children to have the tourism experiences that they never had. The tourism organizations targeting this group must offer exciting destinations but with the added benefits of good value for money discounts, reliability of service and reassurance about safety. The mass-market package holiday companies have been very effective at targeting this group, and most have developed brands specifically for this purpose. Tourism organizations have also tried to take products that have successfully targeted the middle-classes in certain countries and transfer these to other countries (see the Carnival Cruise Line Case Study – 7).

The development of large multinational tourism organizations and the maturity of markets will encourage these organizations to increasingly move across national boundaries with their products and services. The academic debate of whether a global consumer or Euro consumer exists may be quickly overtaken by the budgets of these organizations as they forge ahead with their marketing programmes.

Discussion points and essay questions

1 'The emergence of the global consumer or Euro consumer can be attributed to the marketing activities of large multi-national organisations rather than changes in consumer behaviour' (Horner and Swarbrooke, 1996). Discuss the relevance of this statement.

2 Evaluate the importance of whether a global consumer or Euro consumer exists for the development of tourism products.

3 'The very nature of tourism could allow tourism organisations to target groups of consumers on a European or world-wide basis' (Horner and Swarbrooke, 1996). Discuss this statement.

Exercise

Collect statistical evidence to evaluate whether a Euro consumer does exist for tourism products.

16 The emergence of new markets and changes in tourist demand

The tourism market, world-wide, is going through a period of great change in the current era, in terms of:

- the demand for new types of tourism product
- the rejuvenation of some older established forms of tourism
- changes in the ways in which tourists purchase tourism product
- the growth of outbound tourism from countries that traditionally have generated few international tourist trips.

In this chapter, we will highlight a number of such trends in the global tourism market.

It is important to recognize that some trends are the result of a complex three-way relationship between the tourism industry, the media and tourists.

There is also a need to understand that it is difficult to generalize about such trends, for there are great differences in demand between different market segments.

Figure 16.1 illustrates 13 major emerging markets and changes in demand which we will be considering in this chapter.

The all-inclusive vacation concept

In the early days of package tourism, the all-inclusive package was the norm. It provided security for travellers unused to travelling to other countries. However, in recent years we have seen a trend towards more flexible packages which allow tourists to buy meals outside their hotel, and to plan their own excursions.

In the 1990s we have seen the growth of all-inclusive vacations across the world. For example, many packages to the Caribbean from Europe are based on the all-inclusive principle. They tend to include travel, all needs, drinks, excursions, leisure activities and entertainment.

Figure 16.1   Thirteen major emerging markets and changes in demand

They are popular with those tourists who know exactly how much their holiday will cost when they book it, and enjoy the fact that they will only need to take a small amount of spending money with them.

The all-inclusive concept has proved particularly popular in developing destinations such as the Dominican Republic. This may reflect the fact that:

- in some destinations there is only a very limited choice of restaurants and a poorly developed tourism infrastructure outside the main resort hotels
- because of a fear of crime and language difficulties, many tourists do not feel confident enough to travel away from their accommodation.

All-inclusive holidays tend to flourish at both ends of the tourism market, namely:

- the luxury end where leading players are the Sandals organization in the Caribbean and Club Med on a global scale
- at the budget end many two- and three-star hotels in the Mediterranean are offering two-week all-inclusive packages from a little over £300 per person!

Children's holidays

Children are now tourism consumers in their own right. As well as influencing the choice of family holiday destinations, the industry is now offering holidays for children that are for children only, without their parents.

This market is already well developed in the USA via the summer camp movement, with brand names such as Camp America. However, it is also developing in Europe, as we can see from these examples.

1 In the UK, the operator PGL (Case Study 1) has, over a period of years, developed a range of activity holidays aimed at young people, such as canoeing on the Ardeche river in France.
2 Young people in France can spend time on a 'Gîtes d'Enfants', usually farm-based accommodation where the visitors learn about life and work on a farm.

Sometimes, these two products can be purchased by schools and group trip organizers on behalf of children. However, often they are purchased directly by the family on an individual basis.

For the child or young person the motivator for such a holiday is probably the chance to make new friends and the feeling of being independent and 'grown up'.

However, while the young person is the consumer, the parent is usually the customer, making the final purchase decision and paying the bill. For parents, safety and security is probably the major determinant of the product they choose to purchase. They may also feel better disposed towards products that they feel will make their children healthier, or which are educational.

As children become increasingly targeted as consumers in their own right, with all kinds of interests, it seems likely that this market will grow, and that the young people themselves will play an even greater role in deciding which product their parents should buy.

The international wedding market

Some people have always travelled abroad for their honeymoon. In Case Study 3 on the Japanese tourism market we see that many Japanese couples travel as far as Europe for their honeymoon.

In recent years, we have seen an ever growing number of people travelling abroad to get married, and the industry has quickly sought to exploit this growth market.

For UK couples, popular wedding destinations include:

- the USA, particularly Las Vegas and New England
- Caribbean islands, including St Lucia, the Cayman Islands and Barbados
- Cyprus.

The package offered to couples can include not only the ceremony but also videos, flowers and music, as well as the food and drink.

In many cases the only real restriction on where a couple can get married are residence restrictions before a couple can legally marry in a particular place. In some destinations, there can also be other legal requirements such as blood tests.

As well as 'conventional' weddings in exotic locations there has also been a growth in unconventional weddings, where the couple 'tie the knot' while:

● under water
● drifting down under a shared parachute
● bungee jumping off a tall bridge
● sitting in an ice cave.

There is clearly a status value to being wed abroad, particularly if the location is perceived to be particularly exclusive or exotic.

Visiting sites associated with popular culture

In recent years, there has been a growing trend for tourists to visit places associated with aspects of popular culture. This can include locations where films and television programmes are made, the homes of major figures in popular culture and the settings for best-selling books.

As popular culture has become increasingly global, this phenomenon has become truly a world-wide market. For example, Granada Studios Tours in Manchester, the place where *Coronation Street* is filmed, receives visitors from all over the English-speaking world. This reflects the global sales of the programme to other television networks.

Other examples of this phenomenon of tourists visiting popular culture sites include:

● the coach parties visiting the Avoca Valley in County Wicklow, Ireland, where the TV series *Ballykissangel* is filmed
● the film *Sleepless in Seattle*, which helped put that city on the tourist map
● the British people who used to visit Menerbes in Provence, when it was the home of Peter Mayle, the author of the best-seller, *A Year in Provence*.

In the UK there is even the *Archers* phenomenon, where tourists visit a fictional village which is the setting for a radio programme.

Many tourists who visit television and radio programme locations are older, while those who visit film locations tend to be younger.

A large number of destinations have built their local tourism industry around a chance association with a television programme such as Holmfirth in West Yorkshire, where the *Last of the Summer Wine* series have been filmed.

Trails may be developed to allow tourists to visit places associated with a programme or film. Weekend breaks may also be offered that allow fans to meet characters from the programme.

In the area of popular music, we have already seen that fans are keen to visit sites associated with their heroes. Hence the popularity of Elvis Presley's home at Graceland, and Jim Morrison's grave in Paris.

If we take our definition of popular culture further we can surely include popular sports like soccer, where for many overseas fans a visit to the trophy room at Old Trafford or Anfield would be a lifetime's ambition.

As popular culture becomes ever more commercialized and global, and tourists seem ever more willing to travel to popular culture sites, this market seems set to grow.

Budget cruising

For many years the cruise market was concerned with a small elite enjoying an exclusive leisure pursuit. However, in the 1990s, the emergence of tour operators offering cruises at budget prices has changed all that. Pioneered in Europe by the UK operator Airtours and Thomson, British people have been offered the chance to enjoy a week's cruise in the Mediterranean from around £350. This product innovation has brought a whole new segment into the cruise market. It has also helped to fuel the renaissance in the cruise market as a whole, which was already underway. Cruise companies are using new on-board leisure facilities and themed cruises to attract new younger market segments.

And it is not just cruise companies that are trying to promote the idea of 'budget cruises'. Many ferry companies on longer routes are endeavouring to sell their ferry services as cruise products with similar on-board entertainment and facilities. In the off-peak season they sell these ferry services as two-, three- or four-day 'mini-cruises'. For example, a three-night cruise to Norway from the UK, with a few hours ashore, cost from as little as £50 per head in 1997–1998.

The rise of budget cruises has also made the up-market operators review their prices and offer more discounts. At the same time the luxury end of the market is also flourishing as are the specialist markets of Antarctic voyages, and river cruises, for example.

'No-frills' airline travel

In the global recession of the early 1990s, leisure and business travellers looked for bargains in air travel. As we emerge from the recession, there is evidence that the desire for a good deal has become a permanent feature of the market.

This demand is being accommodated by a range of new 'no-frills' airlines, including South West in the USA. In the UK the best example is 'easyJet', which is the subject of Case Study 16.

Such airlines are taking advantage of the move towards the liberalization of air transport in Europe to other new services. The emphasis is on informality and basic service. As far as possible, such carriers try to keep down costs by being paperless organizations. They also offer no 'complementary' in-flight service. In return they can offer low prices such as single fares of £49 from Luton to Barcelona or Nice, in the case of easyJet in 1998.

Such airlines are becoming fashionable with customers, and not just those on limited incomes. They are also popular with better-off travellers who simply resent paying a higher price for a short journey.

One way of keeping down prices for these airlines is for them to sell direct to clients, rather than paying commission to travel agents. However, as the Irish carrier, Ryanair, found in 1997, this can cause problems too.

It remains to be seen whether this trend towards 'no-frills' air transport will be extended to larger routes or to regions of the world such as South-East Asia.

The direct booking phenomenon

The growth of technologies such as the Internet, Smart Cards and Multi-Media systems has made direct booking easier for both tourist and the industry.

For the client, direct booking holds out the prospect of lower prices because there is no travel agency commission and/or better service.

Many tour operators have founded their own direct booking brands such as Thomson's Portland Holidays in the UK. At the same time, more and more airlines are offering direct booking links for clients. The same is true of ferry companies. In the hotel sector, major chains have set up central reservations systems to give customers direct access to any one of their hotels, anywhere in the world.

The rise of the small specialist tour operator has fuelled the rise of direct booking. These small specialists cannot guarantee a high enough volume of sales to interest most travel agents. Therefore, they have to sell direct to their clients. Direct sell is better in some ways for it should ensure that the tourist receives more detailed information about the product. It also gives the organization the chance to receive direct feedback about its products and their appeal, from prospective clients.

The direct booking phenomenon looks set to increase with people being able to use the Internet to not only gain information, but also to make bookings.

The couples-only market

For many years the industry has focused on the family holiday and also on holidays for single activities, like Club 18–30. But what about holidays for couples without children?

In recent years, this segment has been taken more seriously for several reasons, namely:

- the growing number of couples who are making a conscious decision not to have children
- the relatively high disposable income of this segment and its tendency to take several holidays per year.

For this market, romance and shared interests are a major motivator, as is the desire to be in an adult-only environment, without other people's children.

Some tour operators have launched brands to attract this market specifically, or else have included in their brochures the suitability of particular hotels and resorts for such people.

Many country house hotels are also trying to tempt this market by either banning children or restricting the access of children to the evening. However, in hotels that also want to attract the family market this can be a sensitive issue.

It is important to recognize that even people with children can temporarily enter the couples-only market when they take breaks away from their children, where romance is usually the main motivator.

Travelling for one's health

Travelling for one's health is one of the oldest motivators in tourism. But, today, the range of health tourism products is greater than ever before. Travelling for health covers a multitude of types of demand, including:

- visits to health resorts or 'health farms' which provide a holistic product that is often designed to relieve stress or put right the effect of over-indulgence in people's everyday lives
- activity holidays designed to enhance the tourist's overall level of physical fitness
- seaside resort-based sea-water treatments or thalassotherapy, in France, for example
- natural mud treatments in the Dead Sea area or Ireland, for instance
- mineral water treatments designed to cure or alleviate particular conditions.

Even on holidays where health is not the main concern, it is often still a consideration. Guests may demand healthy menus in hotels, for example, and leisure facilities, such as gyms and swimming pools.

In the increasingly stressful world of work, it seems likely that in the future health tourism will grow, and the concept of health may increasingly encompass mental as well as physical health.

Visits to religious retreats

The pressures of everyday life and the search for new spiritual values appears to have stimulated the demand for trips to religious retreats in two main ways, as follows:

- visits by non-believers or agnostics to conventional religious retreats, not only for religious enlightenment, but also for relaxation and spiritual enrichment. Examples of such retreats are Mount Athos in Greece which only admits men, for a limited period of time, and the Taizé community near Cluny in the Burgundy region of France
- visits to the homes of modern religious cults, and sects, notably in the UK, the USA and Asia.

At the same time, religious retreats are still attracting considerable number of believers as well as visitors.

In most retreats, life is simple and the comforts few. Personal, private, contemplation, is often the core of the experience. The 'customer' is not paying for the services they receive but rather for peace and the space to think.

There appears to be no reason at all why the demand for religious retreats will not continue to grow.

The eco-tourist

Eco-tourism is a global growth phenomenon of the tourism market in the 1990s. The eco-tourist is someone whose main motivator for taking a trip is to see wildlife and communities in their natural habitat. It is linked with other phenomena such as the desire to learn something new while on holiday.

Eco-tourism is also being put forward by some people as being synonymous with sustainable tourism. It is seen as a less exploitative, soft form of small-scale tourism, that has relatively low impact.

It is now difficult to separate the hype from the reality but there is no doubt that seeing oneself as an eco-tourist can give the tourist a feel-good factor, a feeling that their holiday is somehow better than the mass-market beach holiday.

The growth of eco-tourism seems to stem from two main sources, namely:

- the growing concern over green issues which has focused attention on the plight of rainforests and endangered wildlife
- media wildlife and travelogue programmes which have increased awareness of destinations.

Demand has also been stimulated by destinations such as Costa Rica or Belize, which are selling themselves as eco-tourism destinations.

Eco-tourism holidays exist at all price levels from budget overland 'expeditions' to luxury safaris and continent-wide tours.

Eco-tourism products are highly diverse and may include:

- wildlife safaris in East Africa
- journeys up the rivers of Borneo to see native villagers
- visits to endangered rain forests
- natural history walking holidays in the mountains of Europe
- outback trips in Australia
- whale-watching holidays to New England or New Zealand.

For some people, eco-tourism packages constitute their whole vacation. However, in other cases, they are just a day trip on a beach holiday.

At the same time, people on an eco-tourism holiday may also want to use the environment for sporting activities such as white-water rafting. If they do, then is it still an eco-tourism holiday?

There is a controversial dimension to eco-tourism, in that:

- some potentially authentic, wildlife-based activities that should be seen as eco-tourism, such as hunting, may be seen as socially unacceptable
- where eco-tourism grows it can begin to cause major environmental problems, such as is the case with the mass safari market in Kenya.

When all is said and done, eco-tourism is not an altruistic form of tourism. It is as self-indulgent as all forms of tourism. It is about tourists spending their leisure time in the way that gives them the benefits they seek.

Russian tourists

Since the demise of old-style communism and the rise of the market economy in Russia, there has been a noticeable increase in outbound tourism from Russia.

As the new Russian middle class has gained money from whatever source, it has found it difficult to find outlets for its new-found wealth in Russia itself. These Russians have therefore used tourism as a way of improving their status in their own community.

It sometimes seems that in every destination of the world which is famous for shopping – Dubai, Paris, London and Hong Kong – there are Russian tourists spending heavily in the shops. The most graphic evidence of this phenomenon is the huge pile of luggage that seems to be a feature of every Aeroflot check-in around the world!

At the same time, Russian tourists are becoming a vitally important market segment for traditional Mediterranean destinations such as the 'Costas' in Spain. Not only are they visiting these resorts but they are also buying property as second homes. This phenomenon is so well developed that there are even property magazines produced in Russian in resorts such as Benidorm.

In a country of some 200 million people, where only a fraction are currently travelling abroad, there is clearly great potential for future growth, providing that the economic crisis experienced in Russia in 1998 is short-lived.

Outbound tourism from Asian countries

Traditionally, the only Asian country that has generated considerable outbound tourism has been Japan. However, today, with the growth of economies in the region, we are seeing a rapid growth in outbound tourism from other countries, notably South Korea and Taiwan.

Tourists from these two countries are increasingly travelling to world-wide destinations including Europe and the USA. At the same time, tourists from Hong Kong, Malaysia, Singapore and Indonesia are increasingly travelling within South-East Asia, particularly for short-duration shopping trips. This growing phenomenon is being aided by the relatively small distances between these places, and the highly developed airline network in the region.

Two other markets offer potential for massive growth in coming years, namely:

- China, where rapid-economic growth and the growth of a capitalist economy will create a new affluent class who will want to travel abroad for pleasure
- India, which has the largest middle class of any country in the world.

As Asian travellers travel further and further, it will be important for the tourism industry in their destinations to recognize how their culture and the nature of their demand differs from other markets. They must also be careful to recognize that Korean or Taiwanese or Chinese tourists are not like Japanese people. They must guard against stereotyping all Asian tourists as being like the Japanese.

Many South Koreans already visit Las Vegas. However, according to the Las Vegas Visitor and Convention Authority, their behaviour is very different to that of other foreign visitors. For example, they:

- book later than most other tourists
- use packages more than many other national markets
- often visit friends and relatives while in the USA
- stay in the USA for longer than most other visitors
- dine out less than other tourists, but are more likely to visit the national parks than other nationalities
- spend significantly less than tourists from many other countries
- rely heavily on travel agents for advice.

The growth of Asian markets is shown by the fact that between 1990 and 1995, the number of tourists to Las Vegas from South Korea grew from

23 000 in 1990 to 78 000 in 1995, and from China the figure was 54 000 in 1990 rising to 117 000 in 1995. This figure in 1995 meant that Las Vegas received more Chinese visitors than it did French, Dutch, Australian and Spanish tourists. It is important, however, to recognise that the economic crisis being experienced in Asia in 1998 is putting a brake, albeit temporarily, on this trend.

Conclusion

In this chapter, we have looked at a number of different emerging markets and changes in the nature of tourist demand. We have seen how some regions of the world are becoming major generators of foreign trips for the first time, while in traditional markets we have noted new trends. These trends will probably continue into the future but they will evolve and be joined by new, as yet unforeseen, developments in demand.

Discussion points and essay questions

1 Select *three* of the emerging markets and changes in demand outlined in this chapter, and explain their growth.
2 Discuss the extent to which the rise of no-frills airlines, budget hotels and low-priced cruise products is likely to continue.
3 Evaluate the likely impact of the growth of outbound tourism from Asia on the global tourism industry.

Exercise

Choose one of the following markets:

● scheduled airline
● hotel
● mass-market tour operator
● visitor attraction
● retail travel.

For your chosen market, you should produce a report, supported by statistical and qualitative evidence, highlighting current trends in the market and emerging types of demand.

17 Quality and tourist satisfaction

The concept of quality

Quality is a 'buzz word' in all modern industries, and is seen as being the key to achieving customer satisfaction.

In this chapter we will explore what the concepts of quality and satisfaction mean in tourism. Firstly, we must begin by looking at some standard definitions of quality.

Gummesson, writing in 1988, divided definitions of quality into two types namely:

1 technology-driven and product-orientated definitions which defined quality in terms of conformance to requirements based on company specifications
2 fitness for purpose definitions, which are market-driven and customer orientated, and which focus upon customer utility and satisfaction.

In general, the first type of definition tends to be used in manufacturing industries where the main aim is usually standardization and reliability. The second type, with its emphasis on the customer and their satisfaction, is more commonly used in service industries.

Service quality is a more complex concept than manufacturing industry quality because of the unique characteristics of service products, or what Frochet in 1996 (in Robinson, Evans and Callaghan, 1996) described as the:

intrinsic services nature of heterogeneity, inseparability of production and consumption and intangibility.

Because of these characteristics, the standardization of product that is the aim of manufacturing companies is impossible to achieve in tourism. In any event, in tourism, the customer wants to feel that their experience will be different to other people's and tailor-made to match their tastes.

In many people's minds quality is an absolute that is either present or absent from a product. It either is or is not a quality product.

However, in reality, it is more of a continuum from little or no apparent quality to high or even, in theory at least, total quality.

Furthermore, it has often been assumed that quality means premium priced products, at the top end of the market. This is clearly not true if we take the fitness for purpose view of quality, where any product can be seen as a quality product if it meets the needs of the purchaser.

Therefore, a simple youth hostel could be a quality product for a young walker on a limited budget looking for an inexpensive bed for the night. At the other end of the scale, for the tourist who enjoys being pampered, only a five-star hotel with a high staff to guest ratio will meet their desires.

This brings us to the crucial issue at the heart of quality in service industries and the fitness for purpose definitions. They are customer-orientated and every customer is different. Quality is not a fact or a reality in such industries, it is a perception in the minds of the customer. In other words, quality is in the eye of the beholder. Whether or not a tourist will perceive a product as a quality product will depend upon:

- their individual attitudes, expectations and previous experiences as a consumer
- the benefits they are looking for from the particular purchase in question.

These needs and desires are closely linked to motivators and determinants. In terms of a holiday they might include:

- looking for a low cost vacation because of a lack of disposable income
- a desire to gain status from purchasing a particular holiday
- searching for a destination where the tourist will feel safe and secure
- a wish to take a type of holiday that will make it easier for the tourist to make new friends
- a deeply held desire to meet local people, see the 'real' country, and 'get off the beaten track'
- a need for relaxation and to reduce stress levels.

Obviously, tourists may be seeking more than one benefit from a holiday, and these may be conflicting or even contradictory.

The quality jigsaw in tourism

Because of the complex nature of tourism, product quality can be seen as a jigsaw, with many equally important, but different sized pieces, that must all fit together perfectly in order to satisfy the tourist. The jigsaw is illustrated in Figure 17.1 in relation to the purchase of a family's annual summer holiday in a resort hotel.

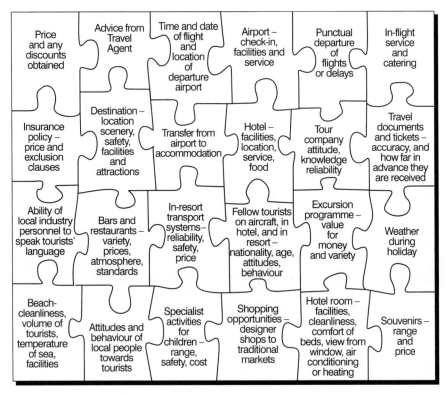

Figure 17.1   The quality jigsaw

The importance of tourist satisfaction

Satisfying the consumer in tourism is important for three main reasons, namely:

1 It leads to positive word-of-mouth recommendation of the product to friends and relatives, which in turn brings in new customers.
2 Creating a repeat customer by satisfying them with their first use of the product brings a steady source of income with no need for extra marketing expenditure.
3 Dealing with complaints is expensive, time-consuming and bad for the organization's reputation. Furthermore, it can bring direct costs through compensation payments.

The tourist satisfaction process

Figure 17.2 illustrates a simplified view of the process by which tourists are satisfied or not.

The tourism product	The satisfaction factor	The outcome
• Tangible element • Service element • Role of Intermediaries and agents	• Perceptions of the tourist experience • Tourist attitudes and expectations • Uncontrollable factors such as and strikes	• Tourist satisfaction • Tourist partial satisfaction • Tourist dissatisfaction

Figure 17.2 The tourist satisfaction process

Key models and techniques

There a number of models and techniques used in service industries in relation to quality and customer satisfaction. Several of these have been applied to tourism by various authors.

The SERVQUAL technique

The SERVQUAL scale was first introduced by Parasuraman, Zeithaml and Berry in 1985. They attempted to develop an instrument that would measure service quality across a range of service industries. It was based on some empirical research albeit not in the tourism industry. They stated that service quality has five dimensions (Parasuraman, Zeithaml and Berry, 1985, quoted in Frochet, 1996, in Robinson, Evans and Callaghan, 1996):

- Tangibles: physical facilities, equipment and appearance of personnel
- Reliability: the ability to perform the promised service dependably and accurately
- Responsiveness: willingness to help consumers and provide consumers with prompt service
- Assurance: knowledge and courtesy of employees and their ability to convey trust and confidence
- Empathy: caring individualized attention the firm provides to its customers.

Based on this idea they developed this technique where customers are asked questions and on the basis of their answers a score is calculated for each of the five criteria, and for subcriteria within these five groups. However, the model has been criticized on various methodological grounds.

A number of writers have attempted to apply the SERVQUAL technique to tourism services. In 1991, Fick and Ritchie found that the tool was most useful in those situations involving companies of one firm with another within a similar market segment.

A particularly interesting attempt to apply the technique in tourism was made in 1996 by Frochet who was studying its application to heritage sites. This study can be found in Robinson, Evans and Callaghan, 1996.

The service gap concept

This concept is based on the idea that dissatisfaction in services such as tourism is caused by gaps between expectations and perceived outcomes.

In 1985 Parasuraman, Zeithaml and Berry identified five such potential service gaps:

1 Differences between consumer expectations and management perceptions of consumer expectations.
2 Differences between management perceptions of consumer expectations and service quality specifications.
3 Differences between service quality specifications and the service actually delivered.
4 Differences between service delivery and what is communicated about the service to consumers.
5 Differences between consumer expectations and perceptions of the quality of the service received. (Parasuraman, Zeithaml and Berry, 1985)

Laws has applied this concept to the airline business. In 1991 he wrote:

In airline advertising, passengers are often shown seated, or reclining in relaxed comfort in spacious cabins. They are attended by elegant and calm stewardesses (more rarely by stewards) and are featured enjoying delicious, carefully presented meals and fine wines. The reality is often very different. The point is that marketing communications are educating passengers to expect a level of service which it is beyond the ability of a carrier to deliver in all but the most favourable conditions. These might occur when there were no strikes, no mechanical failures, the cabin crew were on their peak performance, the plane was less than full, and all passengers were relaxed.

The aim therefore, must be to use our marketing activities to create realistic expectations in the minds of our customers or else dissatisfaction may well result, however 'good' we feel our product is.

The critical incident approach

The critical incident approach to quality and consumer satisfaction is based on the idea that a tourist's satisfaction or otherwise with their experience of a product or service is a result of so-called 'critical incidents'. These incidents are concerned with the interaction of the organization's employees and the customer which can be termed the 'moment of truth' or 'the service encounter'. It assumes that there is a 'zone of tolerance' (Parasuraman, Zeithaml and Berry, 1985). In other words, customers will not notice a situation where the perceived experiences deviates only slightly from their expectations. Critical incidents are those which go beyond this zone of tolerance.

A critical incident is one that can be described in detail and that deviates significantly, either positively or negatively, from what is normal or expected.
                    Bejou, Edvardsson and Rakowski (1996)

Clearly an organization will wish to rectify the problems which caused a negative incident and pacify the customer, while at the same time building on the strengths which contributed to a positive incident.

In 1996, Bejou, Edvardsson and Rakowski published an interesting study of negative critical incidents in the airline industry in Sweden and the USA. In the hotel sector, such critical incidents could include:

- whether or not the check-in process goes smoothly
- if a meal ordered via room service appears quickly and meets the customer's expectations
- whether or not the concierge can provide an item that the guest has forgotten to pack.

These three models or techniques are largely based on an organization's perspective of service quality. This leads us naturally on to the issue of the service staff themselves.

The human resource management dimension

In a service industry like tourism, human resource management is clearly of great significance in relation to quality and tourist satisfaction. Tom Baum (quoted in Ryan, 1997) has described the role of staff as 'making or breaking the tourist experience'.

Tourist satisfaction depends on effective human resource management. It will only occur if staff:

- have the technical skills to carry out their job effectively
- have a positive attitude towards their job and seem committed to pleasing their customers
- operate as a team and there are good working relations between front line staff and managers
- are reliable in terms of attendance at work
- deal with complaints promptly, sympathetically and effectively.

However, in tourism, clients often complain about the quality of service and staff performance, particularly waiting staff, and tour operator representatives. This is probably not surprising as such staff are often employed as poorly paid temporary staff, with little training, and working long hours.

Nevertheless, many tourism organizations have sought to put in place customer care programmes and other measures designed to improve the quality of service for customers. The fashionable technique of 'empowerment' has been used by companies such as the hotel chain, Marriott, to encourage staff to take more responsibility for satisfying customers' needs.

The role of marketing intermediaries

In tourism, a vital role is performed by the marketing intermediaries, most notably travel agents. Their service is of great importance to most tourists and has a major influence on their ultimate satisfaction or dissatisfaction. They:

- provide advice on destinations and hotels and their suitability for the client
- handle bookings and the issue of tickets
- advise the tourist on health issues and immigration formalities in the destinations
- take the clients' money on behalf of the tour operator
- deal with complaints on behalf of the client.

Each of these factors can either enhance or diminish the quality of the tourist experience.

Work carried out in New Zealand by Cliff and Ryan in 1994 outlined consumer concerns about the reliability and performance of travel agents (quoted in Ryan, 1997).

Cliff and Ryan (quoted in Ryan, 1997) identify three dimensions to the travel agent's service quality as follows:

1 tangible elements, e.g. the decor of the premises and the dress of the staff. If these do not satisfy the potential client they will not even think of using that travel agent
2 reassurance that the agent is reliable, and competent. If this reassurance is not given to the client, they may enter the premises, but they will not book via the agent
3 after the travel, if the tourist is not satisfied with the arrangements made by the agent, they are unlikely to use them again.

Furthermore, inadequate performance by the marketing intermediary also affects the reputation and custom of the tour operator. If an agent recommended a family to visit a particular resort and apartment complex in a certain resort that turns out to be lively, loud and not suitable for people with young children, the tourists would be dissatisfied with the holiday they had purchased from a particular operator. Yet, it could have been a perfectly good holiday package, ideal for a young single person. It was just that the agent recommended it to clients for whom it was not designed.

The importance of problem solving

The test of any quality management system is what happens when something inevitably goes wrong and the customer complains. Tourist do not expect perfection, but they do expect prompt action when problems occur.

Indeed, dealing effectively with difficulties and complaints can actively enhance tourist satisfaction. If everything on a holiday goes to plan, tourists tend not to notice. However, if something goes wrong and the organization handles the situation well, then the organization's reputation can be enhanced in the mind of the tourist. However, for this to happen, some basic guidelines need to be followed, namely:

- problems have to be put right as soon as possible. On a two-week holiday, the whole experience can be ruined if clients are not moved from inadequate to satisfactory accommodation within the first day or two
- making it easy for clients to contact resort representatives so they do not spend hours of their precious holiday trying to locate the person who is supposed to be there to help them
- ensuring that any offer of compensation is fair and reflects the gravity of the problem.

Personal factors and satisfaction

There are two important personal factors that affect a consumer's satisfaction or otherwise, notably stress and arousal, and we will now briefly consider both of these.

Stress and tourist dissatisfaction

Stress caused by any aspect of the vacation experience tends to lead to tourist dissatisfaction. This stress can result from a variety of sources, as we can see from Figure 17.3.

We could have listed many others but those shown in Figure 17.3 give a good indication of the range of such factors. The tourist industry is constantly seeking to ameliorate these stresses, particularly at the higher end of the market.

Tourist satisfaction and arousal

In tourism, satisfaction is clearly connected to the concept of arousal. Too little arousal can cause boredom and dissatisfaction. According to Ryan (1997):

The distinction between relaxation, a common motivation for holidays, and boredom is, from this viewpoint, dependent upon a level of arousal that is sufficient for relaxation, but is not so low as to induce boredom.

At the other extreme, there is the concept of 'hyper-arousal, producing panic, frenzy, and possible collapse' (Yerkes–Dodson Law, 1908, quoted in

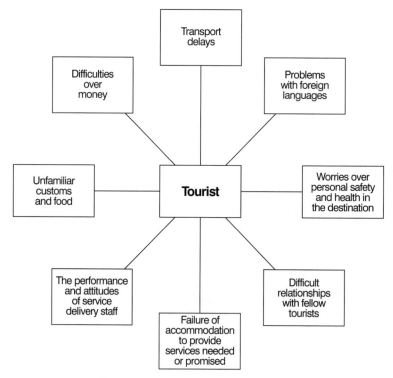

Figure 17.3 Sources of stress for tourists

Ryan, 1997). A classic case of this in tourism might be the fear of flying experienced by some travellers. Hyper-arousal is likely to cause dissatisfaction in general.

However, interestingly in recent years the growth of so-called adventure tourism – white-water rafting and bungee-jumping, for example – has been based on hyper-arousal. This search for hyper-arousal is the exception though, for normally hyper-arousal in tourism arises when something goes wrong or there is an unforeseen occurrence such as an aircraft delay, and it is seen as negative.

Hyper-arousal is closely related to the concept of stress in tourism. So it is appropriate for us to move on to the latter topic at this stage.

Changing expectations of quality over time

Tourists' expectations, in general, have risen over time in response to two influences, as follows:

1 Improvement in their everyday standard of living and housing amenities, which make them always demand something extra when they are on holiday.

2 Product innovation by organizations that are then copied by competitors and become the norm.

We can see the way in which the consumer expectations of the accommodation product have developed over the years in response to both these factors.

At one time, hot and cold running water and shaving points in bedrooms were the height of sophistication. Then in-room radios were introduced and interior-sprung mattresses. After that came televisions, en-suite bathrooms, minibars and automatic alarms. These were followed by cable movie systems and eventually satellite television, jacuzzi baths and in-room computer links. Each of these were state of the art when first introduced but have now become the norm, stage by stage.

The interesting point is that while established generating markets like the UK have passed slowly through all these stages, the recently developed markets such as Korea and Russia have demanded the latest state of the art facilities from the beginning.

At the same time, there are still consumers who are satisfied with less sophisticated in-room facilities, or rather they are willing to accept them in return for a low price.

The importance of uncontrollable factors

A major problem for the tourism industry is the factors that influence product quality or customer satisfaction, yet are outside its control. These include:

- weather, such as unseasonable rain in Mediterranean resorts in the summer, or lack of snow in Alpine ski resorts in the winter
- strikes that affect tourists such as air traffic controllers and ferry crews
- harassment of tourists by beggars and traders
- poor transport infrastructure in the destination country
- poor hygiene and sanitation standards and disease
- the perhaps unrealistic expectations of tourists. Some people, for instance, hope that a romantic weekend in Paris will put life back into a failing – and doomed – marriage
- the behaviour of other tourists in the resort or accommodation establishment
- government bureaucracy and bureaucratic factors such as visa restrictions and departure taxes.

Any of these may cause tourist dissatisfaction with a holiday experience but they are outside the control of the tour operator that sold the holiday.

A good example of uncontrollable factors and tourist dissatisfaction comes from Las Vegas. The 1996 Las Vegas Visitor Profile Study showed that 5 per cent of visitors were dissatisfied because they did not win enough money in the casino! There is absolutely nothing the tour operator can do to solve this problem.

Subjective factors

Another difficulty in relation to quality and tourist satisfaction is that tourists have different attitudes, standards and prejudices. Often their satisfaction or otherwise is based on subjective views about an issue which is important to them, and which they judge in their own unique way.

Again the 1996 Las Vegas Visitor Profile Study shows that:

10% of visitors found the people in Las Vegas rude and unfriendly
8% thought it too expensive
7% said it was too hard to get to
4% felt it was too intense
3% claimed Las Vegas was dirty

All of these factors are subjective opinions based on individual inter-pretations of experiences as tourists. It is difficult to see how the tourism industry can effectively respond in concrete terms to such views.

National differences in quality standards and tourist satisfaction

There is clear evidence that there are national differences in tourist expectations in relation to quality standards. It is widely recognized, for example, that German tourists are more concerned with the environmental quality of resorts than their British counterparts.

The authors' discussions with airline marketing executives also show that passengers from different nationalities have different quality standards. The consensus appears to be that passengers from countries such as Japan and the USA have higher expectations than those from more recently indus-trialized countries.

These national differences in tourist expectations are obviously of great significance to organizations that operate trans-nationally such as hotel chains and major airlines.

There are also national differences in the supply side, in terms of the quality of the product offered. These can lead tourists in turn to modify their expectations if they are planning to visit a particular country, or even to decide not visit a country. The different quality standards can cover elements of the product such as:

● food hygiene in restaurants
● fire safety in hotels
● public transport in destinations
● interpretation techniques in museums
● technical competence and attitudes of guides at heritage sites.

When considering the issue of national differences in product quality and tourist expectations, it is important to distinguish facts from the clichés and stereotypes that exist.

Conclusion

We have seen that quality and tourist satisfaction are inextricably linked. However, they are both subjects about which we still have much to learn. In many cases we find airlines trying to apply models and techniques to tourism that were developed for service industries in general. We have yet to develop convincing models and techniques based on large-scale empirical research in tourism. This will not be easy for we have also seen that many of the factors which affect satisfaction are uncontrollable, and that quality is a highly personal and subjective concept.

Discussion points and essay questions

1 Discuss the idea that the most important factors that determine whether tourists will be satisfied or not are beyond the control of tourism organizations.
2 Critically evaluate the SERVQUAL technique and its potential use to tourism organizations.
3 Discuss the suggestion that quality means high price.

Exercise

Select a small sample of people, perhaps ten, who have recently taken a holiday. You should then interview them to see:

- how satisfied they had been with their holiday
- which factors influenced their satisfaction or otherwise.

You should finally produce a report of your findings, indicating what you have learnt from the survey about quality and tourist satisfaction, while recognizing the limitations of your survey.

Part Seven
Conclusions and Future

At the end of a long text dealing with a complex and only partially understood concept, the time has come for the authors to attempt to draw some conclusions and make predictions about the future.

In this part of the book we will:

- identify the main conclusions that have arisen from the previous 17 chapters
- highlight the need for further research and the development of new consumer behaviour models in tourism
- compare tourist behaviour to that of consumers in general
- suggest some ways in which tourist behaviour may evolve in the future.

18 Conclusions

At the end of such a lengthy book on a very complex subject, it is difficult to try to draw some general conclusions. Nevertheless, the authors will now attempt to highlight some key points which they believe have emerged from the preceding chapters. These are as follows:

1 Tourist behaviour has a long history, dating back over two thousand years. Many 'modern' forms of tourism, such as health tourism, are simply a continuation of a tradition that dates back to Roman times. At the same time, some early forms of mass tourism such as Christian pilgrimages are now specialist niche markets.

2 Many existing models of consumer behaviour in tourism are generally much simpler than general consumer behaviour models. Yet, tourism is a particularly complex aspect of our modern consumer society, so perhaps they are too simplistic.

3 Most of the motivations that make tourists want to take a particular holiday can be divided into six distinct, but related, groups, namely:
   - physical
   - emotional
   - personal
   - personal development
   - status
   - cultural.

4 The motivations of any individual tourist are influenced by their:
   - personality
   - lifestyle
   - past experiences
   - personal circumstances, including family situation and disposable income.

5 Tourists may well have more than one motivator at any one time.

6 Tourists may admit to a socially acceptable motivator while in reality they may be driven by a motivator that is less socially acceptable. They may be conscious or unconscious of this.

7 Different types of tourism product are associated with different motivating factors, e.g. museums and theme park visits are stimulated by different motivations generally.

8 There are two types of determinants of tourist behaviour namely:
- those which are personal to the tourist
- those which are external to the tourist.

9 Those determinants which are personal to the tourist are of four types, as follows:
- their personal circumstances
- their knowledge
- their experiences
- their attitudes and perceptions.

10 The external determinants include the following five types:
- the views of friends and family
- the marketing activities of the tourism industry
- the influence of the media
- national political, economic, social and technological factors
- global political, economic, social and technological factors.

11 The main purchase decision-making models used in tourism, as outlined in Chapter 6, tend to have a number of weaknesses, including:
- they are often based on little or no empirical research
- many are now at least 15 years old and do not take account of recent changes in patterns of purchase behaviour such as the growth of last-minute purchases
- most are based on experiences in the traditional markets such as Europe and the USA, not the new markets like South-East Asia
- they are too simplistic to explain the complex process of purchasing a tourist product.

12 Many academic typologies of tourists are flawed in that they:
- rarely differentiate between different nationalities and cultures
- tend not to recognize that tourists can move between categories and rarely always remain in one category
- do not usually recognize that holiday choice is often a compromise rather than an expression of the true desires of the tourist
- often have methodological weaknesses such as being based on small samples, for example.

13 Typologies of tourists are clearly similar to the concept of market segmentation, although the former are theoretical while the latter is concerned with applications and practice in marketing.

14 In the global tourism market, the major growth in tourist arrivals is being seen in Asia and the Pacific, while Europe is experiencing relative decline in its share of world tourism

15 There are significant differences between countries in terms of tourist behaviour in terms of domestic, outbound and inbound tourism.

16 Tourism is not a single market but is rather a series of submarkets, all of which have their own characteristics. These submarkets include:
- the family market
- the 'back-packer' market
- hedonistic tourists
- those visiting friends and relatives
- day trippers or excursionists

- educational tourists
- religious tourists
- ethnic minority tourists
- tourists with disabilities
- retired people
- short break takers.

17 There are also variations in consumer behaviour within the different sectors of tourism, namely:
- accommodation
- visitor attractions
- destinations
- transport operators
- tour operators
- retail travel.

18 Business tourism is very different in terms of consumer behaviour from leisure tourism, in terms of:
- frequency of trips
- duration of trips
- when purchase decisions are made
- who makes purchase decisions.

19 In business tourism, we see the difference between customers and consumers. The former tend to be the companies that pay the bill, while the latter are usually the employees, the business travellers themselves.

20 Research on tourist behaviour is weak in a number of respects, most notably:
- the fact that much quantitative data is outdated and based on small samples which mean the results are open to question
- the relative lack of sophistication in terms of qualitative research on how and why tourists make their decisions.

21 Consumer behaviour affects every aspect of marketing, in that it should influence:
- product development
- pricing strategies
- distributive channels
- promotional campaigns.

22 There is no such thing as a 'green tourist'; there are instead, 'shades of green' consumers in tourism and indeed there are some tourists who are not at all green.

23 There are significant differences between nationalities in terms of tourists' attitudes towards the environment.

24 The current era is seeing the growth of a number of emerging markets in tourism including:
- eco-tourism
- the phenomenon of direct booking
- children-only holidays
- all-inclusive vacations
- budget cruising

- outbound tourism from Asia and Russia
- 'no-frills' airline travel
- the international wedding market
- couples-only holidays
- visiting sites associated with popular culture such as films and television programmes
- visits to religious retreats
- taking trips designed to improve the health of the tourist.

25 There is no apparent evidence for the idea that we are seeing the emergence of the 'global tourist' or even the 'Euro tourist'.

26 Quality in tourism is a jigsaw where, if any piece is missing, the customer will be dissatisfied.

27 Tourist dissatisfaction is largely a result of gaps between expectations and perceived outcomes, viewed from the perspective of the tourist.

28 The concept of quality and the expectations of tourists change over time.

29 There are many uncontrollable factors that influence tourist satisfaction, namely:
- weather
- strikes
- harassment of tourists by beggars and traders
- difficulties within the destination such as hygiene problems, poor infrastructure and crime
- the behaviour of other tourists.

Hopefully, this book has helped, in a small way, to focus attention on this important field in the study of tourism. As well as the main text we hope that the discussion points and essay questions, exercises, and case studies (see Part Eight) have also helped you deepen your understanding of this crucial area of tourism management.

In the era of so-called 'consumer-led marketing', where organizations are told they must meet the demands of their consumers if they are to thrive, it is obviously vital that we understand the tourist and what makes them 'tick'.

In the next chapter, we will gaze into our crystal ball and attempt to predict what might happen in the future. This is a risky activity at a time when consumer factors appear to be changing at an ever greater pace and new forms of tourism are continually emerging.

19   The future of tourist behaviour

In this chapter, we are going to consider how tourist behaviour might evolve in the future in terms of who will be travelling, what tourists will buy and how they will buy tourism products.

It is likely that future tourist behaviour will be influenced by a range of factors including those illustrated in Figure 19.1.

The impact of these factors, and others, will be four-fold, in that they will lead to:

- the growth of outbound tourism from countries which have previously not been major generators of international tourist trips

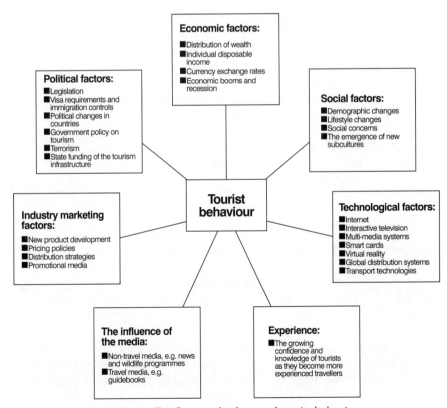

Figure 19.1   Factors that will influence the future of tourist behaviour

- the expansion of tourism demand from certain groups in society
- the development of new types of tourism product
- changes in the way in which we purchase tourism products.

We will now look at each of these in a little more detail.

New generating countries

There are economic, political and social reasons why the major growth in outbound tourism in future years will be seen largely in countries which until recently have generated relatively few international tourist trips. These countries include:

1 Eastern Europe, where political and economic change is slowly creating a growth in outbound trips.
2 Asia and the Pacific, where economic growth has rapidly expanded the market for outbound trips by the residents of those countries. For example, outbound trips from South Korea rose between 1986 and 1995 from 455 500 to 3 819 000, an increase of some 850 per cent in just ten years.

However, in both cases, the growth in outbound tourism will only continue if there is political stability and economic growth in both regions of the world. Recent events (autumn 1998) seem to indicate that this may not be the case with economic problems and uncertainty over the future in both Russia and South-East Asia.

As yet, there is little outbound tourism from most countries in Africa and South America. This may change, however, as:

- some economies, such as Brazil, are growing rapidly
- political change in some countries may lead to a more equal distribution of wealth which may make more of the population able to take a trip abroad.

Market segments that will grow in importance

Social change, the influence of the media and the actions of the tourist industry seem likely to have the following effects on segmentation in tourism:

1 Demographic change in Northern Europe, USA and Japan will lead to growth in the importance of the elderly or 'third age' market. Conversely in countries where the population is becoming more youthful – Southern Europe, South America and South-East Asia – there will be a growth in the 18–30 market segment.

2 As children become ever more consumers in their own right, an increasing number of them will take holidays, separate from their parents.

3 There will be more non-Christians travelling internationally in future which will have implications for the tourism industry world-wide.

4 We may see the growth of segments which share similar characteristics, regardless of their nationality. Students may be the first example of such a segment.

5 As attitudes towards people with disabilities change over time, there should be a growth in the number of travellers who are disabled. They will become a major market which the industry will not be able to neglect.

New types of tourism product

The development of any new types of tourism products will result from:

- the changing tastes of tourists
- whatever the industry chooses to make available to tourists
- technological innovations
- social concerns.

In Chapter 16 we looked at some of the current trends in tourist demand and the products that are now in fashion.

The veteran travel writer, Arthur Frommer, writing in 1996, identified a number of types of tourism products that may grow in popularity in the future. These included the following:

- 'vacation resorts that stretch the mind and change your life'
- 'political travel' which allows tourists to visit countries that are often in the news and see for themselves what everyday life is like there
- 'volunteer vacations' where tourists work for nothing on projects which are good causes, such as conservation work or building a school in a poor country
- taking holidays that involve staying with an ordinary family in another country
- searching for new modes of travel such as freighter ships and sailing vessels
- 'ethical holidays' where the tourist is concerned about the impact of their trip on the host community and the staff who look after them
- health-enhancing holidays.

Frommer also talks about finding 'new ways to visit old destinations', where, he argues, tourists visiting well-known destinations, perhaps for the third or fourth time, will look for new, more off-beat experiences. For example, visitors to London may seek out less touristy neighbourhoods and 'fringe' arts events.

It is also likely that the growing pressures of modern life will lead to more people seeking to use their holiday to reduce stress and/or gain spiritual enlightenment as an antidote to the materialism of modern life. This will increase demand for trips to 'retreats', even amongst those who do not have strong religious beliefs.

As well as the development of new products, many tourists will be encouraged by the industry to take similar types of holidays as they have before, but in new locations.

This might include:

- European tourists taking short city breaks to places further afield such as Cape Town, Samarkand, Tbilisi, Havana and Teheran
- beach holidays being taken in Namibia and Brazil
- skiing trips to Japan, Argentina and Chile
- cultural holidays in Myanmar, Laos and Nigeria.

In general, it seems likely that tourists will travel longer distances for their main vacations, even though their main holiday activity or motivation may be little different from the past.

Virtual Reality and fantasy tourism

One of the major current debates in tourism revolves around Virtual Reality technologies, and the ability to create synthetic substitutes for real tourism experiences. The question is, will Virtual Reality (VR) reduce the demand for conventional tourism or increase it by stimulating even more people to want to take particular trips.

The potential application of VR in tourism, once the technologies themselves have become more sophisticated, is virtually unlimited. We could let people:

- feel the sun on their face, hear waves lapping on the shore, as they lie on a deserted beach on a Pacific Island, all in their own home
- experience a visit to the greatest of the Pyramids in Egypt, without the fear of terrorist activities, stomach upsets or overbooked flights, because they would not need to leave home
- enjoy a romantic 'Bateaux Mouches' cruise on the Seine in Paris, with the love of their life, all from the comfort of their bed at home.

At the same time, Virtual Reality technologies, and other technological innovations, could help us to develop new forms of escapist tourism, by allowing people to live out their fantasies.

Already, the Russians are allowing tourists to experience what it is like to:

- be a cosmonaut training for their first space flight
- be a fighter pilot, on a sophisticated flight simulator.

In this case, it is a result of economic necessity and the desire to attract foreign currency, through the use of well-established VR technologies.

Ultimately, development in VR and related technologies could allow the creation of new fantasy-based resorts.

For example, just as in the film *Westworld*, whole themed resorts could be built where tourists could totally immerse themselves in a fantasy experience. The tourist could be a Roman gladiator, a medieval knight, a wild west gunslinger or a Chicago gangster. They could enjoy playing these roles in a safe environment.

Alternatively, one day we will be able to create artificial environments, where tourists can experience holidays under the sea, or in gravity-less environments.

Perhaps, one day, tourism will be a wholly mental activity, with no need to travel, an activity which takes place purely within the tourist's own home and is limited only by the imagination of the tourist.

Will tourism demand turn full circle?

It is often assumed that the evolution of tourism demand is a linear process of stages which are passed through in a sequence. Figure 19.2 illustrates the widely accepted conventional wisdom about how the behaviour of many British tourists has changed over time.

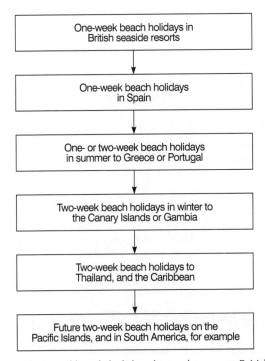

Figure 19.2   The evolution of beach holiday demand amongst British tourists

There are several reasons why this apparent linear process may become more circular in future. It could perhaps turn full circle if:

- diseases such as malaria and AIDS discourage tourists from taking trips to long-haul destinations, where the threat of both is perceived to be high
- the Earth's resources become depleted and it either becomes difficult to justify long-haul trips or the cost of fuel makes such trips too expensive
- the tourism industry makes the coastal resorts of Britain and Spain attractive to tourists for their main holiday. This could involve cleaning up beaches and making more water-based activities available, or offering non-beach dependent attractions such as theme parks, casinos and shopping. Resorts such as Benidorm are already setting a good example in this respect. At the same time, the coastal resorts of Britain and Spain, for example, may begin to be seen as attractive as heritage tourism destinations given that mass tourism is now part of our modern heritage.

We already have examples of how tourism demand can turn full circle. Spa tourism reached its peak in Europe in the eighteenth and nineteenth centuries and then declined early in the twentieth century. Now, however, the spa resorts of Europe are experiencing a boom. Likewise, cruising which went into decline after the Second World War is currently experiencing a real renaissance. In both cases, the change has resulted from social factors and the activities of the tourism industry.

The number of holidays per annum

In many countries, a large number of tourists now take more than one holiday per year, and this trend looks set to continue. This has a number of implications for tourist behaviour, as follows.

1 The main holiday will be the longest, and may well be used for relaxation, stress release and the 'recharging of the tourist's batteries'.
2 The extra holidays may normally be shorter, more active and more specialist in nature.

The extra holiday may be used for intense short leisure experiences, as an antidote to the route of everyday life, including day trips to cities in other countries or 24-hour visits to a foreign mountain range to climb a particular peak.

The unchanging tourist

Before we get carried away by the idea that tourism demand is constantly changing, let us briefly remember that there are some tourists whose behaviour is not following the trends we have been discussing in this book. These are tourists who:

- are doing the same on holiday as they did 20 years ago, namely relaxing on a beach or by the hotel pool, for instance
- are taking their holidays in the same type of destination, or even exactly the same place, as they were two decades ago.

British seaside resorts are still packed with tourists on summer holidays, as are those of all Northern European countries.

There will continue to be a group of tourists who do not wish, or who are not able, to change their behaviour, regardless of what other tourists are doing.

Changes in the way we purchase tourism products

Technological innovations are going to continue to change the way in which we purchase tourism products, in several ways, as follows.

1 The development of the Internet and interactive television will stimulate the growth of direct marketing and direct booking. People will increasingly be able to access information and make bookings from their own home or office. Tour operators, airlines and hotels may help encourage this trend as the Internet is a relatively inexpensive promotional tool and direct selling takes away the need to pay commission to travel agents.
2 The growth of ever more sophisticated global distribution systems (GDS) will help tourists put together individual, tailor-made itineraries, by giving them access to the detailed product information they require.
3 Smart Card technologies will bring with them the benefits of ticket-less travel which will stimulate the growth of last-minute purchases of tourism products.

Developments in technology such as multi-media systems and the Internet are blurring the dividing line between promotion and distribution in tourism. In other words, tourists, through these systems, can both gain information and make bookings at the same time, in the same place.

We may also see changes in the future in terms of who we buy holidays from as the role of travel agents declines and other organizations take their place. These could be:

- high street retailers who will combine selling holidays with the sale of the goods needed by tourists, such as clothes, suntan creams and luggage
- 'tele-shopping' networks that may simply add holidays to the portfolio of products they sell
- banks who provide loans for holidays and sell currency, might go on to sell the holidays themselves

- telecommunications companies which may become involved in selling holidays as their systems play more and more of a role in the distribution of the tourism product.

So far in this chapter we have looked at how the consumer behaviour of tourists might change in the years to come. However, we do need to recognize how important it is for us to become better at researching tourist behaviour so we can identify any changes in behaviour and explain them. Therefore we will now turn our attention to the issue of researching consumer behaviour in tourism.

Towards a new agenda for consumer behaviour research in tourism

In Chapter 12, the authors provided a critique of current consumer behaviour research in tourism.

If we are to better understand tourist behaviour, and use this knowledge to improve marketing within the industry, we need to adopt a new agenda for research. This agenda should contain the following ten points. It should:

1 focus upon the process by which tourists make their purchase decisions
2 recognize the importance of tourists' perceptions and endeavour to find out more about where these perceptions come from
3 pay attention to the need for us to improve our techniques for conducting qualitative research, including the use of focus groups, observation and informal conversations with tourists
4 give a high priority to the issue of quality and tourist satisfaction. We need to better understand how tourists perceive quality and what makes them satisfied or dissatisfied with a particular touristic experience
5 be concerned with the need to conduct longitudinal research that will help us to identify trends in tourist behaviour
6 explore the link between consumer behaviour research and the criteria on which we segment tourism markets, to make segmentation more closely mirror the realities of actual tourist behaviour
7 look at how tourists evaluate the offers of different tourism organizations and decide which one to purchase
8 concentrate some effort on developing techniques that help us to understand why people choose not to purchase particular products
9 place great emphasis on the need to recognize and research variations in tourist behaviour between different nationalities and different cultures
10 explore the links between consumer behaviour in tourism and that in other industries, for people's purchase of tourist products is clearly related to their purchase of other products.

In general, a new approach to research in the consumer behaviour would also involve:

- academics producing techniques and models which have practical applications, and disseminating them as widely as possible, and in as easily comprehensible a form as possible
- practitioners making more use of consumer behaviour research when taking marketing decisions.

Government tourism agencies have a key role to play in bringing both groups together and helping them work together for their mutual benefit, in terms of both:

- the research they themselves commission
- how consumer behaviour data is presented and disseminated.

Summary

We have seen that a range of factors will lead, in the future, to changes in who the tourists are, what they buy, and how they buy it. However, the authors have also noted that the behaviour of some individual tourists will not change noticeably.

At the same time, even within the global tourism market as a whole, we will find that changes in behaviour will be evolutionary rather than revolutionary. We will also see variations in the power of change between different:

- countries
- market segments
- sectors of the tourism industry.

Nevertheless, there is little doubt that tourist behaviour will change in fundamental ways in the years to come. That is why it is so important that we become better at researching consumer behaviour in tourism.

Part Eight
Case Studies

Introduction

This book has used many tourism examples to illustrate the points made in individual chapters. It is useful, however, to consider longer and broader case studies to evaluate some of the main issues in relation to consumer behaviour in more depth.

The case studies that follow show a number of tourism organizations from a variety of countries. These organizations range from small to large, and operate in one or more than one country. Some case studies are short and have been written to explore one particular issue. Others are much longer and give an overview of the whole organization and how they relate to consumers.

The case studies have been grouped together under particular headings to allow the reader to examine issues in relation to consumer behaviour and compare and contrast the approaches of the different organizations. The case studies were researched during 1997 and therefore, like all published case studies, are only snapshots at that particular time. We are aware that the material in the case studies will date but this does not make the lessons that can be learned from them any less valuable.

The case study list is given below. We hope that you enjoy reading the case studies and exploring some of the issues related to consumer behaviour in more depth.

Case studies

Targeting different market segments
1 PGL Adventure Holidays
2 Flying Colours Holidays Limited – Club 18–30
3 The segmentation of the outbound Japanese market

Customer service
4 The Savoy Group of Hotels
5 Cathay Pacific Airways

New emerging tourism markets
6 First Choice Holidays – all-inclusive package
7 Carnival Cruise Lines – the cruise market

Industrial tourism
8 Wensleydale Creamery, Hawes, North Yorkshire
9 Société Roquefort, Roquefort, France
10 Industrial tourism in France

Environmental initiatives
11 British Airways – environmental policy
12 TUI, Germany – environmental policy

Hedonistic tourism
13 Ragdale Hall – health hydro
14 The international spa market

Leisure and tourism
15 Granada Studios Tour

Budget tourism
16 easyJet

Destination marketing and the consumer
17 Las Vegas, Nevada, USA
18 Rural tourism in France
19 Inbound and outbound tourism in the USA – breaking the myths
20 Taiwan – the emergence of a new major outbound tourism market

Activity holidays
21 Susi Madron's Cycling for Softies

Topical issues in tourism
22 Currency exchange rates as a determinant of tourism behaviour

Case study 1
PGL Adventure Holidays

Introduction

PGL Travel Limited is the leading British provider of adventure holidays for young people. The holidays are designed around holiday centres which the company has bought or leased, and developed. Young people go on the holidays without their parents and it is often the first time that they have been away from their family for any length of time. The holidays incorporate a whole selection of outdoor and indoor activities, and accommodation can range from tents to dormitories. The company has also developed substantial business in the school holidays market.

Background

The company takes its name from the initials of the man who started it in the 1950s and who is now the Chairman of the PGL Group of Companies – Peter Gordon Lawrence.

The idea for the company came to Peter when he went on holiday to Austria in 1950 and sailed down the Danube in a folding canvas canoe. In 1957 he started to organize canoe camping trips for young adults down the River Wye. Peter led the groups himself and called his new venture, PGL Voyages. Peter expanded the business to Wales and the Brecon Beacons National Park. In the 1960s and 1970s the PGL holidays were based on canoeing, sailing and pony trekking, with the accommodation in tents. During the early years, the company developed holidays for school groups, and expanded their holidays to include the Ardeche Gorge in the South of France. The company now has a permanently staffed headquarters in France and the UK.

The company gradually grew during the 1980s to become the leading UK provider of adventure holidays. Properties were bought by the company

The authors would like to thank Martin Hudson of PGL Travel Limited for his help in producing this case study.

which were converted to permanent centres. This development included the acquisition of a mansion house in Perthshire, and the flagship 250-acre estate of Boreatton Park in Shropshire.

The company gradually diversified into other markets in the last ten years, including educational tours for schools, and field study courses. There was a considerable expansion into the school's adventure market in 1991/92, when the company acquired the Quest Outdoor Adventure programme from a failed competitor.

The company today

The company now has 40 years' experience and is recognized as being Britain's leading operator of activity holidays for children and teenagers. PGL has 23 centres in the UK and France. The company offers a full range of activities including archery, pony trekking, motorsports, abseiling, canoeing, orienteering, assault courses, sailing, windsurfing, climbing and others. Specialist holidays include Mountain Biking, Dordogne Adventure, Driver Awareness, 'Indiana Jones' Theme Holiday, Farming, Beach Life-guarding, French Language, and Tennis Coaching.

The company has 15 centres in the UK, in Perthshire, Lancashire, Shropshire, South Wales, the Wye Valley, North Devon, Oxfordshire and Surrey. There are also eight centres in France, and two Teenski resorts in Austria. A full range of the holidays offered by PGL to children and teenagers is shown in Exhibit 1.1.

Exhibit 1.1   The full range of holidays for children and teenagers, offered by PGL Travel Limited

Multi-activity holidays in Britain

Ages	Centre	Location
6–9	Thomley Hall	Nr Thame, Oxfordshire
6–9, 8–11	Hillcrest	Nr Ross-on-Wye, Herefordshire
6–9, 8–11, 11–13	Marchant's Hill	Nr Hindhead, Surrey
8–11, 11–13	Boreatton Park	Nr Shrewsbury, Shropshire
8–13, 12–16	Dalguise	Nr Dunkeld, Perthshire, Scotland
8–13, 12–16	Myerscough College	Bilsborrow, nr Blackpool
8–13, 12–16	Beam House	Bideford, Devon
12–16	Court Farm	Nr Ross-on-Wye, Herefordshire
12–16	Tregoyd House	Welsh border, nr Hay-on-Wye
12–16	Tan Troed	Brecon Beacons, Wales
14–18	The Bluecoat School	Horsham, West Sussex
14–18	Moreton Hall	Nr Oswestry, Shropshire

Specialist holidays in Britain

Ages	Holiday Type	Centre
8–13	Indiana Jones Adventure	Boreatton Park
8–13	Robin Hood Adventure	Boreatton Park
8–13, 12–16	Motorsports	6 Centres
12–16	Driver Awareness	4 Centres
14–18	Tennis Coaching	2 Centres
8–13, 12–18	Riding and Trekking	4 Centres
12–18	RYA Sailing and Windsurfing	Royal Oak
12–16	Mountain Biking	Court Farm and Tan Troed
8–13, 14–18	Theme Parks and Activities	3 Centres
12–16	Fishing	Court Farm
12–16	River Canoe Trail	Court Farm
12–16	Espionage and Outdoor Challenges	Tregoyd, Dalguise and Tan Troed
16–18	Personal Development Skills	The Bluecoat School
8–13, 12–18	Drama and Theatre	3 Centres
8–13	Media Skills	Marchant's Hill
8–13, 12–18	English Language for Foreign Children	4 Centres

Multi-activity and specialist holidays in France

Ages	Location	Holiday Type
12–16, 16–18	South Normandy	French Language
14–16, 16–18	South Normandy	House Party
12–16, 16–18	Brive, Dordogne	Multi-activity
12–16, 16–18	Brive, Dordogne	Riding and Trekking
10–14	Hardelot, Nr Boulogne	Multi-activity
12–16, 16–18	Mediterranean	Watersports
16–18	Mediterranean	Lifeguarding
12–16, 16–18	2 Centres, Ardeche and Mediterranean	Watersports
14–18	Embrun, French Alps	Multi-activity

All holidays include care and tuition by well-trained staff, use of specialist equipment and clothing, evening entertainments and full board accommodation.

The adventure centres and activities requires the professional help of 100 Head Office staff. The company also own the Alton Court head office complex which includes over 100 000 cubic feet of warehouse capacity for its storage of all the specialist equipment required for the organization of the holidays.

PGL Travel Limited is recognized by major activity organizations including the Royal Yachting Association and the British Canoe Union.

Pricing policy

The prices for the holidays for the 1997 season are shown in Exhibit 1.2. Prices for the holidays are inclusive and incorporate all food, accommodation and activities.

Accommodation on the holidays ranges from tents to dormitories according to the location and customer requirements.

Exhibit 1.2   Prices for PGL Activity Holidays for children and teenagers – 1997 season

- UK   Weeks from £209
- Overseas holidays   Weeks from £249
- UK   4 nights from £149
- UK   3 nights from £99
- UK   Weekends from £79

Source: PGL Travel Limited

Customers of PGL Travel Limited

The holidays are designed for young people aged 6–18 years inclusive. Customers can choose a range of holidays designed for different age ranges. These include holidays designed for the 6–9, 8–11 and 11–13 year-old age groups. The activities on offer are geared to this particular age group. The

---

Exhibit 1.3   Age of UK guests 1996 season

Age	%
6	2
7	4
8	8
9	11
10	12
11	12
12	14
13	12
14	11
15	8
16	6
17	1
18	1

Source: PGL Travel Limited

young people who go on the holidays are often experiencing time spent away from their families for the first time. This means that the safety and security of the young people is a major priority for the company and these aspects are stressed in the promotional literature for the holidays. The ages of the UK guests for the 1996 season are shown in Exhibit 1.3.

The young people who go on a PGL holiday gain many experiences from their time at the centre. They may be away from home for the first time and

---

Exhibit 1.4   Comments on PGL holidays, 1996

The staff laughed and smiled 24 hours a day!'

'When Matthew met us at the end of his holiday he was wearing a wall-to-wall grin!'

'The first thing Anthony said as he got off the coach was "Sorry I didn't send you a postcard, but I was having too much fun to stop and write it!"'

'Jonathan returned from his holiday over a fortnight ago and is still talking about it – that sums up the experience!'

'If your brother or sister is driving you up the wall, go to PGL – and get away from it all!'

'I'm completely gobsmacked! I loved it and I want to come back!'

'Non-stop fun, from start to finish!'

'Yet again, PGL has succeeded in giving my teenagers an excellent week!'

'Going away on her own wasn't a problem – everyone was so friendly she settled in straight away!'

'Buckets and spades have obviously been replaced by adventure and activities!'

'PGL is a great "Kids only" holiday where you can meet millions of new friends.'

'Congratulations on a very professional organisation. Please give all your staff my thanks.'

'Not a minute went by when I was not having fun. Watch out – I'll be back!'

'It's the ultimate fun experience – Why can't it be next summer already?'

Source: PGL Travel Limited

are learning about leading a more independent life. They may be looking for excitement and adventure in a range of different activities. They may also be looking for new friends and new experiences. Some of the comments which were made by young people who went on PGL holidays during the 1996 season are shown in Exhibit 1.4.

It is the parents of the young people who are the purchasers of the holidays. PGL Travel Limited commissioned a piece of market research in 1994 to discover the type of people who purchase their holidays. This market research was carried out by ICD Marketing Services and provided a full customer and prospect profile analysis for the company. ICD Marketing Services distributes consumer questionnaires throughout the UK and from these it gathers information relevant to their clients.

Customers of ICD Marketing Services can select their own particular information from a series of sources including the National Consumer Database which has information on 38.5 million individuals and/or 22 million households; the British Investors Database which has 6.1 million shareholders; and the Lifestyle Database which is a survey carried out by ICD Marketing Services. The ICD Marketing Services research is designed to help clients improve their sales, usually by direct marketing methods.

The National Lifestyle Report includes information on over 3 million individuals in the UK. The report covers a number of elements including:

● Maps – These show the postal area and TV area distribution of the client's present database and of the prospective target. This can have important implications for integrated national or regional campaigns.
● Lifestyle Cell Clusters – Use Principal Component Analysis and Cluster Analysis to allow the client to arrange individuals into groups which can then be targeted. The Lifestyle Database incorporates 100 different cell clusters utilizing the most significant lifestyle and demographic characteristics available. The numbers of individuals on the client's database is compared to the percentage on the Lifestyle Database to produce a Prospect Index. The logic behind this research is that individuals with similar lifestyle characteristics have similar purchasing intentions. The upper cell ranking comprises those prospects that fit the target best, and these can then be used to generate complex address details for the client.

The results of the survey carried out by ICD Marketing Services for PGL Travel Limited revealed some interesting facts about the customers for their holidays and prospective groups to target. Details of these are shown in Exhibit 1.5.

It can be seen from this research that the customers for PGL holidays are largely from the ABC1 socio-economic groups. They are professional people who read the quality newspapers and have a relatively high standard of living. They live in a good standard of owner-occupied accommodation and often own more than one car.

Information on products sold by PGL Travel Limited in the 1996 season is shown in Exhibit 1.6.

Exhibit 1.5   Lifestyle summary of the PGL customer

- Occupation — Director, Manager, Professional people, self employed, doctors, teachers, other professionals and housewives are particular targets
- Gender — More females than males
- Marital Status — Married people are the predominant group
- Newspaper Readership — *Daily Telegraph, Daily Mail, Sunday Times, Guardian* readers
- Age — 35–54 years is the predominant age group
- Number of Children — 2 children is most common followed by 1 child and 3 children, in that order
- Age of Children — Age 11–15 and Age 5–10 are the most important age groups
- Home Ownership — Most of the customers are owner occupiers
- Property Types — Over half of the customers live in detached houses. The rest live mainly in semi-detached or terraced properties
- House Price — The customers live in houses from a range of price brackets. A particular target in the range £100K to £500K was identified by the research
- Household Income — Household income was found to be predominantly in the £20 000 plus bracket. A particular target was in the £40 000 plus bracket.
- Hobbies and Interests — Customers were found to have a wide range of hobbies and interests. Particular reference was made to:
  - Further Education
  - Gardening
  - Theatre and Arts
  - Wines
  - Watching Videos
- The most popular sporting activities included:
  - Swimming
  - Aerobics/Keep Fit
  - Badminton/Squash
  - Tennis
  - Cycling
- Credit Cards/Bank Accounts — Most of the customers were found to have bank accounts.
  A high proportion also had credit cards and store cards.
- Holidays and Travel — A high proportion of the customers were found to holiday in the UK. Locations in decreasing order were shown to be:
  - The UK
  - Other European
  - Canada
  - Africa
  - Asia/Far East
  - Australia/New Zealand
- Over half of the holidays are taken as weekend or short breaks. Self catering package holidays, or villa holidays are also popular.
- Car Ownership — Over half of the customers own 2 cars, with saloons and estates being the most popular makes.
- Residence — Customers from the Central and Southern half of England were found to be of particular importance.

Source: Research report by ICD Marketing Services for PGL Travel Limited, 1996

Exhibit 1.6   Holiday sales information for the 1996 season

- Numbers of holidays sold   16 500
- UK 87%,   France 13%
- UK split as follows:
  - Multi-activity 68%
  - Motorsport 7%
  - Trekking 6%
  - Other Specialist 19%
- Duration 89% – one week or more
- Overseas guests accounted for 10% of total
- Previous guests accounted for 50% of sales, 20% are recommended by previous guests, and 30% are new guests
- 48% of guests went on their own, 43% went with one friend or sibling, 9% went in a group of 3 or more

---

Source: PGL Travel Limited

Promotion of PGL holidays

The promotional strategy of PGL has helped to sustain the company as the market leader in the activity holidays market. A loyal following of party leaders and children has been built up through an emphasis on quality, safety and value for money, all of which are highlighted in the promotional literature.

PGL focuses on five methods in their communication mix:

- direct mail
- personal selling
- advertising
- public relations
- word of mouth.

The mix of communication methods used is amended according to the product and the effectiveness of each tool relative to the market. Advertising, for example, is more effective for the marketing of holidays aimed at the individual unaccompanied child.

Direct mail

Direct mail is the most cost-effective method of promotion which PGL uses in its communication strategy. It has enabled the company to target their customers accurately and assess qualitatively the success of different campaigns. PGL has developed a central database which has been maintained and enlarged to encompass all existing customers and enquiries. This is used in conjunction with purchased mailing lists. The company uses brochures, newsletters and videos within their direct mail campaign.

The PGL Activity Holidays brochure is a very important part of this direct mail communication activity.

The 1997 PGL Activity Holidays brochure divides its potential customers into three groups, based on their age, and targets a different message at each group, as follows:

Age 6–9   where the sales message uses 'get away from home for the first time'

Age 8–13   with the slogan 'make new friends with children from all over the country'

Age 12–18 where the persuasive message is, 'non-stop action and enjoyment – day and night!'

These slogans reflect the company's perceptions of what children in each age group are looking for on an activity holiday. The brochure also includes the comments of young people who have previously taken PGL holidays.

PGL is a good example of the distinction between consumers and customers in tourism. The young people are the consumers; in other words, they are the people who actively use or consume the holiday product. On the other hand, their parents are the customers in that it is they who pay the bill and have to give their permission for their children to take a PGL holiday.

PGL seeks to promote its product to parents by emphasizing certain aspects of its operation, including:

● it has '40 years' experience of activity holidays
● its staff are 'carefully selected and trained'
● its centres are 'subject to independent inspection by the new Activities Licensing Authority or the British Activity Holiday Association'
● equipment used 'meets all the latest British and European safety standards'
● a good 'staff to child ratio'.

In other words, the sales messages are exciting and offer new experiences for the young consumers, and emphasize safety and reliability for their parents, the company's customers.

Personal selling

PGL has built up a team of Group Travel Advisers who promote products to schools and build up a personal rapport with party leaders. These advisers provide the 'human face' of the organization since the rest of the booking is carried out by telephone or correspondence.

Advertising

Advertising is used in certain circumstances by the company. It is mainly used in conjunction with individual holidays for children and teenagers.

PGL adverts are used in quality Sunday newspapers and supplements, educational supplements, and children's publications.

Public relations

Public relations activities take the form of press releases, advertisements in newspapers and magazines, newsletters, and the provision of holidays for competition prizes. PGL also encourages journalists to send their children on their holidays. In addition, the company works closely with the community close to their centres and supports local fêtes and sporting events.

Word of mouth

Word of mouth is considered to be the most powerful promotional tool for PGL and the company actively encourages positive word of mouth by rewarding existing customers when they introduce a new school or individual to PGL.

Conclusion

PGL Travel Limited have been developing their product to meet the growing interest in holidays for young people wanting to experience quality time away from their families. They offer well-run and secure holiday centres which are staffed by experts in their field. This gives the parents the security of knowing that their children will be looked after in an appropriate environment. For the children, PGL offers exciting adventures and new experiences. Many of the children who go on a PGL holiday can't wait to go back for their next one!

Discussion points and essay questions

1 Evaluate the role of safety in the choice of outdoor pursuits by parents for children.
2 'Buckets and spades have been replaced by adventure and activities'. Explain the reasons for the change in the type of holidays which young people are demanding.

Case study 2
Flying Colours Holidays Limited –
Club 18–30

Introduction

The Club 18–30 brand is owned by Flying Colours Holidays Limited. The Club 18–30 unique holiday formula has remained more or less unchanged over the years and provides holidays for this specific age group of customers to the liveliest resorts in the central locations of major holiday regions. The company currently offers holidays to 14 destinations across the Mediterranean and the Canaries, and flies from eight UK airports. The company has recently modified their product offering and the summer programme is now the only one on offer.

History of the development of the Club 18–30 brand

Club 18–30 has been in existence for over 30 years, and was the first holiday company in the UK to specialize in holidays exclusively for young people. Club 18–30 was, more recently, part of the International Leisure Group (ILG) which collapsed in 1991. The collapse of ILG forced Club 18–30 into voluntary liquidation, despite the fact that it had been a profit-making division.

Five weeks after the collapse, the existing directors of Club 18–30 bought the trade name and re-formed the company. This move received enormous support from the travel, trade and overseas suppliers. The company was prevented from trading under the Club 18–30 name due to ABTA legislation, and hence the re-formed company became known as The Club.

The Club has witnessed enormous growth since 1991 from a small tour operator to a top-ten UK operator. ABTA granted the company permission to trade under the original branding, Club 18–30, in August 1994, and so The Club reverted back to the original name.

The authors would like to thank Clare Burns of Flying Colours Holidays Limited, Club 18–30, for her help in writing this case study.

Flying Colours Holidays Limited are the current owners of the Club 18–30 brand. This company was formed in November 1995 and was backed by a £40 million deal in which a major family tour operator, Sunset Holidays, and Club 18–30, were bought. The management team of Flying Colours Holidays Limited has extensive breadth and depth and was headed until March 1997 by Jeremy Muller, who was formerly Managing Director of Club 18–30. It is now headed by Rosemary Astles, former Marketing Director of Thomson.

The business of Flying Colours Holidays Limited in 1997

Flying Colours Holidays Limited aims to drive ambitious growth through successful market segmentation and positioning. The success of Sunset and Club 18–30 show that well-targeted products using a portfolio of differentiated travel products can provide a successful business strategy in the competitive holiday market. The formation of Flying Colours Holidays Limited has been recognized as a dynamic response to the conservatism which has typified the UK market for overseas holidays.

Club 18–30 carried over 100 000 passengers in 1995. Some facts and figures about Club 18–30 are shown in Exhibit 2.1.

Exhibit 2.1   Club 18–30 facts and figures

Club 18–30 is the market leader in overseas summer sun based youth holidays with a market share in excess of 60%.

More than 100 000 passengers were carried in 1995.

The product is highly respected in the travel trade, and available from over 6000 travel agents. The product is racked and recommended in more than 4000 agents.

Regional flying from eight airports ensures high profile image is maintained throughout the UK.

Constant evaluation of resorts ensures that only the most 'happening' of places makes it into the company brochure.

Over 5000 applications are received annually for jobs as Clubreps. Less than 100 new Clubreps are required.

Source: Flying Colours Holidays Limited

The Club 18–30 holiday concept

The Club 18–30 holiday formula is unique, and has remained unchanged over the years of development. Flying Colours Holidays Limited concentrates on attracting clients in the 18–30 year-old age bracket. Club 18–30 contracts hotels and apartments in the liveliest resorts and in central locations. The Club 18–30 accommodation is usually exclusive to the company's clients because it was recognized many years ago that it was preferable for the clients to have their own separate facilities and accommodation.

The holidays are marketed as 'a fortnight of Saturday nights', and entertainment is available 24-hours a day, seven-days a week. Club 18–30 also offers its clients a range of unique excursions, and Clubreps help make up an unrivalled fun holiday experience for their clients.

Club 18–30 currently visits 15 destinations across the Mediterranean, the Canaries and Florida, and flies from eight airports, offering their summer programme. More details of the Club 18–30 portfolio of products on offer are shown in Exhibit 2.2.

Exhibit 2.2   The Club 18–30 product range – Summer 1997

- Ibiza   – San Antonio
- Majorca   – Magaluf
                       Palma Nova
                       Arenal
- Tenerife   – Playa de las Americas
- Gran Canaria   – Play del Ingles
- Costa Brava   – Lloret de Mar
- Costa Blanca   – Benidorm
- Turkey   – Bodrum
                    – Marmaris
- Cyprus   – Ayia Napa
- Corfu   – Kavos
- Crete   – Malia
- Rhodes   – Faliraki
- Zante   – Laganas
- Kos   – Kardamena

Source: Club 18–30 brochure, 1997

The company has selected resorts in an attempt to put together a Mediterranean party scene. They have chosen the best resorts that stay awake 24 hours a day and have selected accommodation that is near to the centre of action.

San Antonio, in Ibiza, has been selected because it is well known as the dance capital of Europe and the area offers blue zone beaches.

The twin funspots of Magaluf and Palma Nova on Majorca have been selected for their range of bars, lots of pubs, English food and night-clubs. Benidorm and Lloret de Mar on mainland Spain offer good beaches, excellent nightlife and stylish atmospheres. Resorts on Gran Canaria and Tenerife have been selected for their bars, disco bars and clubs. Bodrum and Marmaris in Turkey are well known for their small streets and trendy nightlife. Resorts on the Greek Islands of Corfu, Crete and Rhodes have been selected for their around the clock entertainment.

The Club 18–30 concept is shown in Exhibit 2.3.

The beach and pool are the main focal points of daytime activity with a suntan the priority for most clients on a Club 18–30 holiday. The main action of the holiday, however, starts after dark. The resorts which the company

---

Exhibit 2.3   The Club 18–30 concept

It's about being young, acting young, and living young with a great bunch of ready made mates even if you bring your own. It's about staying out late, sleeping as long as you like, dressing up, dressing down, looking tanned, feeling great, being in the thick of the action and having action all around.

Look, basically it's **A FORTNIGHT OF SATURDAY NIGHTS but no Monday mornings.**

- OK – so we don't visit the Roman ruins and pretend to be interested in botanical gardens.
- But we do give you the wickedest time of your life. And when's the best time of your life to be wicked?
- **RIGHT NOW**
- Pity some people are just too old or grey to grab a piece of the action.

Source: Flying Colours Club 18–30 holiday brochure

picks, have a good variety of local colour and generally have two or three major venues or attractions close at hand. The clients prefer to stay in self-catering or bed and breakfast accommodation, and so the company ensures that there is a good selection of well-priced restaurants and cafés close to the accommodation.

The Clubrep is an important aspect of the Club 18–30 holiday. He or she will be with the clients pretty well around the clock and will act as a party organizer, personally taking the clients to the best bars and nightspots. The ratio of Clubrep to clients is 1:25 because he or she is a social catalyst and the client's best friend. Many of the clients are travelling abroad for the first time, so the Clubrep provides a vital role in making sure the clients have an enjoyable time.

The final aspect of the Club 18–30 holiday is the programme of 'Days 'N' Nights' which give clients the chance to get out and see some of the local sights. These trips include such things as barbecues, beach parties, cruises and trips to local attractions, Clubrep's cabaret and night-clubs by night. The company generally offers eight trips over a two-week period, which are keenly priced and include food and drinks.

Competitors of Club 18–30

Club 18–30 is the original mainstream holiday product targeting this market segment. There is another major company in the UK that specializes in young people's holidays – 'Twenty's', which is owned by First Choice Holidays and Flights. This company carries less than half the passengers of Club 18–30 (at the time of writing). Other holiday companies offer holidays for young people within a broader portfolio of products.

The Club 18–30 client

A summary profile of the Club 18–30 client is shown in Exhibit 2.4.

The predominant age range for clients is 18–26, with an average age of 21–22. Lower age limits are enforced fairly stringently, but the upper limits are fairly vague. If a client feels that the holiday would be suited to them, even if they are older, then they are welcome to go on the holidays. The company has a record of customers coming back, year after year, and some female clients even bring their mothers with them.

Exhibit 2.4   The Club 18–30 client

Average age:	21–22
Male : female ratio:	50 : 50
Socio-economic group:	C1/C2/D
Marital status:	Single
Lifestyle:	In fulltime employment
	Resident in parental home
	Influenced by fashion, music, dance and entertainment (their spending patterns reflect this)
	An 18–30 holiday is usually their first holiday abroad with friends, but without parents

---

Source: Flying Colours Holidays Limited

The male to female ratio is generally 50:50, but varies between 40:60 and 60:40. This is partly due to price as female clients tend to go when it is cheaper, and it is also fashionable for them to get an early suntan in May or June. Most of the clients go on a Club 18–30 holiday with a friend of the same sex. In low season, the average number of people per booking is two. In high season, this rises to three or four with groups of friends sharing apartments.

Most of the clients are fully employed and live at home with their parents. They are single and from socio-economic groups C1, C2 or D. The clients are quite loyal to the product over time and 50 per cent repeat book each year. Clients take two to three holidays with Club 18–30 on average.

Many clients experience their first holiday abroad with Club 18–30. It is a common trend for clients to progress from Spain or the Balearic Islands in year 1, to the Greek Islands or Turkey in year 2, and then the Canaries or Cyprus in year 3. This behaviour reflects a 'trading up' in price.

A unique feature of Club 18–30 clients are the reunions which are held in the UK in November and March. These infamous events are in effect the largest private parties in the world, with up to 10 000 guests getting back together, determined to relive their two weeks' worth of summer holidays, in two weekends.

The advertising campaign

The Saatchi and Saatchi Advertising agency, London, were appointed by Club 18–30 in October 1994 to handle the advertising campaign for the brand. The campaign objectives set by Club 18–30 were to increase bookings for Summer 1995, raise the awareness of the Club 18–30 brand name, and accurately to reflect the nature of Club 18–30 holidays to the appropriate target market.

The campaign that the advertising agency developed, highlighted the fun of a Club 18–30 holiday in a 'tongue in cheek' way. It was designed to speak to the target market (17–25 year olds) via their type of media (48-sheet posters) and in their style of language.

The advertising agency designed a series of posters which incorporated controversial and suggestive statements which were designed to appeal to the target audience. Examples of the poster copy is shown in Exhibit 2.5.

Exhibit 2.5   The 1995 Club 18–30 poster campaign poster copy

'It's not all sex, sex, sex'

'Girls. Can we interest you in a package holiday?'

'It's advisable not to drink the local water. As if . . .'

'Beaver España'

'You get two weeks for being drunk and disorderly'

'Discover your erogenous zone'

'The summer of '69'

Source: Flying Colours Holidays Limited

The initial campaign spend was £250 000, which allowed the company to concentrate a month-long, medium-weight campaign around the area where there was potential for growth. The campaign was nationwide, other than Scotland and London, and was particularly concentrated in catchment areas of regional airports, such as Newcastle, Manchester, Birmingham, East Midlands, Cardiff, Belfast and Bristol. The posters were placed in major town centres where the largest population of young people in the 18–30 age range live and work. Research showed that the target group found the poster campaign humorous and appealing. The campaign also portrayed the products in a true light and consciously discouraged families, and other groups of people who would not enjoy this type of holiday, from booking a Club 18–30 holiday.

The campaign commenced in January 1995, and for the 1995 season Club 18–30 enjoyed record bookings which were 30 per cent higher than the previous year.

The company decided to run an amended version of the campaign in 1996. There had been criticism of the campaign and the Advertising

Standards Authority (ASA) insisted that the Club 18–30 campaign should be vetted by themselves before it was run. The company decided to run a 48-sheet billboard campaign along the lines of the previous 'Jolly Japes' campaign, but the posters urged the reader to look for the real advertisements in magazines such as *Sky, Loaded* and *Company*. These magazines were chosen because they are read by the target audience. It also allowed the company to design press advertisements that were much more explicit, but similar to the first campaign. The awareness and public relations gained from this campaign made an essentially small budget work very hard. The advertising campaign must continue to make sure that the product remains at the forefront of youth culture. The brochure, which is produced on an annual basis, is a major part of this.

The 1997 brochure was designed with this in mind, and it has a strong emphasis on style and fun. It has caused comment in the trade since it was launched. The brochure uses 'Flo' and her 'pensioner pals' to introduce the products and it was designed to be humorous, but informative. The brochure also incorporates advertisements for other companies that sell products targeted at the same market segment.

The company has been criticised for their product range and their controversial advertising campaigns by some pressure groups, in the light of HIV and AIDS. The company decided to take positive action about this and, although they did not consider themselves as moral guardians, they thought it would be sensible to reiterate the 'safe sex' message wherever possible. Young people in the 1990s have been the first group to benefit from the Government Health Authority's advice on sex education. Club 18–30 have recognized that young people may have sex on holiday, and for that reason, the company has reacted positively to the Government Health Education Authority's initiative of 1991, which asked travel companies to help educate young travellers in the dangers of casual sex overseas. Club 18–30 has included information on safe sex and protection within every ticket wallet since 1991. The company will also provide confidential supplies of condoms to clients for their Club 18–30 holiday.

The Government Health Education Authority is seeking to address the problem of Drug Abuse amongst young people in 1997. Club 18–30 has responded accordingly and will be offering realistic advice on drugs and the laws governing their use overseas to clients before they travel.

A statement by the Club 18–30 Managing Director, Stuart Howard, in February 1996 emphasized the point.

We believe it is important to be proactive on these issues. Everybody knows that holidays are a time of romance and excitement, and we have 30 years of experience in dealing with this. Condoms are not as reliably available in many Mediterranean resorts, as they are here. Drugs, unfortunately are widely available everywhere. Although we have no wish to set ourselves up as moral guardians, we believe that it is only responsible to take up these initiatives on our client's behalf.

Club 18–30 is the only tour operator currently to respond positively to the Government Health Education Authority's initiative on drugs.

Conclusion

Club 18–30 is one of the best examples of a UK company which has aggressively targeted a particular market segment and positioned their products to suit the behaviour patterns of their clients. The company has repeatedly targeted the clients with effective and eye-catching advertising which has been controversial enough to attract substantial media attention. The company has also reacted positively to the Government Health Education Authority's campaigns on safe sex and drug abuse. This has meant that the company is seen to be acting positively for their clients in the face of major health concerns.

Discussion points and essay questions

1 Discuss the ways in which Club 18–30 has been very effective in designing holidays to suit the lifestyle of their target clients.
2 Explore the dilemma which a company such as Club 18–30 can find itself in when it is trying to design effective and appealing advertising campaigns without offending society at large. Discuss the ways in which Club 18–30 has overcome this potential problem.

Case study 3
The segmentation of the outbound Japanese market

The Japanese tourists are one of the classic stereotypes of the tourism world. Yet, it is still a market which is little understood by many businesses wishing to attract Japanese tourists.

For those accustomed to the Western European and North American markets, the Japanese market has very different characteristics based on Japanese culture.

Dace (1995) and other authors have identified a number of segments in the Japanese market, including:

- Working Soldiers. Male managers in the 30–50 age group, who have difficulty in finding time for a vacation because of their work commitments. They appear to want to enjoy 'meaningful experiences rather than just visual tours' (Beecham, quoted in Dace, 1995). They are also enthusiastic, discerning shoppers.
- The Silver Greys. 50–60 year olds who have been influenced by growing up in the era of post-war austerity in Japan. They live frugal lives but when on vacation they like to 'let themselves go'. However, they want the familiar when on holiday, including Japanese food and guides who speak their language.
- The Full Mooners. Mature married couples who prefer to take single centre holidays, and are very quality-conscious.
- Technical Visits and Study Tours. Japanese companies use work-related study tours as a way of recruiting and rewarding staff. Most such tourists are men and many such trips are combined with leisure pursuits such as golf.
- Student Travel. School, college and university students take, generally short duration, trips, most popularly in February. They tend to book flights and accommodation only packages.

The authors are pleased to acknowledge that the segments outlined here are based on those outlined in the article by Roger Dace (1995).

- The Young Affluent or Shinginsi. This is a 20–30 year-old segment which has grown up in a period of affluence in Japan. They like to flaunt their money and are independently minded. They rarely take packaged vacations and are major participants in the short break and activity holiday market.
- The Office Ladies. These are unmarried women in their early 20s. They have high disposable income and they tend to be living at home with their parents. They like Western countries and enjoy visiting capital cities like Paris and London, and shopping. They like organized tours although there is a trend towards more independent travel.
- The Honeymooners. A segment defined by the fact that it goes overseas for its honeymoon. This is true for as many as 95 per cent of Japanese couples (Beecham, quoted in Dace, 1995) who choose Asian destinations, European cities or places in the USA.

The Japanese market does have a controversial dimension in terms of:

- the demand of some Japanese tourists that their destinations should offer Japanese food, service, guides and so on. This can alienate some local communities, as has been seen on the Queensland coast in Australia, for example
- Japanese male tourists are a significant proportion of the sex tourism market in many Asian destinations.

Conclusion

The Japanese market example shows that national markets need to be segmented in different ways which reflect the culture of the country in question.

Discussion points and essay questions

1 Compare and contrast the segments of the Japanese market identified by Dace (1995) with those found in the UK market.
2 Discuss the implications of Dace's (1995) segmentation of the Japanese market for UK hoteliers wishing to attract more Japanese customers.

Case study 4
The Savoy Group of hotels

Introduction

The Savoy Group is a group of hotels and restaurants, most of which are located in London, England. The Savoy Group has played host to eminent men and women and provided the setting for glittering social occasions for over a century.

The company was founded in the late 1800s by Richard D'Oyly Carte, the theatrical impresario who founded the Savoy Theatre, and realized that people visiting the theatre also wanted somewhere to stay. The Savoy Hotel was built with every luxury in mind.

The Group today manages a portfolio of hotels and restaurants and is working hard to become known as 'England's most distinguished and individual Hotels and Restaurants'.

The Savoy Group is a public limited company, trading under the name of The Savoy Hotel Plc.

The Savoy Group in 1997

The Savoy Group of hotels and restaurants are located in London. The company also owns The Lygon Arms in Broadway, in the Cotswolds. A full list of the Group is shown in Exhibit 4.1.

The hotels in the Group are represented by 'The Leading Hotels of the World' group. In 1995, the Group embarked on a major programme of work to re-establish itself as the world's leading luxury hotel chain. This programme of work has involved a major period of refurbishment which has tried to maintain the old charm of the hotels, but introduce new comfort and facilities. The programme has also involved an extensive programme of management restructuring and training and new approaches to sales and marketing.

A range of prices for the Savoy and Claridge's is shown in Exhibit 4.2.

The authors would like to thank Beth Aarons of the Savoy Group for her help in the writing of this case study.

Exhibit 4.1   The Savoy Group of hotels and restaurants

THE BERKELEY, Wilton Place, Knightsbridge, London SW1X 7RL
Tel: 0171 235 6000

CLARIDGE'S, Brook Street, Mayfair, London W1A 2JQ
Tel: 0171 629 8860

THE CONNAUGHT, Carlos Place, Mayfair, London W1Y 6AL
Tel: 0171 499 7070

THE SAVOY, The Strand, London WC2R 0EU
Tel: 0171 836 4343

THE LYGON ARMS, Broadway, Worcestershire WR12 7DU
Tel: 01386 852255

SIMPSON'S IN THE STRAND, 100 Strand, London WC2R 0EW
Tel: 0171 836 9112

EDWARD GOODYEAR Court Florist, 45 Brook Street, London W1A 2JQ
Tel: 0171 629 1508

SAVOY THEATRE, The Strand, London WC2R 0ET
Tel: 0171 836 8888

Source: The Savoy Group promotional literature

The hotel group distributes its product by using its sales office in London. The Group also employs a sales manager in New York. The Group has guest histories on a computerized system and can mailshot guests directly. The Group also distributes via travel agents, and is featured in selected holiday brochures. The hotels are part of 'The Leading Hotels of the World' group which acts as a distributor of luxury hotels throughout the world. The Group's hotels are visited by customers from the UK, Europe, the Far East, USA and world-wide.

Financial highlights of the Group

The Savoy Group went through a very difficult financial position in the 1990s. This poor financial performance was accompanied by low occupancy rates, and poor general performance. The new Managing Director, Ramón Pajares, was appointed in 1994 with the specific aim of re-establishing the company into a profitable and successful business. The financial performance of the Group has improved steadily since this period. The turnover for the Group increased to £92m in 1995, but the operating profit increased dramatically from £4.7m in 1994 to £12.0m in 1995.

A summary of the financial performance of the Group is shown in Exhibit 4.3.

Exhibit 4.2 Prices for the Savoy and Claridge's

| | Single | Double or Twin | | Junior or Studio Suite | One-bedroomed Suite | Two-bedroomed Suite |
		1 person	2 persons			
LONDON:						
CLARIDGE'S						
Standard	£210	–	–	£410	From £580 to £680	–
Superior	–	£255	£280	–	–	–
De luxe	£245	£290	£315	–	£1600 (Penthouse suite)	£2100 (Penthouse suite)
Executive De luxe	–	£305	£330	–	From £1050 to £1300 (Royal suites)	–
THE SAVOY						
Standard	£210	–	–	–	From £460	From £740
Superior	–	From £255	From £280	From £360	£550	From £1000 (River view)
De luxe	£235	From £305 (River view)	From £330 (River view)	–	From £675 (River view)	–

Source: The Savoy Group promotional literature, 1997

Exhibit 4.3　Summary of the financial performance of the Group

		1995 £'000	1994 £'000
Turnover		91 978	87 266
Operating profit		12 027	4 661
Profit before tax		11 546	4 437
Profit for the financial year		7 876	3 340
Dividend		4 006	2 003
Key ratios	Operating margin	13.1	5.3
Earnings per share	A Ordinary Shares of 10p each	27.5p	11.7p
	B Ordinary Shares of 5p each	13.8p	5.8p
Dividends per share	A Ordinary Shares of 10p each	14.0p	7.0p
	B Ordinary Shares of 5p each	7.0p	3.5p

Turnover £m		Operating profit £m	
1995	92.0	1995	12.0
1994	87.3	1994	4.7
1993	78.2	1993	2.4

Profit before tax £m		Dividend £m	
1995	11.5	1995	4.0
1994	4.4	1994	2.0
1993	1.7	1993	1.0

Source: The Savoy Hotel Plc annual report and accounts, 1995

A brief history of the Savoy Group

The Savoy Hotel was built by the theatrical impresario Richard D'Oyly Carte. He had built the first theatre in the world with electric lights – The Savoy Theatre – in 1881, and proceeded to commission operettas. Gilbert and Sullivan wrote the operetta *Trial by Jury* ' for Richard D'Oyly Carte, and it proved to be an instant smash hit when it was staged at the theatre.

Richard D'Oyly Carte began to realize that theatre customers often needed overnight accommodation, and in 1885 he started to resurrect the Savoy Hotel on the banks of the River Thames. He recognized that he needed people with considerable talent to run the hotel. He brought César Ritz from Switzerland and Escoffier from France to convert the cooking at the Savoy to an art form. Society flocked to the new creation, to try out the new dishes and soak up the luxurious ambience. The Savoy has been at the heart of the arts in London for over a century. It continues to be the home of leading artists and is a meeting place for journalists, captains of industry and politicians.

D'Oyly Carte quickly decided to expand his interest in hotels, and refurbished Claridge's in Mayfair in 1899. It opened with a flourish and soon became a favourite hotel with royalty. Heads of State and royalty have stayed in the hotel ever since.

The Connaught was built in 1897 and rapidly became the hotel for the landed gentry. D'Oyly Carte also purchased The Berkeley, which was located in Piccadilly. The area started to change after the Second World War, and the Managing Director, Hugh Wontner, was commissioned to seek out a new site for this hotel. Land was found in Belgravia, a very elegant part of London, and the hotel was finally opened in 1972. The Berkeley has become a popular location for social, diplomatic and business gatherings.

The Group also purchased The Lygon Arms in the Cotswolds, and Simpson's in the Strand, London.

A profile of Ramón Pajares – the Managing Director

There have only been five Managing Directors of the Savoy Group since 1889. Ramón Pajares was appointed on 7 November 1994 after a long and distinguished career in the hospitality industry. He had worked for The Four Seasons Hotel, London, in various capacities, finishing as Vice-President Europe for Four Seasons Regent Hotels and Resorts, before his appointment to the Savoy Group.

He was appointed to his role of Managing Director at a difficult time for the Savoy Group. The company was having an extremely bad financial period, due to poor occupancy levels and deteriorating image. He commented extensively about the challenges facing him on his appointment, as follows:

The Savoy Group's collection of hotels and restaurants has always epitomised excellence in service, style, elegance, and cuisine. The combination of the rich history, and the distinguished cast list of guests and staff make it unique. It has also encouraged and trained thousands of young, career-minded people – indeed, it is a 'school' for learning to delivery quality of service.

We have always been at the very heart of innovation, a characteristic of The Savoy Group, and I am delighted to be in a position to help continue this tradition. I enjoy working with the staff, maintaining the existing high standards and enhancing them where appropriate. In this industry, the hotel business and the needs of our guests are constantly evolving, and our job is to make sure that we keep abreast of every change.

We aim to offer the best of both worlds – maintaining respect for the past and an understanding of the future. We have the very latest in technology and efficiency, giving modern comfort, which is combined with the original interiors and traditional standards of service.

The Savoy Hotel plc comprises a group of luxury hotels that is independent and answerable only to its Board of Directors. The Group's key objective is to maintain all the elements of style and service that have made it famous and envied throughout the world.

Customers of the London hotels in the Group

The customers of Claridge's and The Savoy have a differing profile. This is largely due to the history of the hotels and how they have been developed to attract different market segments.

A profile of the customer for both these hotels is shown in Exhibit 4.4. It can be seen from this exhibit that the customers of Claridge's come from high socio-economic groups from the UK and worldwide. The hotel is particularly appealing to royalty, special celebrities and major corporate clients.

Exhibit 4.4   Customers at the Savoy Group hotels

- Claridge's   60% UK   40% Worldwide
                     50% Male   50% Female
                     A/B Socio-Economic Group

  Special Groups – Royalty
                   Special Celebrities
                   Impresarios
                   Film Producers
                   Major Corporate Clients

- The Savoy   60% UK   40% Worldwide
                     66% business travellers 34% leisure guests

  Business travellers   70% male   30% female
  Visitors from the US   50% male   50% female

  A/B Socio-Economic Group   80% of visitors
  Special treat visitors   20% of visitors

  Far East important – 5% guests Japanese

  US, Australia, Europe, Far East important. Japan – emerging market

---

Source: The Savoy Group

The customers at the Savoy also originate from the UK and the rest of the world. There are a large proportion of guests at the Savoy who are there on business (50 per cent).

The guests come from a high socio-economic group (A, B) although a small percentage of guests are from lower socio-economic groups and are visiting the Savoy as a treat. This is very often tied to a visit to the Savoy Theatre.

One market which is growing in importance for the Savoy is the Far East and particularly Japan, which in 1997 only represented 5 per cent of visitors, but this percentage is growing rapidly.

The guests at both hotels are looking for high levels of individual service. Business guests are particularly looking for conference facilities, individual meeting rooms and business technology such as modems, DDI and ISDN lines, and voice-mail facilities. The challenge for the hotel has been the way in which to introduce this new technology, whilst still keeping the old traditional ambience of the hotel. Both hotels keep a comprehensive guest profile on their computers and rely on this information to provide requirements, particularly for repeat guests. If the guest has requested a special type of bed, for example, on their previous visit, this will be automatically provided for their subsequent visits.

The customer survey, 1995–1996

The Savoy Group carried out an extensive customer survey during 1995–1996. This survey was designed to investigate the reasons for the problems which the Group was having with regard to poor occupancy rates and poor profitability results.

This research revealed that guests had a poor image of the hotels and did not consider that the service within the hotels met their expectations. The research also revealed that the hotels were reliant on guests with 'old money', i.e. those who had inherited money from generations before. The hotel was failing to attract guests with 'new money', i.e. those who had made money recently from entrepreneurial activities.

The danger was that all the old clients would simply die in time, and, if the hotel failed to attract new guests with substantial amounts of money, profitability and occupancy levels would continue to suffer.

The research also revealed that guests coming from abroad who were looking to book a luxury hotel in London, would try to book other luxury hotels such as The Four Seasons, or the Hilton on Park Lane first, and then try to book The Savoy or Claridge's, if the others were full. This explained the poor occupancy levels, which were as low as 60 per cent in the early 1990s. It was clear that the Group had much to do in terms of refurbishment and image building for the individual hotels.

The renovation and relaunch

The Savoy Group, under the leadership of Ramón Pajares, began the painstaking process of restoring the hotels within the Group to be the most distinguished and individual hotels in England. The customer survey had noted some particular areas for attention such as general levels of comfort, improved business services and improved levels of personal service.

The Group spent £62 million in their refurbishment programme which is still proceeding in 1997. The project has affected all five hotels in the Group's portfolio and has combined careful restoration work with the installation of state of the art technology. New bedrooms, penthouse suites, luxurious fitness facilities, meeting rooms and modern business amenities have all been incorporated in the ambitious programme. The programme was controlled by Ramón Pajares and was summed up by his maxim:

respecting the past and understanding the future

The refurbishment programme at the Savoy and Claridge's is shown in Exhibit 4.5.

The Group has paid particular attention to the needs of the business executive in their refurbishment project. Business amenities and meeting rooms have been upgraded. The refurbished rooms incorporate ISDN lines,

---

Exhibit 4.5   The refurbishment programme at the Savoy and Claridge's

CLARIDGE'S

A London name to rank alongside Christie's, Harrods and the Victoria and Albert Museum, Claridge's has all the style, elegance and sophistication of an English stately home.

Business at the Top

A central element in the £32 million refurbishment programme at Claridge's has been the creation on the sixth floor of a self-contained conference suite, comprising four interconnecting meeting and dining rooms.

Olympian Fitness

Claridge's magnificent new health and fitness centre, The Olympus Suite, is ideally suited for the international traveller.

Seventh Heaven

Pride of place in Claridge's hotel-wide restoration programme is taken by the two new luxurious Penthouse suites, one traditional, one Art Deco style, and seven Art Deco de luxe double bedrooms on the seventh floor.

Double Award

In two separate readers' polls in 1996, Claridge's has been voted by *Travel & Leisure* magazine one of Europe's 25 best hotels and by *Institutional Investor* magazine, one of the world's 25 best hotels.

THE SAVOY

The Savoy is a London landmark whose history and location are entwined with the capital's vibrant cultural and commercial past. Rich, elegant and flamboyant, the hotel's unique atmosphere makes any visit an event in itself.

Restoring the Glory

The restoration of the famous Front Hall is just one element in an £18 million list of improvements which have brought a renewed sense of style to The Savoy.

Other public areas, including the American Bar, have been sympathetically restored to their former glory.

Big Business

The magnificent Abraham Lincoln and Manhattan meeting and banqueting rooms have been carefully restored to maintain their classical style whilst also incorporating the latest technology.

Past and Future

Guest rooms have been redecorated, their architectural features painstakingly restored and bathrooms throughout upgraded.

Style Vote

The Savoy's stylish interiors and elegance remain as popular as ever with readers of *Institutional Investor* and *Travel and Leisure* magazines, who voted it one of the world's 100 best hotels in their respective 1996 polls. It has just been named Egon Ronay's Hotel of the Year.

Source: The Savoy Group

video cameras, projection screens, high quality sound systems and sophisti-cated audio visual systems. Dual line telephone lines, dedicated fax lines and modem points have all been incorporated. The rooms have individually controlled air-conditioning systems, CD player and a CD library on demand, and the provision of US and European electrical points, voice mail and language facilities.

The refurbishment programme has been followed up with an extensive period of staff training and staff are attending an intensive customer service training programme. The Group is also putting a new focus on sales and marketing. The first stage of this has been to communicate the good news about the refurbishment programme across the world. The Group has established a web site and is travelling to cities around the world, including Tokyo, Singapore and Hong Kong to tell the trade about the dramatic improvements in the refurbished hotels.

The Group has reorganized the sales and marketing departments. Specialists have been appointed who have been given the responsibility of regaining market share by developing key geographic markets (UK, USA, Europe and Japan) and by focusing on individual business and leisure segments. It is hoped that this quality marketing will help to re-establish the company as the first choice for customers who are looking for a luxury hotel in London.

Conclusion

The Savoy Group has had to respond to demands from its guests to see improved facilities and services. The new Managing Director Ramón Pajares has initiated a major investment programme coupled with staff training programmes, and renewed sales and marketing effort to reverse the downward trend. The initial results of the programme of work indicates that it is successful. Particular emphasis has been put on the use of new technology, improve-ments in public rooms and leisure and business facilities.

The focus on particular market segments, designing products to suit their needs and wants, and communicating these develop-ments to them has been a major part of the strategy.

Discussion points and essay questions

1 The restoration programme at The Savoy Group has been based on the maxim of: 'respecting the past and understanding the future'. Discuss the importance of this statement, in relation to the needs and wants of the customers of The Savoy and Claridge's.

2 The Savoy Group carried out marketing research with guests to inform their refurbishment programme. Prepare a detailed plan of the marketing research programme which you would carry out for the Savoy and Claridge's prior to this programme. Suggest an ongoing programme of marketing research with guests which you would implement at the hotels.

Case study 5
Cathay Pacific Airways

Hong Kong based Cathay Pacific Airways has a world-wide reputation for its quality of service. Founded in 1946, the airline had nearly 14 000 employees in early 1997. In the same year, it had a fleet of 58 aircraft and served some 50 destinations.

Cathay Pacific is constantly seeking to improve the quality of its service and the effectiveness of its marketing activities. To help it do this, the airline makes wide use of customer questionnaires.

The main roles of the questionnaires are to:

1 help devise marketing strategy
2 allow the airline to benchmark its performance against its main competitors
3 identify trends, e.g. the growth of women travellers and non-smokers
4 highlight areas where further research is required on important issues
5 test how customers have reacted to new product development.

Questionnaires are distributed randomly in that cabin crew are told the seat numbers to which they should distribute the in-flight questionnaires. However, the company does not always sample the same proportion of passengers on every flight. Instead, the number varies from flight to flight with a higher than average proportion on the major, high yield-generating routes.

The results are interpreted by company personnel and presented on a quarterly basis to the company's Board of Directors. Approximately every six months, the questionnaires are renewed and modified.

One particularly interesting point about the questionnaires is that they can be adjusted to allow for national differences in perceptions of service standards, for example. This is important for an airline like Cathay Pacific which has a multicultural, multinational market.

The authors would like to thank Mr Graeme Carder and Cathay Pacific Airways for their help and for their permission to reproduce their customer questionnaires in this case study.

The Cathay Pacific questionnaires are good examples of customer surveys. On the following pages you will find two different questionnaires used by Cathay Pacific, namely:

- the ground questionnaire, which was used at check-in during 1997
- the in-flight questionnaire, which was in use in 1997.

Conclusion

As this example of good practice illustrates, it is important for organizations to use customer satisfaction questionnaires which:

- cover the issues which are of most concern to their customers
- gather information in a form which means that service improvements can be made as a result
- are analysed by independent people not employed by the organization.

Discussion points and essay questions

1 Using examples, describe the ways in which the data obtained from both questionnaires could be used to improve the quality of service offered by Cathay Pacific to its customers.
2 Discuss the potential problems an airline might face when trying to carry out questionnaire surveys such as those undertaken by Cathay Pacific.

CATHAY PACIFIC

Dear Passenger,

I would like to welcome you to today's flight with Cathay Pacific, and ask you for a few minutes of your time to complete this questionnaire. We need you to tell us how you feel about the ground services you received for today's flight, so that we can use your opinions to improve our check in and boarding procedures and, of course, to enhance our Service Straight From The Heart.

As our way of thanking you for your time, we will enter your completed questionnaire into the Cathay Pacific lucky draw, for which there is a winner every two weeks. The winner will receive two return tickets to or from Hong Kong within the Cathay Pacific network.

Your completed questionnaire will be collected by cabin crew before arrival at your destination or alternatively you may hand it to any crew member during the flight.

Yours sincerely,

David Turnbull
Managing Director
Cathay Pacific Airways

**Complete this form
and you could win
TWO
RETURN TICKETS!**

GROUND

1. GROUND SATISFACTION

Please indicate your expectation of Cathay Pacific, actual experience and level of satisfaction for this flight as shown ⊘. If there is no circle, please write in the space provided.

1. Before starting this questionnaire, which should only take a few minutes, please rate your **Overall Satisfaction** with all Cathay Pacific services experienced **before** you boarded the aircraft. This includes check-in, boarding and departure punctuality - **for this flight only** - plus reservation & ticketing if these were conducted through Cathay Pacific directly.

Totally Satisfied	Mostly Satisfied	Somewhat Satisfied	Somewhat Dissatisfied	Very Dissatisfied
◯ 1	◯ 2	◯ 3	◯ 4	◯ 5

10I

2. RESERVATION & TICKETING

2a. Did you personally contact Cathay Pacific directly with regard to this flight?

◯ 1 Yes, which City _____   ◯ 2 No → **GO TO SECTION 3**   11,12-14

2b. Please rate your overall satisfaction with the service received when you contacted Cathay Pacific.

◯ 1   ◯ 2   ◯ 3   ◯ 4   ◯ 5   15

2c. Did you contact Cathay Pacific

By **Telephone** to
Cathay Pacific Office
◯ 1 Yes
◯ 2 No

By **Personal Visit** to
Cathay Pacific Office
◯ 1 Yes
◯ 2 No   16-17

2d. Were you able to communicate effectively with Cathay Pacific staff?

◯ 1 Yes   ◯ 2 No   18

	Telephone to Cathay Pacific Office	Personal Visit to Cathay Pacific Office	
2e. If you contacted Cathay Pacific, please indicate the reason(s):	◯ 1 To make a reservation ◯ 2 For flight information ◯ 3 To rearrange reservations ◯ 4 For general information on Cathay Pacific	◯ 1 To make a reservation ◯ 2 To collect ticket ◯ 3 For general information on Cathay Pacific ◯ 4 For clarification on tickets or vouchers ◯ 5 For flight information ◯ 6 To rearrange reservations	19-22 23-28
2f. What was the attitude of Cathay Pacific staff?	◯ 1 Friendly and eager to help ◯ 2 Professional, courteous, but not particularly friendly or helpful ◯ 3 Indifferent to my requests ◯ 4 Rude and impatient	◯ 1 Friendly and eager to help ◯ 2 Professional, courteous, but not particularly friendly or helpful ◯ 3 Indifferent to my requests ◯ 4 Rude and impatient	29-30
2g. How knowledgeable and efficient were Cathay Pacific staff?	◯ 1 Good product knowledge, and met my requirements efficiently ◯ 2 Limited product knowledge but met my requirements quite efficiently ◯ 3 Little product knowledge, and was unable to meet my requirements competently	◯ 1 Good product knowledge, and met my requirements efficiently ◯ 2 Limited product knowledge but met my requirements quite efficiently ◯ 3 Little product knowledge, and was unable to meet my requirements competently	31-32

G

1

GROUND

3. CHECK-IN

3a. How would you rate your overall satisfaction with Cathay Pacific's <u>check-in</u> service <u>for this flight</u>?

◉ O 1   ☺ O 2   ☺ O 3   ☹ O 4   ☹ O 5   33

3b. In which city did you check-in for this flight? Please write: _____   34-36

4. Did you check-in by...?

O 1 Express check-in counter   O 2 Normal check-in counter   O 3 Check-in counter at transfer desk   37

5. Was your seat preference met?

O 1 Yes   O 2 No   O 3 Have no seat preference   38

6a. Once at check-in, how long did you queue to check-in <u>for this flight</u>?

Please write: _____ minutes   39-41

6b. How satisfied are you with the queuing time?

◉ O 1   ☺ O 2   ☺ O 3   ☹ O 4   ☹ O 5   42

7a. Check-in staff's greeting of passengers?

	Experience or observation on this flight
• A sincere and natural greeting, making you feel welcome	O 1
• A brief, business-like greeting, polite and acceptable	O 2
• An insincere and rather mechanical greeting	O 3
• No obvious greeting, and not very welcoming	O 4

43

7b. How satisfied are you with the greeting you received from the check-in staff?

◉ O 1   ☺ O 2   ☺ O 3   ☹ O 4   ☹ O 5   44

8a. Check-in staff's attitude?

Expectation of Cathay Pacific		Experience or observation on this flight
O 1	• Friendly and eager to help, responding to individual needs and making passengers feel appreciated and respected	O 1
O 2	• Professional, courteous, but not particularly friendly or helpful	O 2
O 3	• Indifferent, and generally ignoring passengers who did not specifically request attention	O 3
O 4	• Rude or impatient with passengers	O 4

45-46

8b. How satisfied are you with the check-in staff's attitude?

◉ O 1   ☺ O 2   ☺ O 3   ☹ O 4   ☹ O 5   47

G   2

9a. **Manner of providing information by the check-in staff?**

	Experience or observation on this flight
• Eager to provide appropriate information and advice. Sensitive to different passenger requirements	O_1
• Providing basic information, business-like and routine	O_2
• Providing information unwillingly or only on request	O_3
• Providing unclear answers or information, perhaps impolite	O_4

48

9b. **How satisfied are you with the manner in which you were given information?**

O_1 O_2 O_3 O_4 O_5 49

10a. **Queue management at check-in counter?**

Expectation of Cathay Pacific		Experience or observation on this flight
O_1	• Minimum queuing and efficient processing, flexible in opening counters, and direction to available queues and counters when necessary	O_1
O_2	• Queues generally had more than 5 people, but were orderly and staff worked efficiently	O_2
O_3	• The queues were very long and disorderly	O_3

50-51

10b. **How satisfied are you with the queue management at check-in counter?**

O_1 O_2 O_3 O_4 O_5 52

4.   BOARDING GATE PROCEDURES

11. **How would you rate your overall satisfaction with Cathay Pacific's boarding gate procedures for this flight?**

O_1 O_2 O_3 O_4 O_5 53

12a. **Greeting at the boarding gate?**

	Experience or observation on this flight
• A sincere and natural greeting, making you feel welcome	O_1
• A brief, business-like greeting, polite and acceptable	O_2
• An insincere and rather mechanical greeting	O_3
• No obvious greeting, and not very welcoming	O_4

54

G

3

GROUND

12b. How satisfied are you with the greeting you received at the boarding gate?

◯ 1   ◯ 2   ◯ 3   ◯ 4   ◯ 5   55

13a. Staff attitude at the boarding gate?

Expectation of Cathay Pacific		Experience or observation on this flight
◯ 1	• Friendly and welcoming, actively offering assistance to passengers	◯ 1
◯ 2	• Professional and courteous, providing assistance if asked	◯ 2
◯ 3	• Unfriendly and ignoring passengers	◯ 3 56-57

13b. How satisfied are you with the staff attitude at the boarding gate?

◯ 1   ◯ 2   ◯ 3   ◯ 4   ◯ 5   58

5. DEPARTURE PUNCTUALITY

14a. How satisfied are you with the **departure punctuality** of **this flight**?

◯ 1   ◯ 2   ◯ 3   ◯ 4   ◯ 5   59

14b. Did the aircraft leave the gate or parking bay at the scheduled departure time?

◯ 1 Yes → **GO TO SECTION 6**   ◯ 2 No, it was delayed by   60
                                       _____ Hours _____ Minutes   61-62,63-64

14c. How satisfied are you with the way Cathay Pacific handled the delay in departure?

◯ 1   ◯ 2   ◯ 3   ◯ 4   ◯ 5   65

14d. Was there any announcement or explanation about the delay in departure?

By airport staff   By flight crew
◯ 1 Yes → **GO TO Q14e**   ◯ 1 Yes → **GO TO Q14e**
◯ 2 No → **GO TO SECTION 6**   ◯ 2 No → **GO TO SECTION 6**   66-67

14e. ...and if so was it informative?

Airport staff   Flight crew
◯ 1 Yes   ◯ 1 Yes
◯ 2 No   ◯ 2 No   68-69

6. WOULD YOU CHOOSE CATHAY PACIFIC AGAIN?

15a. If you were to travel on **this route again in the same class**, how likely are you to choose Cathay Pacific instead of other airlines?

Extremely likely	Very likely	Somewhat likely	Not very likely	Not likely at all	
◯ 1	◯ 2	◯ 3	◯ 4	◯ 5	70
	GO TO Q16			**GO TO Q15b**	

G   **4**

GROUND

15b. **Which airline would you choose instead? Please write (one only):** _____   71-72

16. **How likely are you to recommend Cathay Pacific to your family, friends or colleagues?**

Extremely likely	Very likely	Somewhat likely	Not very likely	Not likely at all
○1	○2	○3	○4	○5

73

7. YOUR TRAVEL EXPERIENCE

17a. **In the past 12 months, have you taken a flight <u>from this airport</u> on another airline <u>in the same class as you are travelling today</u>?**

○1 Yes   ○2 No → **GO TO SECTION 8**   74

17b. **Which airline was that? Please write (the most recent one) :** _____   75-76

17c. **How would you compare your experience of that airline with your experience of Cathay Pacific <u>on this flight</u>?**

	Much better than Cathay Pacific	Slightly better than Cathay Pacific	Same as Cathay Pacific	Slightly worse than Cathay Pacific	Much worse than Cathay Pacific	
	1	2	3	4	5	
Check-in	○	○	○	○	○	77
Boarding Gate Procedures	○	○	○	○	○	78
Departure Punctuality	○	○	○	○	○	79
Overall Experience with ground service	○	○	○	○	○	80

8. ABOUT THIS TRIP

18a. **Did you personally choose to fly Cathay Pacific rather than another airline?**

○1 Yes → **GO TO Q19**   ○2 No   10ll

18b. **Who made the decision for you to fly on Cathay Pacific?**

○1 Company   ○3 Secretary   11
○2 Travel agent   ○4 Family   ○5 Others (please specify) _____   12-13

19. **What is your main reason for taking this trip? (Please tick one only)**

○1 Company business   ○5 Education
○2 Attend trade show/convention   ○6 Migration
○3 Holiday   ○7 Others
○4 Visiting friends/relatives   14

20a. **Are you travelling in:**

○1 First Class   ○2 Business Class   ○3 Economy Class   15

20b. **What is your flight number? CX** _____   **Departure date:** ____/____   16-18,19-20,21-22
                                                                        Date   Month

G   5

GROUND

20c. Your seat number is:_____   23-25

20d. Are you travelling...

    ○₁ On your own   ○₂ With friends/colleagues   ○₃ With family   26

20e. At which city will you disembark? _____   27-29

---

9.   A B O U T Y O U R S E L F

21. You are

    (a)   ○₁ Male   ○₂ Female   10III

    (b)   ○₁ Smoker   ○₂ Non-smoker   11

22. What is your age?

○₀₁ Under 21	○₀₅ 36-40	○₀₉ 56-60
○₀₂ 21-25	○₀₆ 41-45	○₁₀ 61-65
○₀₃ 26-30	○₀₇ 46-50	○₁₁ Over 65
○₀₄ 31-35	○₀₈ 51-55	

    12-13

23. What is your country of residence (the place where you spent most of the last 12 months)?

    Country _____ City _____ 14-15,16-18

24a. What is your nationality?_____   19-20

24b. Which of these ethnic groups do you belong to?

○₀₁ Caucasian	○₀₅ Malay	○₀₉ Indonesian
○₀₂ Chinese	○₀₆ Thai	○₁₀ Indian
○₀₃ Japanese	○₀₇ Filipino	○₁₁ Middle Eastern
○₀₄ Korean	○₀₈ Vietnamese	○₁₂ Others (Please write) _____

    21-22

25. In what type of work are you employed?

    Job title / position _____ Industry _____ 23-24,25-26

26. Are you a member of / belong to...

	No	Yes	
Cathay Pacific's Marco Polo Club	○₂	○₁ Membership No. _____	27,28-37
Other airline club / association	○₂	○₁ Which airline(s) _____	38,39-44
Frequent flyer programmes	○₂	○₁ Which programme(s) _____	45,46-51

27. Not counting this present trip, have you made any other <u>international</u> air trips in the past 12 months?

    ○₂ No   ○₁ Yes   52

         a.   If yes, how many trips have you made (count each round trip as one)

             Business _____   53-54

             Leisure / Personal _____   55-56

         b.   Approximately how many of these trips were made on Cathay Pacific? _____ 57-58

28. Are you available for further airline research?

    ○₁ Yes   ○₂ No   59

29. Would you like to receive further information from Cathay Pacific?

    ○₁ Yes   ○₂ No   60

G   **6**

GROUND

30. Although we are unable to reply to you personally, we do consider any suggestions and comments you wish to make on improvements to Cathay Products and services.

61

_____

_____

_____

_____

_____

LUCKY DRAW ENTRY

Name: Mr./Mrs./Ms/Miss:(Family Name) _____ (Given Name) _____

Address: _____

62

_____

City: _____ Country: _____ Zip/Postal code: _____

Home phone number: _____ Office phone number: _____

Fax number: _____

≺ THANK YOU ≻

Official Rules for Cathay Pacific's Survey Lucky Draw

1. You are automatically entered in the Cathay Pacific Survey Lucky Draw by filling in the questionnaire, completing it with your name and address and returning it to our cabin attendant prior to landing.
2. Only one questionnaire per person, per flight will be accepted. You may be asked to fill in another questionnaire on each subsequent flight.
3. Cathay Pacific employees and members of their immediate family are not eligible for the draw.
4. The lucky draw will take place every 2 weeks. Winner will be notified by post within 7 days of the draw. Full details and conditions of the prize will be sent to the winner. The name of Lucky Draw Winners will be published in the Inflight Magazine "Discovery" every month.
5. One winner will be selected randomly by the Marketing Strategy, Planning & Research Department of Cathay Pacific. Their decision is final in all matters relating to the draw. No substitution or cash equivalents are allowed in place of the prize.
6. If the winner is resident in Hong Kong, he/she can choose to fly to any of Cathay Pacific's worldwide destinations.
7. If the winner is not resident in Hong Kong, he/she can choose to fly from any of Cathay Pacific's worldwide destinations to Hong Kong.
8. The tickets are for two return flights on a confirmed space basis.
9. This offer is void where prohibited or restricted by law. National, federal, state and local taxes and/or surcharges are the responsibility of the prize winners.
10. If you would like to know who won the draw, please write to the following address, enclosing a stamped address envelope: REFLEX Questionnaire Prize Draw, Marketing Strategy, Planning & Research Department, 15/F, Swire House, 9 Connaught Road, Hong Kong.

FOR OFFICE USE ONLY

QUESTIONNAIRE NO.: [____] 2IV-7

FLIGHT NO.: [____] 16-18

SECTOR: [____] 22-27

DATE: [D M Y] 10-15

VERSION: [G] 19 LANGUAGE: [E] 21

P.T. NO. [____] 28-30

G

7

GROUND

Dear Passenger,

I would like to welcome you on board today's flight with Cathay Pacific, and ask you for a few minutes of your time to complete this questionnaire. We need you to tell us how you feel about your flight today, so that we can use your opinions to improve our cabin interiors and equipment, our cuisine, entertainment and, of course, to enhance our Service Straight From The Heart.

As our way of thanking you for your time, we will enter your completed questionnaire into the Cathay Pacific lucky draw, for which there is a winner every two weeks. The winner will receive two return tickets to or from Hong Kong within the Cathay Pacific network.

Your completed questionnaire will be collected by cabin crew before arrival at your destination or alternatively you may hand it to any crew member during the flight.

Yours sincerely,

David Turnbull
Managing Director
Cathay Pacific Airways

**Complete this form
and you could win
TWO
RETURN TICKETS!**

INFLIGHT

1. INFLIGHT SATISFACTION

Please indicate your expectation of Cathay Pacific, actual experience and level of satisfaction for **this flight** as shown ✇. If there is no circle, please write in the space provided.

1.   Before starting this questionnaire, which should only take a few minutes, please rate your **Overall Satisfaction** with Cathay Pacific services **on-board this flight**.

Totally Satisfied	Mostly Satisfied	Somewhat Satisfied	Somewhat Dissatisfied	Very Dissatisfied
◎ ○ 1	☺ ○ 2	☺ ○ 3	☹ ○ 4	☹ ○ 5

101

2. BEFORE TAKE OFF

2.   How would you rate your overall satisfaction with the services provided by the cabin crew **before take-off on this flight**?

◎ ○ 1   ☺ ○ 2   ☺ ○ 3   ☹ ○ 4   ☹ ○ 5   11

3a.   **Cabin crews' greeting of passengers?**

	Experience or observation on this flight
• A sincere and natural greeting, making you feel welcome	○ 1
• A brief, business-like greeting, polite and acceptable	○ 2
• An insincere and rather mechanical greeting	○ 3
• No obvious greeting, and not very welcoming	○ 4

12

3b.   **How satisfied are you with the greeting you received from the cabin crew?**

◎ ○ 1   ☺ ○ 2   ☺ ○ 3   ☹ ○ 4   ☹ ○ 5   13

3. CABIN CREW

4.   How would you rate your overall satisfaction with the services provided by the **cabin crew on this flight**?

◎ ○ 1   ☺ ○ 2   ☺ ○ 3   ☹ ○ 4   ☹ ○ 5   14

5a.   **Cabin crews' attitude?**

Expectation of Cathay Pacific		Experience or observation on this flight
○ 1	• Friendly and eager to help, and making passengers feel appreciated and respected	○ 1
○ 2	• Professional, courteous, but not particularly friendly or helpful	○ 2
○ 3	• Indifferent and generally ignoring passengers who did not specifically request attention	○ 3
○ 4	• Rude or impatient with passengers	○ 4

15-16

5b.   **How satisfied are you with the cabin crew's attitude?**

◎ ○ 1   ☺ ○ 2   ☺ ○ 3   ☹ ○ 4   ☹ ○ 5   17

6a.   **Cabin crew's service style?**

Expectation of Cathay Pacific		Experience or observation on this flight
○ 1	• Very good at anticipating individual passenger needs, interact naturally with passengers and are always available to assist	○ 1
○ 2	• Good anticipation of general needs, but routine and business-like, not spontaneous in their conversation	○ 2
○ 3	• Not attentive or slow to respond to passenger requests	○ 3
○ 4	• Not responding to passenger requests and needs	○ 4

18-19

1

INFLIGHT

6b. How satisfied are you with the cabin crews' service style?

$\bigcirc_1$ $\bigcirc_2$ $\bigcirc_3$ $\bigcirc_4$ $\bigcirc_5$ 20

7a. Grooming and appearance of cabin crew?

	Experience or observation on this flight
• Well-groomed, professional appearance	$\bigcirc_1$
• Neat, tidy and functional	$\bigcirc_2$
• Untidy, not professional looking	$\bigcirc_3$

21

7b. How satisfied are you with the grooming and appearance of the cabin crew?

$\bigcirc_1$ $\bigcirc_2$ $\bigcirc_3$ $\bigcirc_4$ $\bigcirc_5$ 22

4. FOOD & DRINK

8. Please rate your overall satisfaction with the <u>food and drink</u> provided <u>on this flight</u>?

$\bigcirc_1$ $\bigcirc_2$ $\bigcirc_3$ $\bigcirc_4$ $\bigcirc_5$ 23

	If Applicable			
	Breakfast/ Snack	**Lunch**	**Dinner**	
9. Were you served the following meals on this flight?	$\bigcirc_1$ Yes $\bigcirc_2$ No	$\bigcirc_1$ Yes $\bigcirc_2$ No	$\bigcirc_1$ Yes $\bigcirc_2$ No	24-26
10. Which type of meal did you request?	$\bigcirc_1$ Japanese $\bigcirc_2$ Korean $\bigcirc_3$ Other Asian $\bigcirc_4$ Western $\bigcirc_5$ Special	$\bigcirc_1$ Japanese $\bigcirc_2$ Korean $\bigcirc_3$ Other Asian $\bigcirc_4$ Western $\bigcirc_5$ Special	$\bigcirc_1$ Japanese $\bigcirc_2$ Korean $\bigcirc_3$ Other Asian $\bigcirc_4$ Western $\bigcirc_5$ Special	27-29
11. Did you receive the type of meal you requested?	$\bigcirc_1$ Yes $\bigcirc_2$ No	$\bigcirc_1$ Yes $\bigcirc_2$ No	$\bigcirc_1$ Yes $\bigcirc_2$ No	30-32
For each of the meal(s) you received, please check:				
12. Quantity of the food	$\bigcirc_1$ More than enough $\bigcirc_2$ Just right $\bigcirc_3$ Not enough	$\bigcirc_1$ More than enough $\bigcirc_2$ Just right $\bigcirc_3$ Not enough	$\bigcirc_1$ More than enough $\bigcirc_2$ Just right $\bigcirc_3$ Not enough	33-35
13. Temperature of hot dishes	$\bigcirc_1$ Too hot $\bigcirc_2$ Just right $\bigcirc_3$ Too cold	$\bigcirc_1$ Too hot $\bigcirc_2$ Just right $\bigcirc_3$ Too cold	$\bigcirc_1$ Too hot $\bigcirc_2$ Just right $\bigcirc_3$ Too cold	36-38
14. Visual appeal	$\bigcirc_1$ Appetising $\bigcirc_2$ Unappetising	$\bigcirc_1$ Appetising $\bigcirc_2$ Unappetising	$\bigcirc_1$ Appetising $\bigcirc_2$ Unappetising	39-41

15a. Overall, which statement best describes the food / meal quality on this flight?

Expectation of Cathay Pacific		Experience or observation on this flight	
$\bigcirc_1$	• Tastes freshly cooked, with a good flavour, comparable to a good restaurant	$\bigcirc_1$	
$\bigcirc_2$	• Tastes quite fresh with pleasing flavours, quite enjoyable. Better than most airline food	$\bigcirc_2$	
$\bigcirc_3$	• No different to any other airline food	$\bigcirc_3$	
$\bigcirc_4$	• Tastes like frozen or microwave food, little flavour	$\bigcirc_4$	42-43

I

15b. How satisfied are you with the overall food / meal quality?

$\bigodot$ O_1 $\bigodot$ O_2 $\bigodot$ O_3 $\bigodot$ O_4 $\bigodot$ O_5 44

5. READING MATERIALS

16. Please rate your overall satisfaction with the <u>reading materials</u> provided <u>on this flight</u>?

$\bigodot$ O_1 $\bigodot$ O_2 $\bigodot$ O_3 $\bigodot$ O_4 $\bigodot$ O_5 45

17a. Which type of magazine/newspaper do you prefer? (Choose as many as possible)

Magazine		Newspaper
O_1 Business/Finance O_4 News		O_1 International
O_2 Entertainment O_5 Travel		O_2 International Finance
O_3 Fashion/Lifestyle O_6 Sports		O_3 Local daily (from <u>origin</u> country)
O_7 Others		O_4 Local daily (from <u>destination</u> country) 46-52
		O_5 Others 53-57

17b. Did you obtain your preferred choice of:

Magazine		Newspaper	
O_1 Yes O_2 No		O_1 Yes O_2 No	58-59
$\downarrow$		$\downarrow$	
If no, for what reason(s) (Choose as many as applicable):		If no, for what reason(s) (Choose as many as applicable):	
O_1 Inadequate stock on the plane		O_1 Inadequate stock on the plane	60-61
O_2 Choice /Title not available		O_2 Choice /Title not available	62-63

6. INFLIGHT ENTERTAINMENT

18a. Have you *watched* any of the Inflight Entertainment <u>Video Programmes</u> on this flight?

O_1 Yes O_2 No → **GO TO Q21a**   64

18b. How would you rate your satisfaction with the Inflight Entertainment <u>Video Programmes</u> provided <u>on this flight</u>?

$\bigodot$ O_1 $\bigodot$ O_2 $\bigodot$ O_3 $\bigodot$ O_4 $\bigodot$ O_5 65

19a. How many different movies did you watch? Please write:_____   66

19b. Overall, which statement best describes the selection of movies <u>on this flight</u>?

	Experience or observation on this flight
• Good selection of movies which I have been looking forward to watching	O_1
• Quite a good selection of movies which helps pass the time inflight	O_2
• A selection of movies, many of which I have already seen and do not wish to see again	O_3
• A selection of movies which I do not find very appealing	O_4 67

19c. How do you find the mix of movies and short features?

O_1 Too many movies and not enough short features
O_2 Too many short features and not enough movies
O_3 The mix is about right   68

	Yes	No	
20a. Do you have a personal television available?	O_1	O_2 → **GO TO Q21a**	69

20b. Do you find the personal television:

Working properly	O_1	O_2	70
Has controls which are easy to operate	O_1	O_2	71
Has a clear picture	O_1	O_2	72

3

INFLIGHT

21a. Have you *listened* any of the Inflight Entertainment <u>Audio Programmes on this flight</u>?

    ○₁ Yes   ○₂ No → If you have <u>watched</u> the Video Programmes, please go to   73
                                            Q22a, otherwise please go to Section 7

21b. How would you rate your satisfaction with the Inflight Entertainment <u>Audio Programmes</u> provided <u>on this flight</u>?

😀 ○₁   🙂 ○₂   🙂 ○₃   🙁 ○₄   ☹ ○₅   74

21c. How do you find the selection of Audio Programmes <u>on this flight</u>?

○₁ A good selection of programmes which I enjoy listening to
○₂ Quite a good selection of programmes that helps pass the time
○₃ A selection of programmes which I do not find very appealing   75

22a. Do you find the audio system

	Yes	No	
Working properly	○₁	○₂	76
Has good sound quality	○₁	○₂	77
Has a comfortable headset	○₁	○₂	78

22b. How would you rate your satisfaction with the Inflight Entertainment <u>Equipment</u> provided <u>on this flight</u>?

😀 ○₁   🙂 ○₂   🙂 ○₃   🙁 ○₄   ☹ ○₅   79

7. CABIN CONDITION, SEATING & FACILITIES

23. Please rate your overall satisfaction with the <u>cabin condition, seating and facilities on this flight</u>.

😀 ○₁   🙂 ○₂   🙂 ○₃   🙁 ○₄   ☹ ○₅   10/11

Cabin Condition

24a. Ventilation...	24b. Cleanliness...	24c. Was the decoration?
○₁ Good	○₁ Good	○₁ Attractive, comfortable and relaxing
○₂ Average	○₂ Average	○₂ Ordinary and functional decoration like most airlines
○₃ Poor	○₃ Poor	○₃ Poor decoration, and poorly maintained 11-13

Seating

25a. Overall, how comfortable is your seat?

○₁ Very comfortable   ⎤ **GO TO Q26**
○₂ Quite comfortable ⎦
○₃ Average
○₄ Not very comfortable ⎤ **GO TO Q25b**
○₅ Not at all comfortable ⎦

25b. What would you say is/are the <u>main</u> problem(s) with your seat? (Please indicate as many as applicable)

○₁ Inadequate leg room
○₂ Inadequate seat width
○₃ Inadequate space between adjacent seats
○₄ Inadequate head rest position
○₅ Inadequate padding
○₆ Inadequate back support
○₇ Inadequate recline
○₈ Poor support for legs and feet
○₉ Poorly focused personal reading light
○₀ Seat controls not working   14, 15-24

4

INFLIGHT

26. How would you rate your satisfaction with the <u>cleanliness of the toilets on this flight</u>?

   ◯1   ◯2   ◯3   ◯4   ◯5   25

8. OVERALL SATISFACTION

27. Taking into consideration your <u>total experience (ground and inflight)</u> with Cathay Pacific on this trip, how would you rate your <u>Overall Satisfaction</u> with Cathay Pacific?

   ◯1   ◯2   ◯3   ◯4   ◯5   26

9. WOULD YOU CHOOSE CATHAY PACIFIC AGAIN?

28a. If you were to travel <u>on this route again in the same class</u>, how likely are you to choose Cathay Pacific instead of other airlines?

Extremely likely	Very likely	Somewhat likely	Not very likely	Not likely at all	
◯1	◯2	◯3	◯4	◯5	27
GO TO Q29			GO TO Q28b		

28b. Which airline would you choose instead? Please write (one only): _____ 28-29

29. How likely are you to recommend Cathay Pacific to your family, friends or colleagues?

Extremely likely	Very likely	Somewhat likely	Not very likely	Not likely at all	
◯1	◯2	◯3	◯4	◯5	30

10. YOUR TRAVEL EXPERIENCE

30. In the past 12 months, have you taken a flight on another airline <u>on this route, in the same class as you are travelling today</u>?

   ◯1 Yes   ◯2 No → **GO TO SECTION 11**   31

31a. Which airline was that? Please write (the most recent one) : _____ 32-33

31b. How would you compare your experience on that airline with your experience of Cathay Pacific <u>on this flight</u>?

	Much better than Cathay Pacific	Slightly better than Cathay Pacific	Same as Cathay Pacific	Slightly worse than Cathay Pacific	Much worse than Cathay Pacific	
	1	2	3	4	5	
Service received from cabin crew before take off	◯	◯	◯	◯	◯	34
Cabin crew behaviour/attitude	◯	◯	◯	◯	◯	35
Reading materials	◯	◯	◯	◯	◯	36
Inflight entertainment programmes	◯	◯	◯	◯	◯	37
Inflight entertainment equipment	◯	◯	◯	◯	◯	38
Food and drink	◯	◯	◯	◯	◯	39
Cabin condition	◯	◯	◯	◯	◯	40
Seat comfort	◯	◯	◯	◯	◯	41
Overall experience with inflight service	◯	◯	◯	◯	◯	42

5

INFLIGHT

31c. <u>Overall</u>, how would you compare <u>your total trip experience</u> between Cathay Pacific on this flight and the airline you flew most recently on this route?

   ○ 1 Much better than Cathay Pacific   ○ 4 Slightly worse than Cathay Pacific
   ○ 2 Slightly better than Cathay Pacific   ○ 5 Much worse than Cathay Pacific
   ○ 3 Same as Cathay Pacific

43

11. ABOUT THIS TRIP

32a. Did you personally choose to fly Cathay Pacific rather than another airline?

   ○ 1 Yes → **GO TO Q33**   ○ 2 No

44

32b. Who made the decision for you to fly on Cathay Pacific?

   ○ 1 Company   ○ 3 Secretary
   ○ 2 Travel agent   ○ 4 Family   ○ 5 Others (please specify) _____

45, 46-47

33. What is your main reason for taking this trip? (Please tick one only)

   ○ 1 Company business   ○ 5 Education
   ○ 2 Attend trade show/convention ○ 6 Migration
   ○ 3 Holiday   ○ 7 Others
   ○ 4 Visiting friends/relatives

48

34a. Are you travelling in:

   ○ 1 First Class   ○ 2 Business Class   ○ 3 Economy Class

49

34b. What is your flight number? CX _____   Departure date:____/____
                                                        Date   Month

50-52, 53-54, 55-56

34c. Your seat number is:_____

57-59

34d. Are you travelling...

   ○ 1 On your own   ○ 2 With friends/colleagues   ○ 3 With family

60

34e. In which city did you board this flight? _____

61-63

34f. At which city will you disembark? _____

64-66

12. ABOUT YOURSELF

35. You are
   (a) ○ 1 Male   ○ 2 Female

10III

   (b) ○ 1 Smoker   ○ 2 Non-smoker

11

36. What is your age?
   ○ 01 Under 21   ○ 05 36-40   ○ 09 56-60
   ○ 02 21-25   ○ 06 41-45   ○ 10 61-65
   ○ 03 26-30   ○ 07 46-50   ○ 11 Over 65
   ○ 04 31-35   ○ 08 51-55

12-13

37. What is your country of residence (the place where you spent most of the last 12 months)?

   Country _____ City _____

14-15, 16-18

38a. What is your nationality?_____

19-20

38b. Which of these ethnic groups do you belong to?

   ○ 01 Caucasian   ○ 05 Malay   ○ 09 Indonesian
   ○ 02 Chinese   ○ 06 Thai   ○ 10 Indian
   ○ 03 Japanese   ○ 07 Filipino   ○ 11 Middle Eastern
   ○ 04 Korean   ○ 08 Vietnamese ○ 12 Others (Please write)_____

21-22

6

INFLIGHT

39. **In what type of work are you employed?**

Job title / position _____   Industry _____   23-24, 25-26

40. **Are you a member of / belong to...**

	No	Yes	
Cathay Pacific's Marco Polo Club	○ 2	○ 1 Membership No. _____	27, 28-37
Other airline club / association	○ 2	○ 1 Which airline(s) _____	38, 39-44
Frequent flyer programmes	○ 2	○ 1 Which programme(s) _____	45, 46-51

41. **Not counting this present trip, have you made any other <u>international</u> air trips in the past 12 months?**

○ 2 No   ○ 1 Yes   52

a. If yes, how many trips have you made (count each round trip as one)
Business _____   53-54
Leisure / Personal _____   55-56
b. Approximately how many of these trips were made on Cathay Pacific? _____   57-58

42. **Are you available for further airline research?**

○ 1 Yes   ○ 2 No   59

43. **Would you like to receive further information from Cathay Pacific?**

○ 1 Yes   ○ 2 No   60

44. **Although we are unable to reply to you personally, we do consider any suggestions and comments you wish to make on improvements to Cathay Products and services.**

_____   61
_____
_____
_____

LUCKY DRAW ENTRY

Name: Mr./Mrs./Ms/Miss:(Family Name) _____ (Given Name) _____   62
Address: _____
_____

City: _____ Country: _____ Zip/Postal code: _____
Home phone number: _____ Office phone number: _____
Fax number: _____

≺ THANK YOU ≻

Official Rules for Cathay Pacific's Survey Lucky Draw

1. You are automatically entered in the Cathay Pacific Survey Lucky Draw by filling in the questionnaire, completing it with your name and address and returning it to our cabin attendant prior to landing.
2. Only one questionnaire per person, per flight will be accepted. You may be asked to fill in another questionnaire on each subsequent flight.
3. Cathay Pacific employees and members of their immediate family are not eligible for the draw.
4. The lucky draw will take place every 2 weeks. Winner will be notified by post within 7 days of the draw. Full details and conditions of the prize will be sent to the winner. The name of Lucky Draw Winners will be published in the Inflight Magazine "Discovery" every month.
5. One winner will be selected randomly by the Marketing Strategy, Planning & Research Department of Cathay Pacific. Their decision is final in all matters relating to the draw. No substitution or cash equivalents are allowed in place of the prize.
6. If the winner is resident in Hong Kong, he/she can choose to fly to any of Cathay Pacific's worldwide destinations.
7. If the winner is not resident in Hong Kong, he/she can choose to fly from any of Cathay Pacific's worldwide destinations to Hong Kong.
8. The tickets are for two return flights on a confirmed space basis.
9. This offer is void where prohibited or restricted by law. National, federal, state and local taxes and/or surcharges are the responsibility of the prize winners.
10. If you would like to know who won the draw, please write to the following address, enclosing a stamped address envelope: REFLEX Questionnaire Prize Draw, Marketing Strategy, Planning & Research Department, 15/F, Swire House, 9 Connaught Road, Hong Kong.

FOR OFFICE USE ONLY

QUESTIONNAIRE NO.: [ ]   2IV-7   DATE: [D M Y] 10-15
FLIGHT NO.: [ ] 16-18   VERSION: [I L] 19-20   LANGUAGE: [E] 21
SECTOR: [ ] 22-27   P.T. NO. [ ] 28-30

7

INFLIGHT

Case study 6
First Choice Holidays – all-inclusive package

Introduction

First Choice Holidays is one of the leading package holiday companies in the UK. The company was formed as a result of an extensive relaunch of the Owners Abroad company in 1994. the company offers a full range of package holidays and uses a range of sub-brands. It piloted the idea of an all-inclusive holiday during the 1995 season which led to the successful introduction of the all-inclusive brochure for the 1996/97 season.

Background to the company

First Choice Holidays is aiming to develop and operate a high quality, mass-market package holiday business in the UK and North America. The company's mission statement says that it is not intending to expand vertically into retailing or into accommodation ownership. The company will therefore be able to concentrate all their energies and resources on becoming the best package holiday company and tour operating airline in their countries of operation.

The financial performance of the company has been somewhat disappointing in recent years, which is in common with the rest of the industry. Profits before taxation were down £15.0 million to £1.3 million in 1996. The poor results were primarily due to the extremely difficult trading conditions that prevailed in the UK over the 1996 summer period. The industry was forced into discounting during June, July and August to sell capacity which had been created by weak consumer demand. This can be partly attributed to the hot summer that occurred in 1996 in the UK.

This has meant that it has been increasingly important for the company to establish their new brands, and increase customer awareness through

The authors would like to thank Emma Wadell of First Choice Holidays for her help in the writing of this case study.

effective advertising and promotional campaigns and there is a need for the company to introduce new branded products which will reflect changing consumer demands.

The First Choice product range

The First Choice company is divided into four main group divisions. These include Air 2000, the group airline, Ski-Bound, the ski/lakes and mountains brand, Signature Vacations, the Canadian tour operator, and First Choice Holidays and Flights, the tour operations business based in the UK and Ireland. The relative importance of these different Group Activities can be seen in Exhibit 6.1.

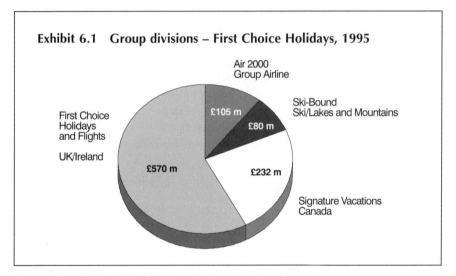

Exhibit 6.1   Group divisions – First Choice Holidays, 1995

Source: First Choice Holidays Annual Accounts, 1995

The company has made some major acquisitions recently.

Ski-Bound which is based in Brighton was acquired in 1996. The company operates 25 hotels in the Alps and incorporates a successful schools ski market programme and is the leader in the UK in the group ski market. The company have integrated the Ski-Bound business into the First Choice Ski, Lakes and Mountains programme.

JWT Holidays was also acquired in 1996. JWT Holidays, prior to acquisition, was the third largest tour operator in the Republic of Ireland and carried approximately 57 000 passengers in 1994.

The current product range for 1996 is summarized in Exhibit 6.2. It can be seen that the range incorporates a number of sub-brands, operating within the First Choice umbrella brand. This is the case for the All Inclusive brand which falls within the UK/Ireland Tour Operations business and operates under the First Choice umbrella brand.

Exhibit 6.2   The product range of First Choice Holidays, 1997

UK/Ireland Tour Operation:

- First Choice – Summer Sun
  - – Winter Sun
  - – Turkey
  - – Cyprus
  - – Portugal
  - – Florida
  - – Tropical
  - – Ski, Lakes and Mountains
  - – Flights
  - – All-inclusive

- Sovereign

- Twenty's

- Free Spirit

- Kids Clubs (branded resort clubs)

- Eclipse (direct sell)

- JWT (Ireland)

- Falcon

Air 2000:   Company Airline

Canadian Tour Operations:
Signature Vacations

Source: First Choice Holidays

Exhibit 6.3   Turnover performance for the company, 1995

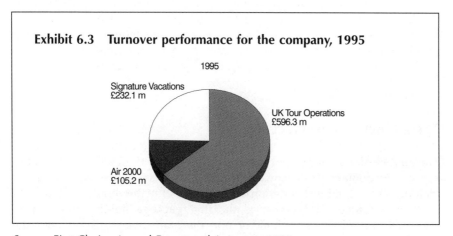

Source: First Choice Annual Report and Accounts, 1995

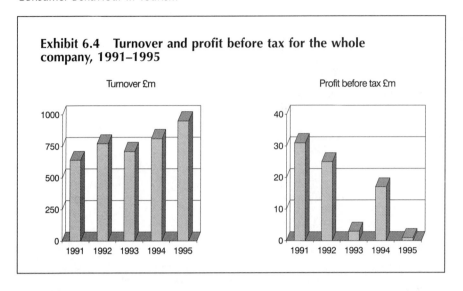

Exhibit 6.4   Turnover and profit before tax for the whole company, 1991–1995

Company performance

A summary of the financial performance for the group is shown in Exhibits 6.3 and 6.4.

The disappointing profit performance over recent years has been largely attributed to the heavy discounting which the company had to undertake during the 1996 season, due to the unusually good summer weather in the UK. There has been an increase in profit, however, during 1996 to £9.3 million.

The Group Chief Executive had an optimistic view for the future of the company in 1995. The summer and winter market shares had been improved to around 14 per cent and the objective for 1991 was to improve the company's margins. The Group was judged to be soundly financed and better balanced with established international brands and a charter airline, Air 2000, which had been judged to be first class. The view of the Chief Executive at this time was that the company would restore group profitability in the year and continue to make progress towards the medium-term objective of achieving industry standard margins.

The all-inclusive product

The all-inclusive holiday concept was developed in the 1990s to respond to a growing demand from consumers for a holiday which was priced to include all food, accommodation and activities for the duration of stay. In 1996, First Choice Holidays was the first package holiday operator to introduce the all-inclusive holiday into the mainstream market with the introduction of a wide range of all-inclusive deals to popular summer

Mediterranean destinations. During this period a NOP Survey was carried out that revealed that 40 per cent of people did not understand the concept of the all-inclusive holiday and thought that it was 'too good to be true'.

A survey carried out in 1995 revealed that the majority of interviewees thought that 'all-inclusive' meant simply a standard package holiday, including only accommodation, flight and transfer.

It became apparent in 1996 that the all-inclusive package holiday had become one of the fastest growing types of holidays in the UK. At the same time, First Choice was voted Number 1 for all-inclusive holidays by travel agents in a MORI survey. A new NOP survey which was commissioned by First Choice Holidays in 1996, shows that people's awareness and support for the all-inclusive holiday have increased during the year.

The 1996 survey showed that less than one in four interviewees now felt this way, and half of the respondents questioned now understood that the all-inclusive holiday includes everything – accommodation, meals, drinks, snacks, entertainment and sport. In the same year, however, less than one in ten interviewees realized that sport and ice-cream were also included in the all-inclusive holiday.

The all-inclusive concept has been well received by the British consumer who is keen to make their pound stretch further. In the 1996 survey 73 per cent of the interviewees stated that there were particular benefits to be gained from purchasing an all-inclusive type of holiday. They made such statements as:

'It would make financial planning easier'

'It provides better value for money'

Other respondents noted the advantages it would bring if they could eat and drink all they wanted every day and the fact that they would be encouraged to be more active on holiday because there was no extra charge for sporting activities.

A sceptical 13 per cent, however, remained to be convinced that such an attractive holiday option exists and think that it is 'too good to be true'.

It has been estimated by First Choice that a family of four, on a week's holiday in a Spanish resort, would spend on average £22.40 on ice-cream for the children (if each child had a minimum of two ice-creams per day) and that the parents would spend on average £103.60 on alcohol (based on each adult having an average of two glasses of wine, two bottles of beer, and a local spirit and mixer per day at local prices). If the extra costs such as those for snacks, soft drinks, teas, coffees, water sports and entertainment are added on, the savings are obvious. The all-inclusive holiday, which is often only £100 per person per week more expensive than the similar half-board holiday, therefore offers extremely good value for money.

Kevin Ivie, the First Choice Group Marketing Director in 1997, has stated that:

First Choice is now a leading authority on Mediterranean all-inclusives. The concept was tested last summer in selected resorts and, following its great success, a full range of all-inclusive holidays were launched for Summer '96. In fact, a MORI survey conducted in 1996 found that more than half of all travel agents advise customers that First Choice provides the best all-inclusive holidays. It has been a trump card this year for First Choice and, ever quick to adopt a good idea, we expect that some of the other leading tour operators may try to copy the all-inclusive theme for next summer.

The all-inclusive product range

First Choice offer a wide range of all-inclusive holidays in the winter and summer programmes. A detailed list of holidays on offer is shown in Exhibit 6.5.

Exhibit 6.5   The First Choice range of all-inclusive holidays

First Choice – all-inclusive Winter 1996/7

Lanzarote	Mexico
Fuerteventura	Dominican Republic
Majorca	Antigua
Costa Del Sol	St Kitts
Costa Blanca	Jamaica
Malta	Margarita
Cyprus	Cuba
Tunisia	
Goa	

First Choice – all-inclusive Summer 1997

Majorca	Crete
Menorca	Zakynthos
Ibiza	Halkidiki
Gran Canaria	Turkey
Lanzarote	Thailand
Fuerteventura	Mexico
Costa Del Sol	Jamaica
Costa Blanca	Barbados
Cyprus	Antigua
Malta	St Kitts
Tunisia	Dominican Republic
Rhodes	Margarita
	Cuba

Source: First Choice Holidays

There is a choice of all-inclusive holidays on offer aimed at specific target market segments, e.g. for families, or exclusively for adults. Honeymooners are also catered for in the all-inclusive tropical selection. Further details of these specially designed packages are shown in Exhibit 6.6.

The all-inclusive range of holidays also offer free child prices, discounts for children and groups, and special offers for tropical honeymooners.

Initial sales results for the all-inclusive range have been very promising for the company. The company has been able to move the concept firmly into the mainstream area of the business and it has proved very popular with holidaymakers. Most of the First Choice all-inclusive holidays for the summer 1996 season were sold out very quickly and there was good initial sales indication for the 1997 season. There has also been good sales of the all-inclusive concept in the winter.

Customers for the all-inclusive concept

First Choice have conducted limited market research on customers returning from all-inclusive holidays. Overall impressions of these holiday-makers seem to be very favourable. There is limited information regarding

---

Exhibit 6.6   Profile of the all-inclusive customer

Age profile:

20 or under	6%
21–30	18%
31–40	29%
41–50	25%
51–65	13%
65+	2%

Marital status:

Married	74%
Single	23%
Divorced/Separated	5%
Widowed	1%

Socio-economic groups:

Professional or Senior Managers	24%
Middle/Junior Managers	12%
Administrators	11%
Self-employed	10%
Students	3%
Housewives	7%
Retired	5%

Favourite newspaper:

Daily Mail, *The Sun* and *Daily Mirror*

Source: First Choice Holidays

the demographic and lifestyle profile of the all-inclusive customer. Highlights of the limited data collected give some ideas of the profiles of this group of holidaymakers. Details of this preliminary market research are shown in Exhibit 6.6.

Conclusion

First Choice Holidays have recognized a change in consumer behaviour in the last few years. Consumers are looking for more security in their financial planning for holidays. The all-inclusive package has been developed to try to offer the holidaymaker better value for money and more security. It will be interesting to see whether this concept develops further or whether it is a passing fad.

Discussion points and essay questions

1 Critically evaluate the reasons for the growth in interest by consumer for the all-inclusive type of package holiday.
2 The all-inclusive holiday was considered to be 'too good to be true' in the early stages of development. Evaluate the possible reasons for this, and suggest ways in which a company could overcome these feelings amongst customers.

There has been a steady improvement in the financial performance of First Choice since 1995. In 1997 the company had an improved full year performance with profits up to £22.0 million and an improved summer performance up 39 per cent on 1996, with profit before tax of £46.3 million. First Choice also recommended an offer for Unijet, one of the UK's leading integrated tour operating and airline groups, during 1998. It also acquired Hayes and Jarvis, a specialist long haul tour operator, during 1998 for £24.0 million.

Case study 7
Carnival Cruise Lines – the cruise market

Carnival Cruise Lines is an American company which was set up in 1972 by shipowner, Ted Arison. He redesigned the concept of the cruise holiday from an upmarket and luxury occasion, to a casual fun experience. He created Carnival to compete with the successful land resorts of Florida and the Caribbean, and to provide an alternative family holiday at sea, which was to be carefree and informal. The cruises were to be reasonably priced so that they would appeal to all generations within an affordable budget.

The Carnival fleet today offers the customer all the attractions, entertainment, sports, activities and shops which they would find in a holiday complex. This allows the customer to be entertained in a resort-like atmosphere, whilst sailing around beautiful areas of the world, such as the Caribbean and Mexico.

The Carnival concept is to offer customers an experience which is just as exciting as the destinations visited during the cruise. The cruises are excellent value for money for customers on a limited budget, since nearly everything – food, parties, shows, activities and entertainment – is included in the initial cruise price. The cabins have been designed to be spacious and feature private facilities, air conditioning, TV, radio and telephone. Carnival's new Superliners also have demi-suites with balconies and luxurious 28 square foot suites.

An outline of the Carnival Corporation is shown in Exhibit 7.1.

It can be seen from Exhibit 7.1 that the Corporation has grown to a position where it earns $2 billion a year, and has invested in other holiday companies with cruise interests. This includes Holland America Line (100 per cent ownership), Seabourn Cruise Line (50 per cent ownership) and Airtours Plc (29.54 per cent ownership). The Corporation currently owns 25 ships and employs 20 000 people world-wide.

The authors would like to thank Lynn Narraway and Carly Perlans of Carnival Cruise Lines for their help in the writing of this case study.

Exhibit 7.1 Carnival Corporation fact sheet

Year Founded:	1972
Headquarters:	Miami, Florida
Chief Executive Officer:	Micky Arison
Cruise Operating Units:	Carnival Cruise Lines Holland America Line (acquired in 1989)
Divisions:	Windstar Cruises – a division of Holland America Line Holland America Westours (Alaska tour operator consisting of 16 hotels, 14 luxury day boats, 390 motor coaches and 8 private domed rail cars)
Joint Ventures:	Seabourn Cruise Line – 50 per cent ownership Airtours Plc – vertically integrated travel company and tour operator serving the European marketplace – 29.54 per cent ownership
Number of Ships:	25 – 11 Carnival, 8 Holland America, 3 Windstar, 3 Seabourn
Employees Worldwide:	20 000
Stock Exchange:	NYSE (symbol:CCL)
1995 Revenues:	$2 billion
1995 Net Income:	$451.1 million
Cruising Areas:	Alaska Bahamas Baltics Caribbean Hawaii Mediterranean North Cape Panama Canal South Pacific Far East South America and other worldwide destinations
Cruise Length:	Carnival Cruise Lines: 3–14 days Holland America Line: 3–98 days (world cruise) Windstar Cruises: 7–15 days Seabourn: 7–23 days
New Ships on Order:	6 – 3 for Carnival, 3 for Holland America

Source: Carnival Cruise Lines

History of Carnival Cruise Lines

The Corporation was established in 1972 by Ted Arison who had the vision of establishing a different sort of cruise company. A brief review of the development of the company can be seen in Exhibit 7.2. The development of the company has been rapid over the last 20 years, and often surprising and astonishing. The announcement by Micky Arison, the son of Ted Arison, that the company was to build three more ships in a short space of time was met by incredulity by commentators at the time who wondered about the profitability of such a venture.

Exhibit 7.2   A brief history of Carnival Cruise Lines

1972   Ted Arison formed a new enterprise aimed at expanding the cruise market from Miami.
Bought *Empress of Canada*, renamed it the *Mardi Gras*.
Mardi Gras ran aground on first voyage with 300 travel agents aboard.

1975   Mardi Gras operating at over 100% occupancy as a 'Fun Ship'.
The *Empress of Britain* is purchased and renamed as the *Carnivale*.

1977   Purchase of the *SA Vaal*. $30 million facelift – renamed as the *Festivale*.

1978   Announcement of construction of brand new passenger ship – *The Tropicale*.

1979   Micky Arison succeeds his father, Ted Arison, as Carnival's President.
Announces that company will build three more ships over next four years.

1984   Diversification into 3–4 day Bahamas Cruises.

1985   The first Superliner, *Holiday*, is launched.
Mardi Gras' service from Fort Lauderdale launched (3–4 day).

1986   *Jubilee* introduced into service.
Festivale sails out of San Juan.

1987   *Celebration* introduced into service.
Announcement of 70 000-ton *Fantasy* with a $200 million price tag.
Public offering of 20 per cent of stock, which netted the company $400 million.

1990   Inaugural voyage of the *Fantasy*.
Ecstasy joins the fleet in late 1990.
Purchase of Holland America Line.

1991   *The Sensation* joins the fleet.
Completion of $250 million, 1500-room mega-resort in the Bahamas.

1995   Investment in Airtours Plc – UK package holiday operation (29.54%).
Fascination, Inspiration and *Imagination* introduced into service

1996   Launch of the *Carnival Destiny* – 100 000 tonnes.

Source: Carnival Cruise Lines

The decision to commission the biggest liner in the world – the 100 000 ton *Carnival Destiny,* was also a bold move in the company's development. The company has invested heavily in other holiday companies in the world to try to spread their interests into related areas. The purchase of the Holland America Line, for example, meant that the company gained substantial interest in the luxury cruise market.

Purchase of 29.54 per cent of the UK vertically integrated travel company, Airtours, brought the company an interest in the European package holiday market, and an opening to develop the cruise market in the UK.

The current Carnival Cruise Lines fleet

The company now has a fleet of Superliners including the *Fantasy, Ecstasy, Sensation, Inspiration, Imagination* and *Fascination.*

The *Carnival Destiny* is the latest Superliner commissioned by the company, and was launched in 1996. This Superliner is the ultimate in cruise liners, with a full range of facilities and public rooms. The poolside entertainment area spans four decks and has four swimming pools, a 200-foot waterslide, two swim-up bars, seven whirlpools and an outdoor amphitheatre. The dining rooms have huge windows which give panoramic sea views. The liner has a two-level Nautica Spa with its own jogging track. The Millionaire's Club is the largest casino at sea and there are excellent shopping malls and nightclubs. The Superliner is ten decks high and has a roofed Grand Atrium Plaza which embodies sophisticated modern design. The company has used the services of world-renowned designers and fitters to create a unique and vibrant interior. Further details of the *Carnival Destiny* are given in Exhibit 7.3.

The company finalized a joint venture agreement with Hyundai Merchant Marine, an Asian-based cruise line, in 1997. This new venture began operations scheduled in the Far East, in the spring of 1998.

In addition, Carnival will have two 70 000-ton Superliners, the *MS Elation* and *MS Paradise,* expected to be launched in February and November 1998, respectively. Holland America Line has three new ships on order, including the 62 000-ton *Rotterdam VI,* scheduled to enter service in autumn 1997, plus two 65 000-ton sister ships for *Destiny* (101 000 ton), the *Carnival Triumph,* scheduled to enter service in 1999, and the *Carnival Victory,* scheduled for the summer of 2000.

Key personnel

Ted Arison, the shipping informal entrepreneur had the initial idea of repositioning the cruise business into an informal fun occasion. A key part of the development of the Carnival Cruise Lines, however, has been completed by Micky Arison, Ted's son, who grew up in the shipping business. Micky Arison is now the Chairman and Chief Executive Officer of the Carnival Corporation. It is his business acumen which has brought the company considerable financial success.

Exhibit 7.3   *Carnival Destiny*

Ship Profile:

Name:	*Carnival Destiny*
Company:	Carnival Cruise Lines
Originally Built:	1996
Refurbished/Built:	N/A
Formerly Named:	N/A
Country of Registry:	Panama
Normal Crew Size:	1100
Nationality of Crew:	International
Officers:	Italian
Hotel Cruise Staff:	International

Size/Capacity:

Gross Registered Tonnage:	101 000
Length:	893 feet
Beam:	116 feet
Total Capacity:	2642 (Dbl Occupancy)

Accommodation:

Outside Cabins:	740
Inside Cabins:	519
Currency on Board:	US Dollars

Facilities:

Fully Air Conditioned and Stabilized
All Cabins with Private Facilities
Three Swimming Pools and Whirlpools (5) + Children's Pool
Ship-to-Shore Telephone
'Camp Carnival' Facilities and Entertainment for Children
Children's Playroom and Teen Club
Closed Circuit TV
Shore Excursions Office
Dry Cleaning and Laundry Service
Duty Free Shops
Beauty Parlour/Barber Shop
Elevators (18)
Full Casino
Gymnasium
Golf Driving Platform
Infirmary
Sauna and Massage/Spas
Shuffleboard and Skeet Shooting
Table Tennis
Library
24-hour Free Room Service
24 hour Pizzeria

Public Rooms

Galaxy Dining Room
Universe Dining Room
The Trattoria
Happy Valley (Chinese)
Sun and Sea Restaurant
Palladium Showlounge
The Criterion Lounge
The Onyx Room
Millionaire's Club Casino
Point After Dance Club
Cheers Wine Bar
Downbeat
Apollo Bar
Destiny Bar
All Star Bar
Cafe on the Way
Virtual World (V. Reality)
Teen Club Disco

Source: Carnival Cruise Lines

Micky Arison is 47 and followed his education with a two-year working experience in the Carnival Cruise Lines sales department. He became Reservations Manager in 1974, and took over the post of Vice President of Passenger Traffic in 1976. He succeeded to the Presidency of Carnival in 1979 and was appointed Chairman of the company's Board of Directors in 1990.

He now oversees diversified travel and tourism holdings including 25 cruise ships marketed under four different brand names, as well as the largest tour operator and hotel chain in Alaska and the Yukon territory.

Financial performance

The company offered 20 per cent of their stock on the New York Stock Exchange in 1987. This netted the company $400 million which allowed further investment in new ships and diversification into other businesses. The turnover and profitability of the company has steadily increased since this time. The 1995/96 results are shown in Exhibit 7.4.

Exhibit 7.4   Financial performance of Carnival Cruise Lines

	1995	*1996*
Revenues for the year	$2 billion	$2.21 billion
Net income for the year	$451.1 million	$566.3 million
Earnings per share	$1.59	$1.95

Source: Carnival Cruise Lines

Distribution of the Carnival Cruise Line products

The company does sell cruises directly to the customer, particularly in the US and Canada. The development of the overseas business for the company has been more difficult and a reliance placed has had to be placed on appropriate package holiday companies in different markets.

The most difficult problem for sales in the UK has been the perceptions of potential customers of what a cruise product is. Potential customers tend to think of cruises as being an upmarket and luxury holiday, where they have to dress up in formal clothes for dinner and engage in intellectual conversations over cocktails. This perception has been built up by the more traditional and established cruises companies which have served the market. The main objective of Carnival Cruise Lines is to overcome these perceptions, and convince potential customers that they are offering an informal and fun holiday which is similar to that which can be experienced in a traditional on-shore resort. One of the ways that this has been achieved is to distribute the products, wherever possible, through mainstream package holiday companies which the customer has dealt with previously for other package holidays. The mainstream cruises businesses in the UK have joined together and spent £80 000 per year to employ a public relations company, BGB Associates, to manage an ongoing public relations campaign to try to get this message across to potential customers via the media.

Carnival Cruise Lines has been working hard recently to improve their sales in Europe. In the UK, for example, the company has worked with a

---

Exhibit 7.5   Distribution of the Carnival Cruises in the UK market, 1997

Product	Operator	Prices from
Carnival Cruises – Baja and Mexican Riviera – Alaska – The Caribbean – Special Voyages – The Bahamas 3–11 days	Equity Group	From £320 (cruise only)
Airtours – Florida and Caribbean (Carnival), Caribbean Cruises, Florida and the Caribbean, Celebration Sun Waves SM	Airtours Plc	From £499, 7 nights inclusive
Carnival Sun Waves, Caribbean, San Juan	British Airways	From £799, 7 nights inclusive
Thomas Cook Holidays, Dominican *Republic, Cruise and Stay*, Dominican Republic and Cruise	Thomas Cook Holidays	From £999, 14 nights inclusive
Florida and Caribbean plus *California and Mexico**, Cruises to Caribbean and Mexico in combination with Orlando	Co-op Travel	From £499, 7 nights inclusive
Florida and Caribbean plus *California and Mexico**, Cruises to Caribbean and Mexico in combination with Orlando	Lunn Poly	From £499, 7 nights inclusive
*Virgin/Lunn Poly Carnival, Florida** and the Caribbean Cruise and Stay Holidays	Virgin Holidays	From £499, 7 nights inclusive

Source: Carnival Cruise Lines; *agreements with high street retailer to produce dedicated brochures

series of major UK tour operators so that the cruises are featured in their packaged holidays programme. This has included companies such as Unijet, Airtours and Virgin Holidays. The company has also negotiated marketing agreements with major high street retailers to produce dedicated Unijet/ Lunn Poly, Unijet/Co-op and Virgin/Lunn Poly Carnival brochures displayed under the banner of 'Florida and the Caribbean Cruise and Stay Holidays'. A large proportion of the UK bookings come via these tour operators, which are shown in Exhibit 7.5.

The company has a target for 1997 to increase their sales in the UK by a further 60 per cent. The company is using two different marketing strategies in 1997. The first target is the tour operation business which is aimed specifically at customers who are planning to take a holiday in Florida and view the Carnival Cruise as an add-on. The second market is the cruise market, which is being targeted with a new Carnival 'Sun Waves' brochure which features seven-night Caribbean cruises on board the *Inspiration* out of San Juan combined with non-stop British Airways flights from London Gatwick.

Customers of Carnival Cruise Lines

Carnival Cruise Lines carries approximately 6 million customers every year. A profile of the customers in 1996 is shown in Exhibit 7.6.

It can be seen from this exhibit that the majority of the customers currently originate from the US and Canada. The company is trying to increase their

---

Exhibit 7.6   Customers of Carnival Cruise Lines – 1996

Numbers	*Average Numbers of Passengers per Year*
World-wide	6 million
of which:	
US/Canada nationals	4.5 million
overseas	1.5 million
UK	15 000
Numbers who gamble on board	½ million

Demographic profile	*Percentage*
Under 35	30%
Teenagers and under	10%
36–54	40%
Over 55	30%

Socio-Economic Groups
Target group is 'Middle American'
Socio Economic Group B C^1 C^2

Source: Carnival Cruise Lines

sales in overseas markets. This case study has already considered the activity involved in trying to develop the UK market, for example. The current customer tends to be older, on average, although the company is keen to develop the market for families and children.

The typical customer has a mid-range income and is probably used to taking resort-based holidays. The company has high levels of repeat purchase, particularly in the US market. The company is trying to target particular market segments with specifically designed products. Children, for example, are being targeted with a Camp Carnival service, and a range of facilities designed particularly for them. These services are shown in Exhibit 7.7.

Exhibit 7.7   Children's services on Carnival Cruise Lines

Camp Carnival – Children's Club

Aim:	to provide a similar atmosphere to American Summer Camps to give parents the freedom to enjoy themselves
Staff:	Each superliner has an Assistant Operations Director, Youth Director and over 50 qualified trained staff who are responsible for the Camp Carnival
Groups in Camp Carnival:	Toddlers 2–4 Juniors 4–7 Teenagers 14–17
Facilities:	Indoor children's playroom and video arcade Music and dancing Play area on deck on the *Carnival Destiny* Family accommodation in cabins

Source: Carnival Cruise Lines

The company has also developed a substantial market in the weddings and honeymoon markets. Customers can now get married either on board or on shore at a selection of locations, and the company offers a wide range of wedding packages to suit different customer requirements. Details of these packages are shown in Exhibit 7.8.

The company has also targeted the health-conscious customer and offers first-class fitness and recreational facilities on all their Superliners. This has been developed to appeal to young people and families – target markets that might not have previously considered a cruise. Each Superliner features a Nautica Spa complex that includes a fully equipped gym, an aerobics room, saunas, steam rooms and a full range of beauty treatments. The Superliners also offer a special healthy Nautica Spa menu which incorporates healthy menus.

Exhibit 7.8   Romantic weddings with Carnival Cruise Lines

Weddings take place in the port of embarkation, on shore, or on board.

Wedding locations are:
– Miami, Florida
– Port Canaveral, Florida
– Tampa, Florida
– Los Angeles, California
– New Orleans, Louisiana
– St Thomas, US VI
– San Juan, Puerto Rico
– Grand Cayman

Different wedding packages:

Just for the Bride and Groom		$490
Welcome Aboard Wedding		$950
Deluxe Romance Wedding		$1100
Puerto Rico:	On Board	$490
	On Island	$625 and $950
St Thomas:	On Board	$490
	On Island	$725
Grand Cayman:	On Board	$525
	On Island	$675 and $750

Wedding licences must be applied and paid for by the couple.

Source: Carnival Cruise Lines

The reasons for customers choosing a Carnival Cruise Lines product

The reasons for customers choosing a Carnival Cruise Lines product vary according to the origin of the customers, and are explained in Exhibit 7.9. The US customer is more likely to go on a Carnival Cruise as an impulse, than those customers who are travelling from overseas before boarding the ship.

Customers often go on a Carnival Cruise to celebrate a special event such as a birthday, honeymoon or wedding anniversary. Customers are often motivated by the desire to have a 'fun time' in a beautiful and changing setting. It is particularly important in the marketing activity for Carnival overseas to communicate the informal theme and good value associated with their holidays. The use of well-recognized package holiday operators and high street retailers, is key to this activity.

Research with customers

The company carries out marketing research with all customers, when their holiday is just about to finish. The Bon Voyage Comment Card is filled in

---

Exhibit 7.9   The reasons for customers choosing a Carnival Cruise Lines product

Motivators:
- Seeking fun and entertainment
- The desire to see new places
- Special occasions – weddings, honeymoons, wedding anniversaries, birthdays
- Entertainment seeking and gambling
- The desire to 'chill out' and get away from it all

Determinants:
- Available by direct sale (particularly applicable in the US)
- Available as part of a package (particularly important in overseas market)
- Good value for money – everything included in the price
- New exciting, informal cruise concept

Source: Carnival Cruise Lines

and returned to the company for analysis. Comments cards which have been completed by customers from outside the US are sent on to the local office after preliminary analysis.

Comments received from these cards are usually very favourable. Some examples of comments received from UK customers are shown in Exhibit 7.10.

The customers often mention particular members of staff in their comments which shows the importance of well-developed customer care programmes. Further scrutiny of the Bon Voyage Comment Cards also reveals the large number of customers that celebrate a special event, whilst they are on the cruise.

Exhibit 7.10   Comments made by passengers from the UK who travelled on Carnival Cruise Lines during 1996/97

'Thanks very much. I have had a really fantastic time. My birthday was on the 24.12.96 and Roel and Mr Paul made it special by singing to me and I also had a cake. Once again, thank you'

'Devin Fleming was absolutely brilliant – and all the staff. We have travelled all over Europe four or five times a year, but this was our best holiday ever. Thank you'

'All your employees have been marvellous and I have enjoyed my holiday with you. The entertainment has been first class, as have all other departments'

Source: Carnival Cruise Lines

Conclusion

Carnival Cruise Lines has developed a new type of mass-market 'fun' cruise and is attempting to attract different market segments into taking a cruise holiday with the company. This has been very effective in the US market, but the company has work to do in other markets in trying to change consumer perceptions of the cruise product.

Discussion points and essay questions

1 The main problem a company has when it repositions a product is the changing of consumer perceptions. Discuss this statement in relation to Carnival Cruise Lines.
2 Carnival Cruise Lines has had to change the product considerably to attract new market segments. Give an outline of this product development process, and highlight the most important features of this programme.

Case study 8
Wensleydale Creamery, Hawes, North Yorkshire

Introduction

Wensleydale Creamery in North Yorkshire, England, is a good example of a company which has combined a tourism venture with traditional food production. The Wensleydale Cheese Experience offers the visitor the possibility of visiting a museum of cheese production, seeing cheese being produced from a viewing gallery, tasting and buying cheese in a well-designed shop. The site also has a restaurant and gift shop. Hawes in North Yorkshire is in one of the most beautiful parts of Britain – the North Yorkshire Dales, which is a picturesque and mountainous area, and has a long tradition as a holiday region.

History

Wensleydale has been inhabited since Iron Age times. The first recorded origins of Wensleydale cheese date back to the period when the Norman conquerors, having settled in the area, brought religious orders from France to found the great abbeys in the Yorkshire Dales. In 1150, a monastery was built at Fors which is four miles from Hawes, and this was later moved to Jervaulx in Lower Wensleydale. The French Cistercian monks continued to make cheese until the dissolution of the monasteries in the sixteenth century.

The art which the monks had developed was then passed on to local farmers' wives who then produced cheese in their own farmhouses.

In 1897, Mr Edward Chapman started the first industrial-scale production of Wensleydale cheese from milk which he purchased from surrounding farms. The industrial depression of the 1930s made trading hard, and the Milk Marketing Board tried to offer contracts to take the milk to a national dairy

The authors would like to thank Alice Amsden of Wensleydale Dairy Products for her help in the writing of this case study.

which was miles away. The dalesmen, led by Kit Calvert, fought against this and established their own Wensleydale Creamery in Hawes with a capital of £1085, £200 of which came from Kit Calvert, the Managing Director.

In 1953, Kit built a new creamery for £15 000 and sales of Wensleydale cheese boomed. In 1966, the Milk Marketing Board purchased Wensleydale Creamery and Kit continued to run the creamery until his retirement in 1967. In May 1992, Dairy Crest, a subsidiary of the Milk Marketing Board, closed the Hawes creamery and transferred the production of Wensleydale cheese to the neighbouring county of Lancashire. The news that Yorkshire's famous cheese was to be lost, because of a decision made by a large conglomerate incensed the public and offers of help to rescue the creamery flooded in.

The ex-managers of the Hawes creamery persuaded the owners to sell the creamery to them in a management buy-out which was finally agreed in November 1992. Cheesemaking in Wensleydale recommenced on the 16 December 1992. The refurbishment of the creamery was completed in January 1993 ensuring a significant increase in the production of hand-made cheeses and the provision of many local jobs.

A Visitor Centre with a viewing gallery was opened in June 1994 and the Cheese Experience was born. This allows visitors to see for themselves the history, tradition and skill involved in the production of Real Wensleydale Cheese.

The attraction was awarded a White Rose Award for Tourism by the Yorkshire and Humberside Tourist Board in 1994.

In recent years, the Wensleydale Creamery has negotiated with the BBC, to use their two animated characters, Wallace and Gromit. Wallace and Gromit, who were created by animator Nick Parks, are well known in their films *The Wrong Trousers* and *A Great Day Out*, for enjoying Wensleydale cheese. The association with Wallace and Gromit has allowed the Wensleydale creamery to use the characters on their cheese products and in their advertising literature.

The Wensleydale Creamery products

The Wensleydale Creamery produces Real Wensleydale Cheese which is creamy-white in colour and has a flaky appearance. The cheese is free from additives and is produced by hand in the traditional way. The texture of the cheese is firm but not dry or hard. The cheese is uneven and open in appearance when it is sliced. It goes well with crisp apple, and is traditionally eaten with fruit cake and apple pie. The cheese is extremely nutritious, rich in vitamins and will keep well at chilled temperatures.

The Creamery makes a full range of Wensleydale cheeses in different shapes and sizes.

The company produces a range which incorporates fruits and another which relies on the traditional art of smoking. The full range of cheeses produced by the Creamery is shown is Exhibit 8.1.

The majority of the cheese sales are through the major food retailers and cheese shops. The company has also a limited direct mail order business,

---

Exhibit 8.1   Range of products made at Wensleydale Creamery, Hawes

- Wensleydale cheese
- Blue Wensleydale
- Matured Wensleydale Range
- Wensleydale with Onions and Chives
- Traditional Wensleydale Kit Calvert
- Oak smoked Wensleydale
- Wensleydale Cow and Ewes Milk blend
- Red Wensleydale with Blueberries
- Wallace and Gromit Traditional Wensleydale
- Wensleydale with Apricots
- Wensleydale with Ginger
- Wensleydale with Cranberries

Cheeses are available in a variety of sizes including miniatures. The Creamery also makes a full range of smoked cheeses, and other regional cheese including Lancashire, Cheshire, Sage Derby, Double Gloucester and Leicester.

Source: Wensleydale Creamery

which it is hoping to develop in the future. Limited sales are also made via the cheese shop on the factory site.

The visitor attraction – the Cheese Experience – opened in June 1994, and has experienced great success since this time. Details of the Cheese Experience are shown in Exhibit 8.2. The attraction is part of the factory

---

Exhibit 8.2   Facilities at the Wensleydale Cheese Experience

- *Viewing Gallery.* The centre opened in July 1994 and includes a Viewing Gallery where visitors can see real Wensleydale Cheese being made. There is a traditional cheeseroom where everything is done by hand. Cheeses are made individually, moulded and wrapped in muslin.

- *The Museum.* The museum portrays the history of 'Real Wensleydale Cheese'. There is a video describing the processes involved in the production of Wensleydale cheese.

- *The Cheese Shop.* The shop offers the visitor the opportunity to purchase a wide range of premium quality cheeses. Free tasting of the 'Real Wensleydale Cheese' is included in the admission price to the museum.

- *Licensed Restaurant.* 'The Buttery', formerly the butter-making room, has been converted to a licensed restaurant where visitors can buy meals, snacks and local ice cream. The 'Creamery Coffee Shop' serves drinks, Yorkshire tea, and a range of home-made cakes, scones and pastries.

Source: Wensleydale Creamery

complex in Hawes village and visitors can reach the site in their own car or by coach. The Cheese Experience features a museum, cheese shop and licensed restaurant. One of the main attractions is the viewing gallery where visitors can see the hand production of Real Wensleydale Cheese. The attraction is open all the year round, except Christmas Day, from 9.00 to 5.30 pm in the summer and 9.00 – 4.30 pm in the winter. Tours of the Creamery are organized daily from 10.00 am.

The optimum cheese viewing times are from 10.00 am to 3.00 pm daily.

Customers of the Cheese Experience

Customers of the Cheese Experience have grown steadily since the opening in 1994. The customers fall into certain categories which are explored in Exhibit 8.3. The Cheese Experience is visited by a growing number of individuals or groups from a wide cross-section of socio-economic groups. Visitors can arrive on foot, in a private car, or on one of the many coach trips which are organized to visit the attraction. The company is currently trying to increase visits by coach parties and offers guided tours to parties of 15 or more. The parties are encouraged to pre-book the restaurant for their visit. The company offers all-inclusive packages which incorporate free admission to the museum if the party books to dine in the restaurant. Restaurant-only bookings and evening visits are also available for party bookings. The facilities are also available for functions and special occasions.

Exhibit 8.3   Main customer of groups visiting the Cheese Experience

1 Individuals or couples arriving by private car.
2 Family groups arriving by private car.
3 Individuals or couples arriving in groups by coach. These customers are given a guided tour.
4 Holidaymakers staying in Hawes arriving on foot as individuals, couples or family groups.
5 Local customers visiting the restaurant only as individuals, in pairs or in family groups.

Source: Wensleydale Creamery

The company has carried out little market research to date to find out details about the visitors to the Cheese Experience. It is clear, however, from the research that has been carried out so far, that the presence of the visitor attraction has boosted cheese sales. Customers who visit the attraction tend to be influenced directly to purchase the cheese when they return home, either in their local supermarket, or by direct mail. The Cheese Experience has also experienced a great deal of press coverage and has received many awards, such as the 1994 White Rose Award for Tourism. This has meant that the Wensleydale Creamery has benefited from substantial indirect publicity, as a result of this press coverage. This raises the awareness of the public at large in the range of products which the company offers.

The company also conducts market research with customers following their visit to the Cheese Experience. It has found that this information, collected from group organizers, has been the most useful in terms of future development of the business. The questionnaire used in this market research is shown in Exhibit 8.4.

Exhibit 8.4   Questionnaire

PLEASE COMPLETE AND RETURN AFTER YOUR VISIT

We believe in providing a quality service at value for money prices.

We are continually monitoring and assessing our Visitor Centre and would be very grateful if you could spare a few moments to fill in this form and return it to us after your visit.

Name _____

Date of Visit _____ Time _____

Please tick the box most appropriate

	Excellent	Good	Satisfactory	Poor
MUSEUM				
Helpfulness of Staff	_____	_____	_____	_____
Knowledge of Guide	_____	_____	_____	_____
Video	_____	_____	_____	_____
Exhibits	_____	_____	_____	_____
Viewing Gallery	_____	_____	_____	_____
Cheese Tasting	_____	_____	_____	_____
DELICATESSEN				
Helpfulness of Staff	_____	_____	_____	_____
Quality of Product	_____	_____	_____	_____

The company is planning to improve its customer database by the introduction of a Creamery Privilege Card, which customers will be encouraged to fill in during their visit. This information will allow the company to target customers with information on current products and encourage mail order sales, particularly during the Christmas period. The application form for the Creamery Privilege Card is shown in Exhibit 8.5.

Exhibit 8.5   Application form for Wensleydale Creamery Privilege Card

NAME _____

ADDRESS _____

_____

_____

POSTCODE _____PHONE NO _____

We promise that your details will will not be passed on to anyone else

CUSTOMER NO _____

Please tick the box if you do not wish to receive details of our special offers or Mail Order ☐

Authorized by _____Date of issue _____

The Wensleydale Creamery has the advantage of offering a product which is tied up with regional tradition. The Creamery is fairly unique in the UK, where many traditional cheese producers have been taken over by larger industrial cheese producers. This link to history, and the fact that the cheese is still hand-made along traditional lines, has meant that the product is very attractive to customers who are seeking nostalgic views of past ways of life. The position of the creamery in the Yorkshire Dales means that a visit can be easily slotted into a holiday itinerary.

The Creamery also has the attraction for customers of offering a view of the cheese actually being made and packed. The viewing gallery means that the visitor feels that they have actually observed the ancient tradition of cheesemaking. This leads to strong feelings of association with the product, which are very memorable.

Conclusion

The Wensleydale Creamery has been successful at combining a traditional food production company with a visitor attraction. The visitor attraction has been very influential in the development of the total cheese business of the company. The company plans to research customer profiles, and views, in more depth in the future, so that it can use this information to target customers more effectively and give them the appropriate products and services. The visitor attraction has also provided the company with extensive coverage in the media which has generated substantial interest in the company.

Discussion points and essay questions

1 Explore the possible reasons for people seeking nostalgic images of the past. Discuss the ways in which a visitor attraction, based on a traditional food process, can exploit these behaviour patterns.
2 The Wensleydale Creamery allows the visitor to see the actual cheese-making process. Evaluate the importance of this feature to the success of the visitor attraction and company cheese sales in general.

Case study 9
Société Roquefort, Roquefort, France

Introduction

Roquefort-sur-Soulzon is situated in the south of France between the regions of Languedoc and Auvergne. The village is perched at about 2000 feet above the town of Millau, near to the beautiful Gorges du Tarn River.

Roquefort is world renowned for the 'king of cheeses', which is made from ewe's milk and matured in the caves at Roquefort. The production of Roquefort cheese is approximately 20 000 tones per year, and approximately 15 per cent of the production is sold abroad, particularly to the United States of America, Belgium, Germany and Switzerland. There are several dozen brands of Roquefort cheese on the market, and the Société group controls approximately 82 per cent of the production.

Société has developed a visitor attraction in the village of Roquefort which allows visitors to gain an insight into this very special cheese production. This attraction is called 'Visite de Caves' – Les plus belles caves de Roquefort'.

The production of Roquefort cheese

Roquefort cheese is made by a number of producers in the Roquefort area from ewe's milk which is the richest milk in cheesemaking. Ewe's milk is approximately three times more expensive that cow's milk which makes the cheese expensive to produce.

The cheese is made in the traditional way at the producers. The *Penicillium Roqueforti* is introduced into the milk in the early stages of production. The cheeses are transported to Roquefort after one day of manufacture, two or three days of draining and five days of salting. The cheeses in this form are white with no internal blue veining. The cheeses are now ready for ripening.

The cheeses are referred to as 'loaves' and are slid into a tray containing 38 large needles which pierce the cheese. This piercing allows carbonic gas

The authors would like to thank Michel Laporte of Société Roquefort for his help in the writing of this case study.

produced by the fermentation of the curds to escape and allows penetration of air into the cheese.

The cheeses placed vertically on trays are placed in the Roquefort caves. The *Penicillium Roqueforti* develops and forms the characteristic blue-green veins inside the cheese which also becomes soft and full of flavour. This process lasts three to four weeks.

The second ripening of the cheese is carried out to develop the *Penicillium Roqueforti*, more slowly, and to exclude micro-organisms from growing on the outside of the cheese. The cheeses are wrapped in pure tin foil and returned to the caves. The master-ripeners will determine when the cheeses are ready, by withdrawing samples of the cheese with a sampling rod. The tin foil is then removed, and aluminium foil is used to wrap the cheeses ready for sale.

The ripening of the cheeses in the caves at Roquefort is key to the production of the Roquefort cheese. The Roquefort mountain was formed by gigantic rock upheaval which formed a mass extending to 1.25 miles in length and 1000 feet in width. Inside the rocks, there are faults or 'fleurines'. These fleurines have draughts of fresh air flowing through them at a constant temperature of 46°F and 95 per cent humidity. This underground breathing is unique in the world, and can be explained by a complex set of issues relating to geological form and climate. The ripening of the cheeses in the Roquefort caves which are fed by the draughts from the fleurine is key to the development of the cheeses.

Roquefort cheese is rich in calories, minerals and vitamins. A large part of the protein present in the cheese is predigested and is therefore directly assimilable. It is rich in B vitamins, and the enzymes in the cheese help with the digestion of certain foodstuffs. These factors along with the very special flavour, make the cheese unique in the world and very sought after.

Visite des Caves

The village of Roquefort has become a very special place to visit in the south west of France. There are a number of Roquefort producers in the village which have developed visitor attractions so that visitors can learn about their very special cheese production methods. Société is the largest producer of Roquefort cheese, and it has developed a sophisticated visitor attraction which appeals to all age groups. Details of the visitor attraction are shown in Exhibit 9.1.

It can be seen that the tour around the attraction lasts about one to two hours, and incorporates the use of special techniques such as a *son et lumière* spectacle with the serious educational information. Visitors can actually see into the special caves, and can view the cheeses maturing on the wooden slats.

The end of the tour incorporates a tasting session of the full range of cheeses and a shop, where cheese and other merchandising items can be bought.

The visitor attraction has developed more sophisticated techniques since it opened in 1957. An excellent film of the cheese production process now forms part of the tour because this does not happen in the Roquefort village, but elsewhere in many small to medium-sized production factories.

Exhibit 9.1   The Visite de Caves – visitor attraction

Location	Roquefort Village
Tour details	1 to 2 hours tour through the caves, exhibitions and museum
Highlights of the tour	• A son et lumière show which shows the production of Roquefort and the development through the centuries • A visit to the ancient caves, dating back to the seventeenth century • A viewing of the fluerines in the rocks which go to the plateau of the Grands Causses • The museum and demonstrations of the *Penicillium Roquefort* • Tasting session of different cheeses and visit to the shop
Cost of the Tour 1997	Adults FF15 Children Free Groups FF10 each
Opening hours	From 09.30 to 18.30 in the summer 09.30 to 11.30 and 14.00 to 17.00 at other times of the year

---

Source: Société Roquefort

Visitor numbers have been growing since the attraction opened in 1957, and over 6 million people have visited the attraction over this period (1957–1996). Details of the visitors can be seen in Exhibit 9.2.

The large majority of visitors come from France, with only 10 per cent of the visitors coming from abroad in 1996. The number of visitors from outside France is growing, however, as the cheese has been marketed throughout Europe on a wider basis in recent years. Most of the visitors to the visitor attraction arrive by car, in independent groups. A small percentage of the visitors arrive as part of an organized tour, and a large

---

Exhibit 9.2   Visitors to the Visite de Caves, 1996

Numbers of visitors since opening in 1957	6 million
Visitors from France	90%
Visitors from outside France	10%
Visitors over 55	9.3%
Groups of schoolchildren/students	4.7%
Visits by organized tours	0.4%

Of the visits by organized tours, 10% of these are from France and 80% of these are American or Japanese

---

Source: Société Roquefort

proportion of these are either American or Japanese. The attraction is also visited by schoolchildren and students. In addition, the visitor attraction is used by the Société as a marketing tool, i.e. to show to corporate clients, such as food retailers.

Young people are encouraged to visit the attraction because they will be enthused with the mystique of Roquefort, and be more inclined to buy the cheese regularly as they grow older. The company is obviously keen to encourage visitors from outside France, because this acts as a powerful marketing tool for the export market, which is an area which the company is working hard to develop.

The visitor attraction is an important part of the tourism strategy for the south west of France. Promotional leaflets for the attractions are distributed widely around the tourism offices, which are very well developed in France. Roquefort is situated in an area of outstanding beauty and there are a number of other attractions in close proximity to the site. This encourages tourism development in this area of France.

The real spectacle of Roquefort, however, is the mystique and legends surrounding the production of such a unique product. The visitor attraction at Société provides the visitor with an excellent insight into an ancient and special tradition.

Conclusion

Société Roquefort is a good example of an industrial tourist attraction which promotes the brand and brings in extra revenue for the organization.

Discussion points and essay questions

1 Discuss the importance of the visitor attraction at Société for the development of an export business for the cheese.
2 The development of the visitor attraction at Roquefort has relied on the appeal of an ancient production process. Evaluate the importance of this for the development of a successful industrial tourism venture.

Case study 10
Industrial tourism in France

In recent years, the industrial tourism market has grown dramatically in France. This is evident in the fact that a publisher now produces guides to industrial tourism for all the regions of France, featuring over 1000 workplaces which open their doors to the public, as well as industry-based museums.

The guides, which are published by Editions Solar, differentiate between three distinct audiences, namely:

- professionals involved in the appropriate field
- school pupils and higher education students
- the general public.

The authors divide the establishments featured in the guides into five groups, namely:

- heritage attractions and museums
- research centres
- manufacturing industries
- artisan or craft workshops
- services.

The 1996 guide to the Bretagne and Pays de la Loire regions of north west France listed some 144 establishments in some nine départements or counties. Perhaps it is not surprising, in France, that a quarter of these were mainstream food and drink manufacturers. Another ten establishments were in fish farming or seafood production and processing.

Industrial tourism permeates most areas of the French economy as can be seen from the following examples of workplaces, included in the guide:

- the local newspaper in Morlaix
- a hydro-electricity power station in Northern Brittany
- potters and wood turners
- working flour mills
- printers

- a cement works in the Mayenne Département
- an abbey where the nuns make cheese
- a local radio station in Laval
- farms producing and selling pâté de foie gras
- wine producers
- oyster 'farms'
- the airport at Nantes
- a bus company
- salt pans on the coast
- a food industry research establishment
- biscuit factories
- a naval dockyard at Lorient
- an Yves Rocher cosmetics plant in Southern Brittany
- an audio-visual production company in St Malo
- textile factories.

The guide also features a number of industry-based museums including industries so diverse as cars and printing, mushrooms and cider, wine and salt. Some of these are what would be termed in France, 'ecomusées', in other words, museums that present heritage themes in their correct geographical setting, and which tell the story of the way in which people have made a living in the area over time.

The vast majority of establishments in the guide offer guided tours, either for the safety of visitors or to allow them fully to understand the processes involved. It can also be essential for security reasons. Many companies do not charge visitors, but a number insist on people making prior appointments. A significant minority offer guided tours in English, German, Spanish and Italian, reflecting the nationality of the majority of foreign visitors.

The experience of industrial tourism in France illustrates a number of consumer preferences when it comes to visiting workplaces. It shows that people particularly like to visit:

- places where famous branded products are produced, for example, Remy Martin Cognac, Cointreau Liqueur and the Ricard brand of Pastis
- unusual products such as oysters
- organizations that provide a public service that is used by everyone, and which is paid for through taxes, such as electricity generating plants
- production processes which are traditional and/or picturesque, including cutlery in Thiers, cheese on farms, and pottery manufacturers
- high technology industries such as computer-aided design
- products and services that are part of everyday life like newspapers, salt, biscuits and banks
- factories where products can be bought at discount prices, such as those textile producers who have on-site factory shops
- establishments where visitors hope to receive free samples of a desirable product, like wine or chocolate, for instance
- controversial organizations including nuclear power stations.

Although a little dated, two reports dating from 1993, in *Tourism Eco* and *La Gazette Officielle du Tourisme*, give an interesting picture of the industrial tourism market in the early 1990s in France. It was estimated that over 5000 enterprises opened their doors to visitors and that, between them, they attracted some 10 million visitors. Four 'attractions' attracted over 100 000 tourists per annum, with the top attraction being a tidal power station in Brittany which attracted some 350 000 visitors in 1992. The other three most popular workplaces were all connected with the food and drink industry (Swarbrooke, 1995a).

The same sources reported that, at the time in question, some 67 per cent of French people had already visited an industrial tourism attraction, while only 57 per cent had visited a major national museum. When questioned, some 75 per cent of French people said they would definitely or probably visit an industrial attraction while they were on holiday.

Conclusion

Many commentators would argue that this popular interest in industrial tourism reflects the growth of post-modernism and the rapid nature of industrial and economic change, in France and beyond.

Certainly we can see evidence of this growing interest in industrial tourism in the UK including Scottish whisky distilleries, 'Cadbury's World' and breweries. In recent years, destinations have developed industrial tourism products including programmes of workplace visits such as 'Quality North' in the North-East, and 'Sheffield Works'. However, interestingly, in both cases the vast majority of workplace visitors have been local people.

Discussion points and essay questions

1 Discuss the main reasons why an enterprise might choose to open its doors to visitors.
2 Compare and contrast the likely motivators for visiting industrial tourism attractions, for the three market segments identified at the beginning of the case study, namely, professional people, educational visitors and the general public.

Case study 11
British Airways – environmental policy

Background

British Airways is the world's leading international airline and one of the most profitable. The financial results of the company continue to set standards for the whole industry. The conversion of British Airways from the public sector to a profit-motivated business, and the accompanying long-term operational and marketing campaign which accompanied this turnaround have been documented by Horner and Swarbrooke (1996).

More recently, the company has established the 'Environmental Campaign' which is a long-term strategy to try to improve the company's performance and reporting measures in this area. The early stages of this campaign have been evaluated by Horner and Swarbrooke (1996). This case study aims to evaluate the development of the environmental campaign of British Airways, and the response of consumers to these initiatives.

Introduction

British Airways is now the 'world's favourite airline', and has an enviable financial performance for an international company in this sector. The Chairman, Sir Colin Marshall, commented on the company's excellent financial performance in the Annual Accounts for the period 1995/96 as follows:

A further year of record performance has been achieved, with profit attributable to shareholders increased by 89 per cent to £473 million. Each of our quarterly results has set a benchmark of record performances.

The company had increased profit and earnings substantially in the 1996 period, compared to the 1995 period. This can be seen in Exhibit 11.1.

The authors would like to thank Dr Hugh Somerville for his help in the writing of this case study.

Exhibit 11.1   Financial performance of British Airways, 1995/96

£ million	1995	1996
Turnover	7760	7177
Cost of Sales	(6903)	(6436)
Gross Profit	857	741
Profits for the Year	473	250
Earnings per share	49.4p	26.2p
Dividends per share	13.65p	12.40p

Source: British Airways Annual Accounts, 1995/96

Exhibit 11.2   The franchisees and Alliance Carriers of British Airways

British Isles
An extensive scheduled domestic network together with close links with franchisees Brymon Airways, CityFlyer Express, Loganair, Maersk Air, and Manx Airlines (Europe), give British Airways the widest coverage in the British Isles.

Europe
British Airways, with its partner airlines TAT European Airlines and Deutsche BA, serve 61 European cities from hubs in the UK as well as Paris and Munich in Mainland Europe.

Middle East
British Airways flies to 13 destinations in the Middle East with dedicated cabin crew fluent in local languages offering superior in-flight service.

Latin America and Caribbean
British Airways serves 16 destinations and major gateways in Latin America and the Caribbean from the UK, including this year's new service to Grand Cayman, and the resumption of flights to San Juan.

Africa
Fourteen flights a week link Heathrow with South Africa, while the airline's biggest network change this year saw the transfer from Heathrow to Gatwick of 11 weekly Central and East African services, making Gatwick the airline's principal African gateway.

Asia/Pacific
British Airways and Qantas connect the UK and Australia offering over 50 flights a week. British Airways flies to 23 cities in the Asia/ Pacific region enabling connections with Qantas flights to over 70 destinations in the region and the USA

Source: British Airways Accounts, 1995/96

British Airways is an international airline which has developed as a result of global strategic alliances with other airlines. The company, together with its franchises and Alliance carriers Qantas, Deutsche BA and TAT European Airlines, now offers a route network which covers 477 destinations in 97 countries. Details of the franchisees and Alliance carriers are shown in Exhibit 11.2.

The airline has had an impressive long-term development concentrating on improvements in operational efficiency and improving marketing operations and customer services. In 1995/96, 32 million people flew on British Airways and the company treated each of them as an individual, offering excellent customer service. Customer loyalty figures suggest that the airline is matching up to their expectations for service levels and value for money. The airline is not complacent, however, and is constantly looking for ways to improve the experience of customers who choose to fly with the airline.

In 1995/96, the company launched a three-year plan, at a cost of £500 million, to improve the travel experience for all passengers. This will involve radical enhancements to every aspect of customer service. The first stage of this programme involved the increase in leg room by 25 per cent in the Club World long-haul business. To help with the programme,

---

Exhibit 11.3   Sir Colin Marshall's commitment to the environment policy of British Airways

The Company's well-established programme to ensure that the 'environmental factor' is taken fully into account in every area of airline activity, is detailed for all to see in our annual Environment Report. The British Airways Tourism for Tomorrow Awards scheme works, for example, on a world-wide basis to encourage environmental care and sustainable development within the travel and tourism industries. During the year, we sponsored and helped organise the first-ever International Children's Conference on the Environment. It was held in Eastbourne, in association with the united Nations Environment Programme, attracting 800 children from many parts of the world. More recently, I was privileged to accept the coveted and rarely-awarded James Smithson Bicentennial Gold Medal from America's Smithsonian Institution for our corporate support of its work to conserve endangered animal species.

The environment, in terms of local relationships, is one of the current themes of our Community Relations programme, along with youth development and tourism and heritage. The Change For Good Scheme, in which cabin crew collect unwanted foreign currency from passengers, continues to raise much needed funds for UNICEF. Our employees organise four charitable ventures, Dreamflight, Operation Happy Child, Cargo Kidney Fund and the Dhaka Orphanage.

Good environmental practice and our wide-ranging community relations programmes are dedicated to our corporate goal. 'To be a good neighbour, concerned for the community and the environment'.

Source: British Airways Annual Accounts, 1995/96

specially designed 'cradle seats' have been introduced with a unique tilting base which gives substantially better support and comfort for the back.

In the same year, the First Class service was improved and customers are now provided with their own individual compartment within the cabin, which they can use for themselves, or as a mini-meeting room, or as a bedroom with a fully flat 6ft 6ins (198 cm) bed.

A new approach to in-flight customer service has also been introduced and staff offer a more personalized style and à la carte menus are now standard. Check-in times have also been improved for First and Club passengers with the introduction of 'queue-jumping' channels.

The airline has also stated publicly that it is committed to the environment. One of the company's corporate values is to be a Good Neighbour, concerned for the community and the environment.

To monitor progress in this regard, the company publishes annually an Environment Report. The Chairman, Sir Colin Marshall, has stated his commitment to the Environmental policy in a very long statement which appeared in his Annual Report for the period 1995/96. This statement is shown in Exhibit 11.3.

Exhibit 11.4   Environmental damage caused by air travel

Noise
- Noise-aircraft noise affects the local community
- Noise from the Ground Power Units
- Noise from engine running during testing

Waste
- Waste from the aircraft and catering
- Hazardous waste from engineering
- Effluent
- Office Waste

Emissions to atmosphere
- Atmospheric impact of aviation
- Local air quality affected by ground transport
- Emissions from ground vehicle fleet
- Emission from maintenance processes

Congestion
- Congestion in the air
- Traffic pressures on the ground

Tourism and conservation
- Impacts at destinations including waste, congestion, emissions and noise
- Conservation issues

Source: British Airways/The Aviation Environment Federation (1995)

Aviation and the environment

The potential for the damage to the environment as the demand for air travel increases has been recognized and documented by many commentators (Archer, 1993; Schumann and Wurzel, 1994; Smith, 1989; WWF International, 1994). A summary of the types of damage that aviation travel can cause to the environment is shown in Exhibit 11.4.

Exhibit 11.4 also shows that although air travel is an integral part of the modern world, with tourism and business travel being recognized as making a major contribution to economic development, it has tremendous potential for damaging the environment. It has been recognized by British Airways that managing the impact on the environment in a responsible and acceptable way is central to the long-term survival of the airline. The Aviation Environment Federation has been established by an independent Federation of interest groups, and is concerned with all the environmental and amenity effects of aviation.

The European Union's programme of policy and action on the environment, 'Towards Sustainability', specifically targets five sectors, including both transport and tourism, as critical to development of a strategy for sustainable development. British Airways define sustainable development as 'the means, in practice, that the global society must seek to use natural resources more efficiently to protect natural "capital" for future generations'.

There has been regulation on aspects of airline operations such as noise, emissions and waste. Fiscal measures have also been applied and may be expanded further. Local noise charges at airports are examples of a fiscal measure. Self-interest of the airline companies involved can lead to environmental measures being taken. Fuel economy in aircraft, for example, can save the airline money in the long term, and give environmental advantages.

British Airways' environmental policy

British Airways has addressed environmental issues, historically, through individual departments. It was considered so important, however, in 1989, that a central Environment Branch was established to focus on this important area. The company now has a clear environmental management structure, consistent with best industry practice, which is shown in Exhibit 11.5. The full statement of the company's environmental policy is published each year in the Annual Environmental Report.

The British Airways Policy for the Environment and the Environmental Strategy are shown in Exhibits 11.6 and 11.7 respectively.

The transparency of the environmental policy and the method of reporting their activities in the Annual Environmental Reports has brought considerable recognition to the airline. In the 1996 Sustainability Report, which looked at company reporting techniques for environmental policies, British Airways scored a highly commendable 4 on a 1–5 scale.

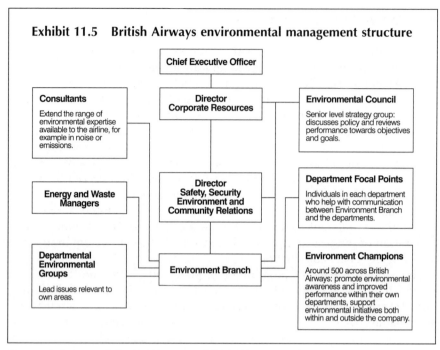

Exhibit 11.5 British Airways environmental management structure

- Chief Executive Officer
- Director Corporate Resources
- Director Safety, Security Environment and Community Relations
- Environment Branch

Consultants
Extend the range of environmental expertise available to the airline, for example in noise or emissions.

Energy and Waste Managers

Departmental Environmental Groups
Lead issues relevant to own areas.

Environmental Council
Senior level strategy group: discusses policy and reviews performance towards objectives and goals.

Department Focal Points
Individuals in each department who help with communication between Environment Branch and the departments.

Environment Champions
Around 500 across British Airways: promote environmental awareness and improved performance within their own departments, support environmental initiatives both within and outside the company.

Source: Aviation and the Environment. British Airways and AEF

Exhibit 11.6 Policy

British Airways will seek:

- to develop awareness and understanding of the interactions between the airline's operations and the environment
- to maintain a healthy working environment for all employees
- to consider and respect the environment and to seek to protect the environment in the course of its activities

Source: British Airways/The Aviation Environment Federation (1995)

Exhibit 11.7 Environment strategy

British Airways will strive to achieve this by:

- setting clearly defined objectives and targets addressing our environmental issues in our commercial decision making
- working constructively with organisations concerned for the environment
- promoting our environmental activities with our staff, customers, and other stakeholders, and letting them know of our concern for the environment
- providing support and advice to staff, suppliers and other stakeholders on environmental matters relating to our operations
- using natural resources efficiently
- monitoring, auditing and reviewing our performance

Source: British Airways/The Aviation Environment Federation (1995)

British Airways tour operations and environmental policy

British Airways operates a tourism business in the British Airways Holidays division. The potential damage to the environment by tourism has been recognized and steps need to be taken to help organizations work towards sustainable tourism practices. British Airways has worked with several organizations that have been set up to raise awareness of the issues related to bad tourism practice. These organizations are summarized in Exhibit 11.8.

British Airways is trying to take positive steps to encourage environmentally responsible tourism. The company has developed a scheme – 'British Airways Tourism for Tomorrow Awards' – which encourages tour operators to protect the environment at resorts. Organizations apply for these awards and the overall winner is chosen from each of five world-wide regional winners and receives the Global Award. There are two special awards aimed at encouraging organizations in the mass tourism sector to behave in a more environmentally friendly manner. The awards are publicized through the British Airways global network and the awards ceremony is shown on the UK travel programme *Wish You Were Here*.

British Airways Holidays is also encouraging a more environmentally friendly approach. An Environmental Co-ordinator was appointed after a review in 1993. A series of programmes and initiatives were started following this appointment. Details of these are shown in Exhibit 11.9. These initiatives are in their early stages of development but are already providing a lead in the tourism industry. An example of an Earthwise Guide for one British Airways Holiday destination is shown in Exhibit 11.10.

Exhibit 11.8   Organizations established to raise awareness of issues relating to bad tourism practice

- **Tourism Concern** – pushing forward the debate about what is good or bad tourism and questioning the direction in which the industry should be moving.

- **Campaign for Environmentally Responsible Tourism (CERT)** – encourages awareness and feedback on experiences as a tourist. Activities include publishing a set of guidelines and distributing them to tour operators to pass on to their clients.

- **The International Hotels Environment Initiative (IHEI)** – targets the hotel sector and encourages positive action.

- **Green Globe** – set up under the auspices of the **World Travel and Tourism Council (WTTC)** – offers a package of practical environmental advice to various sectors of the industry who join as members.

- **ASTA (American Society of Travel Agents Inc.)** and **PATA (Pacific Asia Travel Association)** have published codes of practice.

Source: British Airways/The Aviation Environment Federation (1995)

Exhibit 11.9   British Airways Holidays environmental programmes and initiatives, 1996

1 **Life cycle analysis of a holiday destination** – The company commissioned a detailed study of the impacts of their product at a specific destination – the Seychelles. A number of issues were highlighted including water pollution and exploitation of endangered species for souvenirs.
2 **'Earthwise' guide** – The British Airways brochure for travel from the UK contains a panel with environmental guidelines for holiday-makers.
3 **Traveller donation schemes** – Some brochures contain details of donation schemes in support of conservation projects in places such as Kenya, India, Thailand, Venice, Florida and California.

Source: British Airways Holidays

Exhibit 11.10   Earthwise guide

Fragile Earth – *Wherever you go be a friend to the environment*
British Airways Holidays is committed to improving environmental practice and performance in all aspects of its business. The company held an environmental audit of its operations of 1993 and is working actively as a member of the tourism industry to safeguard holiday destinations for future generations. Through its Traveller Donation Scheme, we actively support important conservation work in countries around the world.

Travel Wisely
- Find out as much as you can about the wildlife, culture and history of your destination. Try to understand the local community and its customs.
- Support the local economy by using locally-owned services and buying regional produce – from souvenirs to the local brew.
- Don't buy products like ivory, coral or tortoiseshell, which are made from endangered species.
- Corals are living creatures, easily damaged just by touch. Avoid standing on them and resist the temptation to collect any corals, shells or other reef species.
- Protect the local environment – dispose of litter carefully and avoid disturbing or damaging wildlife or plants.
- Conserve energy, turn off lights and air conditioning, and save water.
- Ask permission before taking photographs of local people, show respect for religious symbols and rituals. Avoid giving presents or money to local children – if you wish to help youngsters, it is better to give to a local school.
- Dress modestly particularly outside the main tourist areas.
- You can help conservation efforts by visiting parks and reserves. Your support will encourage local authorities to protect their heritage.
- If you witness or encounter environmental abuses, please write to the country's tourist board or an environmental organisation. If you have any comments or suggestions we would be glad to hear from you. Please write to: Environmental Coordinator, Marketing Department, British Airways Holidays, Astral Towers, Betts Way, Crawley, RH10 2XA.

Source: British Airways Holidays brochure

Exhibit 11.11   BA Fact Sheet given to holidaymakers before travel to Thailand

Environmental information

You may find it hard to imagine as you visit some of the more beautiful sites, but the natural environment in Thailand is under massive pressure.

British Airways Holidays want to give customers some background information to help customers to view Thailand through a green lens. It should help you to ensure that your visit to Thailand does not contribute to the growing pressure on the country's environment.

As the population grows and industry booms, so does the demand for land building. Each year, Bangkok – which accounts for about three-quarters of national economic output – concretes over another 8,000 acres of farmland.

Bangkok has virtually no sewage facilities, which puts huge pressures on the city's canals (or klongs) and on the great Chao Phraya River which flows through the city's heart. Happily, there is now an Environmental Protection Act which gives top priority to sewage treatment in Phuket and Pattaya. Business people face fines and even jail sentences for pollution related offences.

If you find yourself wondering why the streets are so congested, just remember this extraordinary fact : vehicle sales have been growing at about 35 per cent a year. An estimated 800 new cars arrive every day – that's an extra two miles of cars bumper to bumper. Thais not surprisingly, are waking up to their environmental problems. Look out for posters featuring a pair of angry 'Magic Eyes', part of a major Bangkok campaign to discourage litter.

Population growth has been phenomenal in recent decades. The population of Bangkok today is larger than the entire population of Thailand in 1910. There is even a Bangkok restaurant dedicated to the theme of contraception. It is called 'Cabbages and Condoms'.

With a surprisingly high number of young Thais involved in some form of prostitution, AIDS is now a growing concern.

Now AIDS is putting sex tourism firmly in the spotlight, with Thailand ranking alongside or possibly ahead of the USA.

For a lesson in eco-history visit the beautiful Vrinannek Teak Mansion in Bangkok. Once the home of King Rama V, the building dates from a time when teak trees were still Thailand's most valuable resource. With 81 rooms, this is said to be the largest building ever made out of golden teak. Teak contains a special oil which helps it resist heavy rain, hot sun and insects. A solid piece of the wood, it is said, can easily last 1,000 years.

But the world's appetite for tropical timber has chewed great holes in Thailand's forests. Coupled with tree-felling by farmers and opium poppy growers, the result was that the country's forest cover was cut in half between 1960 and 1985.

Despite logging bans and attempts to replant logged areas, Thailand continues to lose its forests. Today the country's rainforests and other natural treasures need urgent protection. Remember, this is a country in transition, from an agricultural economy to one based on industry. But ask yourself: can any country afford to lose its natural resources at this rate? The answer, surely is, no. Visit one more of Thailand's wonderful National parks and see for yourself what is at stake.

Source: British Airways Holidays

An example of environmental literature that is given out before travel is shown in Exhibit 11.11. These guides encourage holidaymakers to treat the environment with respect and cause minimum damage while they are on holiday. They also point out special features related to the individual destinations.

The consumer and environmental policy

Research by Laws and Swarbrooke (1996) indicated that the people in the UK do not put sustainable tourism at the top of their list of priorities, when they are choosing tourism products.

British Airways commissioned a piece of primary research in 1996 to investigate consumer perceptions of environmental policies in the tourism industry (Pembroke, 1996). The sample survey was carried out between 4 and 20 June 1996 and involved face-to-face interviews with a total of 402 respondents who were all UK residents travelling outbound for leisure purposes with a range of tour operators.

The survey was based on a Waste Education Model (WEM) developed by the New South Wales Environment Protection Authority. The survey questioned the respondents about the most important issues for aviation in their opinion. This showed that energy conservation was considered an important environmental issue for aviation. Respondents up to the age of 24 (70 per cent), students (61 per cent), activists (57 per cent) said that they would choose an airline or tour operator that took environmental issues into account. These groups also mentioned issues which are not so widely understood, such as loss of cultural diversity at the destination.

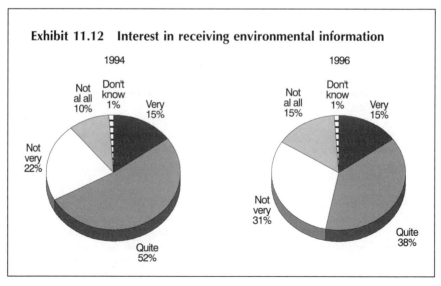

Exhibit 11.12   Interest in receiving environmental information

Source: British Airways

The individuals were then questioned about their interest in receiving environmental information. This research showed that overall interest had decreased since 1994 when a similar piece of research was undertaken. The results of this section of the research is shown in Exhibit 11.12.

The respondents were also asked to comment on the method by which they would like to receive environmental information. The results of this questionnaire are shown in Exhibit 11.13. It can be seen that customers like to receive this information by a variety of techniques and especially in holiday brochures.

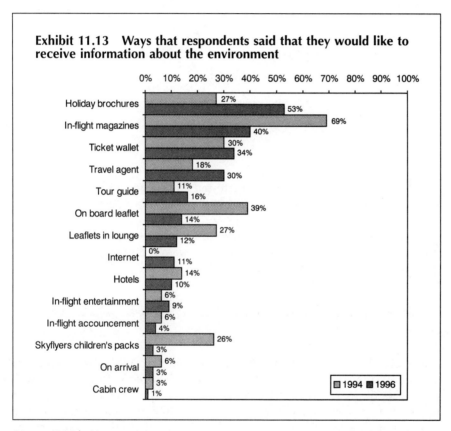

Exhibit 11.13   Ways that respondents said that they would like to receive information about the environment

Source: British Airways

The most interesting part of the research was the question relating to people's purchase decisions to gauge whether the environment was important as a factor when choosing a holiday. The respondents were presented with a range of behavioural statements and asked to choose the most appropriate statement for them. The statements and results of this part of the research are shown in Exhibit 11.14.

The research showed that although there was a level of environmental concern amongst the respondents, there was evidence to suggest that certain subgroups were much more concerned than others.

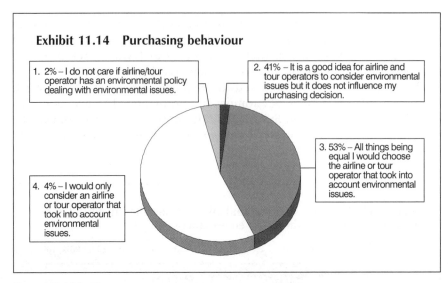

Exhibit 11.14   Purchasing behaviour

1. 2% – I do not care if airline/tour operator has an environmental policy dealing with environmental issues.

2. 41% – It is a good idea for airline and tour operators to consider environmental issues but it does not influence my purchasing decision.

3. 53% – All things being equal I would choose the airline or tour operator that took into account environmental issues.

4. 4% – I would only consider an airline or tour operator that took into account environmental issues.

Source: British Airways

Respondents who were most interested in receiving information were students and young people up to 24. It is important that this group is communicated to because of the growth of tourism to exotic locations, characterized by remoteness and cultural diversity coupled with a lack of understanding of foreign cultures. This was recognized by one tour operator in the Tourism Concern/WWF report (WWF International, 1994):

There has been a boom in exotic holidays, but no boom in awareness of foreign cultures.

This piece of research helped British Airways develop their Environmental Communications Strategy for 1996/97. This has been designed to raise awareness of the fact that the company has an environmental strategy, and to raise awareness of environmental issues and tourism, generally. The target audience which was proposed as a result of the research is as follows:

● aged up to 34
● students
● travelling for holiday purposes
● independent travellers; and
● travelling within Europe and Africa.

This group has high levels of environmental concern, activism, green consumerism and interest in environmental information, and also has low levels of awareness of the BA environmental programme.

Conclusion

British Airways will continue their long-term environmental policy and will be trying to communicate their successes via different communication mediums, including their Annual Environmental Report. Work will continue on trying to encourage people to take a more responsible attitude to tourism in co-operation with such bodies as WWF.

Customers at present, however, seem to have a limited interest in environmental measures, and seem to be more interested in other features such as destinations, facilities, entertainments and price.

Targeting the subgroup that has a particular interest in environmental policies will be crucial in increasing overall awareness and interest.

Discussion points and essay questions

1 Evaluate the reasons for an apparent lack of interest amongst consumers in the UK in environmental issues of tour operation and airlines when purchasing holiday products.
2 British Airways is trying to communicate their environmental policies to customers with the aim of increasing interest and encouraging concern. Discuss the most appropriate way of communicating this information to customers, in your opinion.

Case study 12
TUI, Germany – environmental policy

Introduction

TUI (Touristik Union International) is the largest tour operator in Europe. The company is based in Germany and has developed a wide range of mass-market tourism products which are distributed in major countries throughout Europe. TUI has developed their tourism business by ownership and part investment in a range of tour operators, hotel companies, incoming agencies and distribution companies. The TUI Group is shown in Exhibit 12.1.

It can be seen from the exhibit that TUI participates in the ownership of tour operators in a number of European countries including Germany, Austria, Netherlands, Switzerland and Belgium. It also has substantial interest in hotel companies and incoming agencies in destinations which are of major importance for the TUI Group. Through its participation in hotel companies, TUI safeguards its influence on hotel quality and the group's financial performance. The TUI hotel portfolio consists of the five brands RIU, Grecotel, Iberotel, Dorfhotel and Club Robinson, with over 120 hotels in 16 countries.

The company has been quick to capitalize on an increase in European travel and tourism which occurred in the year 1995/96, despite the difficult economic conditions which occurred throughout Europe.

The TUI Group performed very well in the period 1995/96, and was able to expand its market position nationally and throughout Europe. The four business segments of the TUI Group – business tour operating, hotel companies, incoming agencies and share holdings in distribution, all performed positively in the 1995/96 financial year. The good financial performance, which is shown in Exhibit 12.2, allowed the Group to further enlarge its position as European market leaders in the tourism business.

The Group turnover increased in this period by 19.4 per cent to DM7.7 billion and profits reached a satisfactory level of DM151.2 million. The growth in turnover was largely due to the development of the various business sectors of the Group including Arke, Netherlands, and Airtours International Germany.

The authors would like to thank Dr Wolf Michael Iwand of TUI for his help in the writing of this case study.

Exhibit 12.1   TUI Group, 1997

TUI Konzernunternehmen – **TUI group companies**	**TUI assoziierte Unternehmen –** **TUI associated companies**
Veranstalter – *Tour Operators:*	*Veranstalter –* *Tour Operators:* Jet air – 50%
TUI GmbH & Co. KG – 100% Air Conti Flugreisen – 100% Airtours International – 100% 1–2-Fly – 100% Wolters Reisen – 100% Seetours International – 75% TUI Austria – 100% TUI Nederland – 91% TUI Suisse – 60%	*Hotelgesellschaften –* *Hotel companies:* Cyprotel – 50% Grecotel – 50% Iberotel Marokko – 50% RIU – 50%
Hotelgesellschaften – *Hotel companies:*	*Zielgebietsagenturen –* *Incoming agencies:* Holidays Services – 50% Miltours – 50%
Robinson Club – 100% Dorfhotel – 100% Iberotel Türkei – 100% Iberotel Tunesien – 100% Egyptotel – 60%	Ranger Safaris – 50% Tantur Turizm – 50% Travco – 50% Tunisie Voyages – 50% Aeolos – 49%
Zielgebietsagenturen – *Incoming agencies:* TUI Italia – 100% Ultramar Express – 99% Travel Partner Bulgaria – 95% Airtour Greece – 90% Pollman's Tours + Safaris – 75%	*Vertriebsbeteiligungen –* *Distribution companies:* Reisebüro Enzmann – 50% Tiroler Landesreisebüro – 51% VTB-VAB – 50%
Vertriebsbeteiligungen – *Distribution companies:* TUI UrlaubCenter – 67% Dr. Degener – 100%	

Source: TUI Annual Accounts, 1995/96

Why does TUI have its own Hotel Companies?

- hotel companies are one of the four business segments of the TUI Group besides
  - tour operating
  - incoming agencies and
  - shareholdings in distribution companies
- through its participation in hotel companies TUI safeguards its influence on hotel quality and the groups' financial performance.
- hotel participations provide wide spread exclusivity for the TUI Group and thus guarantees bed capacities

Exhibit 12.2   Financial performance of the TUI Group, 1996/97

	Unit	1996	1997
Number of tour operator guests	thousands	6.267	5.246
Sales	million DM	7.701	6.451
Result of ordinary activities	million DM	182	190
Group profit for the year	million DM	151	165
Cashflow	million DM	204	197
Capital expenditure	million DM	320	276
Fixed assets	million DM	644	513
Securities and bank deposits	million DM	442	538
Shareholders' equity	million DM	335	346
Balance sheet total	million DM	1.644	1.470
Equity ratio	percent	23	24
Asset coverage ratio	percent	69	76
Employees	number	8.802	8.004

Source: TUI Annual Accounts, 1996/97

TUI Hotel Companies – an overview

- the TUI Hotel-Portfolio consists of 5 brands with as per day 118 hotels and 3 other hotel participations with a total of 62 000 beds in 16 countries
- in 1996 those hotels achieved more than 13.5 million overnights generating a total of DM 1.1 billion in revenue
- 37 TUI Hollies, a customer selected award for the 100 most popular hotels, out of about 6 000 contracted TUI hotels were awarded to hotels belonging to RIU, Grecotel, Iberotel, Dorfhotel and Robinson Club in 1997

The brands

 → 58 hotels in Spain, Florida/USA, Cuba and the Dominican Republic

→ 16 hotels in Greece

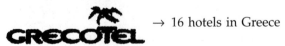 → 16 hotels in Turkey, Tunisia, Morocco, Egypt and Cyprus

 → 6 hotels in Austria

 22 clubs in Greece, Spain, Turkey, Italy,
→ Tunisia, Mexico, Kenya, Sri Lanka, Austria
and Switzerland

The TUI environmental policy

The TUI Environmental policy has been developed as a central strategy of
the Group (Horner and Swarbrooke, 1996).

TUI's environmental strategy is an integral part of the TUI quality
strategy. The TUI corporate policy states:

*the protection of an intact nature and environment are of outstanding importance
to us.*

It is the aim of the Group to try to preserve the national basic substance of
the product that the Group is offering in the form of the sea, the beach, peace
and quiet, landscape, the animal world and nature.

The Group has appointed Dr Wolf Michael Iwand as their Environment
manager to manage the Group's environmental policy. He reports directly to
the Board of Directors. The Group has recognized that it is key for any major
tourism business that it makes major efforts to minimize the environmental
effect on the natural environment which holiday makers are visiting. It is
only by taking a positive approach to environmental planning that tourism
companies will continue to be able to be successful in the future.

The Group has short, medium and long-term objectives in relation to the
environment. These planning objectives are shown in Exhibit 12.3.

It can be seen that this programme outlines a series of measures which the
Group hopes to achieve up to the year 2030. This includes moves towards
'Eco-labelling' and 'Eco-auditing', which originate from Brussels. The Group
has four main aspects to the drive for sustainable tourist development. The
first of these involves reducing pollution by all means and by low-cost
activity. The second aspect is the establishment of financial and technical
feasibility at the destinations. The third aspect is to stimulate environmental
awareness amongst vacationers and clients, and to achieve satisfaction by
environmental quality. The final aspect is to ensure that a measurable return
on investment is secured.

TUI have already commenced the first stage of their environmental
initiatives and are working with experts and environmentalists, local
authorities and hotel partners, to ensure that the holidays on offer are as

Exhibit 12.3   TUI's planning objectives

Time Period	Ecological objectives	Measures	Economic objectives
Short term	Reduction of environmental pollution and impairment	Education/consulting Program organization Hotel management	Quality control Product optimization Ensuring returns
Medium term (up to 2005)	Environmental relief Prevention of environmental pollution and impairment	Environmental standards/ Eco-labelling Environmental information systems Environmental quality goals	Management of risk and opportunities/ innovation
Long term (up to 2030)	Environmental relief Prevention of environmental pollution and nusiance Environmental improvements	Eco-controlling Ecological product control Environmental impact assessment	Securing the future Securing and improving revenues

Source: TUI, 1997

environmentally friendly as possible. The Group has established environmental criteria for their destinations, hotels and carriers. Details of these are shown in Exhibit 12.4.

Information on the TUI environmental programme

Information concerning the environment collected by the Group and stored in the TUI Environmental Database. This information is used in planning and in the holiday brochure. The hotels contracted by TUI are examined using a comprehensive environmental acceptability checklist. The Group works on local environmental action to try to allay problems such as malfunctioning sewage plants or improper tipping of rubbish and bring together tourist officials, local authority representatives, local politicians and hoteliers in 'round table' meetings, in order to find joint solutions. TUI have also worked with their airline partners and other carriers to improve their environmental friendliness on the criteria outlined in Exhibit 12.4.

Customers and the TUI environmental policy

TUI have recognized that an unspoiled environment is key for customers when they are choosing holidays. The main characteristics for 'Quality

Exhibit 12.4   Holiday making and environmental friendliness

TUI Destination Criteria:
- Bathing water and beach quality
- Water supply and water-saving measures
- Wastewater disposal and utilization
- Solid waste disposal, recycling and prevention
- Energy supply and energy-saving measures
- Traffic, air, noise and climate
- Landscape and built environment
- Nature conservation, species preservation and animal welfare
- Environmental information and offers
- Environmental policy and activities

TUI Hotel Criteria:
- Waste water treatment
- Solid waste disposal, recycling and prevention
- Water supply and water-saving measures
- Energy supply and energy-saving measures
- Environmentally oriented hotel management (focus on food, cleaning and hygiene)
- Quality of bathing waters and beaches in the vicinity of the hotel
- Noise protection in and around the hotel
- Hotel gardens
- Building materials and architecture
- Environmental information and offers of the hotel
- Location and immediate surroundings of the hotel

TUI Carrier Criteria:
- Energy consumption
- Pollutant and noise emissions
- Land use and paving over
- Vehicle/craft, equipment and line maintenance techniques
- Catering and waste recycling and disposal
- Environmental information for passengers
- Environmental guidelines and reporting
- Environmental research and development
- Environmental co-operation, integrated transport concepts
- Specific data: Vehicle/craft type, motor/power unit, age

Source: General Information Brochure, TUI Travel, 1997 catalogues

Tourism' were researched by Opaschowski (1993) and are shown in Exhibit 12.5. It can be seen that a large number of the characteristics chosen by respondents were related to the environment.

TUI researches customer views on the environment with a customer questionnaire. The results of their market research and customer letters they receive, are reflected in their environmental measures, which helps to ensure that the Group ensures the best customer orientation from the environmental standpoint.

Tour operators, holiday regions and hoteliers are trying to improve their environmental measures in response to customer demand. The customer

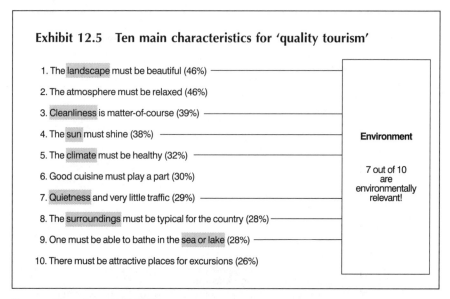

Source: Opaschowski (1993)

has however been spoiled with reduced package prices across Europe, due to intense competition in the market. Customers have also been going to more exotic locations and are seeking more thrilling diversions.

TUI has recognized that the task of persuading these hedonistic citizens of the leisure era to save water and energy, and to avoid discarding litter, even during the most relaxed weeks of their year, is difficult but not impossible. The Group has recognized that reasoned briefing on the ecology of the destination and the environment in resorts, rather than preaching, is required. The publication of sea water analysis and beach qualities are practical examples of this. Publicity for new national parks, cycle tracks and footpaths are other practical examples.

Communicating to the consumer

TUI have recognized that long-term briefing of consumers on their environmental measures is the way to improve recognition of the environment in relation to tourism. Market research in Germany has shown that German tourists are environmentally conscious and consider this when choosing holidays (TUI). It is important that the environmental measures taken by TUI are communicated to the customer in an effective way. TUI produces approximately 30 million TUI brochures every year, which all incorporate information about the environment. This includes both good and bad points about the destination and tries to state realistic facts about the environmental conditions in different parts of the world.

The customer can compare the information which they read in the brochure with the conditions found at the destination. If the environmental situation

Exhibit 12.6　Environmental information in TUI travel brochures

'Nature and environment'

Extracts from TUI catalogues, explaining the 'Nature and Environment' situation for the exemplary cases of Fuerteventura, La Palma and Namibia.

Fuerteventura

Fuerteventura's beaches are acclaimed by our guests as the best in Europe. They are regularly cleaned, and the coastal waters are monitored within the international Coastwatch Network. Five bathing beaches on Fuerteventura were awarded the European Blue Flag in 1995. Due to the low amount of precipitation, the island is one of the driest in the archipelago. The extensive grazing of the many goats has intensified the island's desert character, and erosion, which is perhaps its greatest problem, is increased. Water supply is difficult. Because of the geological conditions, groundwater is scarce. The population is supplied by four seawater desalination plants, while the larger hotels often have their own facilities. For a renewable supply of energy, the 'Parque Eolico' with 45 wind turbines came into operation in 1994. A second wind park is planned. A Nature Conservation Act designates 13 protected zones, amongst which are the unique and particularly endangered dune landscapes of Corralejo and Jandia. Together with the ASCAN environmental organisation, TUI supports the ECO ISLA Fuerteventura project.

La Palma

La Palma boasts one of the ten Biosphere Reserves on Spanish territory, a piece of nature that is unique worldwide. 40% of the island is already protected under nature conservation law. Last year, however, forest fires took toll of some 5,000 hectares. Although the 'Green movement' is strongly represented on La Palma, environmentally sound measures such as the construction of new sewage plants or the introduction of controlled waste management systems are currently only at the planning stage. The new Development Plan makes a positive step forwards: this stipulates that 80% of the island must be held free from development.

Namibia

The government of Namibia has limited the number of tourists per annum to a maximum of 650,000 to preserve the country's unique landscape. Tourist accommodation in nature reserves will continue to be owned by the government in future; ecological sensitive areas like the skeleton coast are protected by strict environmental legislation. More and more lodges are using solar energy for producing hot-water. On account of natural conditions (e.g. climate) Namibia suffers from water shortage. Therefore our request: please use water economically!

'Ecologically sound hotel management'

Extracts from TUI catalogues, explaining 'Ecologically Sound Hotel Management' for the exemplary case of Cyprus

Columbia Pissouri, Pissouri

Own biological sewage plant with re-use of purified water for garden irrigation. Use of solar energy for hot-water supply. Waste separation and composting. Avoidance of disposable products.

The Annabelle, Paphos

Own biological sewage plant; re-use of purified water for garden irrigation. Use of solar energy for hot-water supply, waste separation and use of returnable bottles Automatic tailor-made air-conditioning equipment.

Source: TUI

concerns the customer they will express their dislike at the resort, to the representative, or in writing to the Company, when they return home. They can also fill in questionnaires provided by TUI to express their feelings.

Examples of information provided in TUI travel brochures in relation to destinations and hotels are shown in Exhibit 12.6.

TUI also thinks that the travel agent has a key role to play in the education of consumers on environmental matters. TUI provides seminars for travel agents so that they understand the necessity for good environmental quality. This education of the travel agent is a large task, however, given that TUI goes to about 150 destinations every year. TUI has set up an on-line programme for travel agents containing the latest environmental information to help with the process. The number of travel agents that use this service, at the moment in Germany, is very limited, but TUI hopes this will increase in the future.

The future of the TUI environmental policy

TUI has recognized that their environmental policy will help the company to be successful in 10 to 20 years time. The policy is therefore part of the long-term strategy of the company. TUI has predicted that tourism will have to be organized in a sound, safe and environmentally friendly way in the future. The company does not see itself offering 'eco-tourism' products, but minimizing the environmental impact caused by 5 million TUI customers who travel abroad every year.

The company is predicting that there will be a day in the future when consumers base their travel decision on environmental information provided by the tour operator and travel agent. The key factor in this is the point when the consumer is prepared to pay more for a better environment. Consumer behaviour which favours companies which have well-implemented environmental campaigns is supported by environmental campaigning organizations such as Greenpeace. TUI believes that it is logical for the company to prepare themselves for the day when consumers come and ask for environment-related information before booking their holidays. At this stage, the company that is not in a position to provide the information will lose business.

Conclusion

TUI is the largest tour operator in Europe and has been active in pursuing an environmental policy for all their tour operations business. The company considers that this is an important part of their future strategy, despite the fact that the consumer has limited interest in the environment in relation to tourism, at the present time.

Discussions points and essay questions

1 'Mass tourism and ecological soundness do not go together – but there is much one can do to lessen the impact of one on the other' (Dr Iwand, TUI, 1995). Discuss this comment, in relation to TUI consumers.
2 The desire for consumers to travel to exotic destinations has been accompanied by an almost total lack of interest in the environment. Discuss the reasons for this and explore what a mass tour operator, such as TUI, can do about this situation.

Case study 13
Ragdale Hall – health hydro

Find yourself at Ragdale Hall

Introduction

Ragdale Hall was established in the 1970s as a business which offered customers the opportunity to experience health, beauty and fitness treatments. There have been considerable alterations made to the Hall during the last 20 years. There have been additions made to the original buildings, and facilities have been regularly updated so that the latest treatments and products can always be offered to guests. Ragdale Hall is situated within easy reach of the M1 and A1, between Loughborough and Melton Mowbray in the heart of the Leicestershire countryside. Guests can arrive at the Hall by car or taxi from local railway stations.

Ragdale Hall is set in its own extensive landscaped gardens and combines the charm of traditional Victorian architecture with the most modern facilities, to create one of the most luxurious and relaxing health resorts in the UK.

Ragdale Hall – the company

Ragdale Hall has had many owners during its history. It has been operated as a restaurant and a nightclub with gambling facilities. It became a health hydro in 1972 when Slimming World purchased it. Ragdale Hall changed ownership in June 1990, when it was bought by Gerry Nesbitt and Michael Isaacs – the founders of Our Price Records. These new owners have taken a personal interest in the business and have provided the finance for an extensive refurbishment and extension of the facilities. A financial summary of the business is shown in Exhibit 13.1.

The authors would like to thank Victoria Taylor of Ragdale Hall for her help in the writing of this case study.

Exhibit 13.1   A financial summary of the Ragdale Hall company

	1995
Turnover £	4 953 680
Profit before taxation £	846 798
Net tangible assets £	6 467 200
Return on Capital Employed %	13.09

Source: Ragdale Hall Accounts

The products and services on offer at Ragdale Hall

Ragdale Hall has written a definitive guide to what a health hydro is, so that customers can understand the difference from luxury hotels with a health and leisure spa or upmarket private hospitals and retreats. The criteria which have been developed are shown in Exhibit 13.2.

It can be seen from this list of criteria that the health hydro concept offers customers a very different experience from that at other types of establishments. Customer service in a relaxed and pleasant surroundings is a key part of the product on offer.

Exhibit 13.2   A health hydro – the criteria

- Countryside location with resort-like feel
- Provision of healthy, calorie controlled food on a full-board basis
- Absence of alcohol (wine excepted)
- A no smoking policy in public areas and bedrooms but provision of a small smoking room
- Provision of high quality beauty treatments, some of which are included in overnight packages
- Large variety of exercise classes for all fitness levels provided in the inclusive rate
- Ban on pets and anyone under the age of 16
- A very high guests/staff ratio allowing the very highest standards of personal care, e.g. five-star hotel 1 : 1; Ragdale 2 : 1
- Comprehensive health and beauty consultations to ensure compatibility with treatments and activities offered
- Provision of some medical/dietary advice when necessary but to ensure safety rather than to give any treatment
- Casual dress and leisure wear in all areas at all times
- No conferences, functions or indeed suits!
- An organization geared completely towards caring and total relaxation from the choice of staff, type of decor, ambience of the whole complex to the treatments and activities on offer

---

Source: Ragdale Hall

Ragdale Hall has been designed to allow customers to put together their own mix of activities and treatments. Customers may choose to have an active or more leisurely time. They may want to unwind or tone up, to shed weight or to relieve their worries.

Ragdale Hall offers a full range of services. Guests may choose to purchase a package or may come to stay at the Hall and put together their own programme of activities. The special packages which are on offer at the Hall are shown in Exhibit 13.3. These packages allow the guests to purchase a range of products at one time, and still purchase a range of extra services during their stay. These extra services include body and facial treatment (incorporating Clarins, Declor, Guinot and Kanebo products), fitness activities, and hair and beauty treatments.

Exhibit 13.3   The range of services on offer at Ragdale Hall, 1997

1 Overnight accommodation. Incorporating a luxury hotel with single and double rooms and suites.
2 Restaurant and other catering facilities. A luxury restaurant which offers meals at different calorie levels. There is also a small self-service bar and snack service facility.
3 Retail outlets. Two shops which offer a full range of beauty products, clothing and other merchandise.
4 Health treatment. A range of treatment rooms surrounding an impressive conservatory seating area. These include revitalizing facials, relaxing massages, aromatherapy, reflexology thermal wraps, stress relief and detoxifying treatments.
5 Beauty treatment. A full range of beauty treatments available including manicure, pedicure and expert make-up. There is also a full hair service and a Sun Centre which offers the safest and most modern tanning technology.
6 Exercise areas. A fully equipped gymnasium which includes the latest resistance fitness equipment, bicycles, jogging and rowing machines. There are fitness co-ordinators who look after customers. The Hall also has an exercise studio with fully sprung wooden floor.
7 Water treatment. A luxurious range of water treatments, centred around an indoor pool. Steam room, and a luxurious new spa complex with traditional Scandinavian saunas, plunge pools, hurricane showers, whirlpool spas, floatation tanks and hydrotherapy baths complete this area.

Source: Ragdale Hall

All residential stays include:

● Comfortable accommodation in a bedroom with en suite facilities.
● Breakfast served in the room, three-course buffet lunch and four-course table d'hôte dinner.
● A full introductory tour of the Hall.
● An in-depth consultation with one of the Senior Therapists, including advice on treatments and an individually recommended exercise programme.

- A welcome reception with refreshments, allowing the opportunity to meet the Guest Liaison Officer and Duty Manager who will ensure the break gets off to a great start.
- An extensive daily programme of exercise classes to suit all fitness levels.
- Use of the gymnasium including induction session to cover training principles and safety.
- Use of the indoor and outdoor swimming pools and water exercise sessions.
- The unrestricted use of the Whirlpool Spa bath as well as separate male and female Spa areas with sauna, steam and plunge pool facilities.
- Unlimited use of bicycles, championship standard tennis courts, pitch and putt course, croquet and boules areas.
- The opportunity to relax and unwind, whether it be in one of the relaxing lounges or outside in the beautiful gardens.
- Evening talks and demonstrations covering a wide range of interesting topics.
- Specially tailored packages to suit all needs.
- Weekend breaks, short or longer holidays, Healthy Option breaks geared around a specific objective, i.e. Focus on Fitness, Stress Buster, Slim and Shape, New You, Total Pampering.

New treatments are always being added to the list of treatments on offer. The staff at Ragdale Hall have just developed a new massage treatment called Ragdale Multi Method Massage, which is now on offer to customers. Two highly skilled therapists work in unison to give the customer a feeling of deep relaxation. Music and the use of aromatherapy oils are used during this type of massage. Ragdale Hall is also considering using further holistic treatments such as Kineseology.

The food is considered a very important part of the product at Ragdale Hall. The guest can choose a menu to help them lose weight or they may choose to eat a healthy balanced diet, but with more calorific content. This is particularly important when the guest is taking part in strenuous physical exercise programmes during their stay at Ragdale Hall.

Ragdale Hall has a wealth of experts who can offer advice on special subjects such as:

- bodycare during pregnancy:
  - suitable treatments
  - products which help alleviate the symptoms of pregnancy
  - exercise programmes
- advice for safety in the sun:
  - the best products
  - skin care routines
- care of those forgotten extremities – the hands and feet
- alternative therapies:
  - the concept
  - the difference between each one and who they can help

- stress management:
  - giving up smoking
  - lifestyle
  - diet
- menopause:
  - treatments and activities to counteract its effects.

Ragdale Hall also owns a Health and Beauty Centre at Kings Court, Altrincham, Cheshire. This Centre offers customers of Ragdale Hall a continuous service of beauty and health treatments when they return home. The Centre also has its own clients.

The Centre is non-residential and offers each client a personal consultation in which treatments or a programme is discussed in depth. The Centre has comfortable treatment rooms, changing and shower facilities, and a peaceful relaxation room. Drinks and light snacks are also available for guests during their time at the Centre.

Prices for Ragdale Hall ranged in 1997 from £89 to £135 per person per night (sharing) and include full use of facilities, food and treatments.

Other health resorts in the UK

There are other health resorts available to customers in the UK offering a similar range of products to Ragdale Hall. These are shown in Exhibit 13.4. Customers at Ragdale Hall come from all over the UK, although a significant proportion of these come from areas within a short drive time. It is clear that customers choose the health resort they want to visit according to the range of facilities and treatments on offer and their geographic location. Once a customer has chosen their preferred health resort, they are likely to be very loyal to this and return over and over again.

The guests at Ragdale Hall

A summary of the types of guest who stay at Ragdale Hall is shown in Exhibit 13.5.

It can be seen that the guest of Ragdale Hall is usually female, 35+, working and from a higher socio-economic group. Interest in health and nutrition has been growing rapidly over the last ten years. There has been intense interest in the mainstream media in the UK, and people are generally much more knowledgeable about health and nutrition than they were ten years ago. Treatments such as aromatherapy and floatation are widely recognized by people in general in the UK, whereas ten years ago they were considered rather 'freaky' and unusual. This growing knowledge and education about healthy lifestyles, which has been fuelled by the government report *The Health of the Nation*, has meant that people, particularly women, are much more conscious about their general levels of health and fitness.

Exhibit 13.4   Health resorts on offer in the UK – 1997

Health Resort	Location	Facilities	Price Indication
Champneys	Tring, Hertfordshire	Country house hotel. 82 rooms. Various treatments including alternative therapies	Weekend break. £498 per person (sharing). Including meals and treatment
Henlow Grange	Home Counties	Country house. 170 guest capacity. Various treatments	£224.95 per person. Including meals and treatments. 2-night break
Stobo Castle	Peebles, Scotland	Castle. Range of treatments. 22 bedrooms	£117 per person per night. Including treatments
Lucknam Park*	Near Bath, Wiltshire	Country house hotel with 31 bedrooms and suites. Range of treatments	Two night package. £265–575 per person for room
Gray Shott Hall	Hindhead, Surrey	Victorian house. Range of treatments	£105 –180 per person per day. Includes treatments
Chewton Glen*	Hampshire	18th-century manor house. Range of treatments	£150–250 per person, half board. Treatments extra.

*Hotels with health facilities as an addition
Source: Ragdale Hall

Exhibit 13.5   The guests of Ragdale Hall, 1997

- 92% of guests are female, 8% are male
- Guests are generally in the age range 35–70
- Guests are usually professional or working women, usually from socio-economic groups ABC1
- Guests have a personal interest in health and nutrition and are generally trying to lead healthier lifestyles
- 64–65% of guests have visited Ragdale Hall before. The average number of visits per year is 2/3. Lengths of stay vary but the three-night packages and day packages are very popular
- Guests live in all areas of the UK
- Guests come on their own, but it is more common for them to be pairs or in small groups.

Source: Ragdale Hall

This growing interest has encouraged the development of the health hydro business which offer the guest the opportunity to experience health and beauty treatments and 'chill out' from the everyday stresses and strain of modern living. The health hydro now appeals to people, especially women, from different backgrounds. It is not just the reserve of the 'health freak' or the celebrity model.

The benefits which the guest receives at Ragdale Hall

There is a wide range of benefits which guests say that they receive when they visit Ragdale Hall. These are shown in order of importance in Exhibit 13.6.

Exhibit 13.6   The benefits that guests receive from their visit to Ragdale Hall, 1997

- Relief of stress
- Improvements in looks
- Becoming more healthy
- Escapism
- Losing weight
- A holiday experience
- Recovering from illness
- Getting ready for the 'big day', e.g. marriage or birth of a child

---

Source: Research carried out at Ragdale Hall

Exhibit 13.7   Testimonial of a guest – Ragdale Hall, 1996

To celebrate our 40th birthdays, my friend and I spent a week at Ragdale Hall Health Hydro last July. There we, too, learned not to feel guilty about spending time on ourselves – and about leaving behind our families, pets, jobs and so on, for the first time ever.

A little bit of pampering not only made me look better, but, more importantly, made me feel good and has helped re-establish a sense of my own worth after years of putting myself last in the pecking order. This is having a knock-on effect of making me more pleasant to live with – as my family will testify.

It strikes me that the hectic lifestyles many women lead, well into middle-age and beyond, goes against the natural rhythm of things. Making time for ourselves to relax and feel good must go some way towards redressing the balance and can only benefit our health overall. Long live health hydros and beauty treatments.

Alison Garner, Llandaff, Cardiff

Source: Ragdale Hall

On leaving Ragdale Hall, guests always express feelings of total relaxation and the desire to go back as soon as possible. It seems that the experience is often almost addictive for a large number of guests. The accompanying example testimonial from one guest, shown in Exhibit 13.7, illustrates this point very effectively.

Conclusion

The health hydro concept has developed recently as a response to the growing interest with healthy lifestyles. Ragdale Hall has responded to this trend and offers guests the opportunity to relax and be pampered in luxurious surroundings.

Discussion points and essay questions

1 Evaluate the reasons for the growth of interest in the health hydro concept. How will this develop in the future?
2 Discuss in detail the motivators and determinants for customers of Ragdale Hall.

Ragdale Hall has undergone a period of major refurbishment during 1997–1998. A new swimming pool has been added which incorporates lane swimming, a massage area and a new whirlpool spa. New sauna and steam rooms have also been added. This constant updating of facilities is of major importance to maintain repeat visits by customers.

Case study 14
The international spa market

We saw, in Chapter 3, that spas have played a significant role in the historical development of tourism. While their popularity has declined in countries like the UK, it is still a very large market world-wide, and some spas are enjoying a renaissance.

A report published in 1996 by Deloitte-Touche estimated that every year there are some 160 million visits paid to spa resorts in Europe, the USA and Japan alone. The same document suggested that there were over 2000 spas resorts in Japan, nearly 450 in Italy, and between 250 and 300 each in the USA and Germany.

Deloitte-Touche's research indicated that the proportion of spa visits to overall population was probably highest in Germany and Japan. However, length of stay for Japanese visitors was one of the lowest in the world at around 1 to 2 nights while French visitors were the highest at over 20 nights.

In the same year, the Economist Intelligence Unit published a report on European spas, which was written by Nancy Cockerell. This contained a number of interesting statistics, including the following:

- In Germany, spa towns receive between 40 per cent and 45 per cent of domestic and international tourist trips, and account for around half of all visits to European spas. Spa visiting, in Germany, is popular with both sexes, and all age and income groups. It is also linked to social tourism and the health service in Germany.
- While Germans often also travel abroad in search of spa treatment, most Italians and French tend to stay at home and use domestic spa resorts.
- The market in France is split between traditional thermal spa resorts and the more modern thalassotherapy complexes. Provision for the former is usually subsidized whereas that for the latter is almost wholly commercial.
- The motivation for thermal spas is largely medical whereas that for thalassotherapy is not.
- The thalassotherapy market is also younger than the market for the thermal spas.
- In 1994, it was estimated that the 'European international health holiday market involved around 1.7 million tourists, around 1 per cent of all tourism demand in Europe.

The growing popularity of thalassotherapy is exemplified by the creation of new centres, in recent years, in countries like Cyprus, Morocco, St Lucia, Venezuela, Indonesia and Japan.

Likewise the increased concern with health and beauty is linked to a growth of new types of resort, including:

- pelotherapy (mud treatment) and heliotherapy (sun treatment) in Israel
- seaweed alyotherapy in Ireland.

To ensure their future, spas are seeking to diversity their offer to attract wider market segments. Some thermal establishments have opened themselves up to day visitors, while others have established other health facilities such as outdoor jogging tracks, for instance. Many resorts have sought to become leading venues for major sporting or cultural activities and events. They are also developing better leisure shopping attractions. They are aiming to make themselves attractive to more market segments by offering 'something for everyone'.

A good example of this trend is the famous thermal resort of Vichy, which publishes a glossy brochure, in three languages entitled, 'The Season in Vichy'. Amongst the attractions highlighted in this brochure in 1996 were the following:

- over 50 golf tournaments, so that golfers, who may not have visited Vichy for spa treatment, come for the golf and then often use the thermal spa facilities
- a major tennis tournament
- riding schools
- nightclubs
- an outdoor 'laser spectacular' show
- art exhibitions
- antique fairs
- theatre programmes
- opera performances
- concerts, from classical music to jazz
- horse-racing meetings
- car tours of the surrounding region.

Tour operators are increasingly seeking to exploit the growing interest in health and beauty to develop package holidays, based on different kinds of spa treatments. This is seen, for example, in France. One operator, Vithalité, produced a 76-page full-colour brochure, in 1996, offering holidays to some 88 destinations in 16 countries, all based on health treatments. These included:

- hotels on the coast, in the countryside, and in the mountains of France
- complexes in summer sun destinations such as the Algarve, Costa Brava and Cyprus
- resorts and hotels in North Africa, Israel, Thailand, Abu Dhabi and the Caribbean.

Most of the products were based in upmarket hotels. Their brochure featured details of specialist packages offered to meet the needs of different groups, including:

- women who have just had babies
- those who suffer from migraines
- sports men and women
- people who are trying to give up smoking
- elderly people.

It also included details of conference facilities in its featured hotels so that companies could combine business with healthy activities.

Interestingly the brochure featured advertisements for a range of other products, including:

- a low calorie sweetener
- seawater and seaweed-based cosmetics.

The prices charged by Vithalité, in Summer 1996, including accommodation, meals and treatments in France were typically as follows:

- five nights in Brittany – FF4500–5500
- five nights in Monte Carlo – FF8000–11 500
- five nights in the Alps – FF4500–9500.

Outside France, prices were as follows, including flights, treatments and half-board accommodation:

- seven nights in the Algarve – FF11 000–14 800
- seven nights in Finland – FF9000
- seven nights in Morocco – FF5800–8900
- seven nights in Thailand – FF17 200.

Conclusion

It looks likely that the growing interest in health will create an increasingly large market for health resorts. However, it seems likely that as governments continue to cut subsidies to traditional spas, a growing share of the market will be met by commercial operators. It also seems likely that as consumers become more experienced they will, as in other sectors of tourism, demand new types of product.

Discussion points and essay questions

1 What are the main opportunities and threats that will affect the future growth of the European spa market?
2 Apart from the desire to improve one's health, what other factors might motivate a tourist to visit a spa?

Case study 15
Granada Studios Tour

Introduction

Granada Studios Tour is Europe's only major television and film themed park. The £8.5 million attraction opened to the public on 20 July 1988. A further £12 million was invested to extend and develop the facilities and an additional £5 million was invested at the start of the 1996 season. The accent of the Studios is on real value for money and good family entertainment and the average length of stay at the attraction is five to six hours, making the attraction a genuine day out.

Unlike most theme parks, Granada Studios Tour is open all year round. Granada Studios Tour is situated immediately behind the Granada Television Centre, where many television programmes are made, including the world famous *Coronation Street*. This means that the attraction is intimately linked with the television world and visitors have the opportunity to see the inside of the studios and occasionally see the real stars. The tour is a member of the Granada Entertainments which is a member of Granada Group Plc.

Historical background

Granada Studios Tour is situated on land that originally belonged to Granada Television, which is the largest established Independent Television programme company in Britain. Granada Television was amongst the first producers of television programmes in the UK, originally going on air on 3 May 1956.

The first episode of *Coronation Street* was broadcast on 9 December 1960. It rapidly became a household name and the programme still has a loyal audience of approximately 18 million viewers in the UK.

Work began in 1987 to develop the derelict land which was behind the Granada Television Studios into a major film and television attraction. There

The authors would like to thank Alan MacGregor of Granada Studios Tour for his help in the writing of this case study.

were 3½ acres of land available, which meant that there was ample room for the development. The tour opened to visitors on the 20 July 1988 and was built at an original cost of £8.5 million. The tour gradually expanded and incorporated sets which had been used to film major television dramas, such as the Baker Street set which had been used by Granada Television for the filming of *The Adventures of Sherlock Holmes* and the House of Commons set used to film the serialization of Jeffrey Archer's novel *First Amongst Equals*.

Exhibit 15.1   The development of the Granada Studios Tour

Granada Studios Tour – Opened 20 July 1988

1988   Backstage Tour, Magic Show
1990   Europe's first MotionMaster – Alpha One Cowboy
1991   Coronation Street Experience
1992   New props room on Backstage Tour, new film on MotionMaster, new 3-D show, Sounds Spectacular Special Effects Show
1993   Baker Street Experience, Horribly Squeamish Make-up Show, Sooty Show, MotionMaster 'White Thunder' experience
1994   UFO Zone – the Alien Ride, new visitor car park and Manchester coach park
1995   RoboCop – The Ride – a thrilling new ride on the MotionMaster Haunts of the Olde Country – European premiere of a spooky 3D show, 3D Rock Laser Show, Deadly Effects – a gory special effects show, Coronation Street studio sets – famous interior sets
1996   Futurevision, Cracker Interactive Detective Show, Aliens™: Ride at the Speed of Fright – the new MotionMaster ride

---

Source: Granada Studios Tour

A brief summary of the development of the tour can be seen in Exhibit 15.1.

It can be seen from Exhibit 15.1 that the tour has developed gradually over the years, which is typical of visitor attraction development. New attractions have been added to appeal to all age groups. The latest ride to be added in 1996 was the 'Aliens™: Ride at the Speed of Fright', the new MotionMaster ride which transports the visitor around the tour at frightening speed.

Granada Studios Tour

The tour incorporates a number of different experiences, rides and shows, and has a wide selection of refreshment outlets and souvenir shops, which have all been designed to appeal to a wide cross-section of customers. The full range of these components of the tour is shown in Exhibit 15.2.

There are also a number of recognized photo opportunities available within the tour. These are shown in Exhibit 15.3.

Photo opportunities are important for any visitor attraction, since they ensure that visitors show the photographs to their friends and family, which gives excellent word of mouth promotion.

Exhibit 15.2   Granada Studios Tour

Refreshments:	Deerstalker Pub
	Baker Street
	Rovers Return
	New York Diner – First & Ten
	Mrs Hudson's Potato Shop
Souvenirs:	Madisons
	Laughing Stock
	The Sherlock Holmes Shop
	Cadbury's Shop
	Coronation Street
	Baker Street Shop
	Rosamund Street Shop
	Russell Grant's Astrology Shop
	The Sooty Shop
	The UFO Shop
Shows:	Sound Show
	Live Special Effects
	House of Commons Comedy Debate
	Sooty and Friends
	OB and Emmy's Disco
	Baker Street Show
Rides:	UFO Zone
	Alients™: Ride at the Speed of Fright
Experiences:	Futurevision – This is Tomorrow
	Cracker – Interactive TV Detective Show
	Backstage and Soundstage Tour
	Baker Street
	Coronation Street
	Russell Grant's World of Astrology
	New York Street
	Tele Stars – appear in an episode of Coronation Street
	Chromakey – Jurassic Park

Source: Granada Studios Tour

Exhibit 15.3   Photo opportunities at Granada Studios Tour

- Outside No 10 Downing Street
- On Coronation Street
- Outside 221B Baker Street
- With the Wurlitzer in the Baronial Hall
- With the New York Cops
- With Sherlock Holmes
- With Pearly Kings and Queens
- In the Speaker's chair of the House of Commons
- In the Home of the Future – date 2056

and post a letter from Coronation Street

Source: Granada Studios Tour

Two of the new rides are 'Futurevision: This is Tomorrow' and 'Aliens™: Ride at the Speed of Fright'.

- 'Futurevision' is a new £2 million attraction at Granada Studios Tour. Visitors to 'Futurevision' are guided through a series of stages which allow them to see a vision of the future world. Visitors can see a vision of TV Past and Present, take part in Interactive Television and take part in video conferencing. They can look into the future of shopping and experience 'shopping from your armchair' and learn about the World Wide Web and the Internet. Visitors can also experience the Virtual Classroom and The Mobile Workplace. Finally, visitors can explore the Home of the Future. 'Futurevision' gives the visitor an insight into the powerful forces that are shaping the world for the future.
- 'Aliens™: Ride at the Speed of Fright' is the newest ride at Granada Studios Tour and forms part of the latest £5 million investment in 1996. The ride is based on the hit movie, *Aliens™*, and is a unique ride and cinematic experience that give the visitor the impression of an intergalactic experience. The ride is a mixture of fantastic special effects film footage and seats that move dramatically in time with the on-screen thrills.

One of the best known parts of Granada Studios Tour is the *Coronation Street* Experience. This takes the visitor on a nostalgic journey through over 30 years of the country's best-known drama series. Visitors can stroll past the Rovers Return, pause at the most photographed house on the Street and peep through the shop windows.

The Backstage Tour is a new one-hour guided backstage tour which takes visitors behind the scenes of TV and gives them the chance to operate a camera, read from an autocue and present the weather forecast.

Opening times and prices for the tour

Granada Studios Tour is open all year round. In 1997 the grounds are open Tuesday–Sunday, from 9.45 am with last entry at 3.00 pm on weekdays or 4.00 pm at weekends. Entrance prices are £12.99 for adults and £9.99 for children. There are special discounts available for groups. The price is all inclusive and includes all the parts of the tour.

The success of Granada Studios Tour

The tour has been very successful since it was opened. It is now one of the UK's leading leisure attractions. Over 4 million guests have visited the attraction since it opened, including 45 000 coach parties. The tour has won many awards since it opened. These are shown in Exhibit 15.4.

> **Exhibit 15.4   List of awards won by Granada Studios Tour**
>
> 1 British Interactive Video Association Award – 1988
> 2 Manchester Society of Architects Award – 1988
> 3 English Tourist Board – England for Excellence Award – 1989
> 4 UK Tourism Marketing Award – 1989
> 5 British Tourist Authority – Come to Britain – 1989
> 6 North West Tourist Board Award for Excellence – 1989
> 7 Association of Small and Medium Sized Enterprises – 1989
> 8 Royal Institute of Chartered Surveyors – Inner City Award – 1989
> 9 Regional Loo of the Year Award – 1989
> 10 Development of a Visitor Attraction Award – North West Tourist Board – 1989
> 11 Norweb Beta Award – 1990
> 12 Overall Leisure Award – Leisure Week – 1991
> 13 Best North West Tourist Attraction – North West Tourist Board – 1992
> 14 Best Leisure Attraction – Cellnet Hospitality Awards – 1993
> 15 Best North West Tourist Attraction – North West Tourist Board – 1993
> 16 National and International Award for Baker Street – Greater Manchester Business Through Tourism – 1994
> 17 Finalist – 'Best In-House Public Relations Department' – *PR Week* Awards – 1994
> 18 Silver Award – 'Tourism For All' – England for Excellence Awards given by the English Tourist Board
> 19 Coach Industry Awards – 1995 – Best Group Attraction

Source: Granada Studios

Visitors can now stay overnight next door to Granada Studios Tour at Granada's first luxury 156-bedroom hotel, which opened on the 12 October 1992. The four-star Victoria and Albert Hotel is a grade II listed building constructed on the site of two 150-year-old Victorian warehouses.

Brand proposition and promotion

Granada Studios Tour has been developed as a brand which offers visitors the experience of visiting Europe's most spectacular film and television experience, and providing a unique insight into the TV world behind the screen.

A series of promotions are undertaken to advertise the attraction. These include:

● direct mail to key customer groups
● press advertising
● radio advertising.

Public relations activity is carried out by Mason Williams PR. Specific press promotions as well as photo opportunities and celebrity endorsements are strategies that the company is currently developing. Granada Studios Tour also funds ticket values for joint promotions, with third-party brands such as major multiples.

Visitor profile

Extensive market research has shown that Granada Studios Tour appeals to a wide cross-section of people of different ages and from different social classes. The tour has welcomed guests from 5 to 95 years old, from all over the world. Over 4 million guests have visited the tour since it opened in 1988, and 40 per cent of these guests come from outside the Granada region.

The worldwide popularity of Granada programmes such as *Sherlock Holmes, Brideshead Revisited* and *Coronation Street* has attracted visitors from all over the world, including America, Japan and Canada. Market research has also shown that word of mouth recommendation is the major source of awareness with 70 per cent of repeat visitors intending to come back again. Imaginative catering and merchandising units encourage the visitors to spend as much again as is raised from the ticket spend.

Exhibit 15.5   Demographic data of visitors – Granada Studios Tour

Socio-economic groups – Granada Studios

	Granada Studios Tour	*National*	*Other Theme Parks*
AB	16%	18%	18%
C^1	41%	24%	23.6%
C^2	27%	28%	34.4%
C^1 and C^2	68%	52%	58%
DE	16%	29%	23.9%

Age distribution

Age Range	*All Visitors %*
12–15	13%
16–19	7%
20–24	6%
25–34	22%
35–54	38%
55+	14%

Catchment area
UK, but greatest volume within two hours drive time.

Visitor balance

Male ratio:	49%
Female ratio:	51%

Source: Granada Studios Tour. Market Research Survey, 1996

The demographic profile of visitors to Granada Studios Tour is shown in Exhibit 15.5. It can be seen from the figures that the tour is particularly attractive to families from the C^1 and C^2 socio-economic groups. There is almost an equal ratio of males and females visiting the attraction and a wide age distribution.

One of the most important groups of visitors to the attraction is the coach tour, which forms a major part of the business and includes school trips and other organized coach tours. The attraction is featured on many tour itineraries of bus and coach operators within a two-hour driving radius.

The corporate client is also important for Granada Studios Tour. The attraction provides excellent conference and banqueting facilities with a novel twist. Corporate clients can be accommodated in one of the sets within the tour, can visit the attraction during their stay and can even be addressed by one of the many *Coronation Street* celebrities. This makes Granada Studios Tour a very attractive venue for corporate entertainment and this area of the business is growing.

Visitors to the attraction experience a range of benefits from the facilities on offer. These range from the nostalgic experience gained from the *Coronation Street* set, to the thrills and excitement gained from the new rides at the attraction. Visitors are generally looking to be entertained during a fun-packed day. It is very important that the attraction continues to develop products on offer to attract the whole family.

Conclusion

Granada Studios Tour has become one of the most popular visitor attractions in the UK. It has continued to attract visitors from the UK and abroad since opening in 1988.

Discussion points and essay questions

1 Evaluate the importance of the link of Granada Studios Tour to successful television programmes from the consumer's point of view.
2 Discuss the way in which the Granada Studios Tour Marketing Department has targeted different customer groups and give suggestions for future promotional strategies which the company could use.

Case study 16
easyJet

Background

The European air-travel market is opening up due to the deregulation of the industry and this is predicted to bring about the establishment of a whole variety of cut-price airlines which will offer airline seats at increasingly competitive prices. There is evidence already, in Europe, that air ticket prices are beginning to decrease with the increased competitive nature of the market, although there is still far to go before the fiercely discounted market which exists in the United States of America is achieved.

Stelios Haji-Ioannou – the man and his business idea

Stelios Haji-Ioannou is the son of a Greek shopping tycoon. He graduated from the London School of Economics and gained a Masters degree in shipping trade and finance at the City University Business School.

It was predicted that he would join his father's shipping empire after graduation, but he was keen to escape from his father's shadow and develop himself an autonomous personality. He became increasingly interested in the airline business and proceeded to study the American discount airlines.

He took the American airline company Valujet as a model for the type of business which he thought he could develop for the European market. The Valujet company experienced a tragic crash of one of its planes into the Florida Everglades in May 1996, and this, it is said, showed that his plans for a budget airline would have to incorporate safety features. This aspect was particularly important to him, because he was already facing charges of manslaughter, with his father, because one of the company tankers, the 232 000-tonne tanker *Haven*, had blown up in Genoa in 1991, killing five crew and polluting the Ligurian coastline.

Despite the problems which the American company Valujet had, he became increasingly convinced that the idea of a discount no-frills type of

The authors would like to thank Tony Anderson of easyJet Airline Company Limited for his help in the writing of this case study.

airline would work in the European market. The incident which finally convinced him of this was when he tried to fly to Corfu from London, only to find that the fare was more than the cost of a 14-day package holiday to the same place. This seemed to be a ridiculous situation which should be addressed. Stelios Haji-Ioannou took Freddie Laker and particularly Richard Branson of Virgin airlines as role models for his own idea. He knew that he could not survive in the airline business with just a clever idea, but needed clear business planning and management control. He had the advantage of having the opportunity to get substantial financial backing from his father, but has never played down the fact that this backing was vital to establish the business. The establishment of an airline business, after all, requires considerable investment over a substantial period of time.

He finally approached his father in March 1995, armed with a comprehensive business plan, in order to obtain financial backing for the company. His father backed him with a £5 million advance which meant that he was now in the position of being ready to set up the business he had dreamed about, and planned for.

The business idea which Stelios Haji-Ioannou envisaged was summarized by a statement he made in 1995.

Our research has shown that people in both Britain and Europe are crying out for an American style operation which will give them instant access to really cheap, reliable and safe air travel.

The development of the easyJet business

The development of the easyJet business has proceeded well since the formation of the company in 1995; details of this are shown in Exhibit 16.1.

This development has depended on a simple but clever idea. The airline would offer a no-frills service between a limited set of destinations at the lowest possible price. There would be no in-flight meals and only soft drinks and peanuts would be served. The company would sell direct, cutting out the travel agents' 15–20 per cent commission, and there would be no tickets or fancy staff uniforms.

The business concept was summarized by Stelios Haji-Ioannou in 1995, when he was talking to the press as follows:

If we were a restaurant, we would be McDonald's. If we were a watch-maker, we would be Swatch.

Stelios Haji-Ioannou decided to locate his prefabricated head office next to Luton airport, which is an hour's drive from London. The home base for the flights would be Luton airport where he could get flight slots. He then leased two Boeing 737s complete with pilots. The first flights to Glasgow and Edinburgh commenced in 1995, and were quickly expanded to serve six cities including Amsterdam, Barcelona and Nice. The company is planning to increase the number of flights per day to each location, and expand the network to other European destinations in the future. Places currently being considered include Nordic countries, Geneva, Madrid and Berlin.

Exhibit 16.1   The development of the easyJet company

1994	Stelios Haji-Ioannou has business idea for easyJet.
March 1995	£5 million investment by Loucas Haji-Oiannous. Company established and prefabricated building set up at Luton airport as company headquarters. Two aircraft leased.
18 Oct 1995	easyJet commences selling of seats. Lorraine Chase launched easyJet at Planet Hollywood, London.
10 Nov 1995	First easyJet flight.
24 Nov 1995	Glasgow and Edinburgh services commenced.
26 Jan 1996	Aberdeen service commenced.
1996	Commencement of flights to Amsterdam, Barcelona and Nice. Purchase of first aircraft.
1997	Increased frequency of existing routes. Plans to expand to Nordic countries, Geneva, Madrid, Berlin and Jersey. Purchase of three aircraft and two aircraft leased.

Source: easyJet

The current product

The current easyJet product range and an idea of prices is shown in Exhibit 16.2.

This exhibit shows that easyJet has concentrated particularly on developing their network to Scotland, which has become a lucrative market. This was particularly welcomed by the Scottish Tourist Board which concluded that the development of these flights would encourage both business and

---

Exhibit 16.2   Flight timetable and lowest single fare – 1997

Flights each way from and to Luton Airport UK

Destination	Mon–Fri	Sat	Sun	Price from
Aberdeen	3	1	2	£29
Edinburgh	5	3	3	£29
Glasgow	5	3	3	£29
Inverness	1	1	1	£29
Amsterdam	4	3	3	£35
Nice	2	2	2	£49
Barcelona	1	1	1	£49

Source: easyJet

leisure travellers to visit Scotland for days, and longer periods on a more regular basis.

The Scottish Tourist Board Chairman, Ian Grant (1995), welcomed the new service as a 'huge boost to our promotional efforts in England'.

The price for the flight depends on the chosen travel time and the market conditions. All prices are for single journeys only, and there are no child prices.

The easyJet concept

The concept of a 'no-frills' airline which offered cut price fares has been developed by easyJet and incorporates many features, which are shown in Exhibit 16.3.

Exhibit 16.3   The easyJet concept

Head Office	Prefabricated building. Paperless offices. Located at Luton airport.
Staff	Senior staff headhunted from major airlines. Minimum staffing levels. Large numbers of part time tele-sales operatives paid on commission-only basis.
Uniforms	Cabin crew dressed in orange polo shirts, sweatshirts and black slacks.
Product	Direct sales single journeys to range of destinations. Very low prices. Tickets sold direct with no use of travel agents. Ticketless system. No food – only soft drinks and peanuts served. Open seating.
Company livery	Orange and white livery. Telephone booking numbers emblazoned on side of aircraft in orange for easy recognition.
Positioning	Emphasis on budget accommodation with minimum service levels.

Source: easyJet

The product concept came under criticism by commentators in the travel and tourism industry. One particularly controversial area of the business was the decision by the founder to develop a direct booking service which cuts out the travel agency commission – other airlines have to add this on their final ticket price. Comments concerning this came from all areas of the travel industry, including the potential competitors of easyJet – Tim Jenns, Chief Executive of Ryanair UK commented (1995):

While there is room for two low cost carriers and together we will bring down fares, easyJet is making a huge mistake by ignoring the opportunity of distribution through the travel trade.

There was no doubt in the trade, however, that the easyJet type of operation would be replicated in the market over time. Many analysts have predicted the growth of these type of airlines in Europe. One analyst, Ian Lowden of Simat, Helliesen and Eichner, made predictions in 1995 as follows:

You will see deep, deep discounts being offered by a plethora of 'peanut carriers' creating massive potential savings for ordinary customers.

Competitors

There are already signs that many competitors to easyJet will develop in the future. The current range of cut-price European airlines in Europe is shown in Exhibit 16.4. Some of these new airlines will be close competitors to

---

Exhibit 16.4   Other cut-price European airlines – 1997

Company	Brand Name	Country of Operation
Virgin	Virgin Express	UK
Ryanair	Ryanair	UK
Air One	Air One	Italy
Air Germanica	Air Germanica	Italy
Debonair	Debonair	UK
Denimair	Denimair	Holland

Source: easyJet

---

easyJet, according to the routes that they develop, and the customers that they target. The major airlines will also discount fares and try to stress their particular advantages including more regular flights from mainstream airports; better levels of service and higher safety perceptions amongst customers.

The easyJet customers

Stelios Haji-Ioannou originally envisaged that the customer for easyJet would be the leisure traveller. It is becoming apparent, however, that business travellers are becoming a large part of the easyJet market, particularly on the short-haul day-return routes. It is clear, however, that the company is trying to change the customer buying behaviour patterns that have existed previously, by trying to encourage the impulse purchase of airline travel, rather like the behaviour patterns more commonly associated with the purchase of fast-moving consumer goods, or clothing. In 1996, he commented: 'We are encouraging people to take impulse purchase decisions to fly.'

The company is encouraging this type of impulse purchasing decision by a public relations campaign which describes the price of their airline seats as comparable to or cheaper than that of a pair of jeans.

Research carried out by easyJet has shown that many different market segments are making the decision to fly with easyJet. These are shown in Exhibit 16.5.

Exhibit 16.5   Customers of easyJet – 1997

Socio-economic groups	B C1s
Life-style groups	Working in skilled/professional jobs Living in urban areas within catchment area of airport. Milton Keynes is a major catchment area. Regular travellers abroad
Target groups	Leisure travellers – long stay, weekend, daytrippers VFR travellers Business travellers – (particularly from SMEs) day, overnight, longer stays Students, and people working abroad

Source: easyJet

The main customers for easyJet originate in the UK, although this depends on the route; details are shown in Exhibit 16.6. The customers originate mainly from the catchment area of the airports from which the company operates. The socio-economic profile of the customers is mixed, but tends towards the B C1 socio-economic groups. The customer is usually working in a professional job and lives in an urban area.

The town of Milton Keynes is seen by the company as being particularly representative of the type of area in which the customer of the airline live. Customers of the airline tend to be regular travellers abroad, although this picture may change in the future. Leisure travellers are a particular target group, and the cheap fares mean that they are much more likely to go for a weekend abroad, perhaps, on an impulse. The one-way fares are particularly attractive to customers who do not plan their return travel date. This means

---

Exhibit 16.6   Source of business for different routes – 1997

Scottish routes   50% of customers from Scotland
                             50% of customers from England
(Edinburgh flight – 50% business trips, 25% of flights taken are day return)

Nice route   80% of customers from UK
                             10% of customers from France (mainly expatriate)

Amsterdam route   70% of customers originate from UK
                             30% originate from Holland

Source: easyJet

that the easyJet seats are particularly attractive to students, and to people studying and working throughout Europe on short- or long-term contracts.

easyJet has found that business travellers have become an important target group. Business travellers who work particularly for small and medium-sized enterprises (SMEs) are particularly interested in the easyJet product. This is because the individual will often be responsible for the cost of the airline ticket themselves, and will therefore be very keen to keep the cost of the ticket down. The company has also tried to target purchases of airline tickets within larger companies, in a controversial advertising campaign which stressed the extra cost to the company of buying their staff seats on conventional carriers.

The interest in easyJet from the business community, as a result, has been intense, as is shown by the following statement:

Business travellers can now just hop to more and more cities and the continent. Competition for this business is hotting up.

Business Travel World (April 1996)

This statement stresses the fact that business travellers can travel around the cities of Europe on a much more impulsive basis, pulling off deals and visiting suppliers and customers. The cheaper airfares will encourage them to travel more readily and with less thought.

Students who have previously been put off extensive regular travel around Europe as a result of highly priced airline tickets are now being encouraged by companies such as easyJet who are offering a cheaper alternative, to travel more readily. Students are also being poached from the rail companies because prices are now comparable. This type of behaviour is illustrated in this statement by Barnaby Jenkins, a 23-year-old student, who purchased a long weekend in Barcelona: 'I would not have been able to do this in the past because of the cost. Now it is the equivalent of a rail fare.'

easyJet has also been attractive to professional people who had previously travelled by train to business meetings and events. This is particularly noticeable on the Scotland/England route where rail travel has been relatively expensive and slow; Alan Jackson, an Open University tutor (quoted in *Aberdeen Post and Journal*, 27 January 1996), explains: 'I could have gone by train but when I discovered how much it was with easyJet, I decided this was the way to go.'

The company predicts that the type of consumer profile will continue to develop and change over time as consumer behaviour patterns and competition changes.

The future

It is clear that the deregulation of the airline industry in Europe will continue to encourage small specialist airlines to enter the market. This will result in changing consumer buying patterns as prices drop and competition and choice increases.

Conclusion

easyJet is one of the first airlines to be set up to respond to the changing air travel scene in Europe. The business idea was simple in approach, but required the entrepreneurial spirit and financial backing which Stelios Haji-Ioannou could bring to the company. Longer term development will now be the key for the business to flourish.

Discussion points and essay questions

1 Evaluate the reasons for consumers being increasingly more willing to purchase airline seats as an impulse decision.
2 Analyse the relationship of price and consumer purchasing behaviour in the short-haul airline market.

easyJet have extended their route network since 1997 to include Palma, Majorca, Athens, Geneva, Madrid and also Liverpool to Amsterdam and Nice.

Case study 17
Las Vegas, Nevada, USA

Introduction

Las Vegas is situated in Nevada on the western side of the USA. It is 2591 miles from New York City, 288 miles from Los Angeles and 576 miles from San Francisco.

The city is visited by approximately 30 million visitors each year, and has over 102 000 hotel and motel rooms spread throughout the metropolitan area.

The city's average room occupancy rate is approximately 90 per cent and major projects are planned in the future. These include a 3000-room hotel called Bellagio to be built by Mirage Resorts Inc. at a cost of $1 billion; and Paris, a 2814-room hotel-casino, to be built by Bally Grand Inc., which will evoke Paris just after the turn of the century.

Las Vegas is unsurpassed as a resort because of its impressive range of entertainment, casinos, dining, nightlife and host of other attractions. It has become known as the city that never sleeps, offering the visitor a unique one-stop multi-dimensional vacation.

The history and development of Las Vegas

Las Vegas, which means 'The Meadows' in Spanish, was well-known as an oasis-like valley which attracted Spanish travellers on their way to Los Angeles during the gold rush. John C. Fremont led an overland expedition west and camped in Las Vegas Springs on 13 May 1944.

Nevada was the first US state to legalize gambling. This led to the position today where more than 43 per cent of the state general fund is provided by gambling tax revenue. Legalized gambling suffered a brief lull in 1910 when a strict anti-gambling law became effective in Nevada. Legalized gambling returned to Nevada during the Great Depression. The first major resort growth of Las Vegas was completed by Tommy Hull when he built the El

The authors would like to thank Rossi Ralenkolter of the Las Vegas Convention and Visitors Authority for his help in the writing of this case study.

Rancho Vegas Hotel-Casino in 1941. The success of this hotel-casino fuelled the massive expansion boom which occurred in the late 1940s when construction of several hotel-casinos and a two-way highway from Las Vegas to Los Angeles took place. One of the earliest resorts was the Flamingo Hotel which was built by mobster Benjamin 'Bugsy' Siegel.

The resort was developed extensively during the 1950s. The Desert Inn opened in 1950, and the Sands Hotel in 1952. In the 1950s the Hacienda, the Tropicana and the Stardust hotels opened. The Moulin Rouge Hotel-Casino opened in 1953 to accommodate the growing black population.

The city realized, as far back as 1950, that a way to fill hotel rooms during the slack periods of the year was to encourage the convention business. A 90 000 square foot exhibit hall, the Las Vegas Convention Center, was opened in April 1959. The Las Vegas Convention and Visitors Authority, which is supported mainly by room tax revenue, now attracts more than 2 million convention delegates every year.

Las Vegas has always been at the forefront of gambling and entertainment technology. The resort was one of the first to have multiple slot machines in the 1960s. Video machines were introduced in the 1970s and computerized slot machines were soon to follow.

Las Vegas developed the concept of the mega-resort when it lost exclusive rights to gambling casinos because gaming was legalized in Atlantic City, New Jersey in 1976. The first of these mega-resorts was the Circus-Circus Hotel-Casino, which incorporated an entertainment park, hotel and casino.

Other mega-resorts which have been developed include The Mirage Hotel-Casino (1989), The Excalibur (1990), The Treasure Island (1993) and the MGM Grand Hotel and Theme Park (1993). These mega-resorts involve huge investment plans. The MGM Grand Hotel and Theme Park, for example, cost $1 billion to build its elaborate hotel, casino, theatres arena and theme park.

The city has also been keen to encourage leisure shopping. The multi-million dollar project 'The Fremont Street Experience', was opened in 1995. This shopping centre was designed by the Jerde Partnership to create a lively urban centre which incorporates light, sound and entertainment. A brief summary of the history of Las Vegas is shown in Exhibit 17.1.

Las Vegas in 1997

Las Vegas has become America's top resort destination, offering the visitor an unparalleled range of hotels, casinos and entertainments. The climate is very warm, particularly in the months of April to September. Las Vegas averages 294 days of sunshine per year, and the average daily rainfall is very low. The dazzling strip offers a wide range of entertainment, and 'The Fremont Street Experience' offers the visitor an exciting shopping experience. Las Vegas has its own international airport – McCarran International Airport – where an average of more than 750 scheduled and charter flights arrive every day. Las Vegas has abundant nightlife and offers superstars, five major production shows, and Broadway musicals all year round. The

---

Exhibit 17.1   The history of Las Vegas

1892   Discovered by Spanish explorers
1911   The city of Las Vegas is incorporated
1931   Hoover Dam construction begins
1941   El Rancho Vegas opens
1946   Bugsy Siegel opens Flamingo Hotel
1959   Las Vegas Convention Center opens
1975   Nevada gaming revenues reach $1 billion
1989   Mirage opens – 3039 rooms
1990   Excalibur opens – 4032 rooms
1991   Construction of MGM Grand Hotel and Theme Park begins
1993   Grand Slam Canyon Adventure Dome opens
1993   Treasure Island opens – 2900 rooms
1993   Luxor Hotel opens – 2526 rooms
1993   MGM Grand Hotel and Theme Park opens – 5005 rooms
1994   Work begins on the Fremont Street Experience
1994   Boomtown opens a 300-room hotel-casino
1994   The first non-stop charter service from Europe begins from Cologne, Germany
1994   The Fiesta, the first hotel-casino in North Las Vegas opens
1995   Clark County population is estimated at more than 1 million residents
1995   Visitor Center Hoover Dam opens
1995   Announcement of construction of $420 million Paris Casino Resort
1996   The Orleans Hotel and Casino opens

Source: Las Vegas On-line Visitor Guide (http:/www.pcap.com/lasvegas.htm)

city also has the extravagant strip casinos where visitors marvel at the glittering array of buildings and lights.

Hotels and motels in Las Vegas

The city has approximately 102 000 hotel/motel rooms (1997) which appeal to a wide cross-section of visitors, whether they be holidaymakers, convention visitors or business travellers. The city has accommodation which ranges from multi-suite accommodation, which is bigger than an average home, to low budget one-room hotel accommodation. Many Las Vegas hotels offer a wide range of added-value services, including multilingual staff, gaming lessons for the novice gambler, entertainments, golf courses, travel and entertainment reservation desks, and tour attraction desks. Las Vegas has 13 of the 15 largest hotels in the world and has specialized in the development of mega-resorts, which incorporate hotels, leisure facilities, casinos and attractions.

A review of the main accommodation on offer in Las Vegas in shown in Exhibit 17.2.

A full range of restaurants offering a wide range of cuisines is also available in Las Vegas.

Exhibit 17.2   Accommodation in Las Vegas, 1997

Accommodation	Rooms	Suites	Restaurants
Aladdin Hotel Casino. 3667 Las Vegas Blvd.S. (702) 736–0111, (800) 634–3424	1110	42	6
Alexis Park Resort. 375 E.Harmon Ave. (702) 796–330, (800) 582–2228	0	500	2
Bally's Las Vegas. 3645 Las Vegas Blvd.S. (702) 739–4111, (800) 634–3434	2569	245	5
Boulder Station. 4111 Boulder Hwy. (702) 432–7777, (800) 683–7777	300	0	8
Caesars Palace. 3570 Las Vegas Blvd.S. (702) 731–7110, (800) 634–6661	1392	190	10
Circus Circus Hotel/Casino/Theme Park. 2880 Las Vegas Blvd.S. (702) 734–0410, (800) 444-CIRCUS	3744	126	6
Day's Inn Town Hall Casino Hotel. 4155 Koval Ln. (702) 731–2111, (800) 634–6541	354	3	1
The Desert Inn Hotel & Casino. 3145 Las Vegas Blvd.S. (702) 733–4444, (800) 634–6906 625	625	174	4
Fitzgerald's Casino & Holiday Inn. 301 Fremont St. (702) 388–2400, (800) 274-LUCK	652	0	5
Golden Nugget. 129 E.Fremont St. (702) 385–7111, (800) 634–3454	1907	102	5
Hard Rock Hotel & Casino. 4475 Paradise Rd. (702) 692–5000, (800) HRDROCK	340	28	2
Harrah's Las Vegas Casino Hotel. 3475 Las Vegas Blvd.S. (702) 369–5000, (800) 634–6765	1677	34	6
Hotel San Remo Casino Resort. 115E. Tropicana Ave. (702) 739–9000, (800) 522–7366	711	40	5
Imperial Palace Hotel Casino. 3535 Las Vegas Blvd.S. (702) 731–3311, (800) 634–6441	2475	225	10
Lady Luck Casino & Hotel. 206 N.3rd St. (702) 477–3000, (800) 523–9582	649	143	3
Las Vegas Hilton. 3000 Paradise Rd. (702) 732–5111, (800) 732–7117	3174	275	12
Luxor Las Vegas. 3900 Las Vegas Blvd.S. (702) 262–4000, (800) 288–1000	4474	484	9
MGM Grand Hotel & Casino. 399 Las Vegas Blvd.S. (702) 891–1111, (800) 929–1111	4254	751	8
The Mirage. 3400 Las Vegas Blvd.S. (702) 791–7111, (800) 456–7111	3044	279	10
New York-New York Hotel & Casino. 3790 Las Vegas Blvd.S. (702) 740–6969, (800) NY FOR ME	2035	189	6
The Orleans Hotel & Casino. 4500W. Tropicana Ave. (702) 365–7111, (800) ORLEANS	810	30	6
Palace Station Hotel Casino. 2411 W.Sahara Ave (702) 367–2411, (800) 634–3103	956	74	5
Rio Suite Hotel & Casino. 3700 W.Flamingo Rd. (702) 252–7777, (800) PLAY-RIO0	2554	14	12
Sahara Hotel & Casino. 2535 Las Vegas Blvd.S. (702) 737–2111, (800) 634–6666	1628	81	5
Sam's Town Hotel & Gambling Hall. 511 Boulder Hwy. (702) 456–7777, (800) 634–6371	650	33	10
Showboat Hotel, Casino & Bowling Center. 2800 Fremont St. (702) 385–9123, (800) 826–2800	446	4	4
Stratosphere Resort & Casino. 2000 Las Vegas Blvd.S. (702) 380–777, (800) 99 TOWER	1500	120	6
Treasure Island at the Mirage. 3300 Las Vegas Blvd.S. (702) 894–7111, (800) 944–7444	2900	212	7
Tropicana Resort & Casino. 3801 Las Vegas Blvd.S. (702) 739–2222, (800) 634–4000	1875	197	7

Source: Las Vegas Official Visitors Guide, Winter/Spring 1997

Casinos in Las Vegas

Gambling is one of the major attractions of Las Vegas. The city offers non-stop gaming in a variety of casinos. The gambler can take part in poker, craps, baccarat, blackjack, roulette and slot machines on a 24-hour basis. The resorts also offer classes in gambling for those visitors who are unfamiliar with the games. The range of casinos in Las Vegas is shown in Exhibit 17.3.

The city also hosts year-round gaming tournaments which have their own rules, entry fees and promotional packages that may include a two- or three-day stay, dining specials, parties and banquets. Most tournaments are open to the public and take place at casinos or resorts.

Exhibit 17.3   Casinos in Las Vegas, 1997

- Aladdin Hotel and Casino
- Bally's Las Vegas
- Boulder Station Hotel and Casino
- Caesars Palace
- Circus Circus Hotel/Casino/Theme Park
- Day's Inn Town Hall Casino
- Fitzgerald's Casino-Holiday Inn
- Golden Nugget Hotel and Casino
- Hard Rock Hotel and Casino
- Harrah's Las Vegas Casino Hotel
- Hotel San Remo Casino and Resort
- Imperial Palace Hotel and Casino
- Lady Luck Casino and Hotel
- Las Vegas Hilton Superbook
- Luxor Las Vegas
- MGM Grand Hotel and Casino
- The Mirage
- New York-New York Hotel and Casino
- The Orleans Hotel and Casino

Source: Las Vegas Official Visitors Guide, Winter/Spring 1997

Las Vegas shows

Las Vegas offers the visitor a range of spectacular shows in many of the resorts and hotels in the city. The shows on offer in the 1997 season are detailed in Exhibit 17.4.

Recreation in Las Vegas

A full range of recreation facilities are available for the visitor to Las Vegas. The weather encourages sport on a year-round basis. Most of the Las Vegas

---

Exhibit 17.4   The shows in Las Vegas, 1997

Theatre	*Show*
Aladdin Hotel and Casino	*Country Tonite*
Bally's Casino Resort	*Jubilee*
Caesars Palace	*Caesars Magical Empire*
Debbie Reynold's Hotel and Casino	*Boy-Lesque*
Excalibur Hotel and Casino	*King Arthur's Tournament*
Flamingo Hilton	*The Great Radio City Spectacular*
Golden Nugget Hotel and Casino	*Country Fever*
Harrah's Casino Hotel	*Spellbound*
The Hotel San Remo	*Showgirls of Magic*
Imperial Palace Hotel and Casino	*Legends in Concert*
The Las Vegas Hilton	*Starlight Express*
MGM Grand Hotel and Casino	*EFX*
The Mirage	*Seigfried and Roy*
Monte Carlo Resort and Casino	*Lance Burton, Master Magician*
Rio Suite Hotel and Casino	*Danny Gans: The Man of Many Voices*
Riviera Hotel and Casino	*Splash II, Voyage of a Lifetime*
	An Evening at La Cage
	Crazy Girls – Sensuality, Passions and Pudgy!
Stardust Resort and Casino	*Enter the Night*
	Stratosphere
	American Superstar
Treasure Island at the Mirage	*Mystère by Cirque du Soleil at Treasure Island*
Tropicana Resort and Casino	*Folies Bergères*

Source: Las Vegas Official Visitors Guide, Winter/Spring 1997

resorts have swimming pools and many also have health clubs. Championship golf courses and a host of tennis facilities are available to golfers and tennis players.

Attractions and sightseeing in Las Vegas

The hotels and casinos of Las Vegas offer a varied range of attractions. The latest range of these attractions are shown in Exhibit 17.5.

It is possible for visitors to Las Vegas to visit areas of outstanding beauty in the surrounding area. There are scenic destinations such as the Great Basin National Park in Northern Nevada, the Grand Canyon in Arizona, Death Valley in California, and Bryce Canyon and Zion National Park in Utah. Visitors can travel to these areas by car, bus or aeroplane.

Exhibit 17.5   The range of attractions available in Las Vegas hotels and casinos, 1997

1 *The Stratosphere Tower* – the tallest free standing observation tower in the US. High Roller roller-coaster and Big Shot Ride.
2 *The Fremont Street Experience* – 2.1 million lights in a canopy transform five blocks of downtown into a light and music show.
3 *Theme Park* at Circus-Circus Hotel/Casino, and the MGM Grand Hotel/Casino.
4 *The Dolphin Pool* at The Mirage Hotel, 1.5 million gallon pool with dolphins.
5 *The Pirate Baths* at The Treasure Island. Lifesize British frigate with cannon blasts, explosions, and a sinking ship.

Source: Las Vegas Official Visitors Guide, Winter/Spring 1997

Getting married in Las Vegas

Las Vegas has become known as the wedding capital of the world. There are more than 50 wedding chapels in the city and more than 100 000 couples obtain wedding licences every year in Las Vegas. There is no waiting period and no blood tests are required for weddings in Las Vegas, which explains the reason for its popularity. Any style wedding for visitors can be organized – this can range from a black tie affair, to exchanging vows on a motorcycle at a Chapel's drive-up window. The more exotic type of wedding ceremony includes getting married in a hot air balloon or being married by an Elvis impersonator. The Excalibur hotel can provide medieval costumes for a ceremony reminiscent of Merry Old England. The Tropicana has a thatched roof bungalow in a Polynesian setting, which is also offered for wedding ceremonies.

The Las Vegas Convention and Visitors Authority

The Las Vegas Convention and Visitors Authority (LVCVA) was created in 1995 by the Nevada Legislature to manage the operations of the Las Vegas Convention Center and to promote Southern Nevada throughout the world as a convention location.

The LVCVA has been very successful and there has been remarkable growth of visitors coming to Las Vegas because it is an excellent resort location. The Las Vegas Convention Center opened in 1959 with 90 000 square feet of space. The Center is now one of the largest meeting facilities in the USA, with more than 1.6 million square feet of available space.

The LVCVA also operates the Cashman Field Center with 100 000 square feet of meeting and exhibit space, a 10 000-seat baseball stadium, and a 2000-seat theatre.

The 12 members of the LVCVA Board of Directors have overseen the growth of Las Vegas as a business, conference and resort destination. They have a set policy to increase the number of visitors to Las Vegas and Clark County each year. The LVCVA Board of Directors has representatives from Clark County, the City of Las Vegas, North Las Vegas, Henderson, Boulder City and Mesquite, as well as representatives from the hotel/motel industry, and business and financial communities. The LVCVA Board can use its combined knowledge and experience to help Las Vegas maintain its leadership in the tourism and convention business.

Visitors to Las Vegas

Visitors to Las Vegas have grown steadily over the last ten years. The levels of growth are shown in Exhibit 17.6.

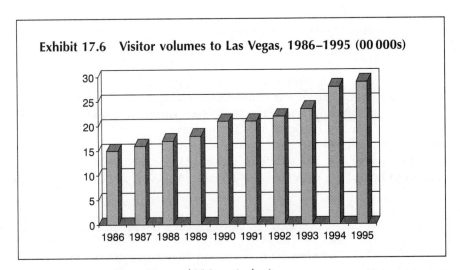

Exhibit 17.6   Visitor volumes to Las Vegas, 1986–1995 (00 000s)

Source: Las Vegas Convention and Visitors Authority

The volume of visitors to Las Vegas is fairly evenly spread throughout the year. This is seen clearly when the visitor figures to Las Vegas for 1995 are considered in Exhibit 17.7.

The spend by visitors to Las Vegas is also growing steadily, with visitor spending a total of $20.7 billion in the Las Vegas area during 1995. The average visitor spend depends on the reason for the visit. Trade show delegates, for example, spent an average of $1420 per visit in 1995. Convention or meeting delegates spent an average of $901 per visit and tourists an average of $465 per visit during the same period (Las Vegas Convention and Visitors Authority). This shows the importance of trade conventions and delegates for the Las Vegas economy.

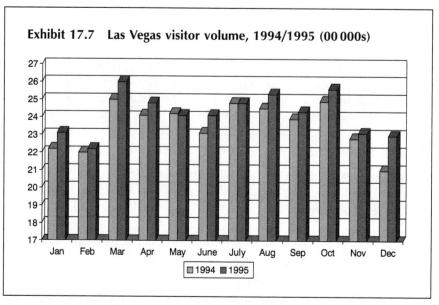

Exhibit 17.7   Las Vegas visitor volume, 1994/1995 (00 000s)

Source: Las Vegas Convention and Visitors Authority

The Las Vegas Convention and Visitor Authority have been trying to encourage the growth of the convention and trade show market in Las Vegas. The success of this activity can be seen when the growth figures for this type of business are considered. The figures for the 1986–1995 period are shown in Exhibit 17.8.

The Authority also has ambitious plans for the growth of the convention market in the future, with bookings already in place up to the year 2004.

Exhibit 17.8   The growth in convention attendance in Las Vegas, 1986–1995

Year	Number of Conventions	Attendance	Non-Gaming Economic Impact ($)
1986	564	1 519 421	1 042 279 651
1987	556	1 677 716	1 197 168 704
1988	681	1 702 158	1 242 227 536
1989	711	1 508 842	1 140 912 624
1990	1011	1 742 194	1 358 243 318
1991	1655	1 794 444	1 482 327 551
1992	2199	1 969 435	1 693 074 125
1993	2443	2 439 734	2 253 526 873
1994	2662	2 684 171	3 034 267 004
1995	2826	2 924 879	3 359 162 165

Source: Las Vegas Convention and Visitors Authority

The demographic profile of visitors to Las Vegas is shown in Exhibit 17.9. It can be seen that there is an approximate equal split of male and female visitors, and a large proportion of the visitors to Las Vegas are from the USA itself. International visitors only represented 13 per cent of all visitors in 1995.

Exhibit 17.9   Las Vegas visitor demographics

	1993	*1994*	*1995*
Male	49%	50%	52%
Female	51%	50%	48%
Mean Age	47.4	47.1	48.9
Retired	27%	26%	27%
Married	68%	66%	68%
US Resident	85%	86%	87%
International	15%	14%	13%

Source: Las Vegas Convention and Visitors Authority, Las Vegas Visitor Profile Study

---

The Las Vegas Convention and Visitor Authority undertakes an annual visitor profile study which reveals some interesting information about the behaviour of visitors when they are in Las Vegas. Highlights of this survey for 1994 and 1995 are shown in Exhibit 17.10.

It can be seen from Exhibit 17.10 that there is high repeat purchase behaviour amongst visitors to Las Vegas, with over 70 per cent of visitors during the 1994/95 period being in this category. The tourist represents a high percentage of visitors to Las Vegas, but business and convention visitors are an important part of the market, particularly as they have a higher per capita spend on average. Arrival by air represents an important part of the market, although arrival by other methods of transport such as car or bus is also important. This will be explored in more detail later. Room occupancy is predominantly in pairs, although single and triple occupancy are also important. Single occupancy is particularly important in the business and convention market.

Visitors to Las Vegas often come on multiple visits during any one year and short stays are more common than longer vacations. Visitors with children represent a small part of the market, which is probably explained by the high incidence of gambling in the resort, which is not always appealing to this group. A large proportion of the visitors to Las Vegas do participate in some gambling during their visit, and often spend a large proportion of the day in this activity. A smaller proportion of visitors also gamble outside Las Vegas. A large proportion of visitors to Las Vegas come from the Western States of America and California (86 per cent in 1995). A smaller percentage of visitors come from abroad (13 per cent in 1995). The large majority of visitors have a white ethnic origin.

Exhibit 17.10   Las Vegas visitor profile highlights, 1994 and 1995

	1994	1995
First vs. repeat:		
First-time visitor	22%	28%
Repeat visitor	78%	72%
Purpose of current visit:		
Vacation/pleasure/gamble	74%	71%
Business/convention	14%	15%
Other	12%	14%
Transportation:		
Air	44%	44%
Automobile	39%	41%
Bus	11%	8%
Recreational vehicle	6%	6%
Room occupants:		
One	14%	13%
Two	70%	67%
Three	11%	13%
Four or more	6%	7%
Other trip characteristics:		
Number of visits in past year	2.5	2.4
Adults in party	2.7	2.6
Nights stayed	3.1	3.5
Visitors with children	8%	11%
Expenditures per visitor:		
Food and drink (per day)	$22.99	$22.53
Transportation (per day)	$14.05	$9.16
Shopping (per trip)	$74.52	$66.18
Shows (per trip)	$20.34	$26.01
Sightseeing (per trip)	$3.77	$4.70
Hotel/motel room (per night)	$52.16	$54.47
Gambling behaviour:		
% who gamble while in LV	92%	89%
Daily hours gambled	5.0	4.1
Gambling budget	$479.77	$513.73
% who gamble outside LV	38%	35%
Origin:		
Eastern States	9%	10%
Southern States	12%	12%
Midwestern States	14%	13%
Western States	50%	51%
CA	33%	35%
AZ	5%	3%
Foreign	14%	13%
Ethnicity:		
White	80%	79%
African American	7%	7%
Asian/Asian American	7%	7%
Hispanic/Latino	6%	6%
Other	1%	1%

Source: Las Vegas Convention and Visitors Authority, Las Vegas Visitor Profile Study

The Las Vegas Convention and Visitors Authority predicted a continuation in the steady growth of visitors to Las Vegas, starting with the 1996 projection. It was estimated that 30.3 million visitors (27.1 million tourists and 3.2 million convention attendees) would visit Las Vegas during 1996, which represents an annual percentage growth rate, since 1995, of 4.5 per cent.

Visitors arriving by air during 1995 totalled 28 027 239. A breakdown of the types of airline in 1995 which visitors used to travel to Las Vegas, is shown in Exhibit 17.11.

Exhibit 17.11   Passengers arriving by air to Las Vegas, 1995

	Numbers	*Percentage change from 1994*
Total Enplaned/Deplaned Passengers	28 027 239	+4.4%
Scheduled Airline Passengers	23 247 015	+7.7%
Charter Airline Passengers	3 799 290	–6.6%

Source: McCarran International Airport

There has been a steady growth in visitor arrivals by air over a ten-year period, especially by passengers travelling on scheduled airlines as opposed to charter airlines, where there has been a small decline. The growth of arrivals by scheduled airline can be explained by the fact that the business and convention visitors are growing in numbers. Convention attendees are much more likely to use scheduled airlines, than charter airlines.

The reasons for visiting Las Vegas have also been researched by the Las Vegas Convention and Visitor Authority. The results of this are shown in Exhibit 17.12.

Exhibit 17.12   Reasons for visiting Las Vegas, 1997

The business convention visitor	Visits Las Vegas for convention. May gamble and carry out other pursuits such as golf while in Las Vegas. May bring partner and/or children.
The tourist	Can be visiting Las Vegas for a variety of reasons including: gambling, entertainment, golf, to get married, visiting friends and relatives, as part of a more extensive package or independent tour of the USA

Source: Adapted from Las Vegas Convention and Visitors Authority information

The increase in scheduled airline travel to Las Vegas has largely been due to the increase in conventions which are held there. Special events such as the National Finals Rodeo, golf tournaments, along with aggressive marketing by the Las Vegas resort industry have all contributed to the increase in convention visitors. Convention visitors come to Las Vegas primarily to attend the meetings and social events associated with the conference, but it is important to remember that they might extend their visit after the conference, and may bring their partners and children with them, which increases their overall spend.

Tourists come to Las Vegas for a variety of reasons. One of the primary motivations is gambling, which is available in the resort at casinos and hotels. Las Vegas also offers the tourist unparalleled entertainment opportunities including shows, eating experiences and attractions.

One of the issues for the hospitality operators in Las Vegas has been the balance between gambling and other activities, particularly when they have been trying to encourage children to visit their operations. The tourist has also been encouraged to visit Las Vegas by the impressive range of golf courses which have been developed around the fringes of the city.

It has become very fashionable to get married in Las Vegas, and the city has become known as the wedding capital of the world. More than 100 000 couples obtain wedding licences in Las Vegas every year, and then get married in more than 50 wedding chapels throughout the city. Many of the large hotels have their own chapels and offer the prospective bride and groom tailored wedding packages. The Excalibur, for example, offers couples the opportunity of getting married in medieval costumes, whilst the Tropicana resort offers couples the chance to get married in a thatched roof building in a Polynesian setting.

It has become popular to get married in Las Vegas because of the lack of formalities required compared to other American states where waiting periods and blood tests are required before the marriage ceremony. This makes getting married in Las Vegas attractive both to domestic and international visitors.

It is also becoming popular amongst foreign visitors to combine a visit to Las Vegas with a more extensive tour of other parts of the USA.

The Las Vegas Visitor Profile Survey

The Las Vegas Visitor Profile Survey is conducted on an ongoing basis so that an assessment of the Las Vegas visitor and trends in visitor behaviour is shown over time. The survey involves personal interviews with a sample of visitors near to hotel-casino and motels (3300 during 1995). Statistically significant differences in the behaviour attitudes and opinions of visitors from year to year are highlighted in the annual report. A summary of the results from the 1995 survey is shown in Exhibit 17.13.

This survey shows that a high percentage of visitors to Las Vegas were white, married and over 40 years old. A high percentage of visitors came for

---

Exhibit 17.13   Summary of the 1995 Las Vegas Visitor Profile Survey

Sample size – 3300 personal interviews

● **Demographic Profile:**
married   68%
employed   63%
retired   27%
white   79%
40 years old or older   68%
from Western USA   51%
household income of $40 000 or more   52%

● **Reasons for Visiting:**
for vacation or pleasure   72% first time visitors
                                                 65% repeat visitors

attendance at convention or trade show   11%
participation in a gaming tournament   3%
as part of an incentive travel programme   1%
for business   6% first time visitors
                                                 11% repeat visitors

● **Trip Characteristics and Expenditures:**
57% of visitors travelled in parties of two
Average party size – 2.6 persons
11% of visitors were in parties including someone under 21
Average length of stay in Las Vegas was 3.5 nights and 4.5 days
78% of visitors stayed in hotels

● **Gaming Behaviour and Budgets:**
9 in 10 visitors said they gambled while in Las Vegas
the average gambling budget was $513.73 in 1995

● **Entertainment:**
46% of visitors attended shows during their stay
visitors who did not visit a show gave reasons such as they did not have
enough time or that they only came to Las Vegas to gamble

Source: GLS Research on behalf of the Las Vegas Convention and Visitors Authority

vacation or pleasure, although attendance at conferences was also important. A large proportion of visitors stayed in hotels, and gambled regularly whilst they were in Las Vegas.

Profile of international travellers to Las Vegas

Las Vegas has managed to attract international visitors to the city and it is now the seventh most popular city to visit within the United States for overseas visitors, surpassed by New York (Number 1), Los Angeles

(Number 2), Miami (Number 3), Orlando (Number 4), San Francisco (Number 5) and Honolulu (Number 6).

The principal source of international travel statistics for the United States and Las Vegas is the International Trade Administration (ITA), which conducts an ongoing survey of international travellers to the United States. The Office of Tourism Industries (OTI) within the US Department of Commerce's International Trade Administration (ITA) is now responsible for reporting international visitor statistics in the United States.

The origin of visitors arriving by aeroplane is shown in Exhibit 17.14.

The top ten overseas travellers to Las Vegas are shown in Exhibit 17.15.

There are differences between travellers from different countries, in terms of the types of activity in which they take part during their stay in Las Vegas

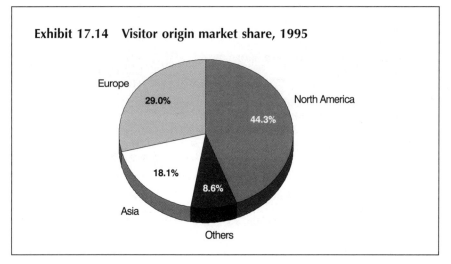

Exhibit 17.14   Visitor origin market share, 1995

Source: Las Vegas Convention and Visitors Authority

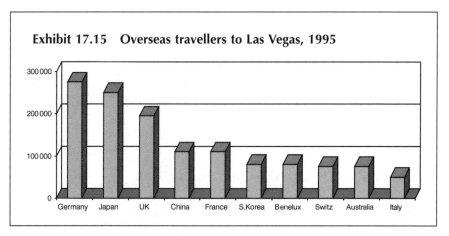

Exhibit 17.15   Overseas travellers to Las Vegas, 1995

Source: Las Vegas Convention and Visitors Authority

Exhibit 17.16 Top ten leisure activities by country, 1995

Percentage of Las Vegas visitors

	All to Las Vegas	RoC	Australia	Japan	UK	S. Korea	Switzerland	France	Germany	Italy	Benelux
Casinos/Gambling	76%	85%	84%	80%	77%	75%	74%	74%	73%	68%	57%
Shopping	88%	92%	94%	87%	86%	80%	90%	88%	90%	85%	89%
Sightseeing of City	82%	87%	89%	70%	88%	76%	88%	77%	94%	82%	95%
Dining in Restaurants	75%	53%	85%	69%	86%	56%	80%	72%	82%	65%	85%
Visiting National Parks	61%	76%	57%	40%	60%	67%	79%	77%	84%	62%	85%

Source: Las Vegas Convention and Visitors Authority; multiple responses allowed

and their average daily expenditure. This is shown in Exhibits 17.16 and 17.17. Exhibit 17.16 shows that gambling and shopping are the top leisure activities for all overseas visitors to Las Vegas. Visitors from countries such as Australia. RoC (Republic of China, Taiwan), Switzerland and Germany are particularly interested in casinos and gambling. The Japanese, an important proportion of all overseas visitors, are particularly heavy spenders in Las Vegas.

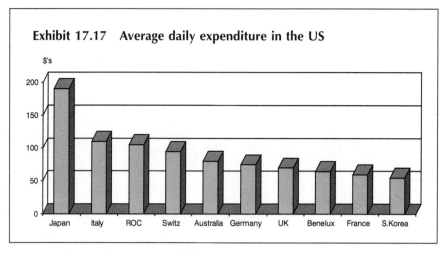

Exhibit 17.17   Average daily expenditure in the US

Source: Las Vegas Convention and Visitors Authority

One of the challenges which the Las Vegas Convention and Visitor Authority will have for the future is how to attract an increasing number of overseas visitors, particularly in the quieter periods of the year. The hotels, resorts and casinos will have to decide on their particular target market and design their products and services accordingly.

Conclusion

Las Vegas has developed as the entertainment capital of the USA. The early development as a gambling centre has evolved into a wider leisure and entertainment base as gambling restrictions were lifted in other areas of the USA. Las Vegas attracts visitors from the USA, and a growing number of overseas visitors who book either independently or as part of package holidays. An important part of the development of Las Vegas as a destination has been the growth of the city as an ideal location for trade fairs, conferences and conventions. The city has ambitious plans for the growth of this business into the next century.

Discussion points and essay questions

1 Las Vegas has been developed as a place to visit for gambling activity. Discuss the opportunities and threats which this could bring to the city in their quest to attract new market segments to Las Vegas.
2 Las Vegas has become the 'wedding capital' of the world. Discuss the reasons for this market development. Outline the opportunities which this development brings to Las Vegas and the wider business community.

Case study 18
Rural tourism in France

France is one of the most popular tourist destinations in the world for international tourists. It also has a large domestic tourism market. Rural tourism in France is highly developed and the market, sophisticated. The data in this case study is largely based on statistics published in December 1996 by the Centre Nationale de Ressources du Tourisme en Espace Rural (CNRTER).

Exhibit 18.1 provides some figures to illustrate the scale of rural tourism in France in the early 1990s.

Exhibit 18.1   The rural tourism market in France, 1993

- 28% of tourist trips in France take place in the countryside
- Around 400 million nights were spent by tourists in rural France in that year
- Tourists in rural France spent around 70 billion Francs in 1993
- Foreign tourists accounted for 16% of the nights spent in rural France and 20% of the expenditure
- 62% of tourist nights in rural France were part of longer holidays while 38% involved short breaks
- On average, 38% of tourist spending was on accommodation, 20% on buying food or drink, 19% on eating out and 10% on leisure activities

---

Source: CNRTER (1996)

While French people now take more holidays in France than they did in the 1960s, the percentage of holidays taken in rural France has fallen significantly, as can be seen in Exhibit 18.2.

Many domestic rural trips by French people involve staying with their friends and relatives or using the second home of friends and relatives, or using their own second home. Relatively few use commercial accommodation.

Rural France is also very popular with foreign tourists. Exhibit 18.3 gives some interesting figures for the international market for the French countryside.

Exhibit 18.2 The evolution of rural tourism demand amongst French tourists

	1964	1980	1994
Number of nights spent on holiday in France by French people (millions)	541	718	742
Percentage of domestic holidays taken in the countryside by French people	35.2	28.3	26.7

Source: CNRTER (1996)

Exhibit 18.3 The international market for holidays in rural France, 1994

- The UK sends most tourists to the French countryside in a normal year. In 1994, 26.4 million tourist nights were spent in rural France by Britons
- The average length of stay by foreign tourists in rural France varies from 6.1 for Spanish tourists to 8.7 for Germans and 11.7 for Canadians
- The use of hotels and rented self-catering accommodation accounts for 34% of tourist nights in the case of Dutch tourists to 94% for Norwegians. On the other hand, camping represents just 1% of nights spent by American tourists compared to a figure of 55% for the Dutch market
- The percentage of foreign tourists visiting the French countryside on a trip to France ranges from 7% with Swedes and Spanish tourists to 29% in the case of UK tourists
- Virtually every national market only visits rural France during July and August

---

Source: CNRTER (1996)

Activity and special interest holidays are becoming more popular in rural France today, including the following:

- horse riding, cycling and walking holidays
- 'fermes pedagogiques' where tourists can find out about life on a farm
- air sports such as micro-light flying and hang-gliding
- golf
- inland waterways holidays.

Finally, the rural hospitality product is developing to meet the aspirations and changing tastes of consumers, as follows:

- the diversification of the 'Gîtes de France' self-catering cottage concept now includes:
  - 'Gîtes de neige' for skiers
  - 'Gîtes d'enfant', where children can stay on farms
  - 'Gîtes de pêche' for fishermen

- the rise of bed and breakfast accommodation, 'Chambres d'hôtes', in rural France
- 'Fermes-auberges', where visitors can enjoy a meal at a farm, using local ingredients
- 'Moulin Etape', a chain of hotels based in converted water mills.

Conclusion

The rural tourism industry in France has shown itself to be innovative in developing new products to attract consumers. However, it has, in respect of foreign markets at least, experienced problems in 1995 and 1996 because of the strong Franc policy of the previous French government. This made France very expensive for British tourists for example, as the exchange rate for the Franc fell from 10 Francs in 1992 to a little over 7 Francs in 1996. Now the rate is above 9 Francs again, the UK market for rural France should increase.

Discussion points and essay questions

1 Discuss the possible reasons why the proportion of holidays taken by French people in rural France fell from 35 per cent in 1964 to 27 per cent in 1994.
2 Describe the likely motivators of those who take holidays in rural France.

Case study 19
Inbound and outbound tourism in the USA – breaking the myths

One of the most enduring myths of consumer behaviour in tourism is that of the American tourist, festooned with cameras, doing a whistlestop tour of Europe. Yet the statistics tell a different story.

Of the estimated 52 million foreign tourist trips taken by Americans in 1996, nearly as many were taken in Mexico than were taken anywhere in the world outside North America. This is not a new situation – it applies throughout the late 1980s. Therefore, in reality, relatively few Americans visit Europe.

The US outbound market is notoriously determined largely by currency exchange rates. Americans tend to travel to places where the Dollar is relatively strong against the local currency. Overall, outbound tourism from the USA has grown steadily in recent years, from around 39 million trips in 1987, to an estimated 52 million in 1996.

At the same time, inbound tourism has also grown overall between the late 1980s and the mid-1990s, from a little over 36 million trips in 1989 to just over 43 million in 1995.

We often fail to recognize that the idea that the typical visitor to the USA is a British family visiting Florida is far from being typical of the market. For example, statistics show us that:

- in most years the USA receives more visits by Mexican tourists than it welcomes tourists from anywhere in Europe
- usually over a third of all visitors to the USA are from Canada
- the proportion of visitors to the USA coming from Asia and the Middle East rose from around 12 per cent in 1993 to nearly 17 per cent in 1995
- in 1995 the USA received 3.5 million visitors from Central and South America.

Conclusion

We can thus see that some of the commonly held perceptions of the US inbound and outbound markets are by no means the whole picture.

Discussion points and essay questions

Discuss the reasons why the perception of the American tourist and the reality appear to be different.

Case study 20
Taiwan – the emergence of a new major outbound tourism market

Taiwan has a population of around 20 million and its economy has grown in recent years at an average rate of nearly 9 per cent per annum.

In the early 1990s, the Taiwanese government has sought actively to encourage its population to take holidays abroad, because it promotes the country's image abroad and helps with international relations for the country which has such an unusual existence, due to its lack of recognition by the People's Republic of China.

Travel restrictions have been relaxed and increased disposable income has stimulated the growth of outbound tourism from Taiwan.

The number of Taiwanese tourists travelling abroad has grown dramatically from 1.6 million in 1988 to a little under 5.2 million in 1995.

Of the tourists who took international trips in 1995, nearly 80 per cent visited other Asian destinations. The only other major destination was the USA, with around half a million Taiwanese visitors.

Indeed, in 1995, around 117000 tourists from Taiwan and the People's Republic of China visited Las Vegas alone (Las Vegas Visitor and Convention Authority). In the same year, by contrast, only 14000 Taiwanese tourists visited Africa.

Of Asian destinations, a few account for the overriding majority of Taiwanese tourists. Hong Kong topped the table in 1995 with a massive 1.9 million visitors, followed by Japan with 500000, Thailand with 400000 and Singapore with a little under 350000.

The average stay abroad is around 10 nights, but there is a variation between a mean of 5.45 nights for trips to South Korea to nearly 17 nights for Canada.

As a recently developed country, Taiwanese tourists are relatively inexperienced and still tend to travel on highly organized group tours.

The authors would like to express their thanks to Professor C. Michael Hall for providing the data used in this case study.

Unlike most Asian destinations, Taiwanese inbound tourism is not growing rapidly. Between 1979 and 1995, foreign tourist arrivals grew from 1.34 million to just 2.33 million. However, the growth in outbound tourism looks set to continue and as the Taiwanese become more experienced tourists they will probably take more independent holidays and explore new destinations.

Conclusion

In 1998 the economic situation in Asia has slowed the growth of the outbound market from Taiwan and has put a question mark over its future.

Discussion points and essay questions

Suggest possible reasons why most Taiwanese outbound tourists choose to visit either the USA or other Asian destinations.

Case study 21
Susi Madron's Cycling for Softies

Introduction

Susi Madron's Cycling for Softies is a limited company established in 1980. The company has developed the market for arranged tours to allow customers to explore France on a bike away from the usual tourist haunts. The company has added the possibility of cycling in the Italian regions of Tuscany and Umbria for the 1997 season. The company is unique in only offering cycling holidays. Other companies have entered the market, but have never gained the reputation of the original.

History of the company

The company was established by Susi Madron and Roy Madron 17 years ago, in 1980. The partners had regularly visited France and experienced the joys of cycling around unspoilt areas rarely visited by tourists. They stayed at small family hotels during these tours and realized that the joys of cycling, coupled with a stay at a reasonable hotel with excellent food, was a powerful and attractive combination. They also noticed that there were no companies offering help to arrange similar tours, in the UK.

Susi and Roy Madron decided to return to the UK and set up a company which would offer customers the opportunity to visit these beautiful areas of France on a bicycle, staying at pre-arranged hotels, offering comfortable accommodation. They decided to call the company 'Cycling for Softies' because the cycling tours would incorporate a touch of luxury – customers would be able to stay at comfortable hotels rather than the more traditional camping experience associated with cycling holidays.

The company was initially run from the back bedroom of Susi Madron's house but, as business developed, it became necessary for the company to obtain premises. Premises in the centre of Manchester were obtained in 1995.

The authors would like to thank Susi Madron of Susi Madron's Cycling for Softies for her help in the writing of this case study.

Over the next 17 years the company grew rapidly. Agents were recruited in France to handle the customers as they arrived in France. Nine bases were established in France which had a good stock of bicycles of various sizes.

Later in 1995 the company moved its headquarters to peaceful office accommodation on the outskirts of Manchester. The company had recruited agents in Australia, New Zealand and South Africa, by this time, to handle their overseas business. These agents were all ex-customers of the company. In 1997, the company expanded their product to Italy, although they still see their main objective as selling their current French products to a wider and more sophisticated market.

Susi Madron and her staff

Susi Madron has provided the inspiration and leadership for the development of the company. It was her initial ideas of providing cycling and accommodation itineraries which established the company. She has a personal interest in providing customers with an exciting and enjoyable experience in a country that she loves.

She has been awarded many prestigious awards for her ideas and business skills, and has written widely on the subject. In 1985, she received BBC Radio 4's Award for Small Business Enterprise. In 1988, her book entitled *Susi Madron's Cycling in France* was published by George Philip, London. Susi Madron has also recruited a loyal and experienced staff from the UK, France and other countries to help her with the development of the business.

Financial performance

Susi and Roy Madron are the main shareholders of the business, each owning approximately 64 000 £1 shares each.

Products

The 'Cycling for Softies' concept is very well defined by the company. This concept is shown in Exhibit 21.1.

The first products offered by the company provided a bicycle for the duration of the holiday, and the hotel booking at the start and the finish of the holiday. Maps and ideas of hotels to stay at en route were also provided. It became clear during the early years that customers would also like the company to book all the accommodation for the whole duration of the holiday. The company therefore started to offer these services if the customer wanted them. The company have developed a close relationship with the proprietors of hotels to allow them to offer this service.

The current product range is shown in Exhibit 21.2 and the regions on offer are shown in Exhibit 21.3.

Exhibit 21.1   What 'Cycling for Softies' actually means

- Lots of warmly welcoming small family-owned hotels
- Food! What the French do best. Always good and authentic, often wonderful
- Cycling along quiet country roads and the little unexpected surprises you might find around any corner. Perhaps the smell of ripe peaches, dropping from the trees, or the fields of sunflowers stretching to the horizon
- The freedom of choosing your own pace and your own route, and cycling as little or as much as you wish
- The friendliness of the people you meet and the sense of well-being you feel as you enjoy each day at a time
- Not having to worry because we do all the planning and organizing for you, so all you have to do is relax and enjoy your own personal adventure in typical French countrysides

Source: Cycling for Softies

It can be seen from Exhibit 21.2 that the customer can choose how much of their holiday is pre-booked by the company and how much is tailor-made or fits in with the arranged holiday route through one of the regions. The company is very flexible and will even arrange special requests for customers. For example, the company can arrange accommodation for customers who have their own bicycles or they can book

Exhibit 21.2   The 1997 product range offered in each destination

- THE GENTLE TOURER. The classic option. – The client stays two nights in each hotel before returning for the last night at the Home Base. Travelling on every other day, means the client can rest on the day off, or if they prefer, they can explore the local region before returning to that same hotel in the evening. The company give lots of information about what to visit and where to go. Terrain and daily distances vary in the different regions, but expect the same comfortable hotels and delicious food everywhere.
- THE TAILOR-MADE. The designer option. – The client chooses hotels and the number of nights they stay in each. The company is flexible in the planning and the client has their very own tour.
- THE SUPER SOFTIE. The softest option. – The whole of the holiday is spent in one hotel, our Home Base. The client can cycle as little or as much as they like. They can explore the region or just relax with a book.
- THE DAISYWHEEL. The two hotel option. – Two hotels and two restaurants. It's a 'soft' option with a little extra variety.
- THE WHIZZ. The energetic option. – After two nights in the Home Base Hotel, the client is out on the road, moving on to a different hotel each night.
- THE ADVENTURER. The independent option. – The company books the client into the Home Base Hotel for the start and finish of the client's holiday. The client arranges their own stays in-between. It gives the client maximum flexibility, and extra choice.

Source: Cycling for Softies

Exhibit 21.3   Regions of France offered by 'Cycling for Softies', 1997

 1 Mayenne and Sarthe
 2 Châteaux of the Loire
 3 La Venise Verte
 4 Cognac and Charente
 5 Dordogne and Garonne
 6 Rivers of the Tarn
 7 Provence and Camargue
 8 Vineyards of the Rhône
 9 Beaujolais and Jura
10 Italy, Umbria
11 Italy, Tuscany

Source: Cycling for Softies

special accommodation equipment and routes for customers with young children or special needs. This means that there is flexibility offered to the customers when they are choosing their particular package.

The length of holiday in the regions shown in Exhibit 21.3 can be 7, 9, 10 or 14 days, according to the customer's requirements.

Prices of the holidays

Prices for the holidays are based on the holiday package excluding travel. Travel can be arranged if required, and prices for this are quoted in the brochure. An example of prices for one of the regions, Rivers of the Tarn, for 1997, is shown in Exhibit 21.4.

Exhibit 21.4   Prices for 1997 – Rivers of the Tarn

Rivers of the Tarn holidays start on Monday, Wednesday and Saturday

Type of Holiday	Gentle Tourer				Super Softie, Daisy	Adventurer
Available	M/W/S	M/S	W	M/W/S		M/W/S
Departures on or between	Prices per person based on 2 people sharing a room					
May 19 – June 28; Aug 24 – Sep 20	517	627	682	902	517	245
June 29 – Aug 23	583	693	748	968	583	272

* 9 night/10 day Gentle Tourer holiday featured.
Compulsory Insurance up to 11 nights £25.50 – up to 18 nights £28.50
NB. Travel Prices Extra

Source: Cycling for Softies

Promotion

Promotion of the holidays is carried out in two main ways. The company produces a colour brochure each year which is sent to customers on request. the company also organizes 'Cycling for Softies' presentations in the North and South of England, and Scotland where prospective customers can meet and talk to staff and chefs from the hotels. These presentations are organized in areas of the country where the bookings record is good and are held in February and March each year. Presentations for 1997 were held in Manchester, Guildford and Aberdeen.

The company advertises in National papers, mainly on Saturday and Sunday at the beginning of the year. This includes advertisements in *The Times*, *Guardian*, *Sunday Times*, *Observer* and *Independent*. Word of mouth promotion is considered to be a key part of the promotion that generates sales to friends and family of past customers.

The company also sends mail shots to the customers who have booked with the company before. A 'welcome home' card is also sent to all customers to be at their home when they arrive back from their holiday. This has proved to be an excellent method of promotion for the company.

Distribution

The holidays are distributed mainly by direct mail. The company relies on newspaper advertisements and word-of-mouth to generate interest. The company sends out a brochure to people who ring in after seeing an advertisement, or hearing about the company from their friends and relatives. A very small amount of sales are handled via travel agents.

The company employs agents in Australia, New Zealand and South Africa, who handle the bookings from these countries, on behalf of the company. The company database of past and present customers is very important in the distribution of the brochure. Past customers are often contacted and a copy of the new brochure is always sent out after publication.

The customers

A profile of the customers of 'Cycling for Softies' is shown in Exhibit 21.5. It can be seen that the holidays attract customers from all over the world. Most people book as couples or families or groups of two or three friends together. Stressed-out professionals, worried academics, relaxing retirees and overworked homeworkers all find the holidays stimulating and refreshing. The customers are mostly 25–65 years old, but the company can arrange holidays for people from other age groups. The customers are interested in 'getting away from it all' or 'chilling out'. They are often busy

Exhibit 21.5   The customers, 1997

Demographic
- 50% Male/50% Female
- Age range – Mainly 25–65, but all age ranges can be accommodated

Socio-Economic
- Mainly A/B Socio Economic Groups
- Some C1s

Lifestyle
- Professional people – 50% of customers are employed in the medical profession; 21% in education. Lawyers, doctors, writers and celebrities, and self-employed business people are also regular customers
- Interested in the healthy outdoor, good diet, and often taking multiple holidays a year

Country of Origin
- Mainly UK based
- Limited business in America, South Africa, Australia and New Zealand
- All figures are approximate

Source: Cycling for Softies

Exhibit 21.6   Comments made by Cycling for Softies customers

'There is the sheer bliss of cycling for an hour or two without seeing a car, and the awful torment of trying to decide which flavour of ice cream to try next'

'France seen from a bike is just blissful'

'We got exactly what we expected, and more. As we hadn't cycled for over 30 years we were a little concerned as to how we would manage, but everything was so well organized; we had no problems'

'On the last day poodling along the river bank back to Chinon was heaven'

'We loved the small hotels and freedom to potter, buy trout, picnic ...'

'I spent one day cycling then the next day walking in the hills and sketching the wild flowers which are glorious in May. The peace and tranquillity took my breath away'

'An elderly gentleman on a very elderly bike stopped and offered to help us. He had a large plastic bag hanging from the handlebars and as we struggled to understand each other, we noticed that several snails were crawling out'

'We particularly liked the more "regional" hotels and food'

'The food was fabulous. You could call it "Cycling for Gourmets"'

Source: Cycling for Softies

professionals who spend little time with their children during the year. This type of holiday allows them to spend a lot of time with their families in a peaceful and stress-free environment.

The repeat purchase business of the company is very high. Approximately 70 per cent of the holidaymakers who book each year have booked with the company before. In the American market, repeat purchase is even higher at 90 per cent. Statements made by the customers in letters written to the company on their return, reflect some of the experiences which they gain from a Cycling for Softies holiday. Examples of these are shown in Exhibit 21.6. The company is now keen to offer the French holidays to customers from a wider geographic area, and is particularly interested in developing the overseas market. Customers are encouraged to fill in questionnaires about every aspect of their holiday on their return. These are scrutinized carefully and if any problems emerge, these are acted on swiftly by the company's management.

Conclusion

Susi Madron's Cycling for Softies is an example of a business which has been developed on the basis of one person's unique and original idea. The cycling holidays in the most beautiful areas of France attract a loyal group of customers who use the company to provide one of their holidays in a year.

Discussion points and essay questions

1 Critically evaluate the way in which the Cycling for Softies business has been developed because of an individual's understanding of the behaviour of a particular group of people.
2 Evaluate the reasons for the growth of interest in cycling holidays for professional people in the UK. In your opinion, will this interest be mirrored in other countries of Europe, and the world?

Case study 22
Currency exchange rates as a determinant of tourist behaviour

Currency exchange rates are clearly a major determinant of tourist behaviour as they have a direct impact on the cost of a holiday. Exchange rates affect:

- the cost of package holidays, leading to tour operators levying surcharges if the exchange rate moves unfavourably, from their point of view
- the cost of living in the resort for tourists.

A good example of the impact of exchange rate fluctuates on tourist flows is the case of the UK and France in the 1990s. In the late 1980s through to 1992, the number of the UK tourists visiting France was growing steadily. Then, in September 1992, the UK withdrew from the European Monetary System while France stayed in. The Pound fell against the Franc by around 20 per cent over the next year. In a very short period of time, a holiday in France that had cost £1000, now cost around £1250. Not surprisingly, many tourists either:

- chose another country for their vacation
- traded down, say, from a hotel to a holiday village, or from a villa to a caravan or campsite.

Several tour operators specializing in higher priced holidays to France went out of business and 'Gîtes de France' was taken over by Brittany Ferries.

Then in 1997 and 1998, the Pound soared against the Franc and France again became a very popular destination for British tourists.

Currency exchange rates have also helped the growth of the tourism industry in Turkey where the Turkish Lira has fallen steadily in recent years against the Pound for example. Holidays to Turkey have therefore been very good value for British tourists, compared to neighbouring Greece, where the Drachma has better retained its value against the Pound.

Transatlantic tourist flows are also heavily influenced by the value of European currencies against the US Dollar.

However, currency exchange rates are not the only economic determinants of tourist behaviour. They are inextricably linked with other factors, most notably inflation rates, and whether the economy of the destination and generating country is in boom or recession.

In Europe, the possible introduction of the European Single Currency could reduce the impact of exchange rate fluctuations, for journeys between European countries. On the other hand, the tour operators and travel agents which make money playing the currency markets or selling currency to tourists may lose out if this happens. They may then have to increase their prices to cover this loss of income.

Outside Europe, it will be interesting to see what impact the current (1998) fluctuations in Asian currencies will have on tourism demand in that region.

Conclusion

It is clear that exchange rates are influential factors in consumers' vacation purchasing decisions. In the current (1998) global climate of economic uncertainty, with great currency exchange fluctuations being seen in some regions, it will clearly remain a major factor in tourist behaviour for the foreseeable future.

Discussion points and essay questions

Discuss the ways in which currency exchange rates affect the price of holidays.

Part Nine
Glossary of Terms

The following glossary of terms is offered as a service to those readers who may be unfamiliar with some of the terms used in this book. It is not meant to be a definitive set of definitions but rather a simple, easy-to-use interpretation of some key words and phrases.

ACORN – a method classifying residential neighbourhoods on the basis of who lives there, for use in marketing research or direct mail.

advertising – any paid form of non-personal presentation of ideas, goods or services by an identified sponsor.

all-inclusive – a type of package holiday where one price covers everything that guests will require in the destination, namely accommodation, food, drink, activities and entertainment.

allocentric – a term coined in 1977 by Plog refers to those tourists who are adventurous, outward-looking and like to take risks.

backpackers – term used to describe tourists who tend to be younger people who take relatively long trips seeking out places which are 'off the beaten track', making relatively little use of the mass tourism infrastructure and trying to minimize their expenses.

brand – the name, symbol, design or combination of these that is used to identify the products or services of a producer to differentiate them from the competitive product or services.

brand loyalty – the propensity or otherwise of consumers to continue to purchase a particular brand.

business tourism – tourist trips that take place as part of people's employment, largely in work time, rather than for pleasure in people's leisure time.

catchment area – the geographical area from which the overwhelming majority of an organization's or product's customers are drawn.

commission – money paid by a producer to an external agent who helps the organization to sell its products, usually expressed as a percentage of the selling price.

competition – the process by which two or more organizations endeavour to gain customers at the expense of the other organization(s).

concentrated marketing – the focusing of the marketing effort on just one or two of the available market segments.

consumer – the person who actually uses or consumes a product or service.

consumer behaviour – the study of which products people buy, why they buy these products and how they make their purchasing decisions.

critical incident – this concept suggests that the tourist's satisfaction or otherwise depends on what happens at times when something out of the ordinary occurs.

culture – the sum total of knowledge, attitudes, beliefs and customs to which people are exposed in their social conditioning.

customer – the person who actively purchases the product or service, and pays the bill. The term is often used interchangeably with 'consumer' but they are different. For example, in business tourism, a company is the *customer* who pays for the travel services, but it is the employee or business traveller who actively travels, and is therefore the *consumer*.

demand – the quantity of a product or service that customers are willing and able to purchase at a particular time at a given price. Where there is a desire to purchase a type of product or experience which is not currently available, for whatever reason, we talk about *latent demand*.

de-marketing – action designed to discourage the purchase of particular products or services.

demographics – the study of population structure and its characteristics such as age, sex, race and family status.

desk research – the collection of secondary data in marketing research.

destination – the country, region or local area in which the tourist spends their holiday.

determinants – the factors which determine whether or not someone will be able to take a holiday and, if so, what type of holiday they will be able to take.

differentiated marketing – the development of a different marketing mix for each market segment.

direct marketing – selling directly from the producer to the customer without the use of intermediaries such as travel agents.

discounting – a reduction in the list price of a product or service to encourage sales.

disposable income – the money which remains once all expenditure has been subtracted from the income of an individual or family.

distribution – the process by which products and services are made available to customers by producers.

domestic tourism – tourism where the residents of a country take holidays as business trips wholly within their own country.

eco-tourist – someone who is motivated by a desire to take a vacation that allows them to see the natural history of a destination and meet the indigenous population.

ethics – the moral values and standards that guide the behaviour of individuals and organizations.

excursionists – people who take leisure trips which last one day or less and do not require an overnight stay away from home.

family life cycle – the stages through which people pass between birth and death, that are thought to influence their consumer behaviour.

FIT – fully inclusive tour.

geodemographics – an approach to segmentation which classifies people according to where they live.

green issues – a common term that is used as an umbrella for a variety of issues relating to the physical environment, from re-cycling to pollution, wildlife conservation to 'global warming'.

growth market – a market where demand is growing significantly.

hedonism – the constant quest for pleasure and sensual experiences.

heterogeneous – a market that consists of segments or subgroups which differ from each other significantly in terms of their characteristics and/or purchasing behaviour.

homogeneous – a market made up of people whose characteristics and/or purchasing behaviour are wholly or largely identical.

inbound tourism – tourist trips from a foreign country to ones own country.

intangibility – the characteristic of a service by which it has no physical form and cannot be seen or touched.

international tourism – those tourist trips where residents of one country take holidays or business trips to other countries.

JICNARS – the Joint Industry Committee for National Readership Surveys.

leisure – leisure is considered to be 'free time', in other words, the time which is not devoted to work or other duties. However, some people also use the term to describe an industry which provides products and services for people to use in their spare time.

leisure shopping – shopping that in contrast to ordinary shopping involves shopping as a leisure activity not as a necessary task of everyday life. It also implies that products are purchased for the pleasure involved in buying and consuming them rather than because of their utilitarian value.

lifestyle – the way of life adopted by an individual or group of people.

market – those consumers who currently are, or potentially may become, purchasers and/or users of a particular individual or group of products are services.

market leader – the product which has the largest share of a single market; in other words, it is purchased by more people than any of its competitor products.

market share – the proportion of sales of a particular type of product achieved by an individual product.

marketing mix – the four controllable marketing variables – product, price, place and promotion – which marketers manipulate in order to achieve their marketing objectives – to influence the target market and determine demand.

marketing positioning – the position in the market which a product is perceived to have, in the minds of consumers, in relation to such variables as quality, value-for-money and level of service.

marketing research – the process of collecting, recording and analysing market-related information. It includes published or secondary data of specific or primary research. It is designed specifically to provide data to help an organization improve the effectiveness of its marketing activities.

media – this can refer to either:
- the news media
- advertising media, in other words, the media in which advertisements may be placed.

model – a representation that seeks to illustrate and/or explain a phenomenon.

motivation – those factors which make tourists want to purchase a particular product or service.

niche marketing – the targeting of a product and service at a particular market segment which is numerically much smaller than the total market.

off-peak – a period when demand for a product or service is habitually lower than at other times, which are termed 'peak periods'.

outbound tourism – tourist trips from one's own country to a foreign country.

perceptions – the subjective interpretation by individuals of the data which is available to them, which results in them having particular opinions of, and attitudes towards, products, places or organizations.

perishability – a characteristic of tourism products whereby they have very limited lives, after which they no longer exist and have no value. For example, an airline seat is no longer an existing saleable product once the aircraft has departed.

point of sale – refers to techniques which are used at the point where tourists actually buy products or services to encourage higher sales. This could involve window displays in travel agencies for example.

post-modernism – a sociological theory that has major implications, if it is a valid theory, for the study of consumer behaviour in tourism. It is based on the idea that in industrialized, developed nations, the basis on which people act as consumers has been transformed in recent years. The theory suggests the traditional boundaries, such as those between high-brow and low-brow culture and upmarket and downmarket leisure activities, are becoming blurred and are breaking down. Authors, notably John Urry, have looked at the implications of post-modernism for the tourism industry.

post-tourist – a tourist who recognizes that there is no such thing as an authentic tourism product or experience. To the post-tourist, tourism is a game and they feel free to move between different types of apparently totally contrasting holidays, from an eco-tourism trip to Belize one year to a sun, sand, sea and sex trip to Benidorm, next year.

product–service mix – the combination of tangible elements and service that is aimed at satisfying the needs of the target market.

promotion – the techniques by which organizations communicate with their customers and seek to persuade them to purchase particular products and services.

psychocentrics – a term coined in 1977 by Plog referring to inward-looking, low risk-taking, less adventurous tourists.

psychographic – the analysis of people's lifestyles, perceptions and attitudes as a way of segmenting tourism markets.

purchase decision – the process by which an individual decides whether or not to buy a particular type of product and then which specific brand to purchase.

qualitative research – research concerned with customer's attitudes and opinions which cannot be qualified.

quantitative research – research concerned with statistical data which can be measured and expressed numerically.

repositioning – the process by which organizations attempt to change consumer's perceptions of a product or service.

seasonality – the distribution over time of total demand for a product or destination, usually expressed in terms of peak and off-peak seasons to distinguish between those times when demand is higher than average and vice-versa.

segmentation – the technique of dividing total markets into subgroups whose members share similar characteristics as consumers.

service gap – a concept coined by Parasuraman, Zeithaml and Berry (1985) which is based on the idea that tourist dissatisfaction is caused by perceived gaps between expectation and actual outcomes.

SERVQUAL – a technique developed by Parasuraman, Zeithaml and Berry (1985) which is designed to measure service quality.

snowbird – people who live in areas which are cold in the winter, who take long trips to warmer destinations to escape the cold weather.

social tourism – a broad area which is primarily concerned with providing opportunities to participate in tourism for those who would not normally be able to go on trips for financial or health reasons, primarily.

target marketing – marketing activity aimed at a particular group of consumers within the overall total population.

tour operator – an organization which assembles 'package holidays' from components provided by other sectors such as accommodation and transport. These packages are then sold to tourists, usually through travel agents.

tourism – the activity in which people spend a short period, of at least one night, away from home for leisure or business.

tourist – a consumer of tourism products.

typology – a classification that divides a group into subgroups sharing similar characteristics.

undifferentiated marketing – a broad-brush approach to marketing in which the market is not subdivided into segments.

upmarket – products aimed at the more expensive, higher status end of the market.

virtual reality – a set of technologies which replicate real-world experiences and can be developed as a leisure product.

visiting friends and relatives (VFR) – tourist trips where the main motivation is the desire or need to visit friends and relatives.

visitor – a widely used term for someone who makes a visit to an attraction. Visitors are not all tourists in the technical sense in that they will not all spend at least one night away from home.

visitor attractions – a single site, unit or entity which motivates people to travel to it to see, experience and participate in what it has to offer. They may be artificial or natural and can be physical entities or special events.

word of mouth – the process whereby consumers who have experienced a product or service pass on their views about the product or service to other people, both positive and negative.

Bibliography and further reading

Adler, J. (1989) Origins of sightseeing. *Annals of Tourism Research*, **16**(1), 7–29.

American Express News Release (1989) *Unique four national travel study reveals traveller types*. American Express, London.

Andreason, A.R. (1965) *Attitudes and Consumer Behaviour: A Decision Model in New Research in Marketing* (ed. L. Preston). Institute of Business and Economic Research, University of California, Berkeley, pp. 1–16.

Archer, L. (1993) *Aircraft Emissions and the Environment*. Oxford Institute for Energy Studies, Oxford.

Ashworth, G.J. and Goodall, B. (eds) (1990) *Marketing Tourism Places*. Routledge, London.

Assael, H. (1995) *Consumer Behaviour and Marketing Action*. International Thomson Publishing. Cincinnati, OH.

Bates, P. (1994) Pilgrims or tourists? *Focus. Tourism Concern*. **11**, 14–15.

Beach, J. and Ragheb, M.G. (1983) Measuring leisure motivation. *Journal of Leisure Research*, **15**(3), 219–28.

Bejou, D., Edvardsson, B. and Rakowski, J.P. (1996) A critical incident approach to examining the effects of service failures on customer relationships: the case of Swedish and US airlines. *Journal of Travel Research*, Summer, 35–40.

Bitner, M.J., Boon, B.H. and Tetreaut, M.S. (1990) The service encounter: diagnosing favourable and unfavourable incident. *Journal of Marketing*, **54**, 71–84.

Boorstin, D. (1964) *The Image: A Guide to Pseudo-Events in America*. Harper and Row, New York.

Bramwell, B. and Lane, B. (eds) (1994) *Rural Tourism and Sustainable Rural Development*. Channel View Publications, Clevedon.

Bray, R. (1996) The package holiday market in Europe. *Travel and Tourism Analyst*, **4**, 51–71.

British Tourist Authority (1996) *Digest of Tourist Statistics. Statistics No. 20.* Martin Withyman Associates.

Buzzell, R.D. (1968) Can you standardise multinational marketing? *Harvard Business Review*, November–December, 102–13.

Calantone, R.J. and Johar, J.S. (1984) Seasonal segmentation of the tourism market using a benefit segmentation framework. *Journal of Travel Research*, **25**(2), 14–24.

Calantone, R.J. and Mazanec, J.A. (1991) Marketing management and tourism. *Annals of Tourism Research*, **18**, 101–19.

Calantone, R.J. and Sawyer, A. (1978) The stability of benefit segments. *Journal of Marketing Research*, 15 August, 395–404.

Calantone, R.J., di Benedetto, C.A. and Bojanic, D.C. (1987) A comprehensive review of the tourism forecasting literature. *Journal of Travel Research*, **28**(2), 28–39.

Calantone, R.J., di Benedetto, C.A. and Bojanic, D.C. (1988) Multi-method forecasts for tourism analysis. *Annals of Tourism Research*, **28**(2), 28–39.

Calantone, R.J. Schewe, C. and Allen, C.T. (1980) Targeting specific advertising messages at tourist segments. In *Tourism Marketing and Management Issues* (eds D.E. Hawkins, E.L. Shafer and J.M. Rovelstand), George Washington University, Washington DC, pp. 149–60.

Cater, E. and Lowman, G. (eds) (1994) *Ecotourism: A Sustainable Option?* John Wiley and Sons, Chichester.

Clark, H.F. Jnr (1987) Consumer and corporate values: yet another view on global marketing. *International Journal of Advertising*, **6**, 29–42.

Cohen, E. (1979) A phenomenology of tourist experience. *Sociology*, **13**, 179–201.

Cohen, E. (1972) Towards a sociology of international tourism. *Social Research*, **39**, 64–82.

Collin, P.H. (1994) *Dictionary of Hotels, Tourism and Catering Management*. P.H. Collin, Teddington.

Cooper, C.P. (ed.) (1991) *Progress in Tourism, Recreation, and Hospitality Management. Vol 3*. Belhaven, London.

Cooper, C.P. et al. (1993) *Tourism: Principles and Practice*. Pitman, London.

Crompton, J. (1979) Motivation for pleasure vacations. *Annals of Tourism Research*, **6**, 408–24.

Crompton, J. (1992) Strategies of vacation destination choice sets. *Annals of Tourism Research*, **19**(3), 420–34.

Culler, J. (1981) Semiotics of tourism. *American Journal of Semiotics*, **1**(1–2), 127–40.

Cullingford, C. (1995) Children's attitudes to holidays overseas. *Tourism Management*, **16**(2), 121–7.

Dace, R. (1995) Japanese tourism: how a knowledge of Japanese buyer behaviour and culture can be of assistance to British hoteliers in seeking to develop this valuable market. *Journal of Vacation Marketing*, **1**(3), 281–8.

Dalen, E. (1989) Research into values and consumer trends in Norway. *Tourism Management*, **10**(3), 183–6.

Dann, G. (1981) Tourist motivation: an appraisal? *Annals of Tourism Research*, **8**(2), 187–219.

Davidson, R. (1994) *Business Travel*. Pitman, London.

Deloitte-Touche Consulting Group (1996) *Highlights of the International Spa Market*. Deloitte Touche, London.

de Mooij, M. (1994) *Advertising World-wide. Concepts, theories, and practice of international multinational and global advertising*. Prentice-Hall International, Hemel Hempstead.

Dhalla, N.K. and Yuspeh, S. (1976) Forget the product life cycle concept. *Harvard Business Review,* January–February, 102–12.

Dibb, S., Simkin, L., Pride, W.M. and Ferrell, O.C. (1994) *Marketing Concepts and Strategies.* 2nd European edn. Houghton-Mifflin, London.

Dibb, S., Simkin, L., Pride, W.M. and Ferrell, O.C. (1997) *Marketing Concepts and Strategies.* 3rd European edn. Houghton-Mifflin, Boston/New York.

Dilley, R. (1986) Tourist brochures and tourist images. *Canadian Geographic,* **30**(1), 59–65.

Douglas, S.P. and Craig, C.S. (1995) *Global Marketing Strategy.* McGraw-Hill, New York.

Douglas, S. and Wind, Y. (1987) The myth of globalisation. *Columbia Journal of World Business,* Winter, 19–29.

The Economist (1998) *The Economist Pocket World in Figures 1998 Edition.* Profile Books Limited, London.

Economist Intelligence Unit (1987) *Choosing Holiday Destinations: The Impact of Exchange Rates and Inflation.* Special Report No. 1109 (A. Edwards).

Economist Intelligence Unit (1988) *International Tourism Forecasts to 1999.* Special Report No. 1142 (A. Edwards).

Economist Intelligence Unit (1989) *Short-term Tourism Forecasts.* Special Report No. 200 (A. Edwards).

Economist Intelligence Unit (1990) *The Japanese Overseas Travel Market in the 1990s.* Special Report No. 2073 (S. Morris).

Economist Intelligence Unit (1992) *International Tourism Forecasts to 2005.* Special Report No. 2454 (A. Edwards).

Economist Intelligence Unit (1995a) Hotel frequent guest programmes. *Travel and Tourism Analyst,* **1**, 84–96.

Economist Intelligence Unit (1995b) 'Prospects for tourism in 1996. *Travel and Tourism Analyst,* **6**, 73–93.

Economist Intelligence Unit (1996) Market segments: spas and health resorts in Europe (by N. Cockerell). *Travel and Tourism Analyst,* **1**, 53–7.

Elkington, J. and Hailes, J. (1992) *Holidays that Don't Cost the Earth.* Victor Gollancz, London.

Engel, J.F., Blackwell, R.D. and Miniard, P.W. (1995) *Consumer Behaviour.* International edn. Dryden Press. Fort Worth, Texas.

Engel, J.F., Kollat, D.J. and Blackwell, R.D. (1968) *Consumer Behavior.* Holt, Rinehart and Winston, New York.

Eshghi, A. and Sheth, J.N. (1985) The globalisation of consumption patterns: An empirical investigation. In E. Kaynak (ed.) *Global Perspectives in Marketing,* Praeger, New York, pp. 133–48.

Euromonitor (1992) *Market Direction Report 19:1. Travel and Tourism.* Euromonitor, London.

Euromonitor (1994) *International Marketing. Data and Statistics 1994.* 18th edn. Euromonitor, London.

Euromonitor (1995) *European Marketing Data and Statistics.* Euromonitor, London.

Euromonitor (1996a) *Market Direction Report 19:1. Travel and Tourism.* Euromonitor, London.

Euromonitor (1996b) *European Marketing Data and Statistics 1996*. 31st edn. Euromonitor, London.

Euromonitor (1997) *European Marketing Data and Statistics 1997*. 32nd edn. Euromonitor, London.

The Europa World Year Book (1997) Vol II. 38th edn. Unwin Brothers, Old Woking, Surrey.

Feifer, M. (1985) *Going Places*. Macmillan, London.

Fick, G.R. and Ritchie, J.R. (1991) Measuring service quality in the travel and tourism industry. *Journal of Travel Research*, Fall, 2–9.

Fisher, A.B. (1984) The ad biz gloms on to global. *Fortune*, 12 November, 77–80.

Formico, S. and Uysal, M. (1996) The revitalisation of Italy as a tourist destination. *Tourism Management*, **17**(5), 323–31.

Foxall, G.R. (1980) *Consumer Behaviour. A Practical Guide*. Croom Helm, London.

Foxall, G.R. and Goldsmith, R.E. (1994) *Consumer Psychology for Marketing*. Routledge, London.

French, T. (1996) No frills countries in Europe. *Travel and Tourism Analyst*, **3**, 4–19.

Frochet, I. (1996) Histoqual: the evaluation of service quality in historic properties. In M. Robinson et al. (eds) *Tourism and Culture Conference Proceedings – Managing Cultural Resources for the Tourist Volume*. Business Education Publishers, Sunderland.

Frommer, A. (1996) *Arthur Frommer's New World of Travel*. 5th edn. Macmillan, New York.

Gayle, D.J. and Goodrich, J.W. (1993) *Tourism Marketing and Management in the Caribbean*. Routledge, London.

Gilbert, D.C. (1991) An examination of the consumer decision process related to tourism. In C.P. Cooper (ed.) *Progress in Tourism, Recreation and Hospitality Management. Vol 3*. Belhaven Press, London.

Ghoshal, S. (1987) Global strategy: an organizing framework. *Strategic Management Journal*, **8**, 425–40.

Gottlieb, A. (1982) American vacations. *Annals of Tourism Research*, **9**(2), 165–87.

Graburn, N.H.H. and Jafari, J. (1991) Introduction to tourism social science. *Annals of Tourism Research*, **18**.

Gray, H. (1970) *International Travel – International Trade*. D.C. Heath, Lexington.

Guido, G. (1991) Implementing a pan-European marketing strategy. *Long Range Planning*, **24**(5), 23–33.

Gummesson, E. (1998) Service quality and product quality combined. *Review of Business*, **9**(3).

Hall, C.M. (1994) *Tourism in the Pacific Rim – Development, Impact and Markets*. Longman, Melbourne.

Hall, C.M. and Johnston, M.E. (1995) *Polar Tourism – Tourism in the Arctic and Antarctic Regions*. John Wiley and Sons, Chichester.

Halliburton, C. and Hünerberg, R. (1993) *European Marketing – Readings and Cases*. Addison-Wesley, Wokingham.

Hampton, G.M. and Buske, E. (1987) The global marketing perspective. In S.T. Cavugsil (ed.) *Advances in International Marketing, Vol 2*, JAI Press, Greenwich, CT, pp. 259–77.

Harcourt, B., Carroll, P., Donahue, K., McGovern, M. and McMillen, J. (1991) *Jovonovich Group*. Monichville, NSW.

Harrison, D. (1992) *Tourism and the Less Developed Countries*. Belhaven, London.

Henley Centre/Research International (1991/1992) *Frontiers*. Henley Centre/Research International.

Herbert, D.T. (1996) Artistic and literary places in France as tourist attractions. *Tourism Management*, **17**(2), 77–85.

Hewison, R. (1987) *The Heritage Industry*. Methuen, London.

Hitchcock, M., King, V.T. and Parnwell, J.G. (1993) *Tourism in South East Asia*. Routledge, London.

Homma, N. (1991) The continued relevance of cultural diversity. *Marketing Research Today*, November, 251–8.

Horner, S. and Swarbrooke, J. (1996) *Marketing Tourism, Hospitality, and Leisure in Europe*. International Thomson Business Press, London.

Horton, R.L. (1984) *Buyer Behaviour. A Decision Making Approach*. Charles E. Merrill Publishing Company, Columbus, OH.

Howard, J.A. and Sheth, J.N. (1969) *The Theory of Buyer Behaviour*. Wiley and Sons, New York.

Hudman, L.E. and Jackson, R. (1990) *Geography of Travel and Tourism*. Delmar Albany, NY.

Inove, R. (1991) An army of Japanese tourists. *Asia Quarterly Review: Special Issue on Resort Development*, **22**(4), 2–10.

INSEAD (1996) *Disneyland® Paris. Case Study on Global Strategy for International Set-up, Marketing, Finance and Management. 'Mickey Mouse' or an American Mouse in France*. Report No. 396–051–1 (A. Etienne-Benz).

Iwand, W.M. (1995) *Cyprus: the impact of tourism on its environment. TVI's Environmental Management System*. Paper presented at 'Tourism and the Environment' seminar, 4 December, Hawaii Beach Hotel, Limassol, Cyprus.

Jafari, J. (1987) Tourism models: the socio-cultural aspects. *Tourism Management*, **8**, 151–9.

Jenner, P. and Smith, C. (1996) Attendance trends at Europe's leisure attractions. *Travel and Tourism Analyst*, **4**, 72–93.

Johnson, P. and Thomas, B. (eds) (1992) *Choice and Demand in Tourism*. Mansell Publishing, London.

Kashani, K. (1989) Beward of the pitfalls of global marketing. *Harvard Business Review*, September–October, 89–98.

Kaynok, E., Kucukemiroglu, O., Kara, A. and Tevfik, D. (1996) Holiday destinations: modelling vacationers' preferences. *Journal of Vacation Marketing*, **2**(4), 299–314.

Keynote Publications (1996) *UK Travel and Tourism. Market Review*. 5th edn.

Kotler, P. and Armstrong, G. (1994a) *Marketing Management: Analysis, Planning, Implementation and Control*. 8th edn. Prentice-Hall, Englewood Cliffs, NJ.

Kotler, P. and Armstrong, G. (1994b) *Principles of Marketing*. 6th edn. Prentice-Hall International, Englewood Cliffs, NJ.

Krippendorf, J. (1987) *The Holiday Makers*. Heinemann, Oxford.

Las Vegas Convention and Visitors Authority (1996) *1995 Las Vegas International Visitor Profile Study.*

Laws, D. and Swarbrooke, J. (1996) British Airways and the challenges of environmental management and sustainable practice. In B. Bramwell et al. (eds) *Sustainable Tourism Management: Principles and Practice*. Tilburg University Press, The Netherlands.

Laws, E. (1986) Identifying and managing the consumerist gap. *Service Industries Journal*, **6**(2), 131–43.

Laws, E. (1991) *Tourism Marketing: Service and Quality Management Perspectives*. Stanley Thornes, Cheltenham.

Le Blanc, G. and Nguyen, N. (1996) An examination of the factors that signal hotel image to travellers. *Journal of Vacation Marketing*, **3**(1), 32–42.

Lett, J. (1989) Epilogue. In V. Smith (ed.) *Hosts and Guests. The Anthropology of Tourism* (2nd edn). University of Pennsylvania Press, Philadelphia.

Levitt, T. (1983) The globalisation of marketing. *Harvard Business Review*, May–June, 92–102.

Levitt, T. (1986) *The Marketing Imagination*. Free Press, New York.

Lewis, R.C. (1983) When guests complain. *Cornell Hotel and Restaurant Administration Quarterly*, **24**(2), 23–32.

Light, D. (1996) Characteristics of the audience for events at a heritage site. *Tourism Management*, **17**(3), 175–182.

Lovelock, C.H. (1991) *Services Marketing*. 2nd edn. Prentice-Hall, Englewood Cliffs, NJ.

Lowyck, E., Van Langenhave, L. and Bollaert, L. (1992) Typologies of tourist roles. In P. Johnson and B. Thomas (eds) *Choice and Demand in Tourism*. Mansell, London.

Lundberg, D.E. (1990) *The Tourist Business*. 6th edn. Van Nostrand Reinhold, New York.

Lunn, J.A. (1974) *Consumer Decision Process Models in Models of Buyer Behaviour* (ed N. Sheth Jagdish). Harper and Row, New York, pp. 34–69.

MacCannell, D. (1989) *The Tourist: A New Theory of the Leisure Class*. 2nd edn. Schlocken Bros., New York.

Mansfield, Y. (1992) From motivation to actual travel. *Annals of Tourism Research*, **19**(3), 399–419.

Maslow, A.H. (1943) A theory of human motivation. *Psychological Review*, **50**, 370–96.

Mathieson, A. and Wall, G. (1982) *Tourism: Economic, Physical and Social Impacts*. Longman, Harlow.

McDonald, M.H.B. (1989) *Marketing Plans – How to Prepare Them: How to Use Them*. Heinemann, London.

Middleton, V.T.C. (1994) *Marketing for Travel and Tourism*. 2nd edn. Butterworth-Heinemann, London.

Morgan, J., Pain, N. and Hubert, F. (1998) The world economy. *National Institute Economic Review*, **1/98**(163), January. National Institute of Economic and Social Research, London.

Moscardo, E., Morrison, A.M., Pearce, P.L., Long, C.T. and O'Leary, J.T. (1996) Understanding vacation destination choice through travel motivation and activities. *Journal of Vacation Marketing*, **2**(2), 109–22.

Moutinho, L. (1987) Consumer behaviour in tourism. *European Journal of Marketing*, **21**(10), 3–44.

Munt, I. (1994) The 'other' post-modern tourism: culture, travel and the new middle classes. *Theory, Culture, and Society*, **11**(3), 101–23.

Nash, D. and Smith, V. (1991) Anthropology and tourism. *Annals of Tourism Research*, **18**(1), 12–25.

Needham, P. (1996) Travel distribution in Germany. *Travel and Tourism Analyst*, **5**, 65–87.

Nicosia, F.M. (1966) *Consumer Decision Processes*. Prentice-Hall. Englewood Cliffs, NJ.

OECD (1996) *Tourism Policy and International Tourism in OECD Countries, 1993/1994*.

O'Guinn, T.C. and Belk, W. (1989). Heaven on Earth: Consumption at Heritage Village, USA. *Journal of Consumer Research*, **16**(2), September, 227–238.

Ohmae, K. (1982) *The Mind of the Strategist: Business Planning for Competitive Advantage*. Penguin Books, London.

Opaschowski, H. (1993) *European Tourism Analysis*. BAT-Leisure Research Institute, Hamburg.

Opperman, M. (1996) Convention destination images: analysis of association meeting planners' perceptions. *Tourism Management*, **17**(3), 175–82.

Otto, J.E. and Brent-Ritchie, J.R. (1996) The service experience in tourism. *Tourism Management*, **17**(3), 165–74.

Ousby, I. (1990) *The Englishman's England: Tate, Travel, and the Rise of Tourism*. Cambridge University Press, Cambridge.

Packard, V. (1957) *The Hidden Persuaders*. Longmans, Green and Co., London.

Parasuraman, A., Zeithaml, V.A. and Berry, U. (1985) A conceptual model of service quality and its implications for future research. *Journal of Marketing*, **49**, 41–50.

Parrinello, G. (1993) Motivation and Anticipation in Post Industrial Tourism. *Annals of Tourism Research*, **20**(3), 233–49.

Pearce, D. and Butler, R. (eds) (1992) *Tourism Research: Critiques and Challenges*. Routledge, London.

Pearce, D.G. and Butler, R.W. (eds) (1993) *Tourism Research: Critiques and Challenges*. Routledge, London.

Pearce, P.L. (1982) *The Social Psychology of Tourist Behaviour*. Pergamon, Oxford.

Peisley, T. (1988) New developments in world cruising. *Travel and Tourism Analyst*, **3**, 5–19.

Pembroke, K. (1996) *The Sustainable Tourist. 1996 British Airways Leisure Survey*. British Airways Environment Report No. 7/96. British Airways, Hounslow, Middlesex.

Perreault, W.D., Dorden, D.K. and Dorden, W.R. (1979) A psychological classification of vacation life-styles. *Journal of Leisure Research*, **9**, 208–24.

Piercy, N. (1992) *Market-led Strategic Change*. Butterworth-Heinemann, Oxford.

Plog, S. (1977) Why destination areas rise and fall in popularity. In E. Kelly (ed.) *Domestic and International Tourism*. Institute of Certified Travel Agents, Wellsbury, MA.

Plog, S. (1987) Understanding psychographics in tourism research. In J.R.B. Ritchie and C.R. Goeldner (eds) *Travel, Tourism, and Hospitality Research: A Handbook for Managers and Researchers*, John Wiley and Sons, New York.

Pompl, W. and Lavery, P. (eds) (1993) *Tourism in Europe: Structures and Development*. CAB International, Wallingford.

Priestley, G.K., Edwards, J.A. and Coccossis, H. (eds) (1996) *Sustainable Tourism? European Experiences*. CAB International, Wallingford.

Quest, M. (ed.) (1990) *The Horwath Book of Tourism*. Macmillan, London.

Reisinger, Y. and Turner, L. (1996) *Comparative Study of the Cultural Differences between Asian Tourists and Australian Hosts*. Proceedings of the 'Tourism and Culture: Towards the 21st Century' International Conference, Northumberland, UK, 14–18 September.

Richards, G. (1996a) Skilled consumption and UK ski holidays. *Tourism Management*, 17(1), 25–34.

Richards, G. (1996b) *Cultural Europe in Tourism*. CAB International, Wallingford.

Richter, L.K. (1989) *The Politics of Tourism in Asia*. University of Hawaii Press, Honolulu.

Ritchie, J.R.B. and Goeldner, C.R. (eds) (1994) *Travel, Tourism, and Hospitality Research: A Handbook for Managers and Researchers*. 2nd edn. John Wiley and Sons, New York.

Ritzer, G. (1996) *The McDonaldisaton of Society*. Rev edn. Pine Forge Press, Thousand Oaks, CA.

Robinson, M., Evans, N. and Callaghan, P. (eds) (1996) *Proceedings of the Tourism and Culture: Towards the 21st Century conference*. 4 vols. Centre for Travel and Tourism/Business Education Publishers, Sunderland.

Ross, G.F. (1994) *The Psychology of Tourism*. Hospitality Press, Melbourne.

Ryan, C. (1991) *Tourism, Terrorism, and Violence: The Risks of Wider World Travel*. Conflict Study 244. Research Institute for the Study of Conflicts and Terrorism, London.

Ryan, C. (1995) Learning about tourists from conversations: the over 55's in Majorca? *Tourism Management*, **16**(3), 207–15.

Ryan, C. (ed.) (1997) *The Tourist Experience: A New Introduction*. Cassell, London.

Savani, G. (1986) Selling travel to the over-50 crowd. *Direct Marketing*, **49**, October, 42–5.

Schofield, P. (1996) Cinematographic images of a city: alternative heritage tourism in Manchester. *Tourism Management*, **17**(8), 333–40.

Schumann, U. and Wurzel, D. (eds) (1994) *Impact on Emissions from Aircraft and Spacecraft upon the Atmosphere*. Deutsche Forschung Sanstalt für Luft – und Raumfahrt, Cologne.

Seaton, A.V. (1994) Tourism and the Media. In S.J. Witt and L. Moutinho (eds) *Tourism Marketing and Management Handbook*. Prentice-Hall, Hemel Hempstead.

Seaton, A.V. (1996) Tourism and relative deprivation: The counter revolutionary pressures of tourism in Cuba. In M. Robinson et al. (eds) *Proceedings of the Tourism and Culture: Towards the 21st Century conference.* 4 vols. Centre for Travel and Tourism/Business Education Publishers, Sunderland.

Seaton, A.V., Jenkins, C.L., Wood, R.C., Dieke, P.V.C., Bennett, M.M., MacLellan, L.R. and Smith, R. (eds) (1994) *Tourism: The State of the Art*. John Wiley and Son, Chichester.

Sharpley, R. (1994) *Tourism, Tourists and Society*. Elm. Huntingdon.

Sharpley, R. (1996) Tourism and consumer culture in postmodern society. In M. Robinson, N. Evans and P. Callaghan (eds) *Proceedings of the Tourism and Culture: Towards the 21st Century conference*, Centre for Travel and Tourism/Business Education Publishers, Sunderland, pp. 203–15.

Sharpley, R., Sharpley, J. and Adams, J. (1996) Travel advice or trade embargo: the impact and implications of official travel advice. *Tourism Management*, **17**(1), 1–7.

Shaw, S. (1990) *Airline Marketing and Management*. 3rd edn. Pitman, London.

Smith, S.L.J. (1996) *Tourism Analysis: A Handbook*. 2nd edn. Longman, Harlow.

Smith, V. (ed.) (1989) *Hosts and Guests: The Anthropology of Tourism*. 2nd edn. University of Pennsylvania Press, Philadelphia.

Solomon, M.R. (1996) *Consumer Behaviour*. 3rd edn. Prentice-Hall, Englewood Cliffs, NJ.

The Statesman Year Book (1997–98) 134th edn. Macmillan Reference, London/Basingstoke.

Stephenson, M.L. and Hughes, H.L. (1995) Holidays and the UK Afro-Caribbean community. *Tourism Management*, **16**(6), 429–35.

Steward, J. (1996) Tourism place: images of late imperial Austria. In M. Robinson et al. (eds) *Proceedings of the Tourism and Culture: Towards the 21st Century conference*, Centre for Travel and Tourism/Business Education Publishers, Sunderland.

Sullivan, M. (1995) The main players in Asia's travel industry. *Travel and Tourism Analyst*, **1**, 54–83.

Sustainability Limited (1996) *Engaging Shareholders. The Benchmark Survey*. The second international progress report on company environmental reporting. Sustainability Limited (UNEP), London/Paris.

Swarbrooke, J.S. (1995a) *The Development and Management of Visitor Attractions*. Butterworth-Heinemann, Oxford.

Swarbrooke, J.S. (1995b) Sustainable tourism and the development and regeneration of rural regions in europe: a marketing approach. In G. Richards (ed.) *Proceedings of the Expert Meeting on Sustainability in Tourism and Leisure*, Tilburg University Press, The Netherlands.

Swarbrooke, J.S. (1996) Understanding the tourist: some thoughts on consumer behaviour research in tourism. *Insights*, November.

Terpstra, V. and Sarathy, R. (1994) *International Marketing*. The Dryden Press, Fort Worth, Texas.

Theobold, W. (ed.) (1994) *Global Tourism: The Next Decade*. Butterworth-Heinemann, Oxford.

Tooke, N. and Baker, M. (1996) Seeing is believing: the effect of film on visitor numbers to screened locations. *Tourism Management*, **17**(2), 87–94.

Toop, A. (1992) *European Sales Promotion*. Kogan Page, London.

Towner, J. (1985) The Grand Tour: a key phase in the history of tourism. *Annals of Tourism Research*, **12**(4), 293–333.

Turner, L. and Ash, J. (1975) *The Golden Hordes: International Tourism and the Pleasure Periphery*. Constable, London.

Urry, J. (1990) *The Tourist Gaze: Leisure and Travel in Contemporary Society*. Sage, London.

Usinier, J.C. (1993) *International Marketing: A Cultural Approach*. Prentice-Hall International, Hemel Hempstead.

Vellas, F. and Bécheral, L. (1995) *International Tourism*. Macmillan, Basingstoke.

Voase, R. (1995) *Tourism: The Human Perspective*. Hodder and Stoughton, London.

Wahab, S., Crompton, L.J. and Rothfield, L.M. (1976) *Tourism Marketing*. Tourism International Press, London.

Walsh, K. (1992) *The representation of the Past: Museums and heritage in the Post-modern World*. Routledge.

Westvlaams Ekonomisch Studiebureau, Afdeling Toerislisch Underzoeu (1986) *Toerishische gedragingen en attitudes van de Belgen in 1985*. Reeks vakontieanderzaeken, Brussels.

Williams, P.W., Andesland, G., Pollock, A. and Dossa, K.B. (1996) Health spa travel markets: Mexican long-haul pleasure travellers. *Journal of Vacation Marketing*, **3**(1), 11–31.

Witt, S.F. and Moutinho, L. (1995) *Tourism Management and Marketing Handbook*. Student edn. Prentice-Hall, Hemel Hempstead.

Wood, K. and House, S. (1991) *The Good Tourist: A Worldwide Guide for the Green Traveller*. Mandarin, London.

Woods, W.A., Chéron, E.J. and Kim, D.H. (1985) Strategic implications of differences in consumer purposes in three global markets. In E. Kaynak (ed.) *Global Perspectives in Marketing*. Praeger, New York.

Wootton, G. and Stevens, T. (1996) Business tourism: a study of the market for hotel-based meetings and its contribution to Wales' tourism. *Tourism Management*, **16**(4), 305–13.

World Tourism Organization (1991) *Yearbook of Tourism Statistics*. WTO, Madrid, Spain.

World Tourism Organization (1992) *Tourism Trends to the Year 2000 and Beyond*. WTO, Madrid, Spain.

World Tourism Organization (1995) *Global Tourism Forecasts to the Year 2000 and Beyond. Vol 1*. WTO, Madrid, Spain.

World Tourism Organization (1996) *Yearbook of Tourism Statistics*. WTO, Madrid, Spain.

WWF International (1994) *Pollution Control Strategies for Aircraft*. Discussion Paper. WWF – World Wide Fund for Nature. CH-1296. Gland, Switzerland.

Yiannakis, A. and Gibson, H. (1992) Role tourists play. *Annals of Tourism Research*, **19**(2), 287–303.

Zaichkowsky, J.L. and Sood, J.H. (1988) A global look at consumer involvement and use of products. *International Marketing Review*, **6**(1), 20–33.

Zalatan, A. (1996) The determinants of planning time in vacation travel. *Tourism Management*, **17**(2), 123–31.

Zaltman, G., Pinson, C.A. and Angelman, R. (1973) *Methodology and Consumer Research*. Holt Rinehart and Winston, New York.